Maurice Rosenblatt

and | *the fall of*
Joseph McCarthy

Maurice Rosenblatt

and | *the fall of*
Joseph McCarthy

Shelby Scates

University of Washington Press
SEATTLE AND LONDON

in association with

History Ink
SEATTLE

© 2006 by Shelby Scates
Printed in Canada
Designed by Marie McCaffrey
11 10 09 08 07 06   5 4 3 2 1

History Ink
www.historylink.org
1425 4th Avenue Ste 710
Seattle, WA 98101

University of Washington Press
P.O. Box 50096, Seattle, WA 98145
www.washington.edu/uwpress

Library of Congress Cataloging-in-Publication Data

Scates, Shelby
Maurice Rosenblatt and the fall of Joseph McCarthy/
Shelby Scates. p. cm
Includes bioliographical references and index.
ISBN 0-295-98594-1 (pbk.: alk. paper)
1. McCarthy, Joseph, 1908 – 1957—Adversaries.
2. Rosenblatt, Maurice. 3. Army–McCarthy
Controversy, 1954. 4. United States—Politics and
government—1945–1953. 5. United States—Politics
and government—1953–1961. I. Title.
E748.M143S28 2005
973.921'092—dc22   2005030042

The paper used in this publication is acid-free
and 90 percent recycled from at least 50 percent post-
consumer waste. It meets the minimum requirements
of American National Standard for Information
Sciences—Permanence of Paper for Printed Library
Materials, ANSI Z39.48-1984.

"Someone must have been telling lies about Joseph K.,
for without having done anything wrong he was arrested one
fine morning." And a few days later, the Police Inspector:
"I can't even confirm you are charged with an offense,
or rather, I don't know if you are. You are under arrest,
more than that I do not know."

—Franz Kafka, *The Trial,* 1937

Contents

Prologue

MY LIFE AS A MERCHANT SEAMAN in the early 1950s came with adventure, discovery, and intense political discussion. It was a pivotal time in United States history, the peak of the demagogic power of Joe McCarthy and the end of Communist influence on West Coast waterfronts—coincidence, not consequence.

There was much to talk about in the engine rooms of vessels where I worked, and time to do it. A likely conversational starting point was the 1934 West Coast maritime strike, which led to enormous improvements in the conditions under which we labored—wages, quarters, meals—for which we were grateful. All veteran hands acknowledged that Communists had led the strike yet failed to gain from its triumph union leadership, much less a first blow in an American revolution. Now, back East, Senator Joe McCarthy was portraying himself, and was being portrayed, as the only force averting Communist domination of our government—and woe to those who dared question him.

Most of what I have just written is long forgotten, if it was ever much known. History moves on. So did I, as a soldier and journalist. Decades later, researching a biography of Senator Warren Magnuson, I went to lunch with Maurice Rosenblatt in his brownstone mansion on New Jersey Avenue in Washington, D.C., a few blocks from the Capitol.

A mutual friend, Joe Miller, a Seattle newsman turned Washington labor lobbyist, brought us together, and as my fellow sailors and I had done in the ship's fireroom, we began talking politics. We didn't quit until suppertime. There was a theme: the extreme stresses placed on American democracy by both the left and the right from 1930 to the climax of McCarthyism in 1955, when real and imagined threats fractured civility, making more victims of innocents than of the guilty. It was a time better described by Franz Kafka than by the *New York Times*. How did democracy and civility survive?

Rosenblatt, a successful lobbyist for nonscheduled airlines, I learned that day, had been a participant in the political action of that turbulent period, a street organizer against New York City's right-wing toughs, a lobbyist for U.S. recognition of the State of Israel, and the man who orchestrated the undoing of Joe McCarthy. He was one who helped preserve democracy and civility.

My much admired union compatriot Bob Casey organized and led the last serious effort of the left—in this case anti-Communist Trotskyites—to take control of a West Coast waterfront local. A rigid ideologue, he failed, which perhaps added to his contempt for "liberals—good only for writing books." But Casey never met Maurice, or anyone quite like him.

Few Americans remain like Rosenblatt who experienced, even remotely, those mid-century political travails. Like his sometime colleague, the writer Ben Hecht, he was a "child of the twentieth century." Even rarer, he was an American participant and activist in a roiling stretch of political history.

From this introduction, I sized Rosenblatt up as a bare-knuckled Ralph Nader, a political organizer comfortable on the streets or in the boardrooms, a liberal, not a zealot, with a personality of velvet and steel. He had a ready sense of humor, a feature usually lacking in ship's forecastles. I was set on meeting him again and soon did so for more political history. What follows came from those talks.

What I learned was this: while history may flow of its own gravity, apparently inexorably, it may be shaped in its course by individuals of exceptionally strong will and high intelligence, an uncommon combination. Maurice Rosenblatt fit the bill: a determined democrat who faced men of great zeal and ruthlessness—from the streets of New York to the corridors of Congress, from Father Charles Coughlin with his anti-Semitic "Christian Front" to Joe McCarthy—men who would have put aside, if not scorned, the due processes given Americans by their Constitution, and stood them down.

Some suggest that McCarthy was his own worst enemy. If so, Rosenblatt was his close rival.

And thus, this narrative.

1 | The Carroll Arms and the National Committee for an Effective Congress

It's GONE NOW, save in the vivid memories of a few old-timers who lived, worked, and played around Capitol Hill in twentieth-century Washington, D.C. The Carroll Arms Hotel and its basement bar, kitty-corner from the old Senate Office Building, was destroyed in 1974, displaced by a parking lot and, post–September 11, 2001, by the ugly juxtaposition of concrete barriers and armed police. Fear of terrorism had replaced the terror of McCarthyism, a legacy of a frequent guest, Senator Joseph McCarthy, R-Wisconsin.

Mark Russell, the political satirist, played the barroom piano at the Carroll Arms in the 1950s and cracked inside jokes as senators, congressmen, and their aides and sweethearts (sometimes one and the same) came to lunch at noon and to drink in the late afternoon. He was very funny. Once asked if he had any writers for his material, Russell said, "Yes, 535 writers—100 in the Senate, 435 in the House of Representatives." Scores of these he entertained.[1]

Sometimes it seemed as if the nation's Capitol had shifted across the street to the Carroll Arms bar. Woody Price, an aide to transportation secretary Brock Adams, recalled one early afternoon, standing room only, aides and congressmen pressed against each other for a two-hour lunch. An Appropriations Committee staffer, Stewart McClure, raised his voice above the tumult to remark, "If a bomb obliterated this place right now, the work of the United States Senate would be delayed by—thirty seconds!" Another round followed.[2]

This was a political no-man's-land, a listening post at First and C Streets Northeast that might be likened to neutral Lisbon during World War II. Senator Barry Goldwater, looking ahead to

1964 and a run for the White House, installed a lawyer pal from Phoenix, Denison Kitchel, in an office in the six-story Carroll Arms under the sham label "Goldwater for Senate." Goldwater's instructions: "Keep your powder dry and listen to everybody. We'll take to the end of 1963 to evaluate the [presidential] political situation."[3] Goldwater would run and lose the 1964 election to Lyndon Johnson.

By 1972, an expanding Congress needed extra room and resorted to the hotel. The first home of the Congressional Budget Office, creature of a budget reform act engineered by Senator Ed Muskie and then Representative Brock Adams, was a leaky room with a three-legged desk in the hotel basement, adjacent to the bar. As late as 1961 a single room could be had at the Carroll Arms for $10 a night. Perhaps it, too, leaked.

Bobby Baker, the Senate majority secretary and prince of Capitol wheeler-dealer-fixers, formed and ran the "Quorum Club," members only, mostly lobbyists selected by Bobby himself. This was above the bar on the hotel's second floor. You could learn about the current barroom lineup from the woman at the lobby newsstand. Otherwise, she wasn't very well informed: she thought Joe McCarthy was a liberal.[4]

Before wrecking balls took it down in 1974, reporters got stories in the Carroll Arms bar, only a few of them fit to print, the line between the public and private affairs of elected officials not yet having been shattered in American journalism. Roy Cohn and G. David Schine, aides-extraordinaire to Senator McCarthy, chairman of the Senate Permanent Subcommittee on Investigations, lived together in a top-floor suite. According to Rosenblatt, they regularly came downstairs in the afternoon to drink with their boss and with Don Surine, a defrocked FBI agent turned subcommittee investigator.

The Carroll Arms began as a "railroad hotel" to accommodate travelers detraining from Union Station, a long walk or a short cab ride up the avenue. It would become backstage to the theater of Joe McCarthy, the high political drama soon to be playing across the street on the Senate floor and in the Senate caucus room, spreading from there onto the front pages of newspapers and through coast-to-coast television into the living rooms of America—a drama the likes of which many had never seen before and would never see again.

When Mark Russell played the piano, not everyone applauded. Some of his political satire must have smacked too close to home. "It really did upset some of them," he said years later. "But in those days there was no satire on television, no irreverence. The barometer was good old Bob Hope. It was the McCarthy era. He had lived in the hotel."

One flight below McCarthy's aides, Cohn and Schine, in a remarkable juxtaposition of friend and foe, if not beauty and beast, Maurice Rosenblatt, late of Vienna, Madison, New York, and New Guinea, shared a suite with the lovely and intelligent Laura Barone, formerly of Monette, Missouri, lately of the John Powers model agency in Manhattan. Laura was Rosenblatt's love and invaluable aide in his increasingly successful lobbying jobs on Capitol Hill. She was a sure-fire means of breaching congressional offices, even those most resistant. Bill Knowland, the new GOP Senate majority leader? No problem. "Laura would get chased around the desk two or three times," said Maurice, "but she would get the message to Knowland."

Having found a postwar home and occupation in Washington, smart, handsome Maurice Rosenblatt needed access. He had closed the doors to his previous organization, the American League for Free Palestine—a driving force behind President Harry Truman's fateful decision to recognize the new State of Israel—and was off and running with a lobbying business. His major clients: nonscheduled airlines. They were a new breed of wildcat operations featuring World War II aviators and surplus Air Force transports. Think of all those unused Douglas C-47s and unemployed hotshot pilots.

Rosenblatt, his former associates suggest, was earning a lot of money, but something was missing. For an athlete, long-distance runner, mountain climber, or war lover, the diagnosis would have been clinically easy: an absence of the adrenaline that accompanies high excitement. Perhaps it was the same for Maurice. After watching Nazi mobs on the streets of Vienna, combating anti-Semitic thugs on the streets of New York, and, with Ben Hecht and others concerned about Jewish survivors of the Holocaust, pushing for the creation of Israel, Rosenblatt needed a fix. He jumped back into high-stakes political action.

As Maurice would come to explain, he worried about the 1946 crop of congressmen, too many of them eager to turn the country away from "foreign entanglements." They began to crystallize around Knowland's predecessor as majority leader, Senator Robert Taft of Ohio. It appeared to Rosenblatt like a rebirth of the America First Committee, which had opposed American intervention in World War II—isolationism all over again. "Did we win the war only to lose the peace?" he asked companions. What loomed was another cause in need of a political organizer's attention.

The upshot was that with Harry Selden, Stewart McClure, and George Agree, old political friends and allies in his earlier political organizations, Rosenblatt formed the National Committee for an Effective Congress (NCEC). The four quickly recruited a nucleus of political and financial support. Eleanor Roosevelt, the president's widow, was a prime recruit.[5] Others included Elliott and Faye Emerson Roosevelt; Harley Kilgore, a West Virginia senator close to President Truman; Oscar Chapman, former secretary of the interior; and Oscar Hammerstein II, the Broadway librettist.

The new committee rustled up $1,000 in seed money from Bernard Baruch, the New York financier and presidential confidante, and carefully screened potential members, nervous over the possibility of Communist infiltration. This was 1948, when such a possibility was perceived to be real. Rosenblatt's aversion to Communist Party members was visceral. He had known them in Manhattan in the 1930s and believed they could not be trusted.[6]

Mary Lasker, wife of the Madison Avenue advertising tycoon Albert Lasker, would help, too—in more ways than one. She gave money, but as a "Knickerbocker" New Yorker she also lent the cause high-society connections and credibility. The "Irish girl from Watertown, Wisconsin," as Rosenblatt called her, had married well.

Baruch was an angel for such liberal causes, a man with enormous wealth and an ego to match. "He wanted you to know," said Rosenblatt, a recipient of the angel's largess, "that he invented everything in politics. FDR did not consider Baruch loyal—he played too many games." But with Baruch's help, the NCEC became the liberal response to the challenge from the "radical right," a term Rosenblatt's associate Russ Hemenway claims Maurice coined.

"We were sure [New York Governor Tom] Dewey would beat Truman in the 1948 election and that would bring in on his coattails an isolationist Senate that would keep us out of the United Nations the way [Massachusetts Senator Henry Cabot] Lodge kept us out of the League of Nations in 1920," said Harry Selden about the NCEC. "So we looked over a list of thirty-three Senate races and chose six we thought could be held by good men who would thwart any isolationist attempt. We raised some money, but it was technical assistance that was important."

For the first organizational meeting, held at the Madison Hotel in Washington, Mrs. Roosevelt sent her son James, a conspicuously unsung hero of World War II, executive officer of a Marine commando battalion commanded by Colonel Evans Carlson. "Carlson's Raiders" fought with knives, shotguns, and piano wire, securing beachheads on Japanese-held islands in the South Pacific. Beloved by their troops, Roosevelt and Carlson went different ways after the war,[9] Roosevelt eventually to Congress, and Carlson to an undeserved oblivion. Though a great soldier, he was politically suspect for his appreciation of the tactics of Mao Tse-tung and Chu Teh's Eighth Route Army, spearhead of China's Communist revolution. He had adapted those tactics—move fast, travel light—to the raider battalion.

James Roosevelt became first chairman of the NCEC, a liberal, nonpartisan, internationalist organization with a board resembling a New Deal alumni gathering, most prominent being the Roosevelts, Chapman, and Harold Ickes. George Agree ran the New York office. Rosenblatt was executive director in Washington, his office in the Carroll Arms. Mrs. Roosevelt signed the first fundraising letters, which yielded wherewithal for the campaigns.

Rosenblatt with his finely honed political talents was at the brink of his most significant achievements: playing a critical role in the election of six liberal senators and orchestrating the undoing of Senator Joe McCarthy. Like his actions in 1938 in New York City's Bronx, where he had pitted a dozen Christian divinity students against a howling mob of "Coughlinites"—anti-Semitic followers of Father Charles Coughlin—these were further exercises in political jujitsu, the art of leveraging minimum strength against maximum force. By 1948, Maurice was a political jujitsu artist.

The committee had to work fast. Elections were coming, and President Truman loomed as a sure loser. But the new organization clicked. It looked east and west for contributions and down the nation's middle for Senate candidates. It aimed to get the most for its money, and campaigns cost less in smaller states. It also wanted candidates concerned with the nation's world policy. By design, the NCEC was a counterforce to the new Republican isolationists.

When it was done, Truman had been reelected. The NCEC had been a critical factor in the election of hard-core liberal, internationalist senators who would endure for nearly two decades. Rosenblatt could take a bow. "He had a jeweler's eye for political talent," said Joe Miller.

"The National Committee for an Effective Congress' assistance to liberal candidates in key states was a decisive factor in [our] election victories. . . . it was practical, down-to-earth activity. Impressive." So wrote the new Senate members, Hubert Humphrey, Estes Kefauver, Matthew Neeley, Guy Gillette, Jim Murray, and Paul Douglas, in their thank-you letter to the NCEC board.[10]

These were tough campaigns. Humphrey, the future vice president and 1968 Democratic presidential nominee, defeated an extremely well-financed incumbent, Joe Ball. Kefauver, a Southern anomaly—liberal, intellectual—beat Boss Ed Crump's Tennessee machine. That was the Portland Beavers beating the New York Yankees. Crump ran his state the way Anaconda ran Montana, but the mining giant also lost. It couldn't defeat the aging Jim Murray, up for reelection in that state.

"We ran the committee out of my back pocket," Rosenblatt would recall. "The six candidates were all strong public leaders, a forward-looking bloc. The committee kept a very low profile. Otherwise it might have been a liability in the South and West. Elliott Roosevelt rang doorbells for money. He had to, given our shortage. The Democratic National Committee put everything into Truman's race, nothing for Congress."

Members of the committee met with the potential candidates in the Mayflower Hotel. Rosenblatt described them as a congenial lot, wary of concentrated wealth and economic power, pro–civil rights, and "respectful of the opinions of others." They were pragmatic liberals, not dogmatic. They were the committee's core force to prevent capture of the Senate by the GOP's radical right wing.

Oddly, in light of what would become a viciously divisive issue in the 1950s, events in China, where the U.S.–backed and generously funded Nationalist government was getting whipped in a civil war by Chinese Communists, failed to surface in these campaigns. "Not on the agenda," said Rosenblatt, their master Democratic architect. "Unlike the matter of Israel, which people took personally and whose arguments could break up dinner parties, China wasn't controversial. It wasn't much known aside from select sophisticates and maybe readers of Max Ascoli's *Reporter* magazine."

On election eve, 1948, Rosenblatt gathered with others at Manhattan's Chatham Hotel on Forty-ninth Street near Grand Central Station to await returns. He took a call from Charles Rose, an Associated Press political reporter. Rose asked which of the six NCEC candidates would win. Rosenblatt answered, "All six." Rose asked if he'd bet his life on that prediction. Rosenblatt paused to review each contest and again answered, "All six." They did.

"That," Maurice wrote in a letter to Selden forty-five years later, "was a night to remember!"[11]

Rosenblatt worked behind the scenes: "If I had been overly visible it would have been detrimental." From offstage he placed NCEC money where it counted. A $1,000 contribution in Tennessee, Iowa, or Montana had more pop than a $5,000 contribution in New York or California. Political jujitsu—maximum force from minimum energy—in this case, money. In Minnesota, a wad—$12,000—was spent on ads reprinting a rundown of Ball's fat-cat contributors.

Maurice took no pay for his work. Compensation would come later, only slightly indirectly, in the form of the help he would get for his lobbying clients from the senators he helped elect. He took some critical heat for this and, pressed, would answer with a question: If a lobbyist can't call on political friends, to whom does he turn?

Boss Crump was unforgiving. So were Tennessee segregationists—a vast majority, especially in West Tennessee, where it was heard said in 1959, when Kefauver had to campaign again, "If that nigger-lover Kefauver comes to town he's liable to get shot." Joe Miller, a sometime business associate of Maurice's and a Democratic campaign operative, heard the grim news and early in 1960 went to Nashville to Kefauver's campaign headquarters at the Andrew Jackson Hotel near the state Capitol. "Aw, don't worry none, Joe," said a local staffer, pouring his nervous visitor a glass of bourbon. "When Ole Estes comes home from the Congress, he'll put a whiskey bottle in one hand, a girl on the other, go up to them hills and get every county."[12] He almost did. But he also carried the overtly hostile west Tennessee counties, a triumph of the senator's strength in county courthouses and his native charm over racist attitudes. An unusual admirer, Teddy White of Boston, Jack Kennedy's campaign Boswell, once said that Estes Kefauver was the best president we never had.[13]

Despite its low profile, word spread about the NCEC, at least among the Washington cognoscenti—Congress and the press, particularly the right-wing press, which was Republican, world wary, and Commie conscious. The 1948 election of Harry Truman and the "NCEC Senate Six" halted the right-wing Republican rush into Festung Amerika isolationism, but not the postwar forces behind it.

Joseph McCarthy, not the NCEC, would be preeminent in the 1950 elections, comeback time for the Republican Party after its 1948 thrashing. From being a Senate nobody, generally shunned by other members, McCarthy, although little respected, became very much feared. With fear installed, who needs respect? He would come to claim that he had Rosenblatt and his NCEC group "booted out of the Carroll Arms." Nonsense, said Rosenblatt, who would remain there until the wrecking ball struck the building. "Another wild, unsubstantiated McCarthy charge."

The NCEC continues to the present, with Rosenblatt serving as chairman emeritus until his death in 2005, but its influence on election results would never be so significant as in its initial effort in 1948. Where it would exert its greatest force was in the conflict with Joe McCarthy.

2 | Tailgunner Joe, Chanker Jack, and "Moose Dung"

AT MID-TWENTIETH CENTURY, there wasn't much to remark in the life of Joe McCarthy, except that he held a U.S. Senate seat and wanted badly to keep it. To grasp his means for doing so—and then doing more—one must turn from Wisconsin to China and go back in time a few years.

American policy in China in the 1930s and 1940s—"the great American illusion," as Winston Churchill called it[1]—was essential raw material for McCarthy and McCarthyism, the stuff on which, more than anything, he debuted his campaign against alleged Communist subversion in a Lincoln Day speech on February 9, 1950, in Wheeling, West Virginia.

"I have in my hand a list of two hundred and five," said Joe, "a list of names that were made known to the secretary of state as being members of the Communist Party and who, nevertheless are still working and shaping policy in the State Department."[2] And never mind that he didn't, a sleepy audience came awake. So did the rest of the country. Forget that he later revised the number downward to 57; reporters and editors in Wheeling would verify the number 205.[3] Joe was under way.

McCarthy had certain unusual talents. He was a solipsist, a man without moral constraints. He could lie and bully and never feel a twinge. And he had a way with alliteration in his speech, as in "the crimson clique in the State Department responsible for our loss of China."[4] Beyond these political gifts, as Rosenblatt noted, "he had cited a plausible danger—there were some Communists in our government and trade unions. In the last analysis, Joe was a creature of our times, not a creator."

Inside the Capitol, McCarthy probably wasn't as well known as his nemesis, Rosenblatt. This would soon change.

"Joe wasn't an interesting rogue but a mean guy, a college boxer," said Rosenblatt, who likened the senator to a classmate at the University of Wisconsin, a heavyweight boxer and, like McCarthy, a bully. "Joe would rather hurt an opponent than win the fight," he observed.

Having magnified a modest war record into a modest political career by posing behind a .50-caliber machine gun in the rear seat of a Marine dive bomber—hence the derisive nickname "Tailgunner Joe"—McCarthy was probably oblivious to the tangled affairs going on between the postwar United States and China. This wasn't federal subsidies for milk and cheese or funds for Wisconsin roads. It was a mess of heightened expectations, the phony suggestion of a Christianized Chinese democracy, an illusion handsomely promoted by the son of a Chinese missionary, Henry Luce, the most influential magazine publisher of the twentieth century. Most Americans fell for it, along with the illusion that the U.S. had "lost" China, thanks to *Time*, *Life*, and *Fortune*.

"Without Henry Luce there would have been no Joe McCarthy," said Gore Vidal, the historical novelist, perhaps pressing too far a hard kernel of truth.[5] Luce certainly provided red-hot raw material for the demagogue. Ironically, *Time* magazine would become one of McCarthy's earliest critics—having "made" him, Luce would help break him.

But much thanks to Luce, Congress was excessively generous to China's Kuomintang (Nationalist) government, led by Chiang Kai-shek. Before their total collapse in 1949, the Nationalists got $125 million from the U.S. Congress, "money that could be spent by that government for anything it wanted—no strings attached," said W. Walton Butterworth, U.S. minister in Nanking. Arms to fight the Commies? "My impression now, a couple of decades later," remarked Butterworth, "is that no military equipment ever landed on the mainland."[6] The $125 million went elsewhere.

Madame Chiang, beautiful and bright, played leading lady in the Kuomintang's pursuit of more American treasure to shore up its collapsing government. But the tap was running dry. In frustration, she called American politicians "clodhoppers" and "boors." President Truman didn't like what she said and, as usual, spoke his thoughts on the Kuomintang leaders: "They're thieves, every damned one of them. They stole $750 million out of the billions we sent to Chiang and it's invested in real estate down there in [Brazil], and some in New York."

"Controls on appropriations in those days were very loose," Rosenblatt noted. It's a sure bet some of that appropriation got kicked back to the U.S. "China Lobby" for its efforts in Washington on Chiang's behalf.

Busy in the corridors on the Hill and in the clubs around it, Rosenblatt was oblivious to China's drift into a civil war between the coalition of warlords under Chiang—portrayed by Henry Luce as the oriental answer to Thomas Jefferson—and the Communists under Mao Tse-tung. He had, however, made Joe McCarthy's acquaintance.

"Our first meeting was somewhat embarrassing," recalled Rosenblatt, already a well-established liberal. "It was breakfast in the Carroll Arms. I invited McCarthy and two or three other senators to talk about the 'non-skeds.' I was surprised he showed up. He never spoke. We behaved stiffly. But it wasn't a brush-off. He feigned concern for my problems on the Hill, offered to sponsor bills, write to the Civil Aeronautics Board, or join any other action to help the nonscheduled airlines. I figured his eagerness to help had everything to do with his eagerness to boost his reputation and win reelection. He needed help.

"There was nothing special about him, except that he was rarely alone. Usually with Roy Cohn, Jay Sourwine—a messy, unpleasant man, most aptly named—or Don Surine, a lantern-jawed, gloomy-looking ex-FBI agent. I was bothered by the characters around Joe. I always figured someone else was picking up the tabs. I had no idea he would soon become one of the most celebrated—notorious—senators. At the time, nothing special."[8]

McCarthy was then fishing for an issue to power his 1952 reelection campaign. Early in January 1950 he lunched at Washington's Colony restaurant with Father Edmund Walsh, dean of Georgetown University's foreign service school, and

William Roberts, columnist Drew Pearson's attorney. Roberts suggested the St. Lawrence Seaway. Joe said, "Not enough sex." Walsh said, "What about the Communist issue? The government is full of Communists."[9]

It clicked. One month later, Joe, the "waterboy for real-estate interests," as Rosenblatt recalled his derogatory sobriquet, had an issue to take to a GOP fund-raiser in Wheeling, West Virginia. Why had the United States "lost China"? Because Commies in the State Department were for Communist Mao and against America's ally, Chiang Kai-shek.

The timing was uncanny. "Creeping Communism" was a popular concern: Eastern Europe had fallen under Soviet hegemony; Stalin had laid a blockade on Berlin; Ethel and Julius Rosenberg had been caught spying and sentenced to execution; Alger Hiss had been caught lying about his Communist past. This had already been sufficient to ignite American hysteria. Now, on top of it, the U.S. had "lost China."

Before Joe's stir-'em-up, shake-'em-down Lincoln Day speech to West Virginia Republicans, it's unlikely that he knew any more about Patrick Jay Hurley than as a name in the newspapers, and even less about Alfred Kohlberg, sometime importer of cheap Chinese textiles, which he sold for a fortune. This would change within a month, and so would American history.

General Hurley, conqueror of homeless ex-soldiers camping in Depression-era Washington—the "Bonus Marchers"—went to China in 1944 as President Roosevelt's choice to settle the conflict between the Communists and the Nationalists. Never mind ideology. This was strategically important for ending World War II. The U.S. counted on South China as the base for launching an invasion of Japan. Only the successful use of the atomic bomb obviated that strategy.

America's soldiers on the scene, General Joseph Stilwell and Colonel Evans Carlson, were concerned that Chiang cared more about fighting Mao than about fighting Tojo. Tojo's Japanese troops were killing American soldiers in the South Pacific, and Roosevelt wanted Hurley to get the two Chinese sides together to fight Japan.

Regardless of Hurley's personality—fancy dresser, name dropper (as in "Joe" for Stalin and "Winston" for Churchill)—this may have been an impossible mission. But Hurley's limited knowledge of China and his deep concern for his own place in history didn't help the U.S. cause. "Overbearing and vindictive" is the description of Hurley from newsman Albert Ravenholt, the United Press bureau chief in Chungking, where he covered Roosevelt's emissary.[10]

Hurley did get Mao Tse-tung ("Moose Dung," as the old cowboy pronounced it) and Chiang Kai-shek ("Chanker Jack") to pose together for a UP photo. They would never get that close again. The mission gained only a short pause in China's civil war—not the Nobel Peace Prize so desired by the would-be peacemaker.[11]

Somewhat surprisingly, the incomparable American soldier-diplomat George Marshall could do no better. Assigned by President Truman to replace Hurley as peacemaker between Mao and Chiang in 1946, he, too, failed. For a man accustomed to success, it was "extremely frustrating," a major disappointment.[12] Marshall continued as secretary of state, helping to save postwar Western Europe from Communism though the use of massive American economic aid, the Marshall Plan.

"Hurley blamed his failure on State Department China experts and vowed to gain revenge," recalled Ravenholt, who spent several evenings over drinks with the ambassador after the collapse of the Chiang-Mao talks. "Hurley would get even by providing Joe McCarthy with names and details of those he accused of thwarting his mission." They included Owen Lattimore, John Davies, John Carter Vincent, John Service, and Edmund Clubb, all State Department advisors or foreign service officers who, according to Pat Hurley, wanted Mao's Commies to take over China. Clubb, a former University of Washington student of China, was chief of the department's China desk. Eventually Hurley would lay the same accusation against General Stilwell, a conservative Republican who was contemptuous of the Kuomintang's corruption and its unwillingness to fight the Japanese.[13]

In March 1945, while Hurley seethed and talked of betrayal, agents of the Office of Strategic Services (OSS) raided the Manhattan offices of *Amerasia,* an obscure fortnightly magazine of a pro-Communist persuasion, where they found State Department documents marked "confidential" or "secret." They called the FBI.

One of these documents, a report on Thailand, had run nearly verbatim in *Amerasia's* January 26 issue. The editor hadn't even called for a rewrite. He was Phillip Jaffe, a Communist sympathizer, if not a party member, a supporter of Joseph Stalin, and a booster of Mao Tse-tung.

Thus the nation got "Amerasia," the spy case that wouldn't die, despite a grand jury investigation based on FBI wiretaps, a House of Representatives probe of the State Department (whence came the leaked documents), and a Senate investigation under the conservative—nay, patrician—Democrat Millard Tydings of Maryland. It would, in a short time, cost Tydings his political career.

None of the investigations found evidence of espionage. Jaffe and an aide were eventually indicted for conspiracy to steal government documents. Five others walked, including John Service, ex-aide to Hurley, who had fired him for being critical of Chiang and too chummy with Chinese Commies.[14] Service may have dished off the documents to get even with Hurley, whom he regarded as ignorant or slightly cracked.

This was hot stuff for conspiracy theorists. In the aftermath of the *Amerasia* affair, William Randolph Hearst's *New York Journal-American* headlined, "Sensational Proof Communists Had Access to Confidential Files." The Hearst chain's other New York entry, the *Mirror,* bannered, "More Arrests Forecast in Spy Hunt." None were made.

In fact, the two indictments, the political equivalents of jay-walking tickets, looked fishy. Had the Truman administration pulled grand jury strings to spare itself embarrassment? There was evidence of a fix of federal prosecutors by Tommy Corcoran, a veteran Democratic wheeler-dealer. He was an operator who could make promises and call in debts. He was also an officer in a company formed to channel U.S. aid to Chinese nationalists.[15]

Corcoran's inside game may have been played with the connivance of Chiang Kai-shek. Given a trial, two certain witnesses would have been Stilwell and Service. Released from a gag order, Stilwell could have spilled the beans on Kuomintang corruption. Service could have told how Chiang slipped around on his beautiful wife—"Mrs. Shek" as Hurley called the imperious madame.[16] The Chiangs had been pumped as Asia's model couple, an oriental Tracy and Hepburn, role setters for an up-and-coming democracy.

Exposure of Chiang's infidelity and misuse of American money would have cost the Kuomintang congressional appropriations, millions of which, wrote Drew Pearson, vanished into private bank accounts.[17] Chiang and his madame never lacked the cash for high living. Equally flush was Alfred Kohlberg's China Lobby. Kohlberg, Senator Wayne Morse alleged, got money from the U.S. Treasury, kicked back through Chiang.[18] Kohlberg was a major force on Capitol Hill who had his way with parts of the American press, most conspicuously the Hearst and Scripps-Howard newspaper chains and the *Chicago Tribune.*

Leftovers from Father Coughlin's Christian Front of the 1930s were Kohlberg's top aides. They included Robert Harris, one-time Coughlin financial advisor; Joseph Kamp, a pro-Nazi propagandist; and William Goodwin, the Christian Front candidate for mayor of New York in 1941, now a $30,000-a-year flack for Chiang in Washington.[19]

From his prewar anti-fascist organizational work in New York City, Rosenblatt had acquired more than a passing acquaintance with the Manhattan gang Coughlin left to Kohlberg. "Kamp was an associate of Allen Zoll, the pro-Nazi agent in pursuit of actress Jenny Parmenter's letters from her lover, George Earle, FDR's pal and ambassador to Bulgaria. Goodwin ran the Christian Front's stronghold in New York City's Queens borough," he said. Subsequently, Kohlberg made a fancy Chinese restaurant on Connecticut Avenue a postwar watering hole and dining hall for the China Lobby. Rosenblatt, an observer, described the food as excellent.

A few weeks after McCarthy's Wheeling speech, Kohlberg, already well connected on Capitol Hill, called for a meeting with Joe and Hurley. They had dinner at the more public Mayflower Hotel in Washington, where the businessman-lobbyist and the ex-diplomat related "the full story of the China sell-out to the anti-Communist senator."[20] Hurley would have his vengeance.

McCarthy's accusations against the State Department could "be traced to Hurley's charges and *Plain Talk*," wrote Ross Koen in his book *The China Lobby in American Politics.*[21] *Plain Talk* was the China Lobby's house organ. Barbara Tuchman put it more forcefully in her epic account *Stilwell and the American Experience in China:* "Hurley opened the journey to the tawdry reign of terror soon to be imposed with such astonishing ease by Senator Joe McCarthy."[22]

By the spring of 1950, with startling speed, McCarthy had Americans under a spell and, in the Senate, a coterie of "Little Joes": Styles Bridges, Owen Brewster, Homer Capehart, Harry P. Cain, Kenneth Wherry, and, most importantly, Bob Taft, "Mr. Conservative." They all seemed to be cheering, "Go, Joe, Go!" Taft declared, "If one case doesn't work out, bring up another."[23]

And so McCarthy did: Phillip Jessup, a State Department consultant, "a man with an affinity for Communist causes"; John Service, "Russia's top espionage agent in the State Department"; and Owen Lattimore, China scholar and political naif.[24] Lattimore had once called the 1937 Moscow show trials of Stalin's enemies—inspiration for Arthur Koestler's dramatization *Darkness at Noon*—"democracy in action."[25] As the columnist Joe Alsop sighed, he was "a man of great learning and befuddled politics."[26] McCarthy declaimed, "The corpse of China bears mute evidence of how valuable the Services, Jessups, and Lattimores have been to Russia."[27]

There was at least one critical reaction. "When I read what McCarthy said about Lattimore, I became very emotional, perhaps determined to do something to right a wrong," said Maurice Rosenblatt. And in time, so he would.

3 | The "McCarthy" Elections, 1950 and 1952

REPUBLICANS HAD A TICKET TO RIDE and a national figure to carry the banner in the next two general elections. In most parts of the nation by 1950 the Communist Party was a phantom, a diminished threat to the democracy not much greater than the Ku Klux Klan. But as portrayed by Joe McCarthy and the "Little Joes," it was a phantom "boring from within"—red-hot campaign ammunition to use against Democrats.

Indeed, by February 1950 a political diagnostician might have said that the country was running a high fever. McCarthy had given the fever a name: "McCarthyism." You could measure it by newspaper headlines: "Plan Roundup of 4,000 Reds," "Soviets Detonate Atom Bomb" (1949), "Red Army Conquers China," "Klaus Fuchs Atom Spy for Soviets," "Alger Hiss Guilty!" of lying about passing secret documents to a confessed Communist.[1] And all of this happening under a Democratic administration. It was a ticket to ride.

"After the Wheeling speech, the Senate nobody [McCarthy] quickly became a national figure," said Maurice Rosenblatt. "Initially, there was little press notice. Then I began to realize that he could get ink. It came one day in the corridor of the old Senate Office Building. I heard a great commotion, a crowd of people. Someone shouted, 'Joe is going to the [Senate] floor.' Sure enough, and followed by a flock of reporters. Wherever he went, he drew a crowd."

Among political sophisticates, there was concern over a switch in global strategy from "communist containment" to "preventive war," as advocated by Senator Harry Cain of Washington State, among others. Norman Cousins, editor of the *Saturday Review of Literature*, wired Marshall Field, the newspaper publisher, of Averill Harriman's concern over "increasing forces pushing for preventive war." Cousins called for a meeting to discuss strategy at the home of Telford Taylor, a New Deal lawyer and the United States' chief prosecutor at the Nuremberg war crimes trials, in early October 1950. "Senate races are critical," he said.[2]

The call was prescient, but a winning Democratic strategy never materialized. With McCarthy out front, campaigning in a dozen states, Republicans won 52 percent of the 1950 general election votes, shrinking the Senate Democratic majority from twelve votes to two, and the House majority from seventeen to twelve.[3] Joe took personal delight in smears against Senate majority leader Scott Lucas and Maryland's conservative Democratic senator, Millard Tydings. Through his aide Jean Kerr, he micro-managed the campaign against Tydings.

Lucas had fatally misjudged McCarthy. In May he allowed that Joe "had made so many charges without proof, people are not paying attention any longer; [McCarthy] will have very little effect on the coming elections." Wrong. Lucas lost his seat. So did Tydings, Pennsylvania's Senator Francis Meyers, and three other Senate Democrats.[4]

"Lucas provided the whitewash when I charged there were Communists in high places in government," said McCarthy in a full-service campaign speech. "McMahon [Senator Brian] brought the bucket, Tydings the brush." Absent Joe, Lucas might have survived payoff scandals in the Cook County Democratic machine to win reelection. He didn't.

"We were overwhelmed," said Rosenblatt, whose new organization, the National Committee for an Effective Congress, had played a critical role in the 1948 election of six new members of the Senate. But that was then; this was two years later, with a new national mood and, as of June, a war in Korea. "McCarthy's group was stronger and had great access to the press," he remarked. "Joe's use of the press was an embarrassment to the whole journalism profession."[5]

McCarthy went way below the belt to get Tydings, whose subcommittee had investigated the *Amerasia* case and found

McCarthy's (and indirectly Pat Hurley's) charges of a Communist conspiracy inside the State Department to be a "hoax and a fraud."[6] Joe was unforgiving. His aides circulated a phony composite photo showing the Maryland patrician posed alongside Earl Browder, the Stalinist Communist Party USA leader. The *New York Times,* among other publications, carried a print of the false picture on November 12 that year. In fact, if not in this faked photo, Tydings and Browder had about as much in common as Dick Nixon and Groucho Marx.

"Tydings had a pedigree and property, a Silver Star decoration for heroism in World War I—he was the squire of Havre de Grace, an opponent of the New Deal," in Rosenblatt's description. No matter to Joe McCarthy. This was a get-even campaign engineered by Joe for Tydings's "whitewash" of "Communists in government," most of them initially targeted by Pat Hurley and his man in Washington, Alfred Kohlberg.

In a Senate floor speech, McCarthy charged that "as a result of the so-called investigation [by Tydings's subcommittee] of the State Department, disloyal persons were shielded from exposure, with the ultimate result that Communist subversion in the government was whitewashed."

The whitewash charge and the faked photo were carried in what Rosenblatt called "the rawest piece of campaign literature ever made," a four-page tabloid labeling Secretary of State Dean Acheson "pro-Communist."

John Marshall Butler's (and McCarthy's) victory over Tydings, according to Joe, "was a great election victory for the people of Maryland and of the nation, a well-deserved defeat for Tydings." Besides, said Joe, Butler ran "an honest, clean campaign." In fact, the campaign against Tydings was dirty enough to merit a Senate subcommittee investigation, which indeed called it questionable but nevertheless allowed Butler to keep his Senate seat.

It was a turning point for Joe—and the nation, Rosenblatt suggested: "McCarthy takes on Millard Tydings—a war hero, senior Democrat, a really important man in the Senate. Suddenly he's brought down. By who? Joe McCarthy. We realize Joe is not just another senator, but a power. You take a nobody—like Joe. He fights. He stays up. All of a sudden you say he's worth watching. It was McCarthy's cumulative power from staying in the ring."

There was a bizarre and unresolved aspect to that now nearly forgotten campaign. McCarthy's designated Maryland hit man was Don Surine, the lapsed FBI agent, a regular along with Joe come evenings in the basement bar of the Carroll Arms. Rosenblatt, who observed him, said, "Surine could have come out of a Dostoyevsky novel, skinny, lantern-jawed, hair disheveled. I never knew when Surine might sneak up behind me and put a knife in my back. But this was McCarthy's man."

Tydings accused the ex-Fed of "Chicago gangland tactics" in his snatch of a Butler campaign aide, William Fedder, and their subsequent six-hour midnight ride around Baltimore. Surine's apparent aim was to secure a letter from Fedder that showed Butler in violation of Maryland campaign laws. Fedder claimed he feared for his life. Surine said no, he had made no threats. The facts of this affair were never made clear.[7]

The investigating subcommittee, with Democrats in the majority, denounced Butler's campaign as "a despicable, back-street type" but stopped short of recommending that he be sent back to Baltimore, expelled from the Senate chamber.[8] The hearing did nothing to arrest McCarthyism or its namesake. On the contrary: the fallout of publicity may have increased its momentum.

Out West, in California, Representative Richard Nixon capitalized on his apparent unmasking of Alger Hiss as a card-carrying Commie to defeat the remarkable Helen Gahagan Douglas for a Senate seat. Mrs. Douglas was an intellect, a beauty, an actress, the wife of actor Melvyn Douglas, and a hand-holding Capitol Hill companion to Lyndon Johnson, a fellow member of Congress.[9] This was Rosenblatt's pre-election summary of that historic California contest and prospects for a new, more enlightened Far Eastern (China) policy, as he wrote it to Agriculture Secretary Charles Brannan in June 1950: "Nixon's chances in California are better than ever. Should he prevail, the Senate will have a cold, adroit inquisitor, a methodical and calculating strategist whose talent for evil far outweighs any of Joe McCarthy's demagogic antics." Maurice figured Nixon would be more attached to the Kuomintang than was McCarthy.[10]

That assessment was nearly pitch perfect, but recall that in June 1950 McCarthy was just getting warmed up and, with the prodding of the China Lobby, had already so poisoned the political atmosphere that hope for a "Titoist" China (a Communist government detached from the Soviet Union) was slim to none. Rosenblatt noted: "No statesman or citizen dares explore approaches to a new Far Eastern policy for fear of being [called] a part of a sinister Communist cabal."[11] That fear would prevail—irony of ironies—for two decades, until President Nixon himself traveled to "Red China" and commenced normal Sino-American relations.

Elsewhere out West, in Washington State, where the Communist Party had considerable influence inside the Democratic Party in the 1930s, the Commie phantom had legs. There was fact to back the insinuations of Red baiters.

One of the more powerful Democrats, Senator Warren Magnuson, seemed vulnerable to McCarthyite charges. After all, he had sought and secured Communist Party support in his first run for Congress. Accordingly, Albert Canwell, now a household name in the Northwest, sought the GOP nomination to oppose Magnuson. He had run a state legislative committee investigation of Communists on the University of Washington faculty. Three professors lost their jobs. Canwell's slogan: "Let's get the Reds out of government and the government out of the Red."[12] Alas for him, the campus Commie hunter lost the nomination to a conservative Seattle businessman. But the force of the Communist issue was undiminished.

Even where Joe didn't intervene directly, McCarthyism—guilt by association—filled his absence. In one example, the *Seattle Times* acknowledged that although Magnuson was not guilty of outright subversion, he was "guilty of giving protection to leaders of the Communist line of thought in the state over the years."

Magnuson barely won the 1950 election, much thanks to his considerable support from the state's business community and McCarthy's indifference to his opponent's campaign. "Maggie" could, as they say, bring home the bacon, in this case hydro-electric dams, military contracts (Boeing's B-17), roads, bridges, welfare, and military bases. Most curious: despite the closeness of this race, Magnuson did not campaign on his own role in purging Communists and "security risks" from the nation's waterfronts. Instead, he stayed silent, perhaps from embarrass-ment or even remorse.

Owen Brewster, the Maine senator and GOP Senate cam-paign chairman, declared McCarthy "decisive" in the party's eight election victories, then lamented that the Red baiter hadn't been used in other states (Washington?). Better use of Joe, said Brewster, would have gained the GOP control of the Senate.[13]

But wait. Another national election was two years hence, and the Communist issue and its major player remained toxic. If anything, the Red scare and the Republicans' use of it ran even stronger in the fall of 1952. Consider a national sample from the 1952 election campaigns. In West Virginia, Revercomb Chapman charged that Senator Harley Kilgore had "aided and appeased Communist causes" and had a record of "continuous sympathy with Communist thinkers." In Maryland, Republican J. Glenn Beall bemoaned the "nation's headlong plunge down the paths of precepts dictated by the teaching of Karl Marx." In Montana, Democratic candidate Mike Mansfield, "a captive of the Truman-Acheson gang[,] helped give China to the Reds." McCarthy was said to have a violent hatred of Mansfield, one of the nation's most distinguished public officials, and prob-ably had a hand in this campaign. Running for reelection to the Senate in Washington State, Harry Cain accused his opponent, Henry Jackson, of "Communist mollycoddling."[14]

In the face of this anti-Commie fever, Robert Sherwood, the playwright, a board member of the National Committee for an Effective Congress, gave an upbeat assessment of liberal pros-pects a month before the elections. "McCarthyism hasn't killed civil liberties and academic freedom—it only threatens," he said.

"This [election] is the hour of counterattack. The results will show if we can be free of the Joe McCarthy [Senate] bloc."[15] Accordingly, his organization supported Democratic candidates Henry Jackson, Dennis Chavez, William Benton, and Mike Mansfield, all elected to the Senate in 1952. Overall, however, election results were mixed.

Breezing to reelection in Wisconsin, McCarthy took time off the 1952 campaign trail in October for a trip from Milwaukee to Minot, North Dakota, to address the Young Republican Club and to hunt ducks. His party of seven included former Minnesota Congressman Elmer Ryan and John Matchette, a sometime Pan-American Airlines pilot and a pal of Maurice Rosenblatt's. They flew west in a DC-3 owned by the boss of Evinrude Outboard Motors. Matchette got aboard courtesy of his friend Al Harvey, who introduced him to McCarthy.

"Al said you don't care much for my viewpoints," said McCarthy. "But Al said you are not dangerous."

"I wish I could say the same about you," Matchette replied.

"With that, McCarthy laughed out loud, a big strong Irish laugh," Matchette recalled. "I was welcomed to the party. Joe was a blustery, hail-fellow-well-met, quite charming when he wanted to be, which was most of the time, being a politician. He didn't play the big shot. He laughed at himself. I think he was sort of ambivalent. He gave a different impression on television in the Army-McCarthy hearings."[16]

Young Republicans scared ducks up from the Souris River to within range of the shooters, "but McCarthy was a terrible shot. He kept missing, and he wasn't drinking. He had a speech to make that night," said Matchette. To retrieve the fowls felled by those who could shoot straight, McCarthy waded into the icy river, taking water down his boots. Back ashore, he lay on his back, raised his legs, allowing the water to pour down, and laughed. Good-time Joe.

The senator's speech that evening attacked Phillip Jessup, the State Department consultant. "He didn't call him a Communist," said Matchette. "If he had, I might have admired him. Instead he said, 'If it looks like a skunk, walks like a skunk, smells

33

like a skunk, it must be a skunk.'" You got the point about Jessup by indirection, as Matchette noted to Elmer Ryan, Joe's close ally. "Why, Jessup isn't a Communist," said Ryan. "He's a pinko."[17]

McCarthy, playing the good-time Joe, may not have been aware of a plot behind the scenes to oust him in the Republican primary election. Pushed by William Hurley (no kin to Patrick Hurley), chief of the Wisconsin State Radio network, the aim was to talk General Douglas MacArthur, a native of the state, into running in the Republican primary. Hurley and his friends were convinced that the American military hero would defeat McCarthy and continue to serve the nation from his Senate pulpit.

It didn't work. MacArthur wanted to run on the 1952 GOP ticket either as Senator Robert Taft's vice presidential nominee or as the presidential candidate himself. Attempts by Hurley and others to talk the general into the Senate race failed. MacArthur underestimated the political appeal of his former aide, General Dwight Eisenhower, whom he did not like. Surprise—a majority of the delegates to the Republican convention in Chicago that year did "Like Ike," a first ballot winner. MacArthur faded away to retirement in Manhattan's Waldorf Astoria Hotel.[18]

Free at home from a formidable campaign, Joe hit the road again to help other Republican candidates, perhaps none more important than Harry P. Cain, a "Little Joe," a strident reactionary seeking reelection to another Senate term from Washington State. He faced Representative Henry M. "Scoop" Jackson, a second-generation Scandinavian American and a straightforward Northwestern progressive. Joe came to Seattle to help. The upshot in this otherwise dreary election year was a burst of political comedy.

The Seattle Press Club arranged a debate between McCarthy and the state's leading stand-up comic, Lieutenant Governor Victor A. Meyers, a former bandleader turned all-time showman. (Sample from the showdown: Q— "Vic, how do you stand on the Communist issue?" A— "Of course, my boy, I'm all right on that one. Next question.") A bully in the Senate, Joe didn't like being the target of laughter, which came in small gales at the Press Club face-off. He stalked out of the club in anger for the studios of KING-TV, to give a televised address.[19]

More frustration. The studio turned him away; no air time for Joe, because of his refusal to strike parts of his prepared speech that company attorneys considered libelous. Never mind. Hearst's *Seattle Post-Intelligencer* took a copy of his speech and ran it verbatim in morning editions, including a paragraph alleging that two members of columnist Drew Pearson's staff were ex-Commies.

And Joe got word out through the ever-eager press that Jackson was "soft on Communism." Taking the cue, Seattle and Spokane newspapers attacked Jackson and Hugh B. Mitchell, Democratic candidate for governor, for their sponsorship of the Columbia Valley Authority. It would have been the Northwest's counterpart to the Tennessee Valley Authority—federal management of the river and its critical hydroelectric generators. The papers called it "Communistic socialistic" and, more poetically, "Communism on the Columbia."[20] The private power companies, Puget Power, Portland Gas and Electric, Idaho Power, Washington Water Power, loved those editorials, if in fact they did not write them.

Election results were split. Mitchell lost the primary election, victim of the "soft on Communism" charge. Jackson won. Both went on to distinguished careers, Mitchell as a businessman, Jackson as a Senate stalwart on behalf of national defense and environmental protection.

Thanks to McCarthy, the 1952 election left the Senate with forty-eight Republicans and forty-seven Democrats, together with Republican President Dwight Eisenhower—who refused to denounce his party's prime demagogue—and Vice President Richard Nixon, who had helped inspire him. It would move Joe McCarthy to chairman of the Senate Permanent Subcommittee on Investigations, the forum that would give the United States "McCarthyism."

It seems odd that McCarthy, who never lacked for money or whiskey, in Rosenblatt's observation, steered clear of the Senate race in Massachusetts—Republican Henry Cabot Lodge against the young war hero, Representative John F. Kennedy. Maurice said the answer to that riddle was easy: father Joe Kennedy intervened on behalf of son Jack with a contribution to McCarthy on the order of $10,000. Accordingly, Joe kept his distance from the liberal Jack.

The father went further in nurturing son Jack's campaign. To secure support from organized labor, Joe Kennedy brought in Gardner Jackson, a friend of Rosenblatt's from his New York days with close ties to the AFL-CIO. Jackson met with Kennedy and his aide, Kenny O'Donnell, in the congressman's Beacon Hill apartment in Boston. Rosenblatt relayed the scene that followed from Gardner Jackson's stunning description:

"They briefly discussed labor support. Jackson had come prepared with the draft of a speech for Jack to deliver to a labor rally. While he was reading the draft Joe Kennedy walked into the room. He stayed silent for a few minutes, listening. Suddenly he jumped up from a chair, grabbed the draft paper, and tossed it across the room.

"'You and your sheenie friends are going to beat my son!' he shouted, stalking out of the apartment. There was dead silence. Finally Jackson said, 'Jack, I don't understand your father. I just don't understand. He's got the whole thing wrong.' I think Joe was reacting to what he saw as a shift by his son to the left wing.

"Finally, Jack responded, telling Jackson, 'Put it down to pride of family, Gardner. Love of family.' Despite the outburst on Beacon Hill, Jackson kept Kennedy in contact with Eastern labor unions while Joe Miller, the Seattle newshawk turned Washington lobbyist, did much the same out West."[21]

The rest is history. Kennedy won the Senate seat and eight years later was nominated by the Democratic Party and elected president. He never resolved his ambivalent feelings about Joe McCarthy. Privately, he must have regarded Joe as a boor, in contrast to his own charm and humor. In public, and for the record, Kennedy was silent, quite possibly in deference to his father.[22]

Apart from the legitimate fear of Communism and the possibility of its subversion of government, McCarthy had tapped a partisan current already running strong in these two general elections. Republicans wanted more than revenge for the loss of the White House to Harry Truman. They aimed for a drastic reversal of U.S. internationalist foreign policy. Here, too, Joe played a role.

Led by Senator Robert Taft of Ohio, with support from Senators Bourke Hickenlooper, William Langer, and William Knowland on the Foreign Relations Committee, neo-isolationists demanded repudiation of the "secret agreements" President Roosevelt had made in his meetings with Joseph Stalin at Yalta near the end of World War II. Those agreements had given the Soviets de facto control of Eastern Europe. The neo-isolationists wanted to "free" those satellite states—never saying exactly how they would go about this potential starter for World War III.

In 1952, with the election of a Republican-controlled House, a nearly equally divided Senate, and a GOP president, the time looked ripe to strike against the deals at Yalta. But when Ike balked (Secretary of State John Dulles said there were no secret deals) and Senator Lyndon Johnson brought Democrats onto the president's side, the matter was dropped—but for lack of votes, not passion.[23] McCarthy maintained a leading role, again, as in Maryland, playing the low road.

Passion carried over into a hot skirmish about the selection of Charles Bohlen, an advisor to Roosevelt at Yalta, as U.S. ambassador to Moscow. On the Senate floor McCarthy claimed to have seen Bohlen's sealed FBI file and that it contained damaging information about the diplomat's "family life." That was 1952 code for homosexuality, and the accusation was too wild even for the vengeful Taft. Bohlen got confirmed. I. F. Stone, in his March 1953 newsletter, summed up the episode as having been carried out by "a coalition of the simple-minded and the sinister in the fight against Bohlen."[24]

Isolationists would also fail to move from the Congress a constitutional amendment that would have forced the president to gain approval from Congress and from state legislatures in order to consummate any international compact. The "Bricker Amendment," creature of Senator John Bricker of Ohio, one of the Taft cadre favoring American withdrawal from most of the world, was fought over for years, finally dying a protracted death. Eisenhower called it "a stupid, blind violation of the Constitution by stupid, blind isolationists."[25]

McCarthy played no significant role in the constitutional battle. He had a larger and more timely agenda: a search-and-destroy mission on behalf of anti-Communism, or anything that seemed in his view to approach it, regardless of international boundaries.

Riding high after the 1950 and 1952 elections, McCarthy, the new chairman of the Subcommittee on Investigations, pushed his Red raids beyond U.S. borders. In early 1953 he dispatched his committee's counsel, Roy Cohn, and its investigator, G. David Schine, to Europe to seek out and ban subversive books in libraries run by the U.S. Information Agency.

Save for his close relationship with Roy Cohn, Schine was an odd selection for an intellectual gumshoe—or for that matter, any kind of gumshoe. A rich kid, son of a hotel magnate, he flashed it at Harvard, where he was served by a personal valet and tooled around Cambridge in a black convertible.[26] He served on the committee without pay, according to Ruth Young Watt, the investigation committee's chief clerk and master of the payroll; he was "just a consultant on his own."[27] At one point, Schine actually proposed to spread democracy in Asia by distributing pictures of pinup girls and establishing "Elks Clubs in Pakistan."[28]

The library hit list uncovered by Cohn and Schine included the papers of General Joseph Stillwell, the *New Republic* and *Nation* magazines, and books by Agnes Smedley, a reporter friendly with Chinese Communists. Back home, McCarthy claimed his sleuths had found "thirty thousand to forty thousand" books by Communists and fellow travelers in U.S.-sponsored libraries.[29] These included *The Maltese Falcon* and *The Thin Man*, by Dashiel Hammett, a sometime party member whose well-written books had everything to do with vicarious entertainment—both made excellent films—and nothing to do with ideology. Even more sinisterly, the dynamic duo cited the absence of anti-Communist magazines, most conspicuously the *American Legion Monthly*. *Newsweek* and Luce's pro-Kuomintang, anti-Commie *Time*, apparently, were insufficient.

Laugh now, but this nonsense captured more press ink than the Rose Bowl, the World Series, and General Motors' new line of zoom-finned automobiles, not all of it spilled by Hearst and the *Tribune*. It also inspired a catch line of those times: "So long, see you tomorrow—come Cohn or come Schine."

McCarthy's ideological press allies aside, a question remains about the lack of skepticism (never mind cynicism) the press showed toward him. It was a faint rationalization to think, What the hell, maybe some of his charges are factually true; deep down we're really doing a good service to the country even if we're doing a disservice to our profession.

Alas, the record shows that McCarthy had little success, if any, in uncovering actual American subversives. This does not diminish his triumph, if that's the word for it, in critically exaggerating a climate of fear and distrust in the United States. Its place in American history endures.

4 | McCarthyism

IT MAY BE IMPOSSIBLE to transmit to later generations how Joe McCarthy—that is, McCarthyism—chilled dissent in our society. "What are you, some kind of Communist?" one might ask in response to an off-center comment, say, a sympathetic word about a movie star tagged with the heresy. In the early 1950s that was a warning, not a joke. Once tagged, the victim was stuck, frequently out of a job, unable to prove his or her innocence. Social scientists labeled those coming of age in the 1950s the "silent generation." They were quiet, and not without reason—self-preservation.

A parable in the *New Yorker* on March 26, 1953, captured the essential McCarthyism: "A squirrel spots a rabbit digging furiously into the earth. Puzzled, he inquires as to why. The rabbit explains that Joe McCarthy is going to investigate all antelopes, so you, pal, should go climb the highest tree. 'You're crazy! I'm no antelope.' To which the rabbit replies, 'Of course not, nor am I, but I'm digging anyway. How can I prove that I'm not an antelope?' " Was it mere coincidence that Franz Kafka, a somewhat obscure middle-European writer of tales about hapless individuals snared in inexplicable traps, suddenly surged to popularity in U.S. academic circles in the early 1950s?

After Communist North Korea invaded South Korea in June 1950, anti-Communism—McCarthy's sometimes wild, usually unsubstantiated charges notwithstanding—gained an increased measure of respectability. Many politically sophisticated people saw the action as a brute extension of Kremlin power. "Red" China was regarded as a Kremlin satellite, à la Poland. Politically, of course, the Korean War and the "loss" of China were blights on the Democratic administration.

Given the political atmosphere, it wasn't much of a stretch from McCarthy to McCarthyism. For instance, on August 6, 1950, at the Astor Hotel in New York City, McCarthy addressed the Veterans of Foreign Wars (VFW) convention, a friendly crowd that shouted, "Give those Reds hell" and "McCarthy for president!" Joe tossed them a warm-up pitch of alleged treason: the State Department's Phillip Jessup "belongs to or was affiliated with not one, not two, but with five Communist Party fronts." Later: "You can't fight this State Department with a lace handkerchief." And finally: "I will not be intimidated by the *Daily Worker* or the *New York Post,*" the latter a liberal, not a Communist, newspaper. Joe made a career of feasting on this missing distinction.[1]

The effect of McCarthy's speech on the veterans' organization may be likened to that of a drop of acid on litmus paper. McCarthyism spread. The VFW subsequently launched its own hunt for Reds in several local organizations around the nation. Suspects were to be turned over to the FBI to determine their "loyalty." As one Kansas chapter stated the case, "We are fulfilling our obligation as loyal Americans."[2] The toll of innocent victims from these ideological vigilantes will never be known.

The net of McCarthyism fell heavily on figures in the entertainment business. By 1950, *Red Channels: The Report on Communist Influences in Radio and Television,* a for-profit newsletter founded in 1947 by former FBI agent Theodore Kirkpatrick, had become a bible for the ever sensitive networks and advertising agencies. Woe to the hapless victim named—just named, no evidence needed—by this media creature of the times.

One such, the poet and anthologist Louis Untermeyer, had just joined Dorothy Kilgallen and Arlene Francis on the panel of *What's My Line,* a popular TV quiz program. CBS ran the weekly show, and mail began pouring into its offices when *Red Channels* tagged Untermeyer as affiliated with something called the "Anti-Fascist Refugee Committee," one of about ninety organizations listed by the U.S. attorney general as at least suspected of being un-American. Following the flood of anti-Untermeyer mail, the Catholic War Veterans Committee began placing stickers in drugstore windows that read, "Stop Stopette until Stopette

Stops Untermeyer." Stopette was an underarm deodorant, and its manufacturer, a sponsor of *What's My Line*. The company complied. Untermeyer was dumped, to be replaced by Bennett Cerf, a book publisher.

Thereafter the well-shaken CBS required its employees to take a "loyalty oath" and cleared its TV guests through *Red Channels*. Some didn't make the publication's grade of real Americanism—among others, symphony conductor Leonard Bernstein, actress Judy Holliday, writer Abe Burrows, singer Harry Belafonte, actress Uta Hagen, and Gypsy Rose Lee, the veteran stripteaser.[3]

In retrospect, it might almost seem as if Joe McCarthy invented anti-Communism as well as giving it his name. But credit belongs elsewhere, and not only to the Washington State Legislature, which beat the senator to the hunt for Communists with an investigation of the University of Washington faculty. President Truman himself set the stage for "guilt by association"—later a hallmark of McCarthyism—when, under right-wing pressure and alarmed by the *Amerasia* case, he instigated loyalty oaths for federal employees. Implicit in his call for oaths was the threat of internal subversion.

Under executive order 9835, dated March 27, 1947, Truman created "loyalty boards," and he told Attorney General Tom Clark to prepare a list of subversive organizations "after appropriate investigation and determination." Loyalty boards could decree government workers guilty of "sympathetic association" with such organizations.[4]

Nearly one hundred organizations, beginning with the Communist Party and an anti-Semitic group known as the Silver Shirts, modeled on Hitler's Brown Shirts, wound up on this de facto black list.[5] (Red, a shipmate in the engine room of the SS *Aleutian*, told me this tale about the Silver Shirts in Depression-era Seattle: "I was shivering in the cold rain on Skid Road when a sailor I'd known on the [SS] *Baranof* came up and said, 'Red, time you joined up with the Silver Shirts, an outfit that's going to take care of the Jews and get us jobs.' I already had a Communist Party card, but what the hell? I was cold. I said, 'Sure, I'll join. Where's the shirt?'")

Other black-listed organizations included Veterans of the Abraham Lincoln Brigade (Americans who had volunteered and fought for Spain's Republican government in the Spanish Civil War of 1936–39), the German-American Bund, the American League Against War and Fascism, the Citizens Committee for Harry Bridges (a West Coast longshoremen's union leader accused of Communism), the Commonwealth College of Mena, Arkansas, the Socialist Workers Party (pro-Trotsky, anti-Stalin), the Industrial Workers of the World ("Wobblies"), and the Washington (State) Commonwealth Federation.[6] In short, Truman gave America the loyalty boards, his attorney general wrote the black list, and McCarthyism gave them both political wings.

The FBI's blacklist of suspected Communists or sympathizers was a worker's curse. A modest example is that of Del Castle, a retired Seattle longshoreman and former Communist Party member. Castle joined the party in 1935, the pit of the Great Depression, also dropping out of the University of Washington for lack of money. Three successive postwar jobs in Seattle lasted about thirty days each before FBI agents notified Castle's employers of his connection to the blacklist. Each time he was fired. To earn a living he went "underground" and found work in California. He lingered in the Communist Party until 1957, after Soviet tanks had destroyed a democratic revolution in Hungary. The party, he said, was by then being run by "democratic centralism," in his view a two-bit term for dictatorship from the top. It was "essentially nondemocratic—a hell of a lot of bureaucratic domination." Eventually he got back to Seattle, a longshore job, and a pension. The road had been rough.[7]

Truman, before his death, conceded in private conversations that his loyalty program had been a mistake, and yes, he said, "it was terrible."[8] By 1951 three million federal employees had been investigated and cleared, and 212 dismissed for questionable loyalty. None would be indicted for espionage. Truman's aide Clark Clifford called the program "a response to the temper of the times." Later, in an interview, he said "it was a political problem—Truman was going to run for reelection in 1948 and that was it."[9]

Too often, as a remarkable document published by the California State Senate Subcommittee on Un-American Activities reported, organizations on the attorney general's list were confused with "extremely liberal groups."[10] These groups, "unjustly accused of being Communist controlled," included the American Friends Service Committee (Quakers), Americans for Democratic Action (stridently anti-Communist), United World Federalists, "and others."

The overwhelming zeal to catch and persecute heretics—Communists or anyone suspected of the slightest sympathy with them—could be likened to using a pile driver to crack a walnut. Collateral damage from this overkill has never been calculated, but anyone who lived through it knows that the ratio of innocent victims to actual Communists or sympathizers was enormous. The hunt was out of control, and worse, due legal process was discarded. Once connected to a "subversive" organization, employees were guilty until they proved their innocence. It took years for the federal courts to unravel this breach of American rights, meager consolation to a lot of employees who lost jobs or, worse, their means of livelihood. Among the latter were nearly four thousand maritime workers, seamen, and longshoremen.[11]

Although it falls under the rubric of "McCarthyism," the purge of seamen was initiated by Truman, with help from, of all people, Senator Warren Magnuson of Washington State, a hero to waterfront workers. The purge preceded the full force of McCarthy's anti-Communism and attracted far less attention. It was quick, clean, and brutal. Irv Hoff, administrative aide to Magnuson, recalled its genesis in July 1950: "Magnuson talked to President Truman (a poker-playing companion) about seaport security. There was fear that a nuclear device could be placed aboard a vessel and sneaked into one of our harbors. Truman said, 'Put in a bill.' He did, and seven days after introduction it passed the Congress and was signed into law." It gave the Coast Guard authority to inspect all incoming vessels, as Hoff recalled.[12]

What Hoff could not recall about the "Magnuson Act" was another provision that allowed the Coast Guard to yank the

U.S. Merchant Marine Document—a seaman's de facto and de jure work permit—from any seaman connected with one of the "subversive" organizations listed by the U.S. attorney general. Innocents, along with card-carrying Communist Party members, went out with the purge.

Some, like George Rogers of the Marine Cooks and Stewards Union, were active anti-Communists. No matter. Rogers had allowed his house to be used for a fundraiser on behalf of Henry Wallace's Progressive Party and had bought a raffle ticket from the Northwest Labor School, a left-wing organization cited by the attorney general. Thus Rogers was ruled a "security risk." The Coast Guard revoked his Merchant Marine Document—his seaman's passport.

The purge ended in the mid-1950s with a ruling by the Ninth Circuit Court of Appeals that the Coast Guard had to afford suspect seamen their rights to confront hostile witnesses and have access to the evidence against them—in short, American civil rights. It came too late for a majority of those seamen left on the beach, victims of a sorry, mostly ignored episode in the Red scare bearing the name of Joe McCarthy.[13]

McCarthy, yes. But Warren Magnuson, a promoter of this outrage? An oversize picture of this maritime hero hung above the dispatch window in the hall of the Sailors Union of the Pacific on First Avenue in Seattle, alongside a crude portrait of a union "martyr" in the 1934 maritime strike. This was Magnuson's explanation to the Senate on July 21, 1950: "Some of the last strongholds of Communism in this country exist in some of the waterfront unions. In my opinion the bill will have the dual effect of helping clean out whatever subversive influences may exist around waterfronts and of protecting the country from sneak attacks."[14]

To understand Magnuson's role in the Magnuson Act, consider waterfront union politics. At the time, maritime unions controlled virtually all jobs on U.S. flag vessels. The Marine Firemen, Sailors Union and the National Maritime Union supported the measure. Their reasons were mixed. There were genuine anti-Communists in these unions, seamen and longshoremen who knew firsthand that Communist Party members sometimes dealt from the bottom of the deck and worked from a hidden agenda. But alongside this ideology was infighting for union shore jobs—in seafaring parlance, "pie cards"—jobs as union agents, patrolmen, dispatchers. Under the Magnuson Act, a business agent wanna-be could remove a rival by snitching to the Coast Guard about the rival's association with a "subversive" organization.

Until the Court of Appeals ruling in 1955, the accused had no right to see the evidence against him or to confront the snitch. The Coast Guard quietly did all the dirty work in the name of national security.[15] Little wonder that Magnuson never boasted of his role in this outrage, not even during his 1950 race for reelection, when he was accused of being "soft on Communism." Perhaps he was ashamed. The Magnuson Act of 1950 was in tune with the times, but not with the senator's conscience.

Joe McCarthy never showed any shame. Off and running with his anti-Communist issue, reckless with his charges, absent a moral constraint about injury to others, McCarthy played the press like a toy drum. If one discounts his ability to ignore facts, this appears to have been his greatest talent. He understood a fundamental truth about reporters: they always sought "play"—more precisely, display with bylines—on the pages of their newspapers. They quickly discovered that Joe was virtually a cinch for play.

It worked like this: in the morning, McCarthy would call a press conference to announce that the names of "Comsymps" or "fellow travelers" would be given to the press in the afternoon. The afternoon papers would publish news of the announcement, and the morning papers would print the names themselves the following day. Next time he would reverse the process, announcing in the afternoon that names would come the next morning. He was playing "fair" with newsmen. Reporters went along with the game, and McCarthy got two cycles of news play for a single announcement of names.[16]

The game prompted Maurice Rosenblatt to comment, "McCarthy was a creature almost entirely of whole cloth, woven on the looms of typewriters. He ran a press circus with himself as ringmaster. His rise can be attributed to a press which covered him with fulsome fascination, as no senator has ever been covered before or since." Rosenblatt recalled scenes in the corridors of the Russell Building (née Senate Office Building), Joe emerging from a "closed" hearing, walking in front of a "gaggle of eager reporters, all looking for his words on what had happened in the hearing room. McCarthy would oblige, never mind how outrageous or unsubstantiated. For these walking, imitation news conferences, substantiation would come tomorrow—but tomorrow never came, and he got away with it."

There is no excusing this sorry episode in American journalism. It did grave damage to the reputations and careers of scores of so-called witnesses, who were in fact being accused either directly or by innuendo and who had scant means of redress or rebuttal. Hadn't McCarthy instructed them not to talk to the press after the closed hearings, and didn't this carry the implicit threat of a contempt-of-Congress citation? The reporters' rationale came from the steady pressure exerted by editors, especially wire service editors with twenty-four-hour news cycles, to "freshen the overnight leads"—the nightly rewrite of morning stories for editions to come the following afternoon. Joe knew this and usually accommodated.

Reporters' typewriters, however, were futile without play back home in their newspapers. No problem. McCarthy had unlimited support from the Hearst chain, with its eighteen newspapers coast to coast, from the wire service International News Service, and from the Midwest powerhouse—even bigger than Hearst in that part of the country—the *Chicago Tribune*. Along with hundreds of other papers, they lapped up Joe's charges, displaying them almost always on the front page. Commies, suspected or accused, were hot copy.

There were critics in newsprint, too: the *New York Times*, the *New York Post* (pre-Murdoch), the *New York Herald Tribune*, the *Washington Post*, the *Baltimore Sun*, the *Portland Oregonian*, the *St. Louis Post Dispatch*, the *Madison (Wisconsin) Capitol Times*—eight of the nation's best newspapers. All made McCarthy's select "left-wing list" for following a "pro-Commie" (that is, anti-McCarthy) line.[17]

But Joe's crusade was cruising past these critics, and Pat Hurley's vengeance was upon the State Department. Bowing to McCarthy's ominous pressure, the department fired ninety-one allegedly homosexual employees in 1952, thus reflecting the notion of Senator Kenneth Wherry of Nebraska that "you can't separate homosexuals from subversives—a man with low morality is a menace to government."[18] McCarthy had already denounced "Communists and queers who have sold 400 million Asiatic people into atheistic slavery . . . [through] powder-puff diplomacy."[19]

Nothing reveals so much about McCarthy's solipsism—his absence of gut convictions other than belief in what was good for Joe on any given day—as his relations with reporters. He liked them and frequently sought them out for drinks; he puzzled about why some of them didn't like him and disapproved of what he was doing. Didn't they know it was just politics? Just a ticket for reelection?[20] But he was getting from them and their employers a political career and, worse, a place in American history.

Sometimes Joe dipped into apparent self-pity over his self-appointed role as political savior: "It's a dirty, disagreeable job I have to do. I don't enjoy doing it, but the job has to be done."[21] Was he ambivalent or simply protesting too much for a man who seemed to enjoy inflicting pain?

In his "dirty, disagreeable job," Joe had no greater accomplice than William Randolph Hearst, a newspaper genius, no Johnny-come-lately to anti-Communism, and no friend of Democrats. In 1934 Hearst, a political Jekyll and Hyde, planted reporters undercover to sniff out Communist faculty members at the University of Syracuse, the University of Chicago, and Columbia University. Decades earlier, William Randolph Jekyll had been a crusading populist, scourge of the beef trust, the oil trust, the railroad trust. As a friendly critic had put it, "Wherever you find foes of Hearst you find enemies of the people." He aimed to "raise hell and sell newspapers" and had no time for Pulitzer Prizes.[22]

But by the mid-1930s, W. R. Hyde had come to hate taxes, the New Deal—the "Raw Deal," the chief ordered his far-flung editors to call it—and above all Communists, or anyone so suspected. He told his readership, "Whether anybody else makes the fight against Communism and mob rule or not, I'm going to make it."[23] And so he did. By 1950, with Hearst's newspapers and one wire service behind it, anti-Communism—more specifically, McCarthyism—had, as they say in show business, legs.

Richard Berlin, first among several equals at the top of the Hearst empire, took charge after Hearst's death in 1951. Berlin did not diminish the anti-Communist crusade he had inherited. On the contrary. With his columnist George Sokolsky, or "Sok," Berlin played maker to the political marriage of Joe McCarthy and Roy Cohn, a federal prosecutor and the right-wing Sok's protégé. Cohn curried the favor of Sokolsky and his Hearst stablemate, Walter Winchell, through courthouse leaks to the columnists.[24]

Sokolsky's background, too, reads like a Jekyll and Hyde story. Early on a Trotskyite—a follower of the Soviet outcast and "enemy of the people" Leon Trotsky—he later became a hired propagandist for the anti-union National Association of Manufacturers and the Iron and Steel Institute. Some said he worked as a flack for imperial Japan. Five days before Japan's sneak raid on Pearl Harbor, in a masterstroke of bad timing, or worse, disinformation, Sokolsky claimed that the Japanese wanted peace.[25]

Sokolsky and Berlin consummated the McCarthy-Cohn connection in a meeting with the senator at the Astor Hotel in Manhattan. They insisted that McCarthy make Cohn his chief counsel on the Senate Subcommittee on Investigations—a problem for the committee chairman. Joe Kennedy, a major McCarthy financial backer, wanted his boy Bobby to have the job.

Maurice Rosenblatt related a scene in which Joe Kennedy drove up in a snowstorm to a Capitol Hill townhouse in the shadow of the U.S. Supreme Court building, where McCarthy and a friendly lobbyist were cooking steaks. Kennedy, wearing a homburg to thwart the snow, left the car's motor running. He met McCarthy at the door with an imperative: "I've got no time.

Bobby won't give me any peace. You've got to give him a job." Joe dodged, saying he'd take it up with the ranking subcommittee Democrat, John McClellan.

With his wherewithal and political clout, Kennedy usually got what he wanted. Not this time, or at least not exactly. McCarthy went with Berlin and Sokolsky: Cohn became his counsel. Bobby Kennedy settled for a job as counsel to the committee's Democratic minority and remained Cohn's enemy for life.[26]

To seal the deal, McCarthy named J. B. Matthews as his committee staff director. According to an unsigned memo leaked from the committee, Matthews's address was 363 Hearst Building, New York City, and his salary was paid by J. A. Clements, a Hearst public relations executive. Joe used Matthews's penthouse during his visits to Manhattan. There, among others, he met Alfred Kohlberg, Mr. China Lobby.[27]

Reinforced with Matthews, McCarthy's Senate Permanent Subcommittee on Investigations kept to the attack, frequently operating behind closed doors and striking at targets less vulnerable than China specialists. While some of his fellow senators pondered what to do about a colleague they considered out of control, McCarthy was bulling his way to a showdown with his nemesis, Maurice Rosenblatt, and the National Committee for an Effective Congress.

5 | The Hunter

"I WASN'T LOOKING FOR A TARGET—the target found me."
That is Maurice Rosenblatt's suggestion that his confrontation
with Joe McCarthy had the kiss, or maybe the curse, of the
inevitable, a fate rooted in the protagonists' history. Indeed,
Rosenblatt had a unique, premature political education, one
that carried through the McCarthy era.

"I had the advantage of gifted parents, a European immersion, an accelerated childhood, and audacious self-confidence.
That was my patrimony," said Rosenblatt. "My parents were children of the Enlightenment, mother a musician. We never owned
a car, but we always had a grand piano. The leitmotiv as we were
growing up was Chopin's preludes."

Frank Rosenblatt, Maurice's father, a native of Kiev with a
Columbia University Ph.D. in political economy, wrote a land-
mark study of the nineteenth-century British Chartists, work-
ing-class reformers of Parliament. Decades later, upon meeting
Maurice, the academic-turned-senator Paul Douglas exclaimed
to him, "Your father wrote a very important book!"

In the 1920s Maurice lived with his family in Vienna, where
his father was director of a privately funded effort to relieve
post–World War I hunger. His father traveled the continent,
once in Russia meeting with Leon Trotsky, a founding Communist revolutionary who, as he told his son, "would just as soon
shoot you as look at you."

At the dinner table in Vienna, Maurice heard continual
political discussions. On the streets outside he witnessed a continent in travail. Hunger, teamed with inflation, brought private
misery, political extremes, and violence.

The family did not suffer. On the contrary—the Rosenblatts lived in Viennese style in the Grand Hotel, where Maurice was schooled by private teachers, rigid disciplinarians paid $1 per day, a splendid sum given economic conditions. But outside Maurice saw panhandlers begging for a meal, workers trying to organize unions as Viennese cops tried to beat in their skulls. "Brot, nicht blut!" (bread not blood) was the chant of workers' demonstrations. As Maurice recalled it, "I was witnessing the decomposition of Central Europe." Across the German border, Adolf Hitler, a fast-rising tyrant, blamed all the trouble on Jews. Soon, so would his American imitators. Rosenblatt carried this premature education, this preconditioning, for the rest of his career.

Back home in a New York suburb, economically depressed like the rest of the nation, Rosenblatt had a brief interlude of his mother's cooking and free board before moving west to the University of Wisconsin. It was cheap—tuition $100 a year—liberal, and excellent. It was also in an uproar. If not as riotous as the streets of Vienna, the Midwest campus was a microcosm of the left-right polarity afflicting the economically distressed nation elsewhere.

This was 1932. Breadlines were growing, Wall Street brokers were peddling apples and, some said, leaping out of tall buildings. Franklin D. Roosevelt was elected president. A few months later Adolf Hitler, wild-eyed, mesmerizing, creature of Vienna's slum hostels, survivor of bedbugs and drunkards, was sworn into office as chancellor of Germany.

Rosenblatt did odd jobs for room and board, sat at the feet of academic icons—Alexander Mickeljohn, the philosopher, and Selig Perlman, the economist—and worked on the student newspaper, the *Cardinal*. He covered a ruckus between members of UW's mighty Badger football team and a rally of the League for Independent Democracy—a right-left encounter. Sans pads and helmets, the Badgers tossed two professors into Lake Mendota.

This was hot news on campus. The jocks had gotten their inspiration, Rosenblatt discovered, along with pocket money, from Badger alums in downtown Madison who wanted UW cleansed of "Commies." What better cleansing than the waters of Lake Mendota? It was Vienna redux, the powerful bullying their lessers. But it was the aftermath to this campus episode that shaped the hunter.

"Liberals on the faculty stayed quiet," Rosenblatt recalled. "The president, Glenn Frank, virtually went into hiding. The call for discipline came from a medieval historian and political conservative, university dean George Clark Sellery. He denounced both the football bullies and the downtown alums who would 'break down the University of Wisconsin.'" Rosenblatt wrote it up in a front-page story for the *Cardinal*. "In the clutch, it was a conservative who stood up, a conservative who had the courage," he remembered.

"It was my moment of maturity, my blooding, a profound lesson," Rosenblatt recalled. And later, when the student had a painful—Is there any other kind?—breakup with a coed, the dean sent him a note: "What care I how fair she be, if she be not fair to me." The young man carried the model of Dean Sellery, along with credentials as an editor of the *Cardinal* and the *Wisconsin Dairymen's News,* from Madison to Manhattan, where, like young people of generations before and since, he sought employment and glory as a journalist.

"What I saw on the streets of New York was what I had seen ten years earlier on the streets of Vienna," said Rosenblatt, who got a job on the *Advance,* a trade union sheet edited by the remarkable J. B. Hardman. It wasn't glory, but it was $25 a week. A job of any kind at that time and place was hard to find.

The violent confrontations he saw in Manhattan made campus conflict between "fascists" and "progressives" in Madison look like kid stuff. Rosenblatt wasn't the only acute observer. As James Wechsler reported in *The Nation* magazine on July 22, 1939:

For six months New York has been somewhat incredulous watching the evolution of an anti-Semitic movement; its manifestations are angry and violent, it uses the streets as a battleground and it

employs all the familiar devices of an ancient crusade. Its spiritual
leader is Charles Coughlin and its book of revelation is his magazine, *Social Justice*. . . . several stabbings, a multitude of street fights,
deepening tensions in neighborhoods where clashes have become
commonplace . . . they have been almost uniformly ignored by
the press, partly because it fears to tread on Catholic toes, partly
because it still believes in the silent treatment for anti-Semitism.

The Coughlin to whom Wechsler referred was Father
Charles Coughlin, a radio speaker with an audience of millions
and leader of the Christian Front, a group of street thugs, mostly
Irish and thoroughly anti-Semitic. In Maurice's description,
Coughlin was "a showman, huckster, and crowd-pleaser." Allied
with him in anti-Semitism was Fritz Kuhn, boss of the German-
American Bund, who got propaganda and inspiration from Josef
Goebbels and, eventually, jail time for theft. Another player in
the anti-Semitic movement in New York was Joe McWilliams,
who led something called the Christian Mobilizers and who rode
through the Manhattan streets in a horse-drawn wagon, holding a lantern in a vulgar replay of Diogenes, searching for an
"honest Jew" and lashing out at "God's frozen people."[1] McWilliams drew crowds but never made the papers.

"Anti-Semites—Coughlin, McWilliams—were taking over
the city," said Rosenblatt. "With the press blackout, politicians
could ignore the danger." Maurice couldn't. This was the high
water mark of American political extremism.

Rosenblatt took his frustration with the news blackout to
the offices of Arthur Hays Sulzberger, publisher of the *New York
Times*, and George Backer, publisher of the *Post*, and then to
James Warburg, international banker and advisor to FDR. He
was smart. He already knew how to open doors in ivory towers.
He pushed the need for press coverage—and got nowhere. The
publishers and Warburg were unmoved. They didn't want to
publicize hoodlums or, fearing an anti-Semitic backlash against
the newspapers, get their hands dirty brawling with thugs.

Still frustrated, Maurice turned from the boardrooms to the
streets, recruiting students, some of whom he had known in

Wisconsin, from Columbia Law School, and the Union Theological Seminary. Soliciting for muscle, he called on John Santo, behind-the-scenes boss of the Transport Workers Union and, it would soon be revealed, the Communist Party organizer in the Bronx. Santo said no and warned, "It's very dangerous, what you are doing."

"Communists repelled me," said Rosenblatt—"too ideological, too dogmatic. They could be witty, as in this CP ditty of the time: 'An economic Tory had an awful scare; he went to sleep on Wall Street and woke up broke on Union Square.'" Although he didn't like Communists, at the moment anti-Semites repelled him more. He took his meager force to the Bronx, 139th Street and Third Avenue, where the dozen or so recruits passed out ecumenical literature and called for peace in the streets. They wore coats and preppy ties for an expected confrontation with 350 proto-fascists, the Christian Front backed up by Kuhn's Bundists. Cops and medics awaited the conflict.

"My heart almost stopped at the sight," said Rosenblatt. "Should I call off the showdown? No. We've come this far. We're not going to back down."

"It's the Kikes. It's the Jews!"—shouts from the mob as it struck. Blood trickled before the cops moved, but no injuries were serious and no arrests made. Next day Rosenblatt found a headline inside the *Daily News:* "Coughlinites Riot; Attack Divinity Students." Bingo! Right-wing Christian thugs attack unarmed demonstrators preaching peace in the streets.

"That headline was priceless," said Rosenblatt sixty years later. It was a breakthrough, the flip side of appeasement. It resonated—an awakening for the city's liberals.

The upshot: formation of the New York City Coordinating Committee for Democratic Action, directed by Rosenblatt and backed by Mary Lasker, wife of the public relations tycoon, and the Protestant Church Council. The committee, through a network of agents, gathered information on right-wing, pro-Nazi activity and published it in its magazine, the *City Reporter.* Rosenblatt's agents included Stuart McClure, a would-be writer, and Jane Gordon, ward of Bernard Baruch. Jane recruited her boyfriend, David McKeekan, a brilliant actor later to light up Broadway and Hollywood as David Wayne. Good scouts all. They were paid $25 a week.[2]

There was ample material for the *City Reporter,* especially concerning efforts by the anti-FDR German embassy to influence the 1940 election. The embassy had an ace on Capitol Hill, poet-propagandist George Sylvester Vierick, who wrote "FDR Is a War Monger, a Man on Horseback" and "Roosevelt Will Plough Under Every American Boy," referring to the New Deal policy of burying crops and slaughtering hogs to inflate farm prices, as well as "Now with unfolding eyes we see the paradox of every fight; that both are wrong and both are right; that friend is foe and foe is friend—and nothing matters at the end." German Foreign Office documents described Vierick as "the most valuable liaison agent."[3]

The committee kept an eye on Abwehr—German intelligence—agents, as well as Charles Lindbergh and the isolationist America First Committee, in which Lindbergh was a prominent figure. Rosenblatt was suspicious of activities going on around 10 Battery Street, headquarters for shipping firms and almost certainly under the watch of Abwehr agents. He passed on his suspicions to the NYPD's Alien Squad, whose members were eager readers of the *City Reporter.* Apparently they helped keep watch on suspected Nazis.

It ended with Pearl Harbor. Rosenblatt closed the committee's doors at 512 Fifth Avenue and joined the army, eventually tracking petty miscreants as a sergeant with the Criminal Investigation Division in New Guinea. As usual, the army found a place in a round hole for a square peg—in this case an expert on Nazi espionage chasing GI moonshiners.

Manhattan postscript: Not so coincidentally, Rosenblatt's New York City was becoming flooded with German Jews, lucky ones who did not doubt the meaning of Adolf Hitler's highly touted theory of a "master race," his code for a population without Jews. Some came to safety through the derring-do of Arno Viehoever, a mechanical engineer turned candle manufacturer in Santa Cruz, California. A written account of Viehoever's exploits, taken from a speech he made to the Santa Cruz Rotary Club in 1988, came to Rosenblatt through their mutual good friend, the lobbyist Joan McKinney.[4] This was the essence of it:

Viehoever, a near miss for a slot as a U.S. Olympic pole vaulter in the 1936 games in Berlin, went to Germany anyway, on money supplied by his rich Uncle Joseph. Arno's job was to finance the escape of thirty-two Jewish employees of Uncle Joseph's leather goods factory in Offenbach.

Hanging around the bar of the Hotel Vierjahrzeiten (Four Seasons), Munich's five-star hotel, favored by Brits and Americans, the playboy cum money launderer met the lovely, inscrutable Unity Mitford, daughter of an aristocratic English family, already famed in those social circles for taking her pet rat to a fancy dress ball.

Arno and Unity went horseback riding together a couple of times. But no romance—the lady was already enthralled by Adolf Hitler, her political hero, whom she had met over kraut, bratwurst, and beer at the Ostera Bavaria, a restaurant favored by the Nazi gang. The dictator already had a live-in, Eva Braun, but he must have felt that the daughter of an English peer was worth stringing along.

Accordingly, Hitler offered, and Unity accepted, several invitations to call at the Berghof, the boss's home in the Alps above Berchtesgarten, along with her Great Dane, Rebel. Arno was her escort on one of these occasions, driving his snappy Horch convertible up the mountain, past platoons of armed guards, as guests at Hitler's forty-seventh birthday party. The gang was all there—von Ribbentrop, Goering, Goebbels, and the birthday boy himself.

As Arno described it, "a fire roared in the Berghof's great fireplace. When Rebel saw Hitler standing in the middle of the massive living room, he ran up, knocking him to the floor, tail wagging, tongue licking. For me, that was the end of a myth: 'If a dog likes him, he can't be all bad.' Nonsense."

The gathering was nonpolitical, said Arno, talk casual— "Where did you learn German? What will you do when you return home? The symphonic music was beautiful. Here I was with the most ruthless man in the world, and what power did I have to do anything about it? Going back to Munich, Unity mentioned she had a revolver in the glove compartment. She looked to see if it was still there. It was, and I thought how close I was to changing history."

Arno's bloated money orders did not escape police attention. He was escorted to police headquarters to explain what he was doing with all that money. He responded, "'I spent it. I'm big spender. I drink a lot. I go to the opera.' I was scared. They said, 'You couldn't spend this much money.' I took a chance and said, 'Gee, the Fuhrer didn't say anything about this when I had lunch with him a couple of weeks ago.' I guess they thought, 'What in hell have we got here!' So they let me go. I was still scared."

Mission accomplished, workers safe in the United States, Arno went home. Unity, in conflict over war between England and love for Hitler, attempted suicide in Munich's English Gardens with her revolver. Brain-damaged but not dead, she lived until 1948.

6 | Postwar and Palestine

MAURICE ROSENBLATT STILL HAD New Guinea mud on his boots when he got back to Manhattan from the South Pacific in 1945 looking for work. What to do? "Wall Street held no lure, neither did business—I wanted to be a journalist," said Rosenblatt, who hooked up with old friends. Among them was Rose Kean, a Broadway star from Missouri and a pal of the playwright Ben Hecht's.

The ambition didn't pan out—a few pieces for *The Nation*, but nothing steady at any of the city's daily newspapers. Something more important loomed. Rose introduced Maurice to Peter Bergson (née Hillel Kook), who had come to the United States from Palestine in 1940, initially to save European Jews from death camps and later to save those who had survived.

"Charming, witty, and seductive—women fell all over him," was Rosenblatt's impression of Bergson, whose postwar cause was a homeland for the one hundred thousand Jews scattered in displaced-persons camps around the European continent. Bergson's charm worked. Rosenblatt was brought into the cause with Bergson's promise of "an opportunity to make history." The same thing worked on Hecht, another key recruit to Bergson's born-in-the-USA organizations, the American League for Free Palestine and the Hebrew Committee of National Liberation.[1]

Almost lost to history, save in the memories of surviving participants, was the divisive, smoldering conflict between Bergson's organizations and the established Zionist groups. Each had the same goal—a homeland for displaced Jews—but they differed over the shape and structure of that Promised Land. Bergson aimed for a secular—not a Jewish—state, and he questioned the right of Zionists outside Palestine to make decisions about the nation-to-be. The two sides would be openly hostile.

"Bergson and his aide, Harry Selden, impressed me," said Rosenblatt. "They didn't talk much about German brutalities. Instead, they talked about the atrocities of indifference—the inaction. Their bitterest scorn fell on the official blindness on the part of the U.S.-backed British and the traditional Jewish organizations." Those organizations regarded Bergson's groups as "terrorists"—with some accuracy, given their backing of the Irgun, the Jewish army in Palestine engaged in a de facto war with Britain. Bergson, in turn, regarded them as "terrified," Rosenblatt said.

Maurice chose sides in the schism when he joined Bergson, his chief aide, Harry Selden, actresses Rose Kean and Ruth Chatterton, and a mix of Capitol congressmen and judges at the "Hebrew Embassy," a sprawling mansion at 2315 Massachusetts Avenue in Washington. In time Rosenblatt would use its fifth floor to pitch his cause to Senators Warren Magnuson, Dennis Chavez, and Wayne Morse—all of whom would have a hand in the creation of the State of Israel. He had a salary and a title— director of Washington operations for the American League for Free Palestine. In plain words, he was the league's Washington lobbyist. He explained that his cause was "to get the Jews out of the ghetto and the ghetto out of the Jews." He would argue for Israel, but—taking a page from Peter Bergson—against Zionists.

Rosenblatt quickly gathered momentum, organizing a committee of one hundred members of Congress who favored recognition of a new Israeli state. He had a magnificent recruiting tool in the ornate, elegant "Hebrew Embassy." Describing Bergson and his headquarters, Rosenblatt said, "Peter had style and a sense of its importance in winning friends and spreading influence." The mansion, built by the Marquis of Reading, one-time British viceroy to India, became party central for the homeland cause. Note that it was the "Hebrew," not the "Jewish," embassy.

"The difference between 'Hebrew' and 'Jew' is the difference between a nationality and a religion," Bergson wrote in a twenty-three-page letter to Chaim Weizmann, president of the

Zionist Jewish Agency, in April 1945.[2] By calling for a "Jewish Commonwealth," Bergson argued, Weizmann was aiming for a theocratic state. If he got it, what would be the status of Palestine's Muslims and Christians? "I propose we abandon the undemocratic idea," wrote Bergson. "We want a free state, not a Jewish state, just as there is no state religion in the U.S. . . . the Zionist position is disastrous for us Hebrews."

That letter put knives on the table. Rabbi Stephen Wise, head of the American Jewish Conference, wrote to Secretary of the Interior Harold Ickes, a supporter of the American League for Free Palestine, describing Bergson's organization as "irresponsible—existing to get money and names of non-Jews like yours."[3] The *Washington Post* described Bergson as a "nuisance diplomat," in contrast to Zionists, who represented "reputable Jewish organizations." Bergson said, "Rabbi Wise won't tolerate any other Jewish organization working for Palestine. He's stealing publicity and honor for himself."[4]

Back in Manhattan, it had been showtime for Palestine. While Rosenblatt was still soldiering in New Guinea, Hecht and Bergson had planted full-page ads in the *Times* and the *Post*, airing the plight of European Jews. More spectacular and bestirring, Hecht produced a pair of enormously successful and frankly propagandistic performances on the same subject. The pageant *We Will Never Die*, with words by Hecht and haunting music by Kurt Weill, opened in Madison Square Garden in March 1943, and the play *A Flag Is Born*, with its scathing criticism of Anglo-American Jews, premiered in September 1946.[5]

New York critics, in chorus, panned the plays as featuring "speeches that are too long, writing that is too purple" (*PM*) and "dubious poetry, political oversimplification" (*New Yorker*).[6] But the playwrights and the plotters got what they wanted: according to Harry Selden, money.[7] Even Mickey Cohen, a Los Angeles mobster better known for murder than for charity, dispatched an enormous "batch of cash." *We Will Never Die* raised more than $1 million while expressing Hecht's disdain for established Jewish organizations. *A Flag Is Born*, starring Paul Muni and a newcomer, twenty-two-year-old Marlon Brando, both working for minimum union scale, raised even more money and concern in New York and on the road in Chicago.[8]

Brando, at curtain time of a brilliant acting career, closed the play with a bitter soliloquy: "Where were you, Jews, when the killing was going on? When the six million were burned and buried alive in lime . . . where was your voice? There was no voice, you Jews of America. Nowhere! A curse on your silence." Later he explained: "I was outraged, along with most people, that the British were stopping ships carrying half-starved survivors of Hitler's death camps to a new life." (The British, between a rock and a hard place—Palestine's Jews and Arabs—wanted to ease conflict in their post–World War I mandate by halting Jewish immigration.) "The play," he said, "made me a zealous advocate for Israel."[9]

"I liked Brando," said Rosenblatt. "He had no sense of money, although given his talent, he could earn all the money he wanted. He was rather odd." *We Will Never Die* may have been forgettable, but Brando's creation of a washed-up prize fighter turned longshoreman ("I cudda been a contender") in *On the Waterfront* and the loutish Stanley Kowalski ("Stel-lah!") in *A Streetcar Named Desire* will endure as long as we favor film and stage.

From theater receipts, the league purchased a Navy submarine chaser and helped fund the Jewish underground—some say terrorist—army in Palestine, the Irgun. And more advertisements calling for a homeland for refugees. The ads played fast and loose with the names of congressional sponsors. In a stinging letter to Bergson in May 1943, Senator Harry Truman ordered his name withdrawn from the "Committee for a Jewish Army." He also noted Bergson's unauthorized use of Senator Ed Johnson's name. "This doesn't mean my sympathy is not with the downtrodden Jews of Europe," wrote Truman, soon to succeed FDR as U.S. president and the critical figure in the creation of Israel. "But you have abused your privilege."[10]

By 1947 the British wanted out. Palestine was a drain on the United Kingdom's depleted treasury, and Jewish-Arab conflicts were a drain on its soldiers' blood. A partition between Arab and Jewish sections by the United Nations was inevitable.

It came in 1947. Could the new State of Israel survive without U.S. recognition?

One of Rosenblatt's first targets in Washington, Warren Magnuson, frequently shared a whiskey with his old Senate buddy, Harry Truman. Magnuson's companion of that time, Ruth Overton, was the daughter of Louisiana Senator John Overton. With the beautiful Rose Kean on his arm, Rosenblatt made his initial contact with Magnuson at a party hosted by Ruth in the senator's apartment. Maurice knew where to hit the proper buttons.

Magnuson was already sympathetic. At the request of friends in Seattle, he had broached the issue of U.S. recognition of Israel with President Truman in the White House. He would go again. Out front, Magnuson put his name on an article for *Answer*, the house organ of the Hebrew Committee of National Liberation, calling for the resettlement of 1.5 million Holocaust survivors. "Before victory [in World War II] can be enjoyed, the future of Palestine must be settled," said Magnuson, sounding much like his new friend Rosenblatt.[11]

As the United Nations headed to a vote on what to do with Palestine, the Truman administration split. The White House, facing elections in 1948, leaned toward recognition of the potential new state; the State Department, under the estimable George Marshall, strongly opposed it. Marshall got so angry that he told Truman he would vote against his reelection if he opted for recognition. The CIA had warned that partition of Palestine and creation of a Jewish state wouldn't work.[12]

So had the American League for a Free Palestine. "We will never accept a partition of Palestine, but we will not use force [the Irgun] against it," Bergson wrote to the United Nations six months before the fateful vote in November 1947. The United States and the Soviet Union voted with the majority for partition, thirty-three to thirteen, and so Israel was created.[13]

There is no indication that Truman or even Magnuson was aware of the schism between Zionist and League aims. As Truman told State Department Mideast diplomats, "I'm sorry gentlemen, but I have to answer to hundreds of thousands who are anxious for the success of Zionism. I do not have to answer to hundreds of thousands of Arabs among my constituents."[14] Conspicuously absent in his exchange with the diplomats was any acknowledgment of Bergson's opposition to partition or his call for a secular Hebrew nation in Palestine. In May 1948, Truman formally recognized Israel, the new Middle East state.

Mission finished, if not accomplished, Rosenblatt closed the doors of the American League for Free Palestine. The dream of an ecumenical Palestine—"the only civilized and rational way to go," according to Maurice—closed with it. Decades later, in July 2003 at his home in Washington, D.C., I asked him whether the dream might have prevailed: "There's no yes or no answer," he said. "But I do feel partition between Arab and Jewish sections was bound to fail. Perhaps if a pluralistic, democratic state could have been imposed on Palestine within a generation, it would have worked."

Half a century after the founding of the new state, Peter Bergson, a founding father, gave a somber summing up. From his home in Shmaryahu, Israel, he wrote to Rosenblatt:

"I presume Israel is still of interest to you—although it may not match my obsession. After years of forced inaction I'm now going to launch a new [educational] campaign. Israelis must get rid of their inferiority complex and realize they are one of the most important nations in the world . . . an important manufacturing nation . . . a potential conduit between the Western republics and the emerging nations. . . . but it still depends very heavily on the United States.

"It is still in a permanent state of war with a hundred million Arabs. It maintains an army which is larger, I believe, than the armies of England, Germany or France. Yet as we approach our 50th year of war we still don't have a foreign policy geared towards peaceful existence. Instead, Israel accepts a destiny of perpetual war.

"We won spectacularly in 1967, and again in 1973. The problem with these great victories is that we aren't winning the war; we are only winning battles. Generals win battles. Statesmen win wars. We have no statesmen."[15]

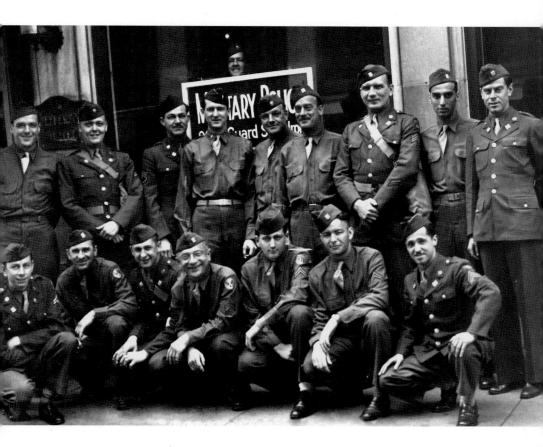

The good soldier Rosenblatt (standing, far right) and his military intelligence unit, South Pacific, 1943. Major assignment: eliminate Army moonshiners.

Roman holiday: Maurice Rosenblatt and Laura Barrone

For Maurice
who almost
got me killed
trying to Save
the Jews!
love —
Davy

*David McKeekan (aka David Wayne), actor and undercover agent for the
New York City Coordinating Committee, inscribed his photograph: "For Maurice,
who almost got me killed trying to save the Jews!"*

*Lobbyist and McCarthy
nemesis Maurice Rosenblatt*

*Maurice Rosenblatt, normally a man of
action, caught in repose*

Political allies and old pals: Eugene McCarthy and Maurice Rosenblatt

In a preview of Joe McCarthy, State Representative Al Canwell swears in a witness before his legislative committee investigating alleged Communists on the University of Washington faculty. Seattle Post-Intelligencer Collection, Museum of History and Industry

Democrats on the "McCarthy Committee": (left to right) Henry Jackson, Minority Counsel Robert Kennedy, John McClellan, and Joe McCarthy.
University of Washington Libraries, Special Collections, UW23623

The Carroll Arms Hotel, back stage to the Joe McCarthy drama.
"Exclusive and expensive," said Manager Jack Kloss. "After all, we cater to members
of the Senate, the world's most exclusive club."
Courtesy Library of Congress

En banc: The Permanent Subcommittee on Investigations. (left to right):
Senators Phil Potter, Everett Dirksen, Karl Mundt, Joe McCarthy (chair),
John McClellan, Henry Jackson, and Stuart Symington.
University of Washington Libraries, Special Collections, UW23624

Mission to Nanking: Secretary of State George Marshall (third from left); to Marshall's right is W. Walton Butterworth, U.S. minister to the Chinese nationalist government, and Chiang Kai-shek. Marshall's attempt to reconcile Chinese Communists and Nationalists failed, and civil war ensued.

Representatives Harold Velde, chair (seated, left), and Morgan Moulder of the House UnAmerican Activities Committee take a break during a hearing in Seattle.
Seattle Post-Intelligencer Collection, Museum of History and Industry

Witness Eugene Dennett knits while his attorney Ken MacDonald (right) studies the next move as they appear before the House UnAmerican Activities Committee in Seattle.
Seattle Post-Intelligencer Collection, Museum of History and Industry

Bergson sent this letter on August 27, 1993. He died a few years later. The war continues.

From Rosenblatt, though, no regrets. "For three years I'd worked for the creation of Israel," he said. "While the pay was only subsistence, the reward came in political capital, sufficient to launch my own lobbyist venture, sufficient for creation of the National Committee for an Effective Congress."[16] And sufficient for the most daunting challenge of any Washington lobbyist's career, the humbling of mighty Joe McCarthy.

Palestine Postscript: Although Maurice never mentioned it, Bergson's Hebrew Committee and Rosenblatt's American League for a Free Palestine were targets of intense FBI surveillance, 1943-47, through wire taps and a pair of snitches inside the organizations identified only as "T-1" and "T-2." The reports were obtained by the David S. Wyman Institute for Holocaust Studies. Apparently, they were instigated by the State Department at the request of the British Foreign Office, which had a "strong suspicion" that Peter Bergson was tied in with Palestinian terrorists—the Irgun.[17]

T-1 produced a detailed internal memo on talks with Senators Morse, Kefauver, Cooper, Gillette, and Jackson; the latter, according to T-1, "a very solid left Democrat." More revealing is the U.S. Communist Party hostility toward the Hebrew Committee ("irresponsible . . . harmful to the rescue of the Jewish people") and Rosenblatt's American League ("Jewish revisionists, fascist-minded agents of imperialism, sponsors of the Irgun terrorist group"). In contrast were the "solid Jewish organizations" and established Zionist groups, such as the American Zionist Emergency Council.[18]

7 | The Cause

WHEN PRESSED TO THE WALL of his comfortable home near the national Capitol, Maurice Rosenblatt was ambivalent, if not contradictory, about his history of political causes—the last, the most conspicuous and dangerous, the cause of exposing Joe McCarthy, a destroyer. Joe didn't tolerate enemies. He terminated them. Coming at the subject long after McCarthy's political destruction and death, Rosenblatt said, "I've never had a predilection for 'causes,' and I cringe whenever I'm assaulted by hard-breathing liberals, who, as Arthur Schlesinger Sr. said, 'are led around on a leash by an underdog.'"[1]

He continued: "When I was in the army, dealing with rookies, I said, 'The idea is not to die for your country but to make the enemy die for his.'" He sounded a lot like the cynical but steadfast prisoner of war played by William Holden in the movie Stalag 17, who is more interested in saving himself than the rest of the world. But the image doesn't quite fit Rosenblatt.

Along with his brief for nonscheduled airlines, Rosenblatt carried around the Capitol the lessons of J. D. Hardman, editor of the *Advance*, Dean George Sellery, the conservative academic who had risen (while liberals sat in silence) to smite the campus bullies in Wisconsin, and Peter Bergson, "the man of action, a man of purpose." He said, "Bergson and Sellery essentially taught me this: 'You've got a role to play—something bigger than yourself. You've got to take bigger steps.' With McCarthy I realized I needed to respond to his threat.

"It didn't come down like a bolt of lightning, but in steps. I realized I had a leadership function, that I could rally others and motivate them. I couldn't defer to others, I couldn't be a Polonius moralizing instead of acting. And I didn't see myself as just another adroit Capitol Hill operator. I had the kind of anger I felt confronting the Christian Front in New York. I wasn't going to yield.

"There were elements of defiance, bravado, adventure, and, yes, adrenaline. I was audacious. Hardman told me, men of purpose will take the gamble. You have to take a chance. Otherwise you won't know for sure you can make it. If you know in advance you can make it, the effort is no fun.

"I didn't see McCarthy as a personal challenge. It was bigger than that, much broader. In a small way, I wanted to make history."

In his twelve-volume *A Study of History*, Arnold Toynbee wrote of civilizations advancing or crumbling, given their response to challenges. Too much challenge and they are overwhelmed and collapse, but with sufficient response to the challenge, they survive and thrive.[2] Where Polonius sat back, talking, Rosenblatt responded, gambling. He didn't go under. Accordingly, he would thrive—and by his notion have fun.

By the new year, 1953, the gamble of his career was under way. Joe had to go—no bolt of lightning, just an accumulation of observations leading to the judgment. "McCarthy was a mean guy—a villain in the democratic process," said Maurice. One especially distasteful event was McCarthy's sneering, bullying, personal attack on the Senate historian, Richard Baker, whom he scorned as a "left-wing Democrat." "It was strictly against Senate decorum to hit on a staff man," said Rosenblatt. "It showed a man so swollen with power he could ignore such institutional disciplines. I didn't like it."

From the Capitol corridors and cloakrooms, Maurice's allies in the Senate, among them Dennis Chavez of New Mexico, began crossing the street to the Carroll Arms for quiet meetings. Senator Lister Hill, an Alabama populist and a favorite of FDR's—"Lister Blister," the president called him—came early one morning at the start of the new year, dispatched by Lyndon Johnson, the Senate majority leader. Washington had not softened Hill's Southern drawl; Rosenblatt said he talked like Stepin Fetchit, the Hollywood comedian who played the stereotypical

Negro servant. But he was ahead of his time as a progressive, helping to legislate education and health-care reforms. Widely respected, Hill also served as Johnson's tie to Southern conservatives.

"'Maw-reese,'" Rosenblatt remembered Hill saying, "'we've got to get that guy [McCarthy] while he's still on the rise. The Leader [Lyndon Johnson] says you've got to get a Republican point man. Democrats will follow.' Then he pushed his knuckle into my chest and repeated, 'You've got to get that rogue!'"

As they talked, Cohn and Schine came downstairs from their top-floor suite, smiling.

On another day, still early in January, Robert Kennedy showed up at the Carroll Arms. It was his first day on the job as a member of Joe McCarthy's investigation staff. Rosenblatt recalled a confrontation: "I was by the newsstand when Kennedy approached me, eyes blazing, hurling a string of curse words at me. 'What's got into you?' I asked. He said, 'You sonofabitch. You know what I'm talking about. Those stories!' I had written a piece for *The Reporter* magazine on his father, Joe Kennedy.

"He continued to curse me. I was speechless. There was a pause. Then he grabbed me and tossed me onto a couch in the lobby. His eyes were still blazing as he went off to meet McCarthy and the senator's entourage. As his father once said, Bobby is a great hater. I subsequently ran into him two or three times at parties. Each time he cut me dead, looking the other way. Bobby Kennedy for president? No!"

The new year, 1953, had begun with bang.

It was a critical time in the anti-McCarthy operation. But had Rosenblatt, Hill, Chavez, and "the Leader" known what McCarthy was doing behind the closed doors of his Subcommittee on Investigations that year, the matter would have taken on even greater urgency. The full story of those hearings lay buried for half a century until, in 2003, the transcripts of the proceedings were released by the Senate.

8 The Closed Hearings:
Vengeance and the VOA

ON FEBRUARY 13, 1953, the *Chicago Tribune*, by its own admission the "World's Greatest Newspaper," bannered across page one, "Uncover Plot in 'Voice' to Sabotage U.S." The byline gave the name Willard Edwards.

"Voice" was Voice of America (VOA), the radio propaganda arm of the United States Information Agency. The time was one of a peak in Americans' concern over Communist infiltration of their government and, not so coincidentally, in the power of Senator Joseph McCarthy, the new chairman of the Senate Permanent Subcommittee on Investigations.

Ruth Watt, the committee's chief clerk, later told Rosenblatt she had informed McCarthy that Senator John McClellan, the outgoing chairman, planned to leave the committee. Quick to respond, McCarthy called the Arkansas Democrat, according to Watt, and said, "You've got to stay on the committee to keep that sonofabitch Joe McCarthy in line." He was capable of humor.[1]

It was not that Americans had no real concerns. Ethel and Julius Rosenberg had recently been convicted in federal court of transmitting to the Soviet Union secrets of the United States' successful effort to make an atomic bomb. They would be executed in an electric chair at the end of that spring. Reds running America's radio propaganda as well as stealing its most guarded atomic secrets? "Comrats" losing China to Communists? So it seemed to many Americans.

Beneath that street-sales grabber of a headline, the Tribune's Edwards wrote: "A Senate investigation of Communist influence in the Voice of America uncovered amazing evidence of a conspiracy to subvert American policy in the nation's radio propaganda broadcasts." And further: "Scores of witnesses have involved high officials in a detailed account which indicates deliberate sabotage of American objectives in foreign propaganda. . . . closed door questioning developed a picture of such appalling proportions [that] executive sessions were ordered. . . . strictest secrecy concerning testimony was ordered by Roy Cohn, chief counsel."[2]

Ruth Watt told Maurice that "witness protection" was McCarthy's reason for closing the doors, "because he was still looking out for people. . . . if there was nothing there, he [the witness] was excused and nothing more was said." The reality was something else.

"Strictest secrecy" at these closed hearings was a joke. Stronger than before the 1952 elections, McCarthy allowed friends, sweethearts, and selected, friendly reporters, such as Edwards, to attend. No television. That would come later, but at the end there was Cohn, Schine, or Joe himself outside the hearing room to greet and brief an eager, compliant press. As he explained, "I always give a resumé [of proceedings] to the press. Otherwise a leak could come from one member and they [the press] get a very distorted picture."[3]

Edwards's story was as phony as Cohn's claim of secrecy and McCarthy's concern about "distorted leaks." Based on innuendos or biased assertions from fewer than half a dozen—not a score of—dubious witnesses, it likely came from leaks by Cohn or McCarthy himself. It is hard to believe that a reporter present at the hearings could have mangled fact and testimony so badly—even one with a determined ideological slant, like Edwards.

We know of McCarthy's conduct of the "closed" sessions, and thus of the distortion of Edwards's report, from transcripts made public in January 2003, fifty years after the fact, by the Senate Committee on Government Operations. "Basically, McCarthy could do anything he wanted," said John Adams, counsel to the U.S. Army. "He gave quite a show, including the impromptu press conferences to say what had happened in the closed hearings."[4]

That was not overstated. After the three Democrats on the committee walked away from it over a personal dispute, McCarthy was questioned about the absence of a quorum. Joe, who was still there, replied, "There is a quorum present. Under rules of this committee one person constitutes a quorum"—so long as the chairman was present. And this, he said, had been approved by the Senate as a whole.

What McCarthy wanted, most of all, was evidence to back his round-the-news-cycle assertions of Communist subversion inside the U.S. government—plus a measure of revenge on his enemies. Never mind the means or due process. Nothing in the four volumes of committee transcripts—four thousand pages of small print—provides redemption for a senator long since deemed a bully, obsessed, unfair, and perhaps a tad off his rocker.

Nor does glory shine upon the Democratic members of his subcommittee, Senators Stuart Symington, John McClellan, and Henry Jackson. With rare exceptions, the transcripts show them as silent witnesses to ruthless interrogations by McCarthy, Cohn, and the committee's unpaid counsel, G. David Schine. They were probably intimidated.

Some five hundred witnesses—credit McCarthy with determination to find a Commie—came before this inquisition. There were two categories: friendly witnesses, convinced that there were subversives inside VOA, and not-so-friendly ones, fearful for their jobs but determined not to be bullied into something they deemed harmful to U.S. interests. The "friendlies" wanted VOA to broadcast hard-core, never-mind-the-subtleties, anti-Communist propaganda.

McCarthy's heart must have leaped with the testimony of Robert Bauer, of VOA's Latin American division. Joe asked Bauer why VOA beamed juvenile adventure programs south of the border, instead of bare-knuckled anti-Commie material. "Was it an honest mistake or a deliberate attempt to sabotage VOA?" asked Joe. In either case, McCarthy's assumption was clear: it was wrong. "I don't know," Bauer answered. "We had a hard-hitting program we wanted to put on . . . but one easy way to sabotage it would be to use [VOA] money for ineffective products. I don't know one person [in VOA's overseas service branch] I would call a good American. . . . I can't say they are

Communists, but—there is that smell."[5]

Another friendly, Nancy Landkeith, testified that the French desk ran "pro-Communist themes." These included a discussion of America's "Negro problem" and comments such as "America has no culture, is incapable of serious thought, unimaginative and materialistic." Besides, said Landkeith, the French desk was loaded with "atheists." She identified herself as a Catholic.

Roy Cohn fed her a pregnant line: "Do you think the scripts show disrespect and disapproval of the American way of life?"

"Yes, I did," Landkeith answered.

"What do you think of Marcelle Henry [a VOA script-writer]?" asked Cohn.

"I think she is subversive," said Landkeith.

"That VOA material [by Henry] would sound more like the voice of Moscow, I gather," said McCarthy.

"Exactly," snapped Landkeith.

"Any programs on religion?" asked Cohn.

"Christian programs alienate the French," she answered. "They are taken to be atheistic."[6]

Ah, the smell.

From the friendly to the suspect. The committee interrogated one Harold Vedeler of VOA's East Europe desk, accused of soft-peddling propaganda into Czechoslovakia.[7] Cohn: "Were you ever a member of a subversive organization?" A— "Not that I know of." Q— "Were you a regular reader of *PM? The Daily Compass?*"—both left-of-center newspapers now long defunct. A— "No." Cohn ordered Vedeler to make a list of all organizations to which he had belonged over the previous decade. Presumably, Vedeler complied rather than face a contempt citation.

Vedeler was small fry compared with a red-hot suspect, Reed Harris, deputy administrator of the International Information Administration, overboss of VOA. What made Harris so hot was his decision to suspend Hebrew language broadcasts to the Middle East. This came at a time when Jewish leaders in Soviet-controlled Czechoslovakia, notably Rudolf Slansky, were on trial for their lives and soon to be executed. McCarthy viewed this as obvious material for hard-hitting anti-Soviet stories broadcast in

Hebrew and aimed at Israel. He was ignorant that at the time, Hebrew, Israel's official language, wasn't the one most commonly used there. German, Yiddish, English, and French were more popular in that five-year-old nation of immigrants.

Nevertheless, on February 23 McCarthy suggested that the decision was "sabotage" and asked Harris, a smart, formidable witness, if he was a Communist. "No," said Harris, "I'm anti-Communist." He had cancelled the Hebrew broadcasts to save money.[8]

But Harris was vulnerable. In the description of an admirer, Maurice Rosenblatt, Harris had been "a college liberal at Columbia, perhaps naive." As such he had edited the campus newspaper, the *Spectator*, and in 1932 wrote a book critical of payoffs to Columbia football players, conditions in the college cafeteria (unclean but managed by the university president's sister), the politics of the American Legion, and the necessity of religious, as opposed to civil, marriages. The book, *King Football*, as Harris would come to acknowledge, was more sophomoric than serious.

Well, said Inspector McCarthy, if Reed Harris wasn't a Commie, then his critique of the American Legion and religious weddings followed "the Communist Party line. . . . If you had been a Communist at the time, this is the type of book you would have written."[9]

Joe surely sensed "the smell." He called witnesses who had known Harris: Nathaniel Weyl and Donald Henderson. Weyl said he "had the impression" in the mid-1930s that Harris was "pro-Communist, but I can't substantiate it."

Henderson, an economics professor at Columbia, took the Fifth Amendment when asked if Harris was a Communist. The chairman judged that this reply implied Harris was a Communist, for otherwise Henderson would have answered the question. Joe had a thing about the constitutional right to avoid self-incrimination: "An innocent man doesn't need the Fifth Amendment."[10]

Harris's book had caused the college president to drop Harris from Columbia. McCarthy told the hearing that Columbia had "expelled him for radicalism." No, said Harris, he was suspended from classes but later reinstated. Help came from a lawyer dispatched by the American Civil Liberties Union (ACLU). Twice in his interrogation McCarthy noted Harris's connection with the ACLU: "Do you know they have since been listed as a front for and doing the work of the Communist Party?" Harris said he didn't know this and how could he have?—the ACLU never having made the attorney general's lengthy list of alleged subversive organizations.

The harrying would go on for hours, by sneaky implication condemning the witness. McCarthy did it like this: "The hearing had been closed because the charges made here against you are of such damaging nature to you, if true, that we felt the committee should examine all aspects of the situation and hear you in executive session." He continued: "I am very, very, interested in getting to the bottom of why certain things happen and finding out who is responsible and if there is incompetence, stupidity, or deliberate sabotaging of VOA. . . . the book you wrote in 1932 is straight from the Communist Party line. Why were you selected for this job? It's almost like [Secretary of State] Dean Acheson selecting me to write his memoirs."[11] That was meant to be a joke. No pals, Joe and Dean.

Exasperated, Harris declared, "I have been an honest and loyal employee of this government from the first moments . . . [and now] you are dealing with something that affects my whole life, the life of my family." Finally, a sympathetic glimmer comes through in this relentless, gloomy inquisition. Senator Henry Jackson, noting Harris's statements of opposition to Communism, asked, kindly, whether he could produce any anti-Communist writings. "I think I could forgive your youthful indiscretions if you have something [in writing] to counteract the book [*King Football*] you wrote in 1932," said Jackson. Harris had nothing of the sort on hand, but in the context of the hearing, it was nice of Jackson to ask.[12]

McCarthy would later examine Harris in a televised hearing, some of it shown, with appropriate comment, in Edward R. Murrow's documentary "See It Now," a deconstruction of Senator McCarthy that aired on CBS on March 29, 1954. "Senator McCarthy succeeded in proving Reed Harris had once written a bad book, which the American people had proved by not buying it," summed up Murrow.

Deeply shaken by the ordeal and, by implication, accused of subversion, Harris resigned from VOA in April 1954, one month after the televised hearings. In a happy twist of fate, he returned to the propaganda agency in 1961, hired back by Ed Murrow, President Kennedy's choice to head the U.S. Information Agency. "Reed never really got over the shock of McCarthy's smear through interrogation," said his friend, former VOA counsel Richard Schmidt. "The hearings were awful for Reed, a decent, intelligent man." Harris died in 1981 of natural causes.[13]

Raymond Kaplan died on March 5, 1953, the last day of the Harris interrogation. He threw himself under a truck on a Boston street rather than face questioning by the Subcommittee on Investigations. The VOA engineer left a suicide note for his wife and son: "I have not done anything in my job which I did not think was in the best interest of the country, or of which I am ashamed. And the interest of my country is to fight Communism hard. I am much too upset to go into the details of the decision which led to the selection of the Washington [State] and North Carolina sites [for VOA transmitters]. . . . My deepest love to all."[14]

Another VOA engineer had claimed in testimony that the transmitter located at Port Angeles, at the top of Washington's Olympic Peninsula, was inferior for broadcasting U.S. propaganda to the Far East and the Soviet Union—a problem with magnetic storms. Better to have placed the transmitter in California. It looked to Joe like another Commie plot to sabotage VOA.

Yet another witness, Dorothy Fried, a secretary in the Washington VOA office, was asked by Roy Cohn, "Are you now or have you ever been a member of the Communist Party?" "No, sir," she answered. "Let me ask you this," McCarthy interrupted. "Do you know whether [Raymond] Kaplan was a member of any

Communist fronts or whether he belonged to the Communist Party?" "I know nothing about his personal life," she replied.[15]

Nor could any other witness connect Kaplan with Communism. But the committee allowed the question—the smear—to linger: Why else would Kaplan have killed himself except to avoid questions about placing a VOA transmitter at Port Angeles and thus undermining America's effort to instruct the Far East? Such insinuations wrecked careers and created headlines but produced no charges against any of VOA's managers or employees. If he had been fishing instead of Commie hunting, McCarthy could be said to have been skunked.

But he was undeterred, not embarrassed even at the testimony of Nancy Stalcup Markward, a snitch for the FBI inside the Communist Party from 1943 to 1945. She had served as "membership director" for the Washington, D.C., cell assigned to recruit new members, which, she cheerfully admitted, she did.[16] It amounted to a make-work project for federal investigators. Markward recruited Commies, and G-men busted them.

Vengeance, not the pursuit of treason, carried McCarthy into the interrogation of Russell Duke and Ed Morgan. This was in January 1953, and the target was Oregon's acerbic Senator Wayne Morse, a particularly troublesome critic of Senator McCarthy's.

Duke was a Portland influence peddler ("public relations executive") close to Morse, and Morgan, a Washington lawyer, was counsel for the subcommittee chaired by Millard Tydings that had found McCarthy's celebrated Wheeling speech "a fraud and a hoax."

McCarthy was unforgiving. He questioned Duke ("I was pretty big in Oregon") on an alleged fee-splitting arrangement with Morgan for settling an income tax claim of $100,000 against Dr. David Tang Lee. Duke supposedly got $8,000, and Morgan, $4,000, for getting Morse to address the Internal Revenue Service. Morse confirmed he had called the IRS on behalf of his constituent, Dr. Lee.

Some embarrassment followed: "My ethics are on trial for communication with this man [Duke]," said Morgan. But no charges. Morse brushed off the business as constituent service. Morgan had gone to Wisconsin to campaign against McCarthy in 1952, and Joe might have felt good about himself in the role of a "Mr. Clean" at work in the Augean stables of payoff politics in Washington, D.C.[17]

Theodore Kaghan, director of public affairs for the U.S. High Commissioner in occupied Germany, labeled Joe's amateur hit men, Cohn and Schine, "junketeering gumshoes" after they told the Berlin press that Kaghan had "strong inclinations to Communism." McCarthy called Kaghan before his committee for several hours of hostile questions.[18]

Kaghan, a newsman, author, and playwright in the early 1930s, had signed a petition to place a Communist on a local election ballot and had worked alongside Joe Barnes on the foreign desk of the *New York Herald Tribune*. McCarthy asserted that Barnes, who had helped General Eisenhower write his memoir, *Crusade in Europe*, was at least a suspected Commie. Worse, Kaghan had roomed with a known (but never named) Communist and had stated in one of his plays that "Communists are people, too." Besides, Roy Cohn didn't take at all kindly to that crack about junketeering gumshoes.

Inspector McCarthy noted all of this and wondered how— wink, glower, nod—if Kaghan had worked with Barnes at the *Herald Tribune*, he could then have come to be pushing an anti-Communist line on behalf of Americans in Germany. But it didn't click. McCarthy got no further than this insinuation against Kaghan, who had a letter from the Austrian chancellor praising his "courageous anti-Communism," as well as security clearances from professional U.S. gumshoes. He apparently kept his job.

Even McCarthy's contempt citations were shaky.[19] Harvey O'Connor, a Seattle radical, ex-logger turned editor of the socialist *Seattle Daily Call*, took the Fifth Amendment when asked if he was a Communist. Outside the hearing room he answered the question: "No," he said, he never had been. Joe cited him for contempt of Congress. He was convicted, given a one-year suspended sentence, and fined $500—a judgment soon reversed by an appeals court. "I got caught in a brawl between McCarthy and the State Department," explained O'Connor, whose books on the Astors and the Guggenheims, nineteenth-century capitalists, were found by Cohn and Schine on the shelves of American libraries in Germany. Schine supplemented McCarthy in questioning O'Connor.

The chairman got even less revenge in his futile effort to settle a score with General Telford Taylor, the chief prosecutor at the Nuremberg war crimes trials after World War II. In a speech to cadets at West Point in December 1953, on May 16, 1954, Taylor had labeled McCarthy "a dangerous adventurer" making "groundless and shameful charges in an unscrupulous grab for publicity." He gave a reprise of that speech to Jewish war veterans in New York on May 6, 1954, noting the "fear and hysteria" aroused in the nation.[20]

Maurice Rosenblatt had first known Taylor in Manhattan. They became reacquainted in Washington, where Maurice found a suitable house for Telford and his wife, Mary, on Connecticut Avenue. "Telford was a New Deal lawyer, a card-carrying liberal, very crisp," said Rosenblatt. "You didn't mess with Taylor, and he couldn't suffer fools. I think he considered McCarthy a card-carrying sonofabitch."

Taylor's New York speech was a reprise of one he had made earlier at West Point. Within a week of his West Point attack on McCarthy, on December 8, 1953, Philip Young, chairman of the Civil Service Commission, was called before McCarthy's committee for questioning about Taylor's confidential personnel file. Someone—never identified—had flagged the report with the note, "unresolved question of loyalty." And someone breached its confidentiality by leaking the file to the investigations committee. McCarthy bore down hard on Young:

Q: Is Taylor loyal?

A: That flag means that if he applies again for a federal job, his file should be rechecked.

Q: But the flag means he is disloyal.

A: The flag itself doesn't mean he is disloyal. It's merely a warning to check his record.

McCarthy managed to squeeze a minor concession from the witness, summarizing by saying, "The flag means there was an investigation showing derogatory material and it was never resolved whether he was disloyal or not."

"A correct statement, sir," said Young.

"That is all," said McCarthy, dismissing the witness.

And that was it, save for the inevitable leaks of innuendo and suggestions of "disloyalty." No call came for Taylor to testify, nor was any investigation made of the alleged "derogatory material."[21] "If Telford had not been so self-controlled, I think he might have physically assaulted McCarthy," said Rosenblatt. "Fortunately, he was smart enough and disciplined enough not to do that."

"McCarthy was judge, jury, prosecutor, and press agent in these hearings," said Erwin Griswold, then dean of the Harvard Law School.[22] Looking back on McCarthy today brings to mind Franz Kafka's Inspector.

9 | The Inspector and His Witnesses

IF NOT NICER, the image of Senator Joseph McCarthy coming out of the fifty-year-old transcripts of his "closed" committee hearings is at least more complex than that of the one-dimensional inquisitor who appeared in the televised hearings in early 1954, the so-called Army-McCarthy hearings. Those later hearings left most Americans with the image of a scowling, bullying abuser of citizens' rights, though some saw a rugged savior of freedom from Communism. TV tended to bring out the darker side of the man.

In the transcripts, several Joes can be seen. There is, of course, Joe the bully, forsaking, in his phrase, the "lace handkerchief" for the gnarled fist in his search for Commie rats inside the recesses of government. There is also Joe the comforter, a kindly sort who really doesn't want to kill your career and ruin your reputation: just the names of Commies, please, which might include you, the witness. Finally, the transcripts, released forty-five years after McCarthy's death from alcoholism, give a rare glimpse of Joe the stymied, a bully getting as much as he gives.

Hanging over the witnesses called before these hearings— and there were hundreds of them—was the threat of a contempt-of-Congress citation and sometimes a threat of perjury charges. Nothing in the techniques "the Inspector" used on these witnesses would come as a shock to anyone in a metropolitan cop shop, where the business is to get a confession, never mind a little verbal dishonesty. It beats bamboo sticks under the fingernails.[1]

In his probe of suspected "subversion and espionage" inside the research facility of the Army Signal Corps, on October 16,

1953, McCarthy called Jack Okun, a radar technician. Roy Cohn asked Okun whether he had roomed with another Signal Corps researcher, one Harvey Sachs. Okun said that for a "few months" he had.

Cohn: "Did you know Sachs was a Communist?"

Okun: "No, sir."

McCarthy: "He [Sachs] never admitted he was a Communist?"

Okun: "No."

McCarthy: "Your testimony is contrary to [that of] other witnesses. . . . Either they perjured themselves or you have been." The matter would be turned over to the Justice Department.

A fortnight later, on the same trail of Signal Corps subversion, McCarthy called Harvey Sachs before the committee and fired a battery of questions at him about his alleged Communist connections. Sachs had little to say. In an earlier interrogation McCarthy had told Sachs, "Go get a lawyer who is not a Communist—a good honest lawyer. Then return and come clean."[2]

"We won't spend any more time to get this information with pliers," McCarthy threatened. "We have testimony about you, a great deal of it. . . . you are not telling the truth, or someone else has perjured themselves."

McCarthy noted that Sachs had roomed with Jack Okun, who was "Communistically inclined." He ordered the witness to prepare a list of all of his roommates, as well as places stayed and the date he started work at the Signal Corps.

Missing in this record is testimony from "other witnesses" alleging that either Sachs or Okun was a subversive. Joe was bluffing, an old cop shop trick. Nor does the record show any charges having been filed against these witnesses for either perjury or contempt. Sachs and Okun might even have kept their jobs.

Chief among the Inspector's weapons was the bluff. As he told Benjamin Wolman at the Signal Corps hearing, "We know something about you. You can go commit perjury if you care to. I do not care." Wolman refused to answer the question of whether his wife was a Communist, but when Joe asked whether she had been a Communist before their marriage, Wolman answered no.

"He has committed perjury," said McCarthy.[3] The record does not indicate that Wolman was so charged.

"You have been identified under oath as a member of the Communist Party and an important functionary in *Amerasia*, a tool for Soviet espionage." So McCarthy opened an interrogation of Harriet L. Moore Gelfen. She had written a book for the U.S. military on Communism. "You are a very, very important functionary of the Communist Party."

It was a tough shot, based, for a change, on actual testimony. That testimony had come from Louis Budenz, by then a professional anti-Communist tattletale with a less than sterling record for tattling the truth. But the record does not indicate that Gelfen broke and turned songbird. This time it was a busted bluff.[4]

Almost sweet is the transcript of the interrogation of Allen Lovenstein, of the Signal Corps laboratory, by committee staffer Robert Jones. "I don't know if you know this," said Jones, "but nothing you say here will go outside this room. . . . it's just [an opportunity] to unload your heart, more or less, and will help us immensely in proceeding."[5] That sweet-talk amounted to a lie. McCarthy and Cohn were prolific in their "off-the-record" leaks of committee interrogations to eager newsmen waiting to lap it up outside the hearing-room doors, apparently unconcerned that they were taking in a slanted version.

One hapless witness admitted, under questioning, that yes, he was a subscriber to *The Reporter* magazine. It's gone, now, still lamented, and not to be confused with the New York City Coordinating Committee's *City Reporter* of the 1930s. While it lasted, *The Reporter* was a liberal, vigorously anti-Communist journal, edited, published, and financed by Max Ascoli. Joe told the witness that the magazine, "as far as we know is the successor to *Amerasia*, a strictly Communist party-line paper. The editor is Mr. Ascoli. He is a Russian who takes it on himself to try and crucify anyone who hurts the Communist party line."[6] *The Reporter* was also anti-McCarthy.

Max Ascoli, born in Ferrara, Italy, in 1898, was a lawyer at odds with Benito Mussolini's Fascist regime. A Jew, he came to the U.S. in 1931 on a Rockefeller fellowship, taught political science, married an heiress, and, in 1949, with her wherewithal, financed *The Reporter*. It paid top dollar for top journalists, including Albert Ravenholt and Joe Miller.[7] Maurice Rosenblatt, an acquaintance of Ascoli's, remembered him as "very Italian, volatile, given to explosions of temper and giving people nasty names." His magazine's demise, ironically, was attributed partly to its hostility toward the radical left in the 1960s. Joe's inability to distinguish an Italian from a Russian immigrant must be attributed to political bias. Sadly, the record shows no attempt by anyone on the committee or its staff to correct McCarthy's errors of fact or to challenge his judgment.

McCarthy comes across as downright soothing in his questions to Carter Lemuel Burkes, a reluctant witness. "This is not a threat," he says. "This is just friendly advice I'm giving you. Do you understand that?" And later he asks Burkes whether he has always preferred "our system of government to the Communist system." When Burkes answers yes, McCarthy immediately replies, "You understand, of course, it is no crime to prefer Communism to our system. You have a right to prefer it. I am not saying you do [prefer Communism], you understand."[8]

The tale told by Victor Rabinowitz, a leftist lawyer whose clients had appeared before McCarthy, is almost poignant. Rabinowitz approached McCarthy in a Senate hallway to make a plea on behalf of Sylvia Berke, a clerk at Public School 50 in New York City's Bronx: "He [McCarthy] stepped out of a Senate elevator, saw me, and with his usual geniality, which he exhibited only in personal relations, he threw his arms around me, shouting, 'Hello, Vic. What can I do for you?'

"We went to a private room adjacent to the elevator. I asked whether he would excuse Sylvia from testifying . . . that it seemed unnecessarily cruel to this young woman to deprive her of employment in a situation that made it possible for her to work and raise a child, albeit on a very low salary.

"She is going to take the Fifth Amendment anyhow, so the committee would get no information from her. McCarthy's answer: 'It's all right with me, but you'd better take it up with

83

Roy.' Cohn was standing nearby . . . his answer was quick and peremptory: 'Nonsense, we can't withdraw the subpoena.' I told him since she was going to take the Fifth Amendment the only result would be that she would lose her job. It made not the slightest impression on Cohn."[9]

So Sylvia Berke came before the committee on November 4, 1953, Rabinowitz at her side. She said no when asked if she was a member of the Communist Party. She took the Fifth Amendment when asked if she had been a member in the past.

"Did you drop out of the Communist Party so you could come here today—under instructions of Communist Party officials—and say you were not a member?" asked Cohn.

"No," she answered.

Cohn was determined not to take no for answer. "Who instructed you to drop out of the Communist Party?" he asked.

"I'm not saying anybody did," Berke replied. "I'm not saying I ever was a member."

McCarthy seemed exasperated at the woman's dance, from her answers about the present to her use of the Fifth Amendment when questioned about her past. He raised the flag of patriotism in an apparent reference to the war in Korea, where U.S. troops were engaged against a Chinese Communist army: "In view of the fact that the Communist half and our half is at war, and a great number of our young men have died in the shooting part, do you think any good American should keep from the proper government officials his or her knowledge of the members of the Communist conspiracy?

"I cite the Fifth Amendment on that," said Berke.

"I'd like to see some of these Fifth Amendment cases in Russia and see them cite the Fifth Amendment," concluded McCarthy, hustling Berke offstage. [10]

The chairman's attitude toward potential witnesses before his committee is best revealed in his warning during an investigation of the Army Signal Corps facility at Fort Monmouth, New Jersey: "Even though you think the man [witness] is completely innocent, keep this in mind, that the most dangerous agent is the man who looks like a Sunday school teacher."[11]

In neither looks nor manner would Paul Hacko have suggested a Sunday school teacher. An employee of General Electric, a veteran of World War II, Company E, 105th Infantry, and a sometime candidate of the socialist American Labor Party for Congress, Hacko had been around. His itinerary, he testified with reluctance, included a stint inside the Communist Party as an FBI snitch. He gave back as much smack talk as he got from the Inspector. Besides, he was grouchy, having responded to a committee subpoena delivered only the night before. McCarthy frequently applied the quickie summons, presumably to catch the witness unprepared and thus more easily intimidated.

It didn't work this time. After McCarthy's now familiar overture to an interrogation—"Are you now or have you ever been, etc."—Hacko interrupted: "You are not going to put words into my mouth. I say this committee is illegal."[12]

Joe: "Don't talk while I'm talking."

Hacko: "Proceed."

Joe: "I'm going to ask you about Communist Party connections and about espionage."

Hacko: "I object. You are stating that I am a Communist and I object."

Joe: "Look, mister, you are going to act like a gentleman."

Hacko: "I am a gentleman and I believe you are not a gentleman."

Joe: "Will you be quiet?"

Hacko: "I will leave."

Joe: "Marshal, stop this witness."

Hacko: "You are taking away my Thanksgiving turkey."

Joe: "Do you want additional time?"

Hacko: "I don't want anything from you. Maybe Mister Schine does."

Joe: "We have testimony you are a Communist."

Hacko: "That's a lie. . . . You make me sick. You are doing more harm to the U.S. government than anyone else."

Joe: "Can you get over being sick long enough to answer questions?"

Hacko: "I haven't even had breakfast. I don't think I can.

You can hold me in contempt. . . . I'm walking out of here."

Joe: "You are not. . . . Are you an espionage agent of the Communist Party as of today? . . . Has the Communist Party ordered you to obtain information about work at GE [General Electric]?"

Hacko: "Who said I belonged to the Communist Party? What do you mean 'ordered'? . . . Why don't you stop that line? . . . I am under your orders. All you need is a swastika and a helmet and you will be right in your place."[13]

Joe: "Look, mister. We have a very important job to do here and it is not pleasant to sit here and listen to people like you rant and rave."

Hacko finally answered no, he was not an espionage agent, or a Communist, and left. McCarthy must have been relieved. It's easy to imagine that Paul Hacko might have left the witness table to cheers and congratulations had the hearing been open to the public.

Hacko would not be asked to appear in subsequent televised hearings.

Nor would Benjamin Zuckerman, another reluctant witness. McCarthy, exasperated, made a hypothetical question from Zuckerman's testimony: "If I told you what you just said, wouldn't you think that either I was the damndest liar you ever heard or that I was a case for a mental institution?"[14]

Zuckerman let the pregnant question hang.

10 The Clearinghouse

POWER MAY CORRUPT ITS USER. Even a little bit may loosen the constraints of morality or judgment. But it may also blind. The user can't see the point at which he goes over the line, at the wrong time with the wrong subject, to become—against his self-interest—an abuser. Joe McCarthy, "the most influential demagogue" in American history,[1] began to have problems with his political vision. Inside the Senate club, Joe got reckless.

His charge of disloyalty against Owen Lattimore, an obscure scholar and State Department advisor with an unfortunate facial twitch, might bestir negative emotions from a not-yet-prominent Washington lobbyist like Maurice Rosenblatt. But—and McCarthy knew this by intellect and instinct—it played well with a large number, possibly a majority, of everyday Americans, who were already suspicious of "eggheads" and not yet suspicious of the Wisconsin senator.

The "club" was something else. Early in 1952, from the Senate floor and thus safe from a legal charge of slander, he accused an aide to Senator Carl Hayden of having given a security clearance to an economist who was the subject of no fewer than "twelve separate FBI reports." The accused aide had worked for the State Department's loyalty board.[2]

Hayden didn't like it. He demanded that McCarthy prove his charge. McCarthy blew the demand aside, dismissing Hayden as an "old, blind fuddy-duddy."[3] McCarthy made an enemy. Hayden did have eyesight trouble, but which of the antagonists was the more blind? Another carelessly created enemy was Harry Byrd of Virginia, chairman of the Senate Finance Committee and, like Hayden, a conservative Democrat.

But McCarthy's fall was far from certain in 1952, much less imminent, despite liberal outrage against him in the Senate. William Fulbright (whom Joe called "Halfbright"),[4] Herbert Lehman, Mike Monroney, and Guy Gillette, as well as Carl Hayden, made anti-McCarthy speeches. Another, and the most conspicuous, was by William Benton, who said, "McCarthy is a hit-and-run propagandist of the Kremlin model."[5] They all complained of McCarthy's "un-Senate-like behavior—his breech of the club propriety."[6] These critiques fell as harmlessly as butterflies against a brick wall. For a time they may even have worked to McCarthy's advantage outside the Washington beltway. For a spell, the words "courageous" and "McCarthy" came together for a vast number of Americans caught up in anti-Communist emotions: here's a straight-shooting guy standing up to those Commie-coddlers, who can't take his kind of Americanism.

When Guy Gillette invited Joe to appear before the Subcommittee on Privileges and Elections to reply to Benton's charges of impropriety, McCarthy was insulting: "Frankly, Guy, I have not and do not intend to read, much less answer, Benton's smear attack. I'm sure you realize the Benton-type material can be found in the *Daily Worker* [Communist Party newspaper] any day of the week and will continue to flow from the mouths and pens of camp followers as long as I continue my fight against Communists in government."[7]

The futility of efforts by Joe's liberal critics was obvious. "I saw a tremendous vacuum," recalled Rosenblatt. "Men with good intentions, like Bill Benton and Herbert Lehman, standing out in a no-man's-land, attacking McCarthy—and not making a dent. With my background of opposition to right-wing extremists, it was inevitable that the committee [National Committee for an Effective Congress] and I would become involved with Joe McCarthy."

To fill the vacuum, in the spring of 1953, while Joe waged his investigations behind (sort-of) closed doors, Rosenblatt formed the McCarthy Clearinghouse as a congressional watchdog arm of the NCEC. He analyzed the need for it and stated its aims in a fifteen-hundred-word confidential memo to Robert

Nathan, chairman of Americans for Democratic Action (ADA), on March 4, 1953:

"[We] must start operating on the [Capitol] hill . . . no question that this is the only way [to stop McCarthy] and that nobody is doing it or even thinking about operating in any concrete realistic fashion. . . . The strategy involves working with [congressional] Committees. . . .

"The McCarthy–[William] Jenner–McCarran group are going after the machinery of government. . . . McCarthy has already created the precedent of being able to control-by-inhibition the State Department and our foreign policy because he has blitzed the personnel. . . . McCarthy exists only in the vacuum liberals have created.

"Can't liberals use the simple [lobbying] techniques of a God-damned power company?"[8] The NCEC would raise the money; the Clearinghouse would do the legwork.

Organizational help came from Dean Francis Sayre, the Washington Episcopal bishop; Harry Selden, late of the American League for Free Palestine; and Stewart McClure, Maurice's New York aide turned administrative assistant to Alabama Senator Lister Hill, "Maw-reece's" partner in the anti-McCarthy operation. To keep a record of McCarthy's speeches, news clips, and assorted other data—material that became ammo for the McCarthy opposition—they hired a full-time researcher, Lucille Lang, and rented a one-room office in the Carroll Arms. Wherewithal came from well-heeled liberals, among them Marshall Field and Paul Hoffman, a pal of President Eisenhower's and president of Studebaker autos.[9] Money flowed through the NCEC.

"Our purpose was to contain and oppose McCarthyism at the source of its power—the Congress," said Rosenblatt in an interview. In a memo, unaddressed but apparently meant for Clearinghouse backers, the organizer noted, "A head-on assault can't really hurt McCarthy since this is not a logical contest but a struggle for power."

In June 1953, a breakthrough. Rosenblatt spied a one-paragraph story on a back page of the *Washington Post*. It said that McCarthy had appointed one J. B. Matthews as staff director of the investigations subcommittee. Bells rang. Maurice asked Lucille Lang, the $75-a-week Clearinghouse researcher, for a background check and, if it turned out as he expected, to spread the word to friendly reporters.[10] These included the *Post's* Murray Marder, Clark Mollenhoff of the Cowles newspaper chain, Phil Potter of the *Baltimore Sun*, and the columnist Jack Anderson.

Lang found what Rosenblatt suspected in an old copy of the *American Mercury* magazine, in a piece titled "Reds in the Churches," written by J. B. Matthews. In it Matthews said that "the largest single group of the Communist apparatus in the United States today is composed of the Protestant clergy." He specifically shook an accusing paragraph at G. Bromley Oxbam, bishop of Washington, D.C., and close friend of Senator Harry Byrd. Lang spread the word.

J. B. Matthews had a jigsawed political background. He was a native of Hopkinsville, Kentucky, where church and state were close enough to ignore the differences and where church came before play, the Holy Bible before the local newspaper. The only institutional rival to the church was the Hopkinsville Hoppers, the Class D baseball club of the oldest organized minor league, the Kitty League. Matthews, a Methodist with a pleasant smile and a paunch, became an ordained minister. He would move from the social Gospels of the New Testament to Marxist socialism and then reject that conversion to preach the new gospel of anti-Communism.

Matthews taught the early edition, the socialist one, at Fisk University in Nashville, a predominantly black college, and he wrote a book, *Partners in Plunder*, a denunciation of capitalism cum Christianity. It claimed that J. P. Morgan ran the Episcopalian Church and Andrew Mellon bossed the Presbyterian congregations. Then Matthews flipped sides.

The "new" Matthews called *Partners* a "nasty stinking book" and asked the Lord for forgiveness. Turning hard right, he became a rising star, feeding anti-Commie material to his favorite columnists, Fulton Lewis Jr. and Westbrook Pegler, both Hearstlings.

In February 1953, soon after Matthews's conversion, the Christian Front gave a dinner in his honor, with Hearst columnist George Sokolsky as master of ceremonies. The guests included a who's who of America's right-wing militants—Roy Cohn, Alfred Kohlberg, Merwin K. Hart. Sokolsky read a message from Vice President Richard Nixon, a "white-collar McCarthy" in Adlai Stevenson's description. The event marked Matthews's turn from a liberal "gospel" to a right-wing one.[11]

Even before he found McCarthy, Matthews found a pulpit before the House Un-American Activities Committee, where he declared Adolf Hitler's dictatorship nicer than Joseph Stalin's,[12] which is akin to saying the needle is nicer than the rope for executions. Maybe, as Stalin once said of a rival before he had him shot, Matthews had become dizzy with success. His charge that "at least 7,000 Protestant clergy in the United States are serving the Kremlin's conspiracy" wasn't very smart.[13]

News produced by the Clearinghouse about Matthews's attack on preachers "stirred up the biggest hornet's nest you ever saw," said Ruth Watt, chief clerk to the Subcommittee on Investigations, who otherwise described the ex-Communist turned preacher turned tattletale as an able administrator. The news was too much for Senators Henry Jackson, John McClellan, and Stuart Symington, the Democrats on the subcommittee. They demanded that McCarthy fire his new staffer. When he refused, the three resigned from the subcommittee in July 1953.

Months later, under some pressure from Eisenhower, McCarthy relented. He dumped Matthews and agreed to hire Robert Kennedy as counsel for the committee minority. Accordingly, the Democrats resumed participation.

It was a telling episode. For perhaps the first time, the man who had turned anti-Communism into a spectacular political career had suffered damage. As Rosenblatt noted, the Matthews affair "demonstrated McCarthy's vulnerability." Word began to filter through the Senate cloakroom.

One anti-McCarthy speech, based on data collected by the NCEC's Clearinghouse and delivered on the Senate floor, hit a nerve with both Democrats and Catholics. In it, Senator Dennis Chavez of New Mexico, a frustrated member of the Senate Democrats' Policy Committee, chaired by Lyndon Johnson, denounced Louis Budenz, an ex-Communist turned professional anti-Communist informer. Rosenblatt recalled that he helped Chavez draft the speech, but not its most memorable line: "This man [Budenz] is using the Catholic Church as a shield. My ancestors brought the cross to this country"—Chavez was a descendant of early Spanish colonists of New Mexico—"and this man is using it as a club."

What prompted this speech, Chavez told Rosenblatt, who related their conversation in an interview, was the unwillingness of Johnson and the policy committee to attack McCarthy. On the contrary, "they talked about stealing Joe's thunder by attacking the State Department and chasing homosexuals. They didn't want to go over McCarthy. They wanted to go under him." Chavez was disgusted.

Jim Farley, the Democratic Party chairman, called on behalf of New York's Cardinal Spellman to rebuke Chavez. The archbishop of Santa Fe demanded that he recant, a demand reflecting the Catholic Church's tolerance of McCarthy. Chavez answered that this was none of the church's business—it was a matter of politics, not faith and morals.

McCarthy kept charging. In early July 1953 he told the army's congressional liaison, General Miles Reber, that he wanted a direct army officer's commission for G. David Schine. His investigator was about to be drafted as a buck private. It was a few weeks later that his committee began investigating Army Signal Corps employees in New York and alleging that subversives were operating at Fort Monmouth, New Jersey. Having savaged American Far East experts, Voice of America, and U.S. libraries in Europe, McCarthy's rampage escalated from the State Department to the U.S. Army.

For thirty-five days in the late spring of 1954, the question "Who promoted Irving Peress?" would overshadow domestic and foreign affairs, including the loss of Dien Bien Phu by French colonials to a force of Vietnamese guerrillas. Who was Peress? He was an army major, a dentist, who was given automatic promotion to lieutenant colonel. A sometime civilian lefty, he might have been characterized by McCarthy as drilling from within. Actually, Peress was a pretext for tackling another established authority, the U.S. Army, which had refused, for obvious reasons, to give G. David Schine an automatic officer's commission.[14]

Ruth Watt, the veteran committee clerk, said the pressure on behalf of Schine came from his close buddy, Roy Cohn: "Well, Roy worked with Schine all the time and they went on trips—of course we couldn't pay his [Schine's] expenses, but he didn't have to worry about money—where he got a lot of it, I don't know . . . he wasn't on the payroll. Then he went into the army and Roy was the one who did all that stuff trying to get him out. Of course Joe McCarthy could have cared less, but he did it for Roy." (Mrs. Watt later described McCarthy as "a very kind man, very thoughtful of people working for him.")[15]

The Clearinghouse opposition still wondered what to do. In July 1953 Rosenblatt met with Paul Hoffman, Francis Sayre, Harry Selden, George Agree, Millard Tydings, Robert Nathan, William Benton's attorney Gerry Van Arkel, and Drew Pearson's attorney Warren Woods—the gifted hard core of McCarthy's enemies. "We all had agreed to challenge the demagogue," said Rosenblatt. "Obviously we were doing something wrong. We needed to reexamine our assumptions. Where should we turn? Nobody wanted to take that step [to a censure motion], to lead the fight. To tangle with McCarthy was a very, very scary thing. He was abusive. There was no exit. . . . most people had nothing to hide, but it was a contagious fear."[16]

Gerry Van Arkel helped crystallize the group's strategy. As revealed in a letter to Benton, he likened the tactics of "Taft conservatives"—a reference to the Senate allies of Robert Taft of Ohio—in 1953 to the nurturing of Adolf Hitler by German industrialist-conservatives in the 1920s and 1930s. The German conservatives thought Hitler would be useful to them, just as the "Taft group" thought they could use McCarthy. "Tragically mistaken," said Van Arkel of both groups. It was only a matter of time, in his view, before McCarthy turned on Eisenhower and his secretary of state, John Foster Dulles.[17]

Stewart McClure refined Van Arkel's analogy into the keystone of opposition tactics. "Why, hell," he burst out at a Clearinghouse meeting, "McCarthy isn't even anti-Communist." Instead of fighting Communists he was pursuing Americans—Lattimore a prime example—who didn't conform to his attitudes. He wasn't a conservative but a radical, an extremist in tactics and objectives bent on tearing down leaders and institutions of the republic.

"In Stewart's analysis," said Rosenblatt, "McCarthy was fighting the establishment. What we had to do was to pit him against those establishment pillars. We had a firm strategy." Their game plan: jujitsu.

The new Senate minority leader, Democrat Lyndon Johnson, kept an eye on the Clearinghouse opposition from the sidelines. As Rosenblatt analyzed it, "Democrats are milling around without leadership or purpose—but they might back [an anti-McCarthy] move by Republicans.[18]

Indeed, Johnson would rationalize McCarthy as "a Republican problem." He was acutely aware, however, that he and Joe shared common benefactors in Hugh Roy Cullen, Clint Murchison, and H. L. Hunt, Texas oil and gas tycoons of right-wing persuasion. Besides, he commented, "Joe will go the extra mile to destroy you."[19]

As a service to his petroleum patrons, Johnson had stooped as low as Joe to destroy the chairman of the Federal Power Commission, Leland Olds, a pro-consumer New Dealer regarded by the Texans as hostile. At confirmation hearings in 1949, Johnson cited Olds's early writings to insinuate that he had been a Communist sympathizer in the 1920s. The oil-and-gas boys dug up the dirt; Johnson used it well. Olds's confirmation was rejected, his spirit wrecked. But gas profits rose.[20] It was a textbook example of personal demolition, a lesson Joe might have taken.

For the balance of 1953, McCarthy kept moving toward his showdown with the U.S. Army, questioning the promotion of a suspected "Comsymp," Peress. Lucille Lang kept stashing McCarthy data in the Clearinghouse files. And public adoration of the make-believe tailgunner soared to poetry. Two samples, with my apologies to Sir Walter Scott:[21]

> *A Tear for the Beautiful* (author unnamed)
> Breathes there a man with soul so dead
> Or interest in affairs so slight
> Who never fervently has said,
> "How I admire McCarthy's fight."

> *McCarthyism Is Patriotism*
> Come one and all and hear me say
> About a knight this very day
> Whose armor bright is truth and play
> 'gainst foes who would this land betray.
> The lefties and the eggheads spout
> In press and radio
> To spread their potent lies about
> There are no depths they will not go.

In late December 1953, Rosenblatt and his companion, Laura Barone, took time out. Given entrée by Senator Chavez, they went to Rome to call on Pope Pius II, the former Cardinal Pacelli, a one-time emissary to the Church in Bavaria. Rosenblatt's aim was to flip the Catholic leadership away from its sponsorship of McCarthy. He and Laura also needed a vacation. Laura took an apartment in Rome's modern section, and Maurice pulled more wires to gain the meeting with Pius II.

His Holiness was well-traveled and sophisticated, and Rosenblatt figured he could talk straight with him on topic A—Joe McCarthy. He wanted to explain that McCarthy was a liability to the Church and get the message back to Cardinal Spellman in New York. Father Cosgrove, of the American College in the Vatican, opened the last door, and Maurice got his interview with the pope.

"Where are you from, my son? How are the [Brooklyn] Dodgers doing?" the baseball-savvy pontiff inquired when introduced to Maurice, who closed to the point. "Your Holiness has added status to McCarthy," he said. "McCarthy is exploiting your approval." The pope listened carefully, and years later Rosenblatt described him as "an eighty-nine-year-old chief executive with amazing energy. It's hard to measure the impact of our meeting, but at least, word got back to the U.S. that Joe didn't speak for the Vatican. Subsequently, U.S. bishops sent out a letter [stating] that Joe didn't speak for the pope."[22]

Laura and Maurice stayed on for six weeks, meeting Rome's American press at the bar in the Excelsior Hotel, hitting the night spots along the Via Veneto, where the American singer Bricktop starred, and purchasing paintings from Mario Russo, a popular Roman artist of the time. The press bought the drinks at the Excelsior and wanted Maurice to fill them in on His Holiness. Rosenblatt obliged: "He was dressed plainly, except for red slippers; slightly stooped but very alert and bright. The clatter of Olivetti typewriters fills the Vatican's inner chambers—a very busy place." Later he described the pope as "a shrewd and worldly politician, in certain ways resembling Lyndon Johnson." A key difference, said Maurice: "Pacelli's wit was sophisticated, Johnson's earthy."

Back in the United States, beneath the prose and poetry surrounding the mighty Joe, was the reality of the U.S. Senate, a house evenly divided between Republicans and Democrats in 1953, leaving Republican Vice President Richard Nixon decisive. The Senate was where McCarthy's fate would be settled, a fact most apparent to McCarthy and the Little Joes, or, as Rosenblatt labeled them, "the Snaggle-Tooth Gang"—Senators Herman Welker, Styles Bridges, and Mollie Malone. Harry Cain had lost his place in the Snaggle-Tooth lineup by losing his seat to Henry Jackson in 1952.

With the loss of Cain, a change of one member in the ornate chamber would have greatly comforted McCarthy and his backers. The gang got a break on June 9, 1953, when Lester C. Hunt Jr., son of the senator from Wyoming, was arrested in a Washington park and charged with soliciting a homosexual act from an undercover cop.[23] Senator Hunt, a popular conservative Democrat, was up for reelection in 1954. If he could be persuaded to step aside, to forgo a reelection race . . .

Hunt, Rosenblatt said, didn't like McCarthy, "a drunk, liar, and opportunist" in the description of the small-town dentist turned politician. Apart from those unattractive characteristics, McCarthy had come to the defense of German soldiers charged with killing 150 U.S. prisoners of war at Malmedy, Belgium, after the Battle of the Bulge in World War II. This happened during a Senate hearing on the massacre, and Joe, no doubt, was making a play for Wisconsin's German-American vote. Hunt didn't like it at all.[24]

Shortly after junior's arrest, Hunt got word, relayed from Senator Herman Welker, that his son would not be prosecuted for this misdemeanor—thus avoiding the newspapers in Washington, D.C., and Wyoming—if the senator did not seek reelection. Hunt's response: he refused to be blackmailed. Three weeks later, on July 3, the *Washington Times Herald* carried a story about young Hunt's homosexual solicitation. Subsequently, he was judged guilty and fined $100.

Having made the D.C. press, the story of Hunt Jr.'s disgrace would surely become a campaign issue in Wyoming. Senator Hunt was in deep conflict over his obligation to fellow Democrats and the adverse publicity his run for reelection would create.

On a Saturday morning in his Carroll Arms suite, Maurice Rosenblatt took a call from Mike Manatos, Hunt's administrative assistant. The man sounded so distressed that Maurice asked, "What's the matter?" The matter was the suicide of his boss, who could no longer handle the conflict. He had killed himself inside his Senate office with a .22-caliber rifle shot to the head.

Newspapers played the suicide on Hunt's admission of poor health. The columnists Drew Pearson and Marquis Childs came closer to the truth. They linked his death to the threat of blackmail by Welker and his ally, Styles Bridges. Welker, the Idaho senator, appeared bereft of outrage or propriety. He gave a eulogy on the Senate floor for the late Hunt. His brass brought this response from Hunt's cousin, William Spencer, of

Chicago: "I was shocked when I read this [Welker's eulogy]. I recall vividly my conversation with Senator Hunt a few weeks before he died, wherein he recited in great detail the diabolical plot you [Welker] played following the episode in which his son was involved.

"Hunt told me without reservation the details of the tactics you used to induce him to withdraw from the Senate. It seems apparent you took every advantage of the misery the poor fellow was suffering at the time in your endeavor to turn it to political advantage. I understood too, from Hunt, that Senator Bridges had been consulted by you and approved of your action."[25]

In the last analysis, McCarthyism appears not only to have savaged many political reputations but also to have corrupted several of its followers and even killed one of their Senate colleagues. It seems to have had a life of its own—indeed, one that endures in some Americans to this day, more than four decades after the senator's death. McCarthy is "a misunderstood American hero," says Ann Coulter, a television commentator and author of *Treason: Liberal Treachery from the Cold War to the War on Terrorism.*[26] Coulter's thesis is that McCarthy, by himself, "saved America from itself for thirty-plus years" and that "the myth of McCarthyism is the greatest Orwellian fraud of our times."[27] In her terminal judgment, "the primary victim of persecution in the McCarthy era was [Joe] McCarthy." Her solution to the contemporary riddle of anti-American terrorism: "We should invade those [Muslim] countries, kill their leaders and convert them to Christianity."[28]

McCarthy and his "ism" surely resonated.

Flanders and the Fall

FOR ALL THE CALCULATION AND SKILL of the Clearinghouse opposition, the sound and fury of his determined liberal critics, and the enmity of powerful Democratic conservatives, Senator Joe McCarthy's ultimate Senate foe was an "outsider," a self-made Vermont businessman turned Republican senator, Ralph Flanders. He would also be the most visible foe, but working with him closely behind the scenes would be Maurice Rosenblatt and his Clearinghouse colleagues.

Unconcealed but so far unpublicized, the Rosenblatt opposition was busy. It had a network of Capitol Hill operatives—congressional aides, staffers, insiders with access to congressional offices—not formally organized but in agreement that "Joe must go."

"You can't use hacks or fanatics to work the Hill," said Rosenblatt of this ad hoc network. "They were practical people who knew their way around."[1] But they were insiders, not directly connected with the American political mainstream.

One of them working inside the belly of the beast was Gracie Johnson, a snitch employed by McCarthy's Senate investigations subcommittee. A good-looking woman with a heart of gold, she had been recruited through Rosenblatt's friend Chickie Chaiken, a member of Senator Gillette's staff—no love lost between Gillette and Joe. Gracie was a close friend of Senator John McClellan, a crusty Methodist from Arkansas and a member of McCarthy's subcommittee. She was somewhat girlish about their relationship: As she explained to Rosenblatt, "Everybody knows I have a guest room."

For a time she kept a room at the Carroll Arms, the transfer point for committee documents headed into Lucille Lang's

Clearinghouse data bank. Gracie provided inside dope on who was who and doing what in the McCarthy apparatus. This heightened the role of the Carroll Arms as backstage to the McCarthy theater playing on the Senate floor.

A detailed record of telephone calls from subcommittee headquarters in December 1950 exposed McCarthy's high-powered contacts. Gracie's purloined telephone log showed calls from committee investigator Don Surine to the gifted right-wing columnist Westbrook Pegler and to William Randolph Hearst Jr., eventual successor to his father as boss of the Hearst news empire. J. B. Matthews called his boss, W. R. Hearst Sr., from the office. Another Hearstling, George Sokolsky, used the telephone to talk with Archbishop Cushing in Boston. His compatriot Ralph DeToledano called Richard Nixon from committee offices. Thank you, Gracie.[2]

By early 1954, American hysteria over treason on behalf of Communism had a household name, "McCarthyism," and such potency that no seer could have foreseen the rush of events that within a year would destroy McCarthy as well as his hold on public opinion. He was heading into a fight with the U.S. Army and an unflattering spectacle on coast-to-coast television.

Signs, however, still indicated a demagogue on the rise.

In February, McCarthy's committee got a $214,000 appropriation to investigate what the senator called "very, very current espionage" at Army Signal Corps headquarters at Fort Monmouth, New Jersey. More telling, votes for this appropriation came from liberals Hubert Humphrey, Estes Kefauver, Warren Magnuson, John Kennedy, and Mike Mansfield. The only vote against more money to fund Joe McCarthy's stumbling investigations was that of William Fulbright. McCarthy was still frightening. Those liberals, minus Fulbright, felt vulnerable.[3]

Joe's prose turned rancid, as in this sample from a floor speech: "Men and women wear the [Democratic] party label, stitched with the idiocy of Truman, rotted by the deceit of [Dean] Acheson, corrupted by the Red slime of [Harry Dexter] White." White was a high official in the Treasury Department who may, in fact, have been a Communist.[4]

Riding high, maybe giddy from that fat appropriation, McCarthy went further, labeling Democrats "the party of betrayal," responsible for "twenty years of treason." A week later he declared General Ralph Zwicker, a soldier of proven bravery, "not fit to wear the uniform," for he had "coddled Communists" by promoting Major Irving Peress, the army dentist.[5]

That was a bit much for the mild-mannered army secretary, Robert T. B. Stevens. He denounced McCarthy's "humiliating treatment" of Zwicker. Not so, replied Joe. His treatment was "too temperate," and moreover, Stevens was "one of the finest dupes I ever met."[6] Presumably that was meant as a compliment.

Later, in his accustomed quick, "off-the-record" press conference, McCarthy gloated, "I made that little sonofabitch [Stevens] get down on his hands and knees and beg to me." On this day, however, a reporter balked. Phil Potter of the *Baltimore Sun* told Joe he would not observe "off the record" and would report his comment on Stevens. And so he did. It was a key factor, said Potter's friend Albert Ravenholt, in turning President Eisenhower against the senator.[7]

In the midst of these exchanges, Senator Flanders took the floor to caution that McCarthy was diverting attention from "dangerous problems abroad" and splitting the GOP at home. Problems abroad would have included the real or perceived threat of a Soviet invasion of Western Europe—the United States was hastening to re-arm Germany and transfer two new army divisions to reinforce NATO—and the war between French colonials and Vietnamese guerrillas in Southeast Asia.[8]

Flanders, a self-educated machinist who had worked his way up from machine shop apprentice to mechanical engineer, had already taken his measure of McCarthy and found him wanting. He might well have agreed with Albert Ravenholt's appraisal of the man: "a fake." McCarthy's defense of the 1944 German massacre of American prisoners did not go down well with the crusty Vermonter.

Joe was undaunted. Flanders carried little weight in the Senate club. And there was this business with the army. McCarthy wasn't getting anywhere with his demand that G. David Schine, soon to be drafted as a buck private, be given an officer's commission. Then, inexorably, it was showtime. In a bizarre twist in McCarthy's conflict with the army, open hearings before a Senate committee were carried live via television into virtually every American living room and tavern, starting on April 22, 1954.

For the next three months, in what were called the Army-McCarthy hearings, Americans would see Joe as he was—an unattractive bully, scowling, impolite, intemperate—not as he came filtered through the files of the Associated Press, United Press, and International News Service. The menacing growl, "Point of order, point of order," became his ugly trademark. High-school kids began using the expression in mockery.

In her retrospective, Ruth Watt always described her boss, Joe McCarthy, as "a very kind man, very thoughtful of people working with him, but when he got in the hearings he was on a tirade sometimes. Whether he was playing to the press, or just taken with it, he did get off a tirade sometimes." Such was his televised tirade against the army for its tolerance of alleged Commies.

Cross-examination by Joseph Welch, the sixty-three-year-old, almost wistful defense attorney, was the legal equivalent of viewing a heavyweight counterpuncher KO an overconfident slugger. Welch brought out the worst in McCarthy, who rumbled into an accusation that Fred Fisher, a young attorney in Welch's blue-ribbon Boston law firm, had once been a member of the Lawyers Guild, an alleged Communist front. Fisher had indeed had a brief stay in the guild, long enough to learn of it and get out.

Explained Joe to Welch, his voice dropping with ominous sincerity, "I have been rather bored with your phony requests [to get] every Communist out of government before sundown." This was Joe's attempt at Senate sarcasm.

It was a needless, stupid swing by slugger Joe. The counterpuncher came back with an uppercut: "Until this moment, Senator, I think I never really gauged your cruelty or your recklessness. . . . little did I dream you could be so cruel and so reckless as to do injury to that lad." Fisher would remain with his law firm, said Welch, but "I fear he shall always bear a scar needlessly inflicted by you. If it were in my power to forgive you for your cruelty, I would do so. I like to think that I am a gentle man, but your forgiveness will have to come from someone other than me."

KO.

Scores inside the caucus room and the multitude of Americans in front of television sets watched this live drama and judged Joe McCarthy. Suddenly, he was the villain, no longer the hero, in a political morality play. Joe didn't seem to know what hit him. When Welch finished, the senator looked about the committee room as if seeking reassurance that he hadn't done something inappropriate. Little was forthcoming from either his live or his TV audience. McCarthy was in trouble, and suddenly he knew it.

Once finished in late spring and off the nation's airwaves— though still at the peak of public awareness—the Army-McCarthy hearings would leave Joe McCarthy critically wounded. Nevertheless, only the Senate, where no TV camera intruded, could apply the coup de grace. And the Senate remained unsettled in mid-1954.

To this point, the opposition's connection with Senator Flanders had been marginal. In keeping with the NCEC's nonpartisan agenda, it had sent the senator a $1,000 contribution for his 1952 election campaign, which, scrupulous man, he promptly returned because he didn't need it. Not until mid-heat of the Army-McCarthy hearings did he figure in the NCEC Clearinghouse's strategy.

Lyndon Johnson had made explicit the need for a Senate Republican, not a Democrat, to lead the charge against McCarthy. Regardless of their common benefactors, Johnson had a visceral dislike of McCarthy, Rosenblatt said. But Johnson was a realist. Political survival took precedence over personal feelings. After his visit from Senator Hill a year earlier, Rosenblatt had called Johnson, suggesting that his leadership against McCarthy would show "the Brits and other sophisticates that he's not just another Texas cowboy but a major leader. He remained quiet, unmoved. We had to get a Republican."[9]

John Sherman Cooper, the Kentucky Republican, had worked with Rosenblatt in the effort to save European Jews—"a strong man." Rosenblatt turned to him: "'We need someone to cut down McCarthy's committee.' Cooper wanted something to work with. We drafted a motion to remove McCarthy as subcommittee chairman. Senator Cooper was with us, but the move didn't work." Help would come from elsewhere.

Ralph Flanders was made of different stuff than Lyndon Johnson. He might not have been a Senate power, but in Rosenblatt's estimate he was a tough man of integrity "acting solely on his principles." Aware of Flanders's feelings about McCarthy, Rosenblatt wrote him a flattering note, calling him a bipartisan hero who gave courage to his colleagues, and describing McCarthy as a "national problem along with the boll weevil, hoof and mouth disease, etc." The note was pro forma, perhaps an inducement, but not an invitation to join the opposition. It was the way a shrewd lobbyist lined up allies whose votes might be needed sometime.[10]

The two men would soon become allies, with Rosenblatt writing some of Flanders's material, yet Flanders marched to his own drummer. He did not await invitations. Early into the Army-McCarthy hearings, he made fun, of a New England sort, of McCarthy's investigations: "He dons warpaint and goes into a war dance, emitting warwhoops. Then he goes into battle and proudly returns with the pink scalp of an Army dentist. We may assume this represents the depth and seriousness of the Communist penetration in the country at this time."[11]

On June 1, 1954, Flanders, the Senate nonentity, made a speech suggesting a homosexual connection in the Cohn-Schine-McCarthy anti-Communist machine. Today, such an attack might seem crude and reflect more poorly on the accuser than on the accused, but at the time it was a bold volley, and one not unknown in McCarthy's own arsenal. "Does Cohn have some hold on Joe?" asked the senator. "The [Army-McCarthy] hearings are not going to the heart of the mystery which concerns personal relations." And Flanders kept going: "There is the relationship of staff assistant to the Senator. The relationship of the staff assistant to the Army private. It is natural he would want to retain the services of an able collaborator, but he seems to have an almost passionate anxiety to retain him. Why? And then there is the Senator himself. . . ."[12]

The innuendo in this speech inspired the playwright Lillian Hellman to label the dynamic trio "Bonnie, Bonnie, and Clyde." Others would call McCarthy's staff couple "the Leopold and Loeb of the 1950s."[13] This was long before the homosexual rights movement began to lift some of the stigma surrounding homosexuality.

In fact, not innuendo, the twenty-six-year-old Cohn was homosexual. He was a brat turned brilliant legal fixer in Washington and New York. According to Mark Russell, he had the boorish habit of eating food from others' plates in the Carroll Arms restaurant. Whether, as hinted, he and Schine complemented their work for McCarthy with a homosexual relationship is unknown. Cohn died of AIDs in 1986.[14]

The call to arms came on June 10, 1954. McCarthy, under questioning before TV lights and cameras in the Senate caucus room, was handed a note by Flanders. It said that on the following day he aimed to deliver an anti-McCarthy speech and move that he be stripped of his subcommittee chairmanship.[15] It is this way with gentlemen: give fair notice so that the assailed may respond.

The next day, Flanders "just came in and broke everything up," remembered Ruth Watt. "I thought Flanders was off his rocker. He interrupted proceedings. I was not impressed." McCarthy responded on the spot. He called Flanders senile and smirked, "They should get a man with a butterfly net and take him to a good quiet place." Flanders's motion would not carry, but the opposition had discovered their point man.

Ralph Flanders never flinched. On July 20, 1954, he served notice to the Senate of a second resolution regarding McCarthy's conduct, which was, as it said, "unbecoming a member of the U.S. Senate, contrary to senatorial traditions and tends to bring the Senate into disrepute. . . . such conduct is hereby condemned."

The nation snapped to attention. So did major players in the Republican establishment. Quickened by the resolution, Maurice Rosenblatt, too, came calling. Waiting in Senator Flanders's outer office, he watched the powerful treasury secretary, George Humphrey, walk in. In a short while, Humphrey, homburg in hand, stalked out, unsmiling, "looking neither left nor right."

"You could feel the heat," Rosenblatt recalled. "When I entered his private office Flanders was smiling. Humphrey had told him to defer the censure motion, to put it off in favor of an agriculture bill. I asked, 'What did you say?' Flanders said, 'No, I think the crops will grow anyhow.'"

Then came Senators Irving Ives, Leverett Saltonstall, and H. Alexander Smith, "the pallbearers," as Rosenblatt called the GOP moderates, none of them very friendly with Joe McCarthy but all of them fearful of him. Maurice quoted Flanders as saying that the three believed that despite their dislike for McCarthy, a censure vote would cost them reelection, so please, they urged, drop it. "What made you invent that thing [the censure motion]?" Smith asked Flanders. "You know I am an inventor—I've got twenty-two patents," he answered. Saltonstall's appeal almost brought him to tears. "I have no choice," Flanders finally answered. "This [censure motion] is a moral imperative."[16]

By this time Joe McCarthy had greater national renown than Dwight Eisenhower, Franklin Roosevelt, and Al Canwell combined. Ralph Flanders? Out in California, the *Sacramento Bee* commented that "when he launched his campaign to censure McCarthy, Flanders rose like a genie from a cracker barrel without warning or sufficient preparation for the role."[17]

Colonel McCormick's *Chicago Tribune* knew better. The day after Flanders served notice, the *Tribune* carried a banner headline across page one: "Bare Lobby Plot to Condemn McCarthy." Under it, reporter Willard Edwards revealed that "so-called liberals," working from suite 303 in the Carroll Arms Hotel, were behind Flanders's resolution of condemnation. Edwards accurately reported that the "well-heeled" group included Studebaker autos chairman Paul Hoffman; Arthur Schlesinger Jr., co-chairman of the "leftist" Americans for Democratic Action

(ADA); John Cowles and Ralph McGill, newspaper editor-publishers; union leaders Walter Reuther and Albert Hayes; and a dozen other members of the American establishment.

"This organization is functioning under the directorship of Maurice Rosenblatt of New York and Robert Sherwood, a playwright who once wrote speeches for Franklin Roosevelt," Edwards reported, half right. Sherwood was a name on the letterhead. He also noted that Senate majority leader William Knowland had gotten it wrong when he cited the AFL-CIO and the ADA as chief plotters behind the anti-McCarthy campaign. It was, Edwards corrected, "the National Committee for an Effective Congress."[18]

Edwards's tale wasn't exactly a major scoop. Although he played it in a low key, Rosenblatt never tried to hide the NCEC campaign. But having Flanders out front, carrying the campaign against McCarthy, certainly came as a surprise to conservative readers of the *Tribune*.

A stealth warrior, a Republican conservative, Flanders was anything but a liberal à la Herbert Lehman or William Benton. Edwards got it right about Flanders's support from the NCEC Clearinghouse—facts, speechwriters, lobbying forces on Capitol Hill, political backup for his campaign. "I was well-prepared by the NCEC," Flanders would say. "I gratefully accepted their help."[19]

Rosenblatt had advance notice of the Flanders resolution. On the day of its presentation, Maurice wrote to Dean Clara Mayer of the New School for Social Research in New York City that "the situation is ripe for a showdown with McCarthy. Television has unmasked his personality, which the press had concealed." A few days later he reminded "the Leader," Lyndon Johnson, that as requested, a Republican was leading the charge against Joe. Thus, he said, "it's time for the Democratic leadership to take a stand."[20]

Internal memos written by Rosenblatt at this time characterize Flanders as "completely motivated by principle," while congressional Democrats are "milling around without leadership or purpose." Lyndon Johnson had yet to act against McCarthy, and he would never get in front of this campaign as he would do as the American president in 1964 on behalf of civil rights. "The Senate has come to act like a Greek tragedy," said Senator Paul Douglas. "All the action takes place offstage, before the play begins."[21] This was a remark aimed at Johnson's backroom manipulations. But in the case of Joe McCarthy, it was better applied to the NCEC.

"Most significant," wrote Rosenblatt—witness to Vienna in the 1920s and New York in the 1930s—"is the inability of Americans to see the totalitarian menace" posed by McCarthy-ism. In the wake of Flanders's resolution, Rosenblatt said the task was "essentially a job of publicity and pressure—to work the [congressional] representatives, befriend the press, pressure Republican leaders—John McCloy, Paul Hoffman, C. D. Jackson [a Luce publisher]—publicize Flanders. The ball is in play. Can we score?"[22]

Senator McClellan had come around. He told Ruth Watt, "I'm fond of Joe McCarthy, but he's getting out of hand and we have to do something to control him."

The Senate punted. Instead of acting on the resolution, it assigned the matter to a select committee chaired by Arthur Watkins, a Utah Mormon, for "study." Wisely, Johnson named three conservative Democrats to serve under Senator Watkins, an "Old Testament kind of man, a hanging judge," in Rosenblatt's description, who "got under McCarthy's skin. Joe didn't hate Flanders. He hated Watkins."

While the selects deliberated, Rosenblatt warned Flanders to expect a counterattack from McCarthyites. No sooner warned than a California woman wrote to the Vermonter, "I hope God strikes you dead for your wicked attack on Senator McCarthy."[23] But a Senate counterattack never materialized. The floor of McCarthy's support inside and outside Congress had collapsed.

McCarthy made his usual show of forceful imprudence before the select committee. This time it backfired. With attorney Edward Bennett Williams at his side, he launched a tirade against Senator Edwin Johnson of Colorado, calling him a biased partisan unfit to serve on the committee. He demanded that Johnson be removed.

It was too much. "Out of order," gaveled chairman Watkins, who went on to rebuke McCarthy for his accusation against Johnson. "Shut up and sit down." McCarthy was stunned. For perhaps the last time, Joe McCarthy had overstepped. "This is the most unheard thing I ever heard of," he retorted.[24]

Joe was whipped. His stammering response to Watkins showed it. Passage of the censure resolution was now a formality. When his "condemnation" was approved by the Senate, sixty-seven to twenty-two, on December 2, Joe quipped, "It was not exactly a vote of confidence, but I don't feel like I was lynched."[25]

By that time he had come to understand the force behind that fatal Senate vote. Speaking of himself in the third person, à la Julius Caesar, McCarthy told Scripps-Howard columnist Arthur Edson, "The National Committee for an Effective Congress and Maurice Rosenblatt masterminded the censure of Joe McCarthy."[26] Rosenblatt said he had never received a greater compliment.

Joe's days as America's greatest demagogue were done. "It was very sad," Ruth Watt remembered. "After the censure the press completely ignored him. If he sent out a press release you never saw it unless it was on the back page—and he was into the press stuff pretty much, I think it had gotten into his blood. He didn't get invitations. I think it affected him greatly. I think it broke his heart, really."

Soon after the censure President Eisenhower, who didn't like McCarthy, sent invitations to a White House party to every member of the Senate save one. In anticipation, McCarthy had an aide sit by his office telephone awaiting his call. It never came. Ruth Watt remembered: "Senator McCarthy kept calling me and saying, 'Ruthie, go ask Mary Driscoll [a secretary] if I've heard from the White House yet, if I've gotten an invitation.' I'd call Mary and she would say, 'You know very well he hasn't—he's not going to get an invitation to that party tonight.'"

But if Joe was finished, his legacy to American politics was not. McCarthyism was too hot to cool down.

A pro-Joe counterattack targeted the NCEC, accompanied by the heavy metal music of anti-Semitism. "Why are [enemies of the United States] spending millions of dollars in propaganda and smear techniques against [Senator William] Jenner, Joe McCarthy and J. Edgar Hoover?" asked *The Cross and the Flag,* organ of Gerald L. K. Smith's "Christian National Crusade." "Treason is the answer. Flanders' speech was done under the pressure of a special committee headed by a Jew whose name is Rosenblatt. The mystery of the hour is the strange and secret way forces mobilized against McCarthy without the Communist Party or its fronts."[27]

"My Dear Morrie," opened a letter to Rosenblatt from one Julian von Alpenfels of Cicero, Illinois, no doubt a reader of the mighty *Tribune.* "I have followed with great interest the noble work you are doing in conjunction with the stupid Gentile stooges, like Flanders, Hoffman and others, to drive McCarthy from the scene.

"Has the senator from Wisconsin uncovered too many Communist kikes in government? . . . really surprising, isn't it, the number of sheenies pulled out of the woodwork, like the vermin they are, by committees engaged in ousting subversives." Von Alpenfels's signature was floridly beautiful. Rosenblatt had no recollection of having known the man.[28]

Hearst went to banner headlines at the turn of events. The New York *Journal-American* led its editions on December 4, 1954, the day of the vote on the censure resolution, with: "Link Leftist Group to McCarthy Censure." Backup for that headline was a story by Hearst's Washington bureau chief, David Sentner, saying that unnamed "McCarthy investigators" had found that "24 of the 39 NCEC board members are affiliated with pro-Communist groups" and that Senator Everett Dirksen of Illinois had labeled the NCEC "left-wing" and "in bed with Flanders to get McCarthy." What the NCEC really aimed to do, concluded Sentner, was "to stifle the investigation of Communism."[29]

Next day the *Journal-American* followed up its allegation with another banner: "Leftist Foes of McCarthy Face Congressional Probe." Again, no names, but a report that "McCarthy supporters" planned to push for a probe of the NCEC to determine whether it had violated anti-lobbying laws.[30] The newspaper stretched it with this piece. It had the credibility of Capitol corridor speculation hyped into headlines, perhaps by wishful thinking. But nothing happened.

Two years later, Joe's sidekick Senator Jenner of Indiana called for a probe of the NCEC. There was no response, save for a few back-page stories in the usual newspapers. This stirred Fulton Lewis Jr., a widely circulated right-wing columnist, to write: "The National Committee for an Effective Congress, a shadowy lobby for so-called liberal causes, used Flanders to paralyze the work of the Senate investigation of Communism and to destroy the chairman of the committee, Joe McCarthy . . . it [also] operates as [an] assassination cabal against anti-Communist candidates for Congress."[31]

Still no response to Jenner's call for a probe.

"Don't quit the fight," Rosenblatt cautioned the other major Chicago newspaper publisher, Marshall Field. "The Cromelin-Stratemeyer 'Committee for Ten Million Signatures for McCarthy' is under way, a nationalistic group pushing for preventive war [against China] in Asia."[32] A dynamic duo of the far right, retired Admiral John Cromelin and retired Air Force General George Stratemeyer were World War II heroes bonded in their fear of democracy as well as of Communism. Testifying before Senator McCarran's subcommittee on internal security in 1954, Stratemeyer allowed that "right up to this minute, there is some hidden force, some hidden power, or something, that is influencing our people. They don't act like Americans. Americans are supposed to have guts, and our policy is wishy-washy, appeasing."[33]

Despite the bluster, nothing happened to rally ten million to save Joe McCarthy or to heed the call of the China Lobby for war against Red China on behalf of Chiang Kai-shek, the fallen Chinese leader now in refuge on Formosa (Taiwan).

And Joe was fading faster than his friends.

On October 2, McCarthy turned up sick. He said his nerves were "shot," and he was hospitalized at the Bethesda Naval Hospital. Nerves or booze? McCarthy made no effort to hide his increasing taste for hard liquor. Evenings downstairs at the Carroll Arms were getting longer.

Down, but out of the hospital in mid-December 1954, McCarthy made a Senate floor speech calling for a blockade of Red China and demanding that the U.S. "unleash Chiang Kai-shek" from his Taiwan fortress to "attack the soft underbelly of China." He was carrying the cause of his friends Cromelin and Stratemeyer and the China Lobby. When Eisenhower, who had passed up the chance to rebuke McCarthy in 1952, refused to heed this call for war with China, McCarthy snarled at the president's "shrinking show of weakness towards combating Communism."[34] Was anybody still listening?

In June 1955, as Eisenhower prepared to meet Soviet leaders in a summit conference in Geneva, McCarthy offered a resolution to the Senate aimed at limiting the president's freedom to negotiate. For openers, it commanded that Eisenhower discuss the matter of East European satellites with the Soviets before the conference could commence. It looked as if it might be comeback time for Tailgunner Joe, a show of force on the Senate floor he had once dominated, a reminder and a renewal of the power of fear. The resolution failed, seventy-seven to four. Three of what Rosenblatt had called the Snaggle-Tooth Gang—Mollie Malone, William Jenner, and William Langer—stuck with their leader. The rest rejected him.

McCarthy was humiliated and, worse, isolated. He was also drinking harder, fading fast toward death from a whisky-diseased liver. "By the end of 1955 he was in pretty bad shape and we knew he had cirrhosis of the liver," said his friend Ruth Watt. "I was told that he told Senator McClellan that he knew he had something and was not going to get any better." He died two years later.

"He never believed his colleagues could—or would—do it [censure him]," wrote Fulton Lewis. "When it happened, he was a changed and a disillusioned man. . . . it was all done under a sinister, unseen, outside pressure . . . a shadowy, unidentifiable group called the National Committee for an Effective Congress, without fingerprints, pushing the feeble and aging Flanders."[35]

Flanders, the antagonist, had a kinder, gentler reaction to

McCarthy's death. He was "a man to be pitied," said Flanders. "He had a deep inferiority complex. For this he found relief in bullying witnesses, slamming associates, and garnering head-lines."[36]

Decades later, when the public memory of McCarthy had dimmed to a twilight, Maurice Rosenblatt reflected on his role in the demise of the demagogue's assault on American civil rights: "The essential lesson learned at the University of Wis-consin, confirmed in the Bronx in the late 1930s, and finally applied to McCarthy in the 1950s is that the way to defeat an extremist is with the conservative establishment."

Easy to say, but getting church leaders and seminary stu-dents to oppose the Christian Front, and Wall Street tycoons and Midwestern industrialists to confront Joe McCarthy, took a political jujitsu artist. Such was Maurice Rosenblatt—in *Time* magazine's description, "an American original, a reformer in the great American tradition."[37]

What Maurice and the National Committee for an Effec-tive Congress had done was to employ McCarthy's own excesses against him. They had a lot to use: ambition, scorn for fair play, lack of empathy, insecurity, and booze.

Epilogue

LONG AFTER THE FEDERAL COURTS corrected its excesses, the worst being a denial of due process in proceedings against an accused, the frost of McCarthyism continued to chill dissent in the United States. It took perhaps a generation to thaw.

Fear of heterodoxy lingered, as in, "My God, maybe I'd better cool my opinions—I could be named." The House Un-American Activities Committee, especially under a hustling former FBI agent, Representative Harold Velde, kept up the hunt for Commies—real or suspect—as well as for publicity. But the main event was over. The big tent of this political circus had gone down with Joe McCarthy.

"It took a long time for the country to recover," observed Maurice Rosenblatt, retired and reflective. "For a time nobody knew where they stood in the Cold War orthodoxy."[1]

Could it happen again? That question about American democracy also lingered. "Personally, I felt enormous relief," said Maurice. "I slept better. I recognized we were the instrument of McCarthy's destruction, but I felt no guilt. Just fatigue and relief. I was exhausted. I didn't feel like crusading again."

New York *Journal-American* headlines behind him, Rosenblatt took a brief fling to Las Vegas with his nonscheduled airline clients, payoff for his work obtaining certification for the nonskeds to fly passengers—$80 a ticket—between New York and Miami. There, in a temporary lapse of his normal self-discipline, he got drunk and married his companion, Laura Barone. It was Christmas 1954 and not a good decision. "I was always a rover," he said. A few months later, just as abruptly, they divorced. She died of leukemia later in 1955. Her memory haunts: "She was loyal and beautiful. I couldn't have done a thing without her." Rosenblatt would not wed again.

No more crusades, perhaps, but much more public business for a master of Capitol Hill's customs and corridors. Alarmed at the decline in numbers of American voters, he formed the Committee for the Study of the American Electorate. As usual, it had a blue-ribbon board, including diplomat Cyrus Vance, Abigail McCarthy, wife of Senator Eugene McCarthy, and Democratic political advisors Ted Van Dyk and Anne Wexler, and a crackerjack director, Curtis Gans. Three decades later it remains in business (Maurice was president). Voter absenteeism still increases, but they are working on it.

If not a crusade in the mode of his past activities, Rosenblatt's lobbying on behalf of CBS, the television network, and its president, Frank Stanton, was a historic blow on behalf of the First Amendment, the right to free speech. In striking it—for a splendid $5,000-per-month retainer—Maurice saved Stanton from a congressional contempt citation and a possible jail sentence.

"The Selling of the Pentagon," a CBS documentary, followed the mode of Edward R. Murrow's "See It Now," his gloves-off exposé of Joe McCarthy, a damaging blow to the demagogue. Broadcast in 1971, the CBS show took the sheets off the Pentagon's huge expenditure of public funds to sell citizens on the Vietnam war—a sales job desperately needed, considering the war's unpopularity.

The Richard Nixon White House went ballistic. Hawkish Representatives Eddie Hebert, hotter than a Cajun sauce, and Harley Staggers, hard-nosed chairman of the House Commerce Committee, went for Stanton's throat. Hebert called it "the most horrible thing I've seen in years . . . the greatest disservice to the military I've ever seen on TV."[2]

Staggers got his committee to subpoena Stanton to come forth and bring all the network's notes and unbroadcast material ("outtakes," in TV jargon) dealing with the critical program. Refusing, Stanton faced a contempt citation and a jail cell.[3]

Stanton balked but did not fold. Instead, as Rosenblatt

recalled, the network dispatched "ten or fifteen lobbyists in Gucci shoes and a fleet of limousines" to work the House floor against the contempt citation, which had been approved by the Commerce Committee. The limos were conspicuous, lined up outside the Capitol's Cannon Building, where congressmen nested.

Someone wisely suggested adding Rosenblatt to the CBS Capitol lineup. Rosenblatt said he'd take the lobbying assignment, given a handsome payday—and provided he could order the others to keep a low profile, stop scattering money around the Hill, and take off those $200 shoes. In sum, move over and let a pro take charge. He did.

"They wanted to go for the liberals," said Rosenblatt. "No, no—you've got the liberals. You need Republicans, conservatives. The issue wasn't a matter of conservatives versus liberals. It was a matter of whether business, free enterprise, had a right to protection from Congress." Or so he framed the issue, and to work it he enlisted the support of several conservative businessmen. Political jujitsu all over again.

The key was Representative Gerald Ford, the House GOP leader and future president, whom Maurice, helped by those businessmen, turned into a supporter of the First Amendment, if not a fan of CBS. As Rosenblatt recalled it: "I talked with him in his office. He listened to me. He acted as though I was telling him things for the first time. Ford liked to look innocent. Sometimes maybe he was."

The Republican floor leader was one critical convert. The other was Wilbur Mills, chairman of the House Ways and Means Committee (the federal "check-writing" committee) and, no less important, of the House Committee on Committees, positions that made him a rival in congressional power to Lyndon Johnson.

Mills was educated and brilliant but fading from booze and his ill-fated romance with Fannie Foxx, a local nightclub stripteaser turned page-one celebrity for her fling with the former small-town boy from Arkansas. Mills, vulnerable, also succumbed to the charms of a high-powered communications lawyer, dispatched by Rosenblatt and concerned with freedom of the press.

The upshot: Staggers led the floor fight for his contempt resolution in July 1971 but came up short of support from Republicans—thank you, Gerry Ford and Wilbur Mills. He lost 226 to 181, a rare, if not unprecedented, repudiation of a committee resolution.

There are conflicting accounts of White House–CBS intrigue lying behind that slap at the powerful Eddie Hebert, chairman of the House Armed Services Committee, and Harley Staggers. No disputing it, a meeting took place between Nixon aide Charles (Chuck) Colson and Frank Stanton. Stanton's lawyer said the network needed White House help in avoiding congressional condemnation.[4]

Behind their meeting was Nixon's preoccupation, nay, obsession, with favorable treatment in the news. He wanted to pry sweeter stuff from CBS, and the contempt business pending before the House looked like a lever. Colson's version in a memo to his boss read: "If we help on the subpoena, Stanton will cut a deal—will play ball with us." Stanton's version: He promised Colson to give attention to any White House complaints about CBS but "made no commitments about news coverage." In his words, no deal was struck.[5]

Frank Stanton was rightly hailed as a hero for his fight for the First Amendment. Books and treatises followed in celebration, one by Garth Jowett duly noting the event's chief significance: "a clear statement that the networks could not be made to bend to government control in the technological era."[6] There's no mention in any of them of the CBS vice presidents in limos and Gucci shoes, Fannie Foxx, or even Maurice Rosenblatt, huddled over whiskey with Gerald Ford.

Having slain another dragon, Rosenblatt settled into lobbying on behalf of commercial clients, working from his handsome brownstone on New Jersey Avenue, two blocks from the Capitol and a few steps from the discreetly inconspicuous Democratic Club, where he frequently entertained. The Cold War dragged on in Vietnam, but relations with the nuclear-armed Soviet

Union eventually warmed.

By now, the usually reticent Rosenblatt had the eye of Capitol observers. *Time* magazine, in August 1965, had called him "an astute lobbyist with a green thumb for controversy." Writer Larry Leamer caught him better in a piece on Washington's power wielders. He quoted a parable from Rosenblatt's lobbyist playbook, a power story:

"There was a total power failure in this [mythical] town. The wisest and smartest engineers ascended on the power plant examining machinery, trying to get it working again. They could not. In desperation they called a university professor who asked for a hammer. With it he tapped a generator. Wheels turned and power surged forth. The lights went on again. So the professor presented the delighted utility bosses a bill: $1,000.07. Puzzled, they requested an accounting. 'Seven cents for tapping, $1,000 for knowing where to tap,' he answered."[7]

Rosenblatt aptly described himself in his own summing up, "Rattling the Cages: Memoir of a Passionate Citizen." He wrote: "I was a knight errant for democracy. I graduated from an academy run by Spinoza [the seventeenth-century Dutch pantheist-philosopher] and the Three Musketeers [fictional do-gooders]. My degree was in political realism."[8] Few in our democracy have put such education to better use.

Notes

MR	Maurice Rosenblatt
HUAC	House UnAmerican Activities Committee
LC	Library of Congress
NCEC	National Committee for an Effective Congress
NYCCC	New York City Coordinating Committee
NYC	New York City
NYT	*The New York Times*
Seattle P-I	*Seattle Post-Intelligencer*

The papers of Maurice Rosenblatt and of the National Committee for an Effective Congress (NCEC), placed together in the Manuscripts Division of the Library of Congress but uncatalogued, were examined by the author and by researcher Evelyn Braithwaite in October 2002 and March 2005. They are identified in the notes by box and folder number. The author's interviews with Rosenblatt took place at the latter's residence in Washington, D.C., in March 2001; February, May, September, and October 2002; January and May 2003; March 2004; and March 2005. They were recorded on seven tapes for approximately ten hours and are in the author's possession. Yet another collection of Rosenblatt's papers ("MR private papers") consist of uncatalogued letters and news clippings, which remain at Rosenblatt's Washington, D.C., residence. Uncatalogued papers of Harry Selden were viewed at his residence in Rockville, Maryland.

1 / The Carroll Arms and the National Committee for an Effective Congress

1. Interviews, Mark Russell and Maurice Rosenblatt, Washington, D.C., March 2003.
2. Interview, Woodruff Price, Washington, D.C., March 2003.
3. Interviews, Woodruff Price, Joe Miller, and Maurice Rosenblatt, Washington, D.C., March 2003; MR papers, box 54, folder 6. Rosenblatt himself quoted Barry Goldwater.
4. Interview, Joe Miller, Washington, D.C., March 2003.
5. Interviews, Russ Hemenway, New York City, July 2002; Maurice Rosenblatt, Harry Selden, and Joe Miller, Washington, D.C., July 2002.
6. Interview, Maurice Rosenblatt, June 2000. See also Harry M. Scoble, *Ideology and Electoral Action* (San Francisco: Chandler Publishing, 1967).
7. Interview, Maurice Rosenblatt, March 2001.
8. Selden papers.
9. Interview, William Henry, ex–Marine Raider Battallion (aka "Carlson's Raiders"), Seattle, July 1997.
10. NCEC papers, LC, box 5, folder 3; interview, Maurice Rosenblatt.
11. Selden papers: Rosenblatt to Seldon, November 1993.
12. Interview, Joe Miller, Washington, D.C., May 2002.
13. Interview, Theodore White, Cambridge, Massachusetts, March 1963.

2 / Tailgunner Joe, Chanker Jack, and "Moose Dung"

1. Jon Wayne Loftheim, "Hurley in China" (Master's thesis, University of Washington, 1973), p. 113.
2. See www.coursesa.matrix.msu306/documents/McCarthy.html
3. *Wheeling (West Virginia) Intelligencer,* 10 February 1950, p. 1.
4. MR papers, LC, box 18, folder 1.
5. Gore Vidal tribute to Henry Luce, PBS–Channel 9, Seattle, 3 May 2004.
6. W. Walton Butterworth, Oral History, 6 July 1972, Truman Library, Independence, Missouri.
7. Chiang obituary, *New York Times,* 25 October 2003, p. A29.
8. Interview, Maurice Rosenblatt.
9. David G. McCullough, *Truman* (New York: Simon and Schuster, 1992), p. 764.
10. Interview, Albert Ravenholt, Seattle, November 2002.
11. Interview, Ambassador Charles Cross, Seattle, November 2002.
12. McCullough, *Truman,* p. 475.
13. Interview, Albert Ravenholt, Seattle, November 2002.
14. Harvey Klehr and Ronald Radosh, *The Amerasia Spy Case: Prelude to McCarthyism* (Chapel Hill: University of North Carolina Press, 1996), pp. 8, 110, 114, 123-24, 129, 152, 217.
15. Klehr and Radosh, *The Amerasia Spy Case,* p. 124.
16. Joseph Keeley, *The China Lobby Man: The Story of Alfred Kohlberg* (New Rochelle, N.Y.: Arlington House, 1969), p. 3.

17. MR private papers: Pearson column in the *Washington Post,* 16 and 24 August 1951.
18. Keeley, *China Lobby Man,* p. 150.
19. MR papers, LC, box 14, folder 6: New York Times, April 1950.
20. Keeley, *China Lobby Man,* p. 3.
21. Ross Y. Koen, *The China Lobby in American Politics* (New York: Octagon Press, 1974), pp. 30, 178.
22. Barbara Tuchman, *Stilwell and the American Experience in China* (New York: Macmillan, 1970), pp. 525–26.
23. McCullough, *Truman,* p. 766.
24. MR papers, LC, box 12, folder 14: McCarthy floor speech, 22 September 1950; box 14, folder 13: McCarthy floor speech, 9 August 1951.
25. Interview with Albert Ravenholt, Seattle, November 2002
26. Ibid.
27. MR papers, LC, box 12, folder 14: McCarthy floor speech, 22 September 1950; box 14, folder 13: McCarthy floor speech, 9 August 1951; Thomas Reeves, *Life and Times of Joe McCarthy* (New York: Stein and Day), pp. 251, 255, 257.

3 / The "McCarthy" Elections, 1950 and 1952

1. Thomas Reeves, *Life and Times of Joe McCarthy* (New York: Stein and Day), pp. 129–334.
2. The Cousins quotations are from MR papers, LC, box 62, folder 3: Wisconsin State Journal.
3. David G. McCullough, *Truman* (New York: Simon and Schuster, 1992), p. 813.
4. MR papers, LC, box 14, folder 3: Wisconsin State Journal; Reeves, *Life and Times of Joe McCarthy,* pp. 334, 339.
5. MR papers, LC, box 14, folder 5: Raleigh (N.C.) *News and Observer.*
6. The McCarthy-Tydings conflict described in the following paragraphs is documented, as reported in the *Milwaukee Journal* and the *Congressional Record,* A7264, in MR papers, LC, box 14, folders 3–5. For the faked photo of Tydings and Browder, see McCullough, *Truman,* p. 814.
7. Reeves, *Life and Times of Joe McCarthy,* pp. 340–43.
8. MR papers, LC, box 14, folder 4: *Milwaukee Journal,* 10 January 1951.
9. Robert A. Caro, *Master of the Senate* (New York: Alfred Knopf, 2002), p. 142–45.
10. MR private papers: Rosenblatt to Brannan, June 27, 1950.
11. NCEC papers.
12. Shelby Scates, *Warren G. Magnuson* (Seattle: University of Washington Press, 1997), p. 151.
13. Ibid., p. 153.
14. Reeves, *Life and Times of Joe McCarthy,* pp. 450–53.
15. Selden papers, October 1952.
16. Interview, John Matchette, Palm City, Florida, July 2003.
17. Ibid.

18. Interview, Albert Ravenholt, Seattle, July 2003.
19. Interview, Joe Miller, Washington, D.C., September 2002.
20. Scates, *Warren G. Magnuson,* p. 137.
21. Interview, Maurice Rosenblatt, March 2003.
22. Arthur M. Schlesinger Jr., *A Thousand Days: John F. Kennedy in the White House* (Boston: Houghton Mifflin, 1965), pp. 12–13.
23. Caro, *Master of the Senate,* pp. 524–28.
24. Reeves, *Life and Times of Joe McCarthy,* pp. 468–69.
25. Stephen Ambrose, *Eisenhower* (New York: Simon and Schuster, 1984), vol. 2, p. 154.
26. MR papers, LC, box 19, folder 4: *Reporter* magazine, 21 July 1953, p. 9.
27. Ruth Young Watt, interviewed by Donald Ritchie, September 1979, www.senate.gov/artandhistory/history/oral_history/Ruth_Young_Watt.htm.
28. MR papers, LC, box 19, folder 4.
29. Ibid.; Reeves, *Life and Times of Joe McCarthy,* pp. 488–90.

4 / McCarthyism

1. MR papers, LC, box 54, folder 6: *Milwaukee Sentinel,* 7 August 1950, p. 2; *New York Times,* 29 October 1953.
2. MR papers, LC, box 14, folder 1: *New York Times Magazine,* 13 January 1991.
3. Ibid.
4. Eleanor Bontecou, *The Federal Loyalty-Security Program* (Ithaca, N.Y.: Cornell University Press, 1953), pp. 29, 31, 35.
5. The Silver Shirts had been organized by William Dudley Pelley, son of a Methodist preacher turned Hollywood script writer for Saturday cowboy idols Tom Mix and Hoot Gibson. See Karen Hoppes, "William D. Pelley and the Silver Shirt Legion" (Ph.D. dissertation, University of Washington, 1992), pp. 3, 46.
6. Bontecou, *The Federal Loyalty-Security Program,* pp. 352–57.
7. Interview, Del Castle, Seattle, March 2003.
8. David G. McCullough, *Truman* (New York: Simon and Schuster, 1992), p. 552.
9. Ibid.
10. Report of the California Senate Subcommittee on Un-American Activities, http://sunsite.berkeley.edu/uchistory/archives.
11. David Chute, *The Great Fear: The Anti-Communist Purge under Truman and Eisenhower* (New York: Simon and Schuster, 1978), pp. 394–99.
12. Interview, Irv Hoff, February 2003.
13. Shelby Scates, "Marine Oilers, Watertenders, and Wipers Union," U.S. Coast Guard Merchant Marine Document Z-948-754, Marine Firemen's Union B2540, 1951.
14. *Congressional Record* (Washington, D.C., 1950), p. 10794.
15. Scates, "Marine Oilers."
16. Interview, Maurice Rosenblatt; Edwin R. Bayley, *Joe McCarthy and the Press*

(Madison: University of Wisconsin Press, 1981), pp. 126–28.

17. Nicholas von Hoffman, *Citizen Cohn* (New York: Doubleday, 1988), pp. 129–30.

18. Senate Committee on Government Operations, Permanent Subcommittee on Investigations, 1953 Executive Session, vol. 1 (Washington, D.C.: Government Printing Office, 2003), p. xxv.

19. Bayley, *Joe McCarthy and the Press.*

20. MR papers, LC, box 54, folder 6.

21. W. A. Swanberg, *Citizen Hearst* (New York: Scribner's, 1961), pp. 477–79.

22. Ibid., p. 506.

23. Interview, William Theis, reporter for the International News Service, U.S. Senate, January 1969.

24. Von Hoffman, *Citizen Cohn,* p. 107.

25. Ibid., pp. 140–43.

26. Joseph Keeley, *The China Lobby Man: The Story of Alfred Kohlberg* (New Rochelle, N.Y.: Arlington House, 1969), p. 112; Reeves, *Life and Times,* pp. 248, 498–500.

5 / The Hunter

Apart from cited sources, the survey of American political extremes in the 1930s and 1940s presented in chapters 5 and 6 came from extensive use of the following books: David H. Bennett, *Demagogues in the Depression: American Radicals and the Union Party, 1932–1936* (New Brunswick, N.J.: Rutgers University Press, 1969); John Carlson, *Under Cover* (New York: Dutton, 1943); Ladislas Farago, *The Game of the Foxes: British and German Intelligence Operations and Personalities which Changed the Course of the Second World War* (London: Hodder and Stoughton, 1972); Richard Kirkendall, *The United States, 1929–1945: Years of Crisis and Change* (New York: McGraw-Hill, 1974); Rafael Medoff, *Militant Zionism in America: The Rise and Impact of the Jabotinsky Movement in the United States, 1926–1948* (Tuscaloosa: University of Alabama Press, 2002); James Ryan, *Earl Browder: The Failure of American Communism* (Tuscaloosa: University of Alabama Press, 1997); Howard M. Sachar, *A History of Israel,* 2 vols. (New York: Knopf, 1976–87); and Donald I. Warren, *Radio Priest: Charles Coughlin, the Father of Hate Radio* (New York: Free Press, 1996). Voice recordings of Father Charles Coughlin were provided by Richard Schrock, Seattle, 2002.

1. Interview, Maurice Rosenblatt.

2. MR private papers: *City Reporter,* 6 January 1942.

3. Niel M. Johnson, *George Sylvester Viereck, German-American Propagandist* (Urbana: University of Illinois Press, 1972), pp. 176, 181.

4. MR private papers.

6 / Postwar and Palestine

1. Ben Hecht, *A Child of the Century* (New York: Signet Books, 1954), pp. 484, 512.

2. MR papers, LC, box 79, folder 10: Bergson to Weizmann, 2 April 1945.
3. Palestine Statehood Papers, no. 690, Series I and II, Manuscripts, Sterling Library, Yale University, New Haven, Connecticut: Wise to Ickes, 22 December 1943.
4. MR papers, LC, box 79, folder 11: *Washington Post*, 13 October 1944.
5. Stephen Whitfield, "The Politics of Pageantry," in *American Jewish History*, vol. 84 (Simon and Schuster, 1986).
6. Ibid., 247.
7. Selden papers.
8. Whitfield, "Politics of Pageantry," pp. 221, 251.
9. Marlon Brando, *Songs My Mother Taught Me* (New York: Random House, 1994), pp. 107, 110.
10. Palestine Statehood Papers.
11. MR papers, LC, box 74, folder 4.
12. Richard Curtiss, "Washington Report on Middle East Affairs," May 1991, p. 17 (http://www.washingtonreport.org/backissues/0591/9105017. htm); David G. McCullough, *Truman* (New York: Simon and Schuster, 1992), p. 604.
13. Palestine Statehood Papers.
14. Curtiss, "Washington Report," p. 17.
15. Selden papers: Bergson to Rosenblatt, 27 August 1993.
16. MR papers, LC, box 74, folder 4.
17. Mimeograph pages obtained under the Freedom of Information Act; confidential telegram from U.S. Embassy (signed by Gallman), London, to U.S Secretary of State.
18. MR private papers; memo written by Sidney Wilkinson to Maurice Rosenblatt, March 8, 1947.

7 / The Cause

1. This chapter is based on interviews with Maurice Rosenblatt, March 2004.
2. Arnold Toynbee, *A Study of History*, abridgement of vols. 1–6 (New York: Oxford University Press, 1946), pp. 60–87.

8 / The Closed Hearings: Vengeance and the VOA

Virtually all the material in this chapter comes from transcripts of Executive Sessions of the Senate Permanent Subcommittee on Investigations of the Committee on Government Operations (4 vols.). The hearings, held in 1953, were not transcribed and made public until January 2003. Volume and page numbers of citations are given in the following notes.

1. Interview, Maurice Rosenblatt.
2. Vol. 1, p. 457.
3. Vol. 4, p. 3642.
4. Vol. 1, p. xix.
5. Vol. 1, p. 555.

6. Vol. 1, p. 573.
7. Vol. 1, p. 599.
8. Vol. 1, p. 615.
9. Vol. 1, p. 697.
10. Vol. 1, p. xxii.
11. Vol. 1, p. 673.
12. Vol. 1, p. 683.
13. Interview, Richard Schmidt, May 2003.
14. Vol. 1, p. 769.
15. Vol. 1, p. 787.
16. Vol. 2, p. 1440.
17. Vol. 1, pp. 13–31.
18. Vol. 2, pp. 1073–1114.
19. Vol. 2, p. 1231.
20. Martin Gilbert, *History of the Twentieth Century,* vol. 2, p. 857 (Toronto: Stoddart, 1999); Thomas Reeves, *Life and Times of Joe McCarthy* (New York: Stein and Day, p. 524.
21. Vol. 4, p. 3637.
22. Vol. 1, p. xiii.

9 / The Inspector and His Witnesses

Again, volume and page numbers in the following notes refer to transcripts of the Executive Sessions of the Senate Permanent Subcommittee on Investigations, 1953.

1. Vol. 3, p. 2667.
2. Vol. 4, pp. 3010–12; vol. 3, p. 2709.
3. Vol. 3, pp. 2701–14.
4. Vol. 3, p. 1919.
5. Vol. 3, p. 2175.
6. Vol. 4, p. 3285.
7. Ascoli papers, Special Collections, Boston University; interview, Albert Ravenholt, Seattle, 2003.
8. Vol. 4, p. 3244.
9. Vol. 4, p. 3013.
10. Vol. 4, p. 3023.
11. Vol. 4, p. 3296.
12. Vol. 4, p. 3566.
13. Vol. 4, p. 3573.
14. Vol. 3, p. 2551.

10 / The Clearinghouse

1. Robert Sherrill, quoted in Robert A. Caro, *Master of the Senate* (New York: Alfred Knopf, 2002), p. 542.
2. Caro, *Master of the Senate,* p. 547.
3. Ibid.
4. MR papers, LC, box 19, folder 7.

5. Thomas Reeves, *Life and Times of Joe McCarthy* (New York: Stein and Day), p. 296.
6. Ibid., p. 362.
7. NCEC papers, box 19, folder 7.
8. Robert Griffith, *Politics of Fear: Joseph R. McCarthy and the Senate* (Amherst: University of Massachusetts Press, 1987), p. 227; MR papers, LC, box 18, folder 14.
9. MR private papers: letter to George Backer; *New York Post*, 20 May 1953.
10. Interview, Maurice Rosenblatt; MR private papers: *Washington Post*, 9 June 1953.
11. The information about J. B. Matthews in the preceding paragraphs is from MR private papers: *Washington Star*, 9 July 1953.
12. Report of the House Un-American Activities Committee, August 1938, p. 915; MR papers, LC, box 54, folder 11.
13. This charge, originally made in *American Mercury* magazine ("Reds in Our Churches") was also reported in Reeves, *Life and Times of Joe McCarthy*, p. 499.
14. Manchester, *The Glory and the Dream* (Boston: Little, Brown, 1974), p. 700.
15. Interview, Maurice Rosenblatt, October 2002.
16. Ibid.
17. NCEC papers; Van Arkel to Benton, 26 February 1953.
18. Interview, Maurice Rosenblatt, October 2002.
19. Caro, *Master of the Senate*, p. 545.
20. Ibid., pp. 252–89.
21. MR papers, LC, box 54, folder 2: *The Cross and the Flag* (publication of Gerald L. K. Smith's "Christian National Crusade").
22. Interview, Maurice Rosenblatt, March 2003.
23. Rick Ewig, *Annals of Wyoming*, vol. 55, no. 1 (1983).
24. Interview, Maurice Rosenblatt.
25. Ewig, *Annals of Wyoming*.
26. Ann Coulter, *Treason: Liberal Treachery from the Cold War to the War on Terrorism* (Crown Forum Press, 2003), p. 104.
27. Ibid., p. 10; also Coulter, MSNBC, 7 July 2003, quoted "All Hail Ann Coulter," James Campion Hackwriters.com
28. *New York Times*, 20 July 2003, sec. 9, p. 1; MSNBC, 9 July 2003.

11 / Flanders and the Fall

Quotations from Ruth Young Watt come from an interview she gave to Donald Ritchie in September 1979, which can be found at www.senate.gov/artandhistory/history/oral_history/Ruth_Young_Watt.htm.
1. Robert Griffith, *Politics of Fear: Joseph R. McCarthy and the Senate* (Amherst: University of Massachusetts Press, 1987), p. 227.
2. NCEC papers, box 12, folder 7; interview, Maurice Rosenblatt, October 2002.
3. Manchester, *The Glory and the Dream*, p. 705.
4. MR papers, LC, box 54, folder 8: Washington City News Service.

5. Robert A. Caro, *Master of the Senate* (New York: Alfred Knopf, 2002), pp. 549, 551.

6. Interview, Albert Ravenholt, Seattle, March 2003.

7. Ibid.

8. NCEC papers, box 54, folder 8; Thomas Reeves, *Life and Times of Joe McCarthy* (New York: Stein and Day), pp. 562–63.

9. MR papers, LC, box 18, folder 14; interview, Maurice Rosenblatt, March 2005.

10. MR papers, LC, box 18, folder 14.

11. MR papers, LC, box 54, folder 8.

12. Von Hoffman, *Citizen Cohn,* pp. 230, 365–68; MR papers, LC, box 54, folder 12: Congressional Record.

13. Ann Coulter, *Treason: Liberal Treachery from the Cold War to the War on Terrorism* (Crown Forum Press, 2003), pp. 104, 110.

14. Von Hoffman, *Citizen Cohn,* pp. 20–26; interview, Mark Russell, March 2003.

15. *Facts on File,* 9 March 1954, 1 June 1954, 11 June 1954.

16. Interview, Maurice Rosenblatt, September 2002; Ralph E. Flanders, *Senator from Vermont* (Boston: Little, Brown, 1961), p. 267.

17. *Sacramento Bee,* undated clipping in MR private papers.

18. *Chicago Tribune,* 21 July 1954, p. 1.

19. Flanders, *Senator from Vermont,* p. 267.

20. MR papers, LC, box 18, folder 14: Rosenblatt to Mayer, 27 June 1954.

21. *New York Review of Books,* 21 November 2002, p. 14.

22. MR papers, LC, box 18, folder 14.

23. United Press (Washington, D.C.) wire service dispatch by Roy Calvin, 22 July 1954.

24. Reeves, *Life and Times of Joe McCarthy,* p. 649.

25. Ibid., p. 663.

26. MR private papers: undated news column.

27. *The Cross and the Flag,* MR papers, LC, box 54, folder 12.

28. MR private papers: Von Alpenfels to Rosenblatt, 13 December 1955.

29. MR papers, LC, box 9, folder 16.

30. Ibid.

31. Fulton Lewis Jr., Reading (PA) Eagle, 13–14 December 1955, MR papers, LC, box 23, folder 1.

32. MR private papers.

33. R. D. Mahoney, "The Tragedy of Southeast Asia," in *New American Magazine,* February 1, 1988, pp. 33–34 (*American Opinion* magazine reprinted by the John Birch Society, 19 December 2002. Appleton, WI: Publishing Inc.).

34. MR papers, LC, box 23, folder 1: undated, from *Washington Star,* p. 1.

35. MR papers, LC, box 23, folder 1: undated, from *Reading (Pennsylvania) Eagle.*

36. Flanders, *Senator From Vermont,* p. 268.

37. MR private papers: undated, from *Time* magazine.

Epilogue

1. Interview, Maurice Rosenblatt, January 2003.
2. Corydon Dunham, *Fighting for the First Amendment* (Westport, Conn.: Praeger, 1997), p. 16.
3. Ibid.
4. *Washington Post*, 1 December 1997, p. 1.
5. Dunham, *Fighting for the First Amendment*, p. 179.
6. Garth Jowett, "Selling of the Pentagon," in *American History/American TV: Interpreting the Video Past*, ed. John O'Connor (New York: Ungr Publishing, 1983).
7. Interview with Laurence Leamer, 19 July 2005, MR private papers.
8. MR private papers: unpublished memoir, 1984.

Index

Iron Gods

The Spin Trilogy by Andrew Bannister

Creation Machine
Iron Gods
Stone Clock

Iron Gods

Andrew Bannister

TOR

A Tom Doherty Associates Book
New York

IRON GODS

Copyright © 2017 by Andrew Bannister

A Tor Book
Published by Tom Doherty Associates
120 Broadway
New York, NY 10271

www.tor-forge.com

Tor® is a registered trademark of Macmillan Publishing Group, LLC.

The Library of Congress Cataloging-in-Publication Data is available upon request.

ISBN 978-1-250-17920-3 (trade paperback)
ISBN 978-1-250-17921-0 (ebook)

Our books may be purchased in bulk for promotional, educational, or business use. Please contact your local bookseller or the Macmillan Corporate and Premium Sales Department at 1-800-221-7945, extension 5442, or by email at MacmillanSpecialMarkets@macmillan.com.

First published in Great Britain by Bantam Press, an imprint of Transworld Publishers.

First U.S. Edition: July 2019

Printed in the United States of America

0 9 8 7 6 5 4 3 2 1

Dedicated to Thomas and Felix, whose uncritical faith was leavened with the occasional timely deflating comment

The Spin

*E*ighty-eight planets and twenty-one suns; all artificial down to the last particle.

More than ten thousand years before, there had been a pact. It had begun what people then called the Stable Age and it was still holding, even though everyone had forgotten about it.

Almost everyone. A few people still remembered – but they had forgotten what it was they were remembering.

But we remembered.

Three Quarter Circle Harbour

When Belbis had first made the Long Walk he had been eleven years old. It had taken him almost three greater moons, and for the first twenty days his legs had trembled and ached from rise to set. Seven years later he was far stronger. It should take him little more than a greater moon – but he would still be tired when he got there.

He walked steadily, using the terse economical stride that all his people were taught from their very first steps. Walking was important and it had to be done properly. When Belbis was younger he had taken this so seriously that he had driven his teachers to the edge of madness.

But then Belbis took everything very seriously. Otherwise, what was the point? Things were *there* to be taken seriously. How else should he take them? Most people seemed not to understand that, but Belbis didn't mind because he knew very well that he didn't understand most people. On that at least, he and his teachers had agreed. He had therefore taken the only obvious route in life, and everyone including him had been relieved. Besides, the Circle's last Painter had died the winter before, and the Predigers were sternly certain that there was only a limited period of grace allowed to find another, so Belbis the Odd had become Belbis the Painter quickly and smoothly.

He took on the grey robe of the Novice – the lowest rank of the Order, but the highest a Painter was allowed – almost with relief. Simple certainties suited Belbis.

The route of the Long Walk was not complex. By tradition it began at the furthest point out to sea of the longest dock at Circle Harbour. From there it plodded on to dry land, past the slipways with their vivid smells of tar and human waste, past the rope walks and oil stores, and past the flensing yards where the great, prized bull-fins were sliced apart with razor-edged spades, leaving the remains to flow back down the glistening gut-ramps and into the back harbour where lesser creatures waited, their mouths open. The lesser creatures were themselves the prey of creatures in some ways even lower, as far as society was concerned: the starving, the ill and the old, who waited above them with clubs and sticks, watching for a chance. When you were too old or too ill to fish, Circle Harbour had no use for you, and no food either.

Belbis didn't like strong smells. He hastened through the first part of the Walk with his eyes fixed on the ground and his throat tensed, in case he should commit the blasphemy of retching.

After the flensing yards the route jinked round the Quay Sergeant's hut, with its own particular smells of fried food and tube smoke and stump brew, and became more agreeable. Or mostly more agreeable; Belbis didn't like the part when he passed the big dwellings at the upper end of Founders' Green. This was where the wealthy had their town-houses, great halls built with massive timbers resting on low walls of mortared schist. The wealthiest had roofs of schist, too, instead of thatch or turf, and the smoke from their chimneys smelled not of dried seaweed but of scented wood. Sweet-smelling or not, Belbis had observed the unsayable fact that the wealthier the family, the more agnostic they became. Never overtly atheist, of course, that would have been suicidal, but even so Belbis never lost his astonishment at how much doubt one could entertain without actually being a formal unbeliever. Especially if one was rich.

His astonishment didn't protect him from the taunts and the occasional flung stone. He could ignore them. Such things had always been part of his life. He supposed they always would be. The Order was unpopular – he had been told that one of the main functions of a priesthood was to be resented, especially in times when the fishing was poor. Not that any of the Predigers ever went fishing.

After Founders' Green the Long Walk passed the great public park of Founders' Fields, kinking inwards as the park narrowed at the upper end to skirt the Ending Place, where a few people every week met their end on the edge of the Dispatcher's axe: criminals, certainly, and traitors, and also those who were possibly less doubting than the residents of the big houses of Founders' Green but also less rich.

The Dispatcher wore the darkest black robes, indicating seniority over all but the ten highest Klerikers. Belbis had heard townspeople whisper that black didn't show bloodstains, but that wasn't the real reason. The Dispatcher had people to deal with blood, on robes or elsewhere.

The channel from the Ending Place wound its way down the town, avoiding the wealthiest neighbourhoods, until it joined the gut-ramps near the harbour. Belbis had heard that things were added to the blood to keep it fluid. He didn't know for sure, but it seemed reasonable. These things could be done, as he knew very well from his own profession, and after all you wouldn't want the channels to block.

The Ending Place marked the outskirts of the town. After that the Walk wandered out through private estates and farmland until it had climbed off the coastal platforms that nurtured the town and the harbour and was heading for the mountains. Day by day the landscape drew in around him as broad valleys became narrow rocky slots, often with cold rivers hissing down them. Night by night he slept as he had been taught, sprawled under his cloak with his cheek resting on his arm and his eyes turned away from the stars. He would not see the stars until his journey was over. No Painter ever did.

Towards the end of the Walk he always became very hungry. Down on the plains there had been berries and a few larger fruits. By tradition the Painter could forage only within ten paces to either side of the Walk, and some of the older farming folk planted bushes within reach, and watched and nodded as the Painter took the food. But as he climbed away from the fertile lands the food thinned out and he had to rely on the baked ration from his little pack. It was not enough, but then it wasn't meant to be. The Painter should arrive at the Watch House with his eyes large and his blood thin, people said.

Belbis reached the Watch House on the evening of the third day before the full dark of the last greater moon of the year. It was an auspicious time. The skies were clear and black with frost and bright with stars.

The Watch House perched on the top of a narrow peak at the highest point in the Spine Range, so called because it crossed the continent in a shallow S-curve that looked like deformity. The House was wooden, a battered castle of a place wedged and propped off the top of the mountain on great rough trunks socketed into the grey rock. There was only one entrance, a swaying unguarded timber walkway that sprang off the end of a shelf of rock just big enough for a man to stand on, if he pressed himself back against the rock wall behind him.

The walkway – a spiritual challenge in itself – was twenty paces long. At its other end the three Housekeepers stood waiting, faint and grey in the starlight. They carried no lanterns; in deference to the needs of the Painter, the Watch House at night was kept in complete darkness, and so were its keepers. As Belbis came nearer he could see their empty eye sockets, blacker shadows in the grey. He had shuddered when he first saw them.

11

Painters were chosen young, but Keepers were selected at birth.

He bowed to the Housekeepers as he had done for the last seven years. With the enhanced senses of the lifelong sightless they somehow registered his bow – he always wondered how; air currents? The rustle of his robe? – and bowed in return. Then they stood aside and gestured him into the Watch House.

His feet knew the way. He walked up steps, and then up narrower steps, to the Painters' loft. The bench was empty except for the two shallow antimony bowls, as wide as the palm of his hand. The rest of the tools were his. He opened his pack, took out the leather roll and unrolled it on the bench between the bowls. The tools came into view one by one: the pens with their different-sized nibs, from thin to bulky. The brushes, and then the other tools. And the dressings.

He thought for a moment before selecting one of the glass shards. He took it between finger and thumb, lifted aside his robe to expose the top of his thigh, and made a quick slicing movement.

Blood welled in dark berry drops. He put the shard back on the leather, picked up a bowl and pressed its edge into his thigh just below the cut. A slow trickle collected in the bottom of the bowl.

Belbis waited until he had a pool two fingers across. Then he put the bowl on the table and pressed a dressing against his cut, shutting his eyes against the sting and counting to ten to give the astringent time to seal his flesh. Then he picked up a fine outline pen, dipped it in the bowl and poised it above the sheet of paper. Only then did he reach up with his other hand to pull the cord which opened the moon shutters.

For a moment he stared, wide eyed. Then he screamed.

For the first time in his life, for the first time in five hundred lives, the sky held the wrong number of Gods.

His scream brought the Housekeepers. At first he babbled

12

and pointed at the patch of sky between the moon shutters but they shook their heads and gestured at their empty sockets. So then he told them.

The old men conferred. Then, looking grim, they waved Belbis to follow them. They led him down flights and flights of stairs he had barely noticed to a part of the Watch House he had never visited before: a chamber that must have been carved out of the peak of the mountain itself because unlike everything else in the Watch House it was made not of wood but of stone, as dry and dusty as ancient death. In the middle of the chamber there was a single black waist-high pillar that looked like a cannon, mounted vertically with its blank mouth gaping upwards.

The oldest of the Housekeepers passed his hand over the mouth of the thing just once. Then he stood back.

For a moment nothing happened. Then Belbis jumped. A quiet voice had spoken out of nowhere. The accent was outlandish but the words were clear. 'Ignition active,' it said. 'Please vacate the area.'

Belbis looked at the Housekeepers. They had linked hands to form a circle round the pillar. 'The thing said to go,' he said. 'Where should we go?'

The oldest spoke, without turning his face towards Belbis. 'Go as far as you can.' Then he clamped his lips firmly closed.

Belbis turned and ran. He had reached the outer walkway when the light exploded soundlessly behind him.

Down on the plains, people looked up and wondered at the fierce green beam that pierced the sky.

Hive World High Orbit, Spin Inside

It was late and Seldyan's nose and mouth were dry with the abrasive dust which was everywhere in here. She huffed down her nose, feeling the warm breath escaping across her face through the perished seals of the filter mask.

Most nights that would have bothered her very much, but tonight she didn't care. She squinted through the haze; Hufsza was in front of her, his shoulders squirming in the confined space as he moved a vac nozzle over the surface of the duct. They were paired off. Of the others, Kot and Lyste were out of sight, working in their own duct. She could hear occasional scrapes and clangs as they cleaned. There was no sign of Merish, but that was a good thing. There wasn't supposed to be, yet.

They were inching their way through the sinistral whorl of the rear branch of the main carbon dioxide manifold. If it had been running, they would have been blown backwards out of it and into the billion cubic metres of the biggest single biomass plant in the Spin – a huge, enclosed forest in its own space-going cube. But not before they had been asphyxiated by all the growth-encouraging carbon dioxide.

Unfortunately the carbon dioxide didn't just encourage the biomass. It also nurtured a whole ecosystem of moulds and fungi, some of them unique to the micro environment. At least one of the moulds was actually parasitic on a combination of two others, and most of them seemed to give off spores that accumulated in sooty, gritty black clumps. They piled up in corners, built up into filter-clogging cakes, and broke apart into drifting clouds of unbelievably pervasive dust.

Cleaning was a horrible, regular, manual job, done by people with vacs and wire brushes and no rights and no choices.

It probably said 'Hive Technicians' on the order. They were duct monkeys to everyone else. Two teams of two people crawling along in the heat and the dust with their cramped limbs aching, and one banksman watching their backs from the entrance. Two people manually scratching the black stuff away with wire brushes and sucking it up with moaning vac nozzles, until their backs ached and their knees ached and the palms of their hands were raw – and who would be punished if they didn't meet a daily target.

She shook herself. Today was not about death, and she needed to concentrate. She resettled the mask on her face and peered through the dust past Hufsza. In the sameness of the ducts it was hard to gauge distance, but surely they were almost there? If they had missed the place there would be no more chances. Or if there had been a refit. Or if . . .

She reached out and tapped Hufsza's foot. He glanced over his shoulder, eyebrows raised. She nodded and gestured ahead.

A few metres in front of them, there was an extra seam in the metal surface. A metre further on was another.

Seldyan felt a grin scratching against the mask. It was still there.

A movement in front of her made her realize Hufsza had seen it too; he sat back on his heels, his head brushing the top of the duct, and switched off the vac.

It fell silent. Seldyan slapped the metal in front of her sharply, twice. The echoes clanged and fell away. She listened intently. On the edge of hearing came the sound of vacs winding down, and then, much louder, two slaps.

Everyone was in place. Or, rather, both teams of two were in place. She just had to hope Merish was too. She slapped the metal just once more, then shut her eyes and began counting silently. She got to five.

Boom.

It was a deep, soft sound that she felt through the metal of the duct almost before she heard it. As it faded, a perfect rect-angular smoke-ring of dust rolled along the duct towards them. She nodded to herself. Merish was on the case.

There was an electrical-sounding buzz and a sharp smell of burning. The two seams glowed dull red, then quickly climbed the spectrum to a fierce yellow-white. Then the metre-long sec-tion of metalwork between the seams dropped out.

The unofficial, unnoticed exit was open.

Seldyan took a deep breath. 'Go,' she said. It was unneces-sary; Hufsza had already shunted himself forward. He dropped through the gap and disappeared.

Seldyan shuffled to the edge of the gap. She had wondered if she would hesitate when she got to this part. She didn't; the worst she could expect by following Huf was a quick death. The best she could earn herself by staying put was a very slow one.

She shut her eyes and launched herself.

She dropped like a stone.

No one in the Hive ever talked openly about escape. But then, no one talked about survival either, and yet they all thought about that all the time, too.

'Hive' stood for 'high value'. Hivers took that as a bitter joke.

The Hive was the biggest forced-labour colony in the Spin. It was the economic well-spring of the Inside, a space-borne city state within a state. Its million or so inhabitants were hired out to do anything at all, for anyone at all. It was slavery, on a more-than-industrial scale, and Seldyan had never known any-thing else.

Her stomach yawned with the acceleration and her body yelled at her to open her eyes, to flail, to save herself. She managed to ignore it, curling instead into the tightest ball she could and keeping her eyes screwed shut. Right now the best and simplest thing she could do for herself was just to fall in a straight line.

The cube's internal monitoring, if any of it had survived Merish's attention, would now be showing four desperate escapees falling to certain death. A straight line was the only sure way to prove it wrong. If she glided off track by more than a hundred metres or so, she was jelly.

Well, fairly sure. Her terminal speed in the thick humid atmosphere of the cube shouldn't be too high, Merish had said, but it seemed high enough. She could feel herself tumbling, and a wind that behaved like a solid battered at her. The temptation to open her eyes was almost unbearable, but she had schooled herself to resist it.

Then something else struck at her, something that felt like being whipped with fog.

She shouted with relief. The line had been straight enough – she had hit the Feather Palms.

From their oily sap the Feather Palms provided almost half of the basic vegetable fat consumed by the Inside. Each tree was over a hundred metres tall. Their roots were shallow, and to compensate for this and to resist the high winds on their native planet they clumped together so tightly that their trunks came close to touching. Even here in this regimented environment they were planted in a hexagonal close-packed array just a metre apart. Thankfully no one had yet managed to engineer out their soft, dense, wastefully deep canopies.

At her speed soft was a matter of opinion, but deep was undeniable. Even curled up, Seldyan slowed in a series of wrenching jolts that felt as if every joint had been dislocated. Any extended limbs would certainly have been torn off. But she slowed, and eventually she felt she had lost speed enough to open her eyes and take control.

Branches were thrashing past her; she grabbed at one and lost her grip and some skin, but it had trimmed her speed to stoppable. The next one she held on to, breathing hard. Her hand hurt and her nose was full of the sickly oily smell of the palm, and she could feel her grin trying to split her face.

She waited until her breathing had got halfway back to normal. Then she hand-over-handed her way down through the remainder of the canopy until she could angle down a single branch to the main trunk. The trunk was smooth, and slender enough at this height for her to close her arms around it. She slid down for thirty metres or so until it became too thick for her to span, then took stock. The palms really were close together; if she stretched out a leg like *this* she could get a foothold on a neighbouring trunk. She turned her back to her own tree, braced herself against it and shunted herself down, ignoring the pain in her back.

She almost made it to ground level before her foot slipped on an oily patch.

'Shit!' The yelp was out before she could stop it. She hit a lot of roots with the small of her back. It knocked the breath out of her, and she lay there panting for a moment. Then, as the spasms in her diaphragm quieted, she rolled over into a crouch, looked around through the dim light – and saw nothing at all except trees, and heard nothing except a thick woody silence.

She didn't dare try to stand. The forest floor wasn't really a floor. The palms relied on sprawling above-ground root spreads for what little stability they had, and their vast thirst shrank the soil so that ground level became a knotted rooty obstacle course littered with loose fallen branches that were even more treacherous than the roots. The next part of the plan really had to work. Otherwise, a few years hence, she was going to be found on this exact spot, stone dead and smelling of tree oil.

She cast about carefully in the branch brash and selected a

strong-looking limb about half her own height, picked it up, hefted it and then took the hardest swing she could manage at the trunk of the tree she had shinned down.

Electronic communication was out down here, for the same reason it was out up in duct-world, but hitting things was fine.

The tree rang like a musical instrument.

She listened as the sound faded away. She didn't have to wait long; almost immediately there were three answering sounds. She nodded. All safe.

The next part was down to Merish. As had been the last, but Seldyan didn't feel guilty about that; she and the other three had a major job to do later. If they got as far as later.

Besides, she knew herself well enough, feeling guilty wasn't her strong suit.

She did her best to sit down on a root. It wasn't easy, but in the end she managed a kind of perch, if she braced one foot against another root. It was miserably uncomfortable, but she didn't care. Even uncomfortable could feel good, if it was a step away from the Hive.

I'm never going back, she thought. The word felt like a chant. *Ne-ver, ne-ver, ne-ver.*

A few minutes later she looked up. The woody silence had stopped being a silence – she could hear a regular knocking, about twice the speed of a heartbeat. She looked around quickly, and then nodded to herself. A few trunks away two big parallel roots formed a bridge she could just about stand on.

Beneath them was a void big enough to curl up in. That would do. She hoped the noise was Merish, but it might not be. Hiding could be good, if it was someone else.

She teetered on to the bridge, leaned against a trunk and peered cautiously round it towards where she thought the sound was coming from. When she saw it she wanted to laugh, partly out of relief that it was Merish rather than someone else, but mainly because it just looked – funny.

He was standing up, but she wasn't sure how. He was on a platform which looked as if it was using the tree trunks like vertical monkey bars. It was grasping its way from one trunk to the next, about a metre above the rootscape, using things that looked like tree-sized lock-grip pliers. Somehow it managed to stay more or less horizontal, but some side-to-side wobble was inevitable. There was a T-shaped handle at waist height, and Merish looked as if he was having to hang on to it quite hard.

She leaned out and waved. He nodded and did something to a control on the handle. The platform slowed, coming to a stop a couple of trunks away.

She grinned at him, and then saw his expression and stopped grinning. 'Okay,' she said. 'Tell me. No clear run, right?'

He nodded. 'Definitely no clear run. There's an extra shift on, fuck knows why.'

She felt herself tensing. 'A *whole* extra shift? Ten bodies?'

'Yes. I'm sorry, Sel.'

'Why? You didn't invite them. I'd like to know who did.' She stared into the distance for a moment, calculating. 'Are the main shift sorted?'

He nodded. 'Sure. Confined in a half-exploded control room by an inexplicable series of systems failures. That bit worked okay. But there's enough of the extra shift to cover the ways out.'

'Are there any inside the Planter?'

'I don't know. There could be.'

'We'd better assume there are then. Let's get the others. We might need to think of another definition of exit.' She gave the platform a jaundiced look. 'You're fine on that thing, for a given value of fine, but it's only big enough to torture one at a time. What about the rest of us?'

His eyes flickered and he pointed over his shoulder.

She followed the gesture. 'Oh . . .'

There was a line of four platforms behind him.

He looked embarrassed. 'They were all I could manage. They're slaved to this one. When they're not hugging trees they just float. It's pretty comfortable.'

She nodded. 'You know, Merish, comfortable doesn't really bother me? Freedom, now that I care about, and you've done your job.' She squared her shoulders. 'Let's go and find the team. It's our turn now.'

He looked away for a moment, and she saw his lips twitching.

Ten minutes later they had picked up the others and formed a wobbly line of five with Merish in the lead. Seldyan was feeling sick, partly from the uneasy jolting of the platform and partly from the pervasive smell of oil from the Feather Palms, but she still didn't care. They were closing on the edge of the plantation and another step towards freedom, even if there were extra obstacles; reaching the edge also meant that they would soon be floating, not gripping. That was good under any circumstances, even these.

They had talked quickly about those circumstances once the five of them were together. They had a plan. It would have to do, because none of them could think of anything cleverer.

As they reached the edge of the stand of Feather Palms they split up. No one said anything.

The Planter was divided into strips a hundred metres wide. Every second one was palms; the others were mainly low-growing succulents that acted as combined moisture moderators and firebreaks. Seldyan turned her platform down the strip and gunned it so that it tilted forward and built up speed until the wind rush scoured her eyes and tried to tear her hands from the T-bar. She hugged the margin of the palms just in case it might shelter her from anyone who might be looking, but someone was bound to see her soon. Speed was the thing.

The end of the strip was rushing towards her. She held her speed as long as she dared, then reared the platform steeply

21

backwards at the last second, threw it round a right angle that made her inner ears dance and into the narrow space between the end of the strips and the inner curtain wall of the Planter. She held on to the turn by a miracle, then leaned forward and twisted the grip to full power. There wasn't much room; her speed built up an air dam in front of her which racketed into the end of the palm stand and bounced off the trunks with a staccato whistle that hammered at her eardrums. Then she was past the palms and hissing through the open air at the end of another low strip.

She covered the kilometre to the far corner of the Planter in just over twenty seconds, and hauled the platform to a halt. Her face felt abraded, her arms ached and her ears were ringing, and it wasn't over yet.

She had had the furthest to go. Everyone else should be in place, but she didn't have any way of checking because they were too far apart to communicate by hitting trees, so she would just have to assume.

That meant the time was now. She powered down the platform and it sank to the ground. Inert, it was surprisingly light. She flipped it over without much effort, examined it for a second and then ran a finger over a rectangular seam on the smooth base. The seam popped open, revealing two greyish squares covered with ominous-looking symbols in a language she couldn't read. No user-serviceable parts inside, she thought.

'Platforms have two cell packs,' Merish had said, 'but they can get by for a while on one.'

She had looked at him for a moment, and then asked, 'Long enough?'

There had been the slightest pause before he nodded. She didn't think anyone else had noticed.

Now she reached into the space and pulled at one of the squares. It turned out to be the square end of a cube about two hands across. As it came free there was a faint crackle. She turned it over; there was a recessed contact array hedged about with even more ominous symbols.

The wire brush she had used to scrub the surface of the duct was still hanging at her belt. She unhooked it. Then she replaced the cover and righted the platform, took the cell pack and walked towards the edge of the palm stand. Ten paces into the trees she stopped and put the cell pack down, contacts upwards. She took the wire brush and held it out, bristles downwards. She gulped, dropped it straight down towards the contacts, and was running by the time it landed.

Even with her back turned the arc was bright. There was an angry buzz, and then a wet-sounding explosion. By that point she was at the platform. She jumped on, gripped the bar and leaned the thing as far forward as she dared.

The acceleration almost tore her arms off. She allowed herself just one glance to the side – the first few palms in the stand were already on fire, set off by the electro-chemical inferno at their bases.

The whole stand of oily trees would burn. She just had to hope that the fire-front would be fast enough.

But not too fast. She tried to force the grip further, but it was at maximum. She didn't know what the top speed of the platform was, or how long it could keep it up on only one cell pack, or if the whole mad scheme would work, or anything.

She still felt like whooping.

Then something screeched and slammed behind her, and a wall of sub-sonic noise shook the platform.

She risked a glance over her shoulder. The first firebreak had dropped. Now the first hundred flaming metres of the Planter were isolated by a thousand tonnes of mineral-fibre curtain wall. It was the next-to-last defence of the Planter, designed to isolate just about any problem.

Except for five improvised incendiary bombs all at once. She glanced again – the trees in front of the firebreak were smouldering.

As she looked, flames leapt. She faced forward and gritted her teeth. Even this far ahead of the fire the air smelled of burning oil.

Slam. That was the second wall. Eight to go. She didn't look this time; she had felt herself slowing the last time she had turned. Speed was everything. The burning smell was getting stronger.

Slam. The concussion seemed stronger too. She was losing ground. Seven to go. She could feel radiated heat on the back of her head.

Slam. It was getting harder to breathe. By now there should have been an air-wash blowing back across the Planter, driving the fire into itself, but instead the air was full of billowing oily smoke.

She remembered. They had broken the ducts. The air-wash couldn't help, either by clearing the smoke or slowing the fire-front. She wanted to thump the controls, but she didn't dare.

Slam. She blinked. That one had seemed quieter. For a moment she thought she must be gaining, but that couldn't be right; the heat and the smoke were even stronger. Then she realized. It wasn't that the firebreak had been quieter – everything else was louder. There was a thrumming roar. Now she risked another look over her shoulder, and immediately wished she hadn't.

Where there should have been trees, there was boiling black smoke shot through with expanding bubbles of fire. It was far too close, and it was getting closer.

It wasn't going to work after all. Then she corrected herself: it wasn't going to work for her. She hoped the others were ahead of her. It was supposed to be impossible for Hivers to break out; four impossibles out of a possible five would be pretty good going.

Besides, she wasn't done yet. She leaned forward as far as possible, drew her elbows into her body to streamline herself

24

and twisted the control so hard she thought it would break, thinking that if this was what freedom felt like – then it felt good.

Better than good. Better than anything she had ever experienced.

And then she felt the platform slowing down.

She actually laughed. When she saw Merish she would tell him that 'long enough' was not long enough, after all. Except that now it looked like she wouldn't be seeing Merish again.

The platform dropped to the ground and she threw herself off it and into a dead run. She had no idea how far she was ahead of the fire-front, or how far behind the last firebreak and when it would drop. All she knew was running, and trying to breathe air that was no longer proper air but smoke and soot and heat that rasped her throat and fouled her lungs. Her heart hammered and her vision began to fade.

The screech and slam of the last firebreak were dead overhead. Her legs gave way; she dropped and rolled awkwardly, hoping it was still forward.

She came to a stop and for a second there was nothing. Then she heard the fire and knew that it was all over.

Then she felt arms on her, uncurling her.

'Seldyan! You okay?'

She opened her eyes. It was Merish. At first she wanted to throw her arms round him and she tried to raise herself. Then she realized, and fell back. If he was here they must both have failed. She corrected herself – she had failed both of them.

'Seldyan! Shit, will you snap out of it? You need to be ready.'

She shook her head. 'Ready for what?'

'What do you think? You still got your vac tab?'

It was hard to think, and besides, he was talking nonsense. She humoured him, patting the upper pocket of her coverall. 'Yep, still there. So what?'

'Then fucking *take* it!'

She opened her eyes properly and stared at him. 'Seriously?'

'Of course seriously! Take it *now*!'

Still staring at him, she fumbled the little pill out of her pocket. It was standard issue for anyone who went space-side, even Hivers. Boiling away into a vacuum, if you were exposed to it, wasn't good. The vac tab bought you minutes.

Her brain came back to life. If she was taking a tab then that must mean . . .

She took it, and looked at Merish. 'How long?'

He shrugged. 'Should be ten seconds.'

'Right. We'd better hold on, then.' She rolled over, extended her hands and drove her stiffened fingers into the soil between the succulents. For a frantic moment she found nothing. Then her fingers met something and curled around it. It was the geo-textile mesh that held the soil together. It should be strong enough.

She saw Merish lying down next to her, his hands pushing down as hers had. Then she heard it – louder than the crash of the firewalls, louder than the roar of the burning trees, it was a sound that had meant frozen boiling death to ten thousand generations of space-faring animals.

It was the howl of air racing out of something very fast.

Seldyan looked up and felt her eyes widen. The vaulted roof was splitting into segments like the skin of a fruit. If she had needed confirmation, here it was; they had made it to the last cell after all, and now the Planter had activated its ultimate defence. When the fire can't be contained, sod the biomass – save the structure. The whole thing was opening itself to vacuum.

She held on.

A hurricane gripped her. Shrieking winds hauled her body off the ground. A vortex of plants, burning tree fragments and even the soil itself was flicking up towards the void. The force on her arms was massive – but manageable.

Then she saw one of Merish's hands grasp at the soil, and

flail, and fly loose. The other, still buried, was shaking. As she watched, the hooked fingers began to uncurl.

Her muscles made the decision before her brain could intervene. She undid the fingers of her right hand, yanked it out of the soil and flung it out and back just as Merish yelped and lost his grip completely.

She caught his shoulder then lost it, his upper arm then lost it, and finally felt his hand close on hers. She gripped back as hard as she could, and gritted her teeth as his mass tried to tear her in half. Her shoulders were close to dislocating and her fingers screamed at her.

She ignored them. *It's just pain*, she told herself. *This time it's pain you're choosing. Take it.*

She took it.

They were buffeted by a storm of shattered timber and smouldering leaves, and she shut her eyes and got ready to be battered to death. Then, at last, the pull lessened and she opened her eyes.

A cloud of ice crystals fogged the view, forming a swirling vortex that followed the clashing debris out through the open roof. When it had gone, so had the last of the air. Without the vac tab she would have had about twenty seconds; with it, maybe three minutes. It was enough, if the hurried plan they had made in the plantation worked out.

As the wind had died the Planter's grav had reasserted itself. They dropped to the ground fairly gently with Merish on top in the total silence of a vacuum. He let go of her hand and rolled off, and she gingerly uncurled her buried fingers from the mesh.

Letting go managed to hurt even more than holding on. She squeezed her hand shut, and fascinatedly watched a drop of blood boil away into the vacuum.

She shook herself. Merish was gesturing towards the end wall and she saw his platform, somehow still sitting obediently on the ground. There were several questions she had no time to

ask him, and no breath either; they ran. Merish hauled the platform upright, jumped on and gestured to Seldyan. She climbed
on behind and locked her arms round his waist.

Even with two aboard the platform was very, very fast in a
vacuum. They were at the end wall in twenty seconds – Merish's
remaining power cell had obviously taken far less of a hammering than hers – and standing in front of an oddly old-fashioned-
looking gas-tight door with a control wheel in its middle. She
looked at it and mouthed, 'Fully manual?'

He nodded. They gripped the rim of the wheel and turned. It
resisted, gave and rotated through a whole turn before taking up
the load. Another full turn and it stopped with a sound that Seldyan
felt as *clang* even if she couldn't hear it, and the door swung open.

They bundled past it into the airlock. The door shut behind
them, and there was the ice-crystal kiss of air freezing as it
expanded into a vacuum.

There was an indicator patch on the wall. Seldyan watched
it, feeling her heart beginning to pump against her ribs. She was
fighting the urge to try to breathe, as while the patch was red
breathing would be a bad idea: even the vac tab couldn't stave
off the effects of thin cold air on starved lung tissue. She had to
wait until the lock thought its own atmosphere was warm
enough and thick enough.

Green. There. It was okay to breathe.

It still hurt though. The chill rasped at nerves she had never
noticed before. She rode it out and then looked at Merish.

'Thanks.'

He nodded, reaching out to take her hand. She winced, but
let him turn it over and gently uncurl her fist. It was filthy with
soil, but the deep cuts at the bases of her fingers had stained it a
glistening purple.

He looked sharply at her. 'Oh, shit . . .'

She shrugged. 'It was that or let go. There'll be meds in the
shuttle. I assume the shuttle *is* our next stop?'

'Yes. The other three should be in the next lock along. Sorry, Seldyan.'

'Don't be.' She grinned, and it felt good. 'Because you know what we're going to do next? With your help, technical maestro, we're going to borrow a shitload of money.'

He smiled slowly. 'I can do that,' he said.

Hive, Juvenile Unit

Seldyan's childhood had seemed normal as far as she could remember. The Hive had been – everything. She remembered food and sleep, and adults that were tall and remote and occasionally forbidding and mostly irrelevant.

But then, she supposed, most childhoods probably did seem normal until something arose to challenge the seeming. Her challenge had come late. It hadn't been when she was four, when she had been taken out of class one day and hurried to a room she had never seen before, and she had been told to take off her shift and curl over, and something sharp had pressed against her back near the top of her bottom and then it had hurt so horribly, and she had howled until her throat hurt as much as her back but she couldn't move because they were holding her.

They had let her rest for the afternoon, and with the evening bowl they had given her something that made her sleep. When she woke the next day she felt almost all right, just a bit sore. When she got to class she heard someone say she had been chipped. It was a new word, and she remembered it.

It hadn't been when she was just beginning to bud and the Supervisor had wangled her a single room instead of a dormitory space, and had visited her on the very first night just when she was feeling so lucky. She had known men were different, obviously, but she hadn't known it could be that sore. She had tolerated his fumbling and grunting and his *mess* for two weeks. Then one day while they were all chanting a lesson, there was a sharp *pop* overhead and one of the light globes became a spray of glassy shards. A big one landed on the surface in front of her; she managed to snatch it and conceal it up the sleeve of her shift. It cut her a little but she didn't care.

Later, it cut the Supervisor much better.

She expected to be punished but for once nothing happened. She never saw the Supervisor again. She supposed he couldn't be a supervisor without what she had cut from him.

She had never seen so much blood.

No. The challenge to her seeming had come later, when she was fifteen. Someone had smuggled in a book, an actual old-fashioned book such as she had heard of but never seen. It had a screen, and buttons to advance the pages, and it used two words that she had never heard, but whose meaning became clear very quickly as she read on, oblivious to risk.

The risk became reality. They found her and took her away, and this time she was truly punished, oh yes, punished until she wished her body didn't belong to her. Until she knew in intimate close focus, one at a time and several times over, what that chip could do. But she remembered the words, and what they meant.

Mother, and father.

A little while afterwards they moved her out of the dormitory and into one of the Villages and she learned another word she wasn't supposed to know.

It was *slave*.

Three Quarter Circle Plains

His feet knew the way and his nose knew the air, but it still took him a long time to retrace his steps. He could feel the changing ground, the way that the jagged rocks of the peak became the smooth worn surface of the lower path. He could feel the change from rock to moss, and from moss to grass if he strayed from the path. The sound of falling water guided him down the sharp-edged little river valleys, and he learned with wonder how dense and detailed the soundscape could be. Even the slightest turn of his head changed it, telling him that *here* the water poured over a boulder and *there* the bed broadened and slowed. The air, too. Not only did it become thicker as he descended – how much thicker he could hardly believe – but the scent! Rock had a smell. Wet rock smelled different to dry rock, and one rock smelled different to another. Not knowing the real names of any of the rocks, he gave them his own names according to their smell. Saltstone, Bitterstone and Sulphur Rock.

Smell guided him to food, too. At first he dared not leave the path but as his hunger and his confidence grew he began to make short side-trips to follow the scents of berries and toadstools.

Somehow, despite his blindness, Belbis didn't quite starve.

Even the times of day changed. Day and night had no meaning

for him, except that night was a bad time to sleep because he would wake up cold and damp. Instead he marked his own daily cycle, and again gave it his own names. Mouse Quiet, for example, that was the time at the end of the night when the night-seeing hunters had finished but the day dwellers were still sleepy or asleep. If he stood very still and listened very hard he could hear the diffident little rustles of the smallest creatures taking advantage of the lull to – well, what? Scavenge, he supposed, or dig a burrow. Perhaps just to breathe without having their tiny breath triangulated by death in the air.

Mouse Quiet was followed by Dew Time, and he usually walked as briskly as he could through that to fight off the cold and to keep dry until the time he named Sun Greet.

His feet were telling him he was near the outskirts of Three Quarter Circle town when his ears and nose alerted him to something. At first he wasn't sure what it was. He stopped and thought.

The sun felt directly above him and an onshore wind was in his face. At this hour the harbour should have been busy no matter the state of the tide. He should have been able to smell the oily reek of the rendering vats with its undertone of burning peat. There should have been the click of ropes against masts and the distant grinding breath of the old steam engines that ran the hauling winches. Especially there should have been the cries of the merchants.

Instead there was quiet. No, that wasn't right; instead, there was the absence of familiar noises. They had been replaced by an odd undertow, almost at the limit of his hearing. And the air did smell, but that was wrong too.

Without thinking about it he found he had broken into a run. Senses he had developed on the downward journey mined the unconscious knowledge of half his lifetime – there were familiar cobbles beneath his feet. From here, downhill two hundred paces, until the cross-shore wind struck his right cheek, and

33

then to the right, and he would be at the Prater House. They would look after him there, and when he had told the Klerikers what had happened they would be able to explain it to him. They would know what to do.

Meanwhile his nose sought the smells that should have been there, and his ears the cries, and then he felt his pace faltering. And now there were cries and there was smoke, yes. But the cries were angry and the smoke smelled of wood and tar and something worse, something that made his gorge rise, and as he came to a halt in front of what should be the Prater House he felt a hot wind on his cheeks. Suddenly his mind supplied an image of burning buildings.

Now the cries were coming quickly closer, and had become focused as if the men had something to shout about.

'Another blood-sucking priest!'

'Didn't we get them all then?'

'Guess this one's been a-wandering . . .'

He turned in panic, but hands seized him.

'Drag him in front of the Merchants.'

'To hell with that. Who put them over us? They're as bad as the fucking priests. Hang him up with the rest of the black bastards!'

'No! Wait . . .'

Someone pushed him to the ground, and there was the warm damp breath of stump spirits in his face. One breath, two breaths, three, and he knew he was being inspected.

'Young. Grey robes. Oh sweet shit, let it be him . . .'

'If it's him he'll be scarred.' Another voice.

'They have potions to stop that.'

'Or witchery . . .'

'Just bloody look, will you?'

Hands took his robes and dragged them upwards, and he felt the hot wind on his thighs.

'Well now . . .'

'What?'

'It's him. It's the Idiot.'

Voices roared around him. Through the roar he sensed the warmth of a face close to his, and more stump brew. The voice was harsh and hoarse.

'What did you do?' Hands took his robe and he felt himself lifted and thrust back so that the back of his head struck the cobbles. Red-green stars fizzed across his darkness and he felt the breath whistling out of him as if it would never return. 'What – did – you – DO?'

It was so hard to make words. For the whole of his life Belbis had treasured the thought that if he could only find the right words, someone would understand him, just for once. He made a supreme effort, expelling each word on a gust of breath. 'Counted Gods. Wrong number.'

There was a pause, while the roaring voices went on roaring. Then came a sound like a grunt of disgust and the hands let go of his robe.

Then the first blows landed. The blows became kicks from men who grunted with effort, loud enough to be heard over the crowd noise. He covered his head and began to cry. It hurt to breathe, and through his tears he realized that the clicks he heard within himself were his own ribs breaking.

After a long time he felt himself lifted and thrown. He landed on a hard slick surface and immediately began to slide. He cried out and the pain in his sides would have made him sick, if the smell hadn't already. They had thrown him into one of the gut-ramps.

Now he had no sense of distance but his speed seemed terrifying. The ramps weren't straight; he slammed round corners and through sharp-edged sumps. Once he held out his arms to try to slow himself. One of them caught against something and for a moment he slowed, but then he felt his elbow twist through an impossible angle.

There was an audible *snap*.

Belbis screamed. He tumbled down the smooth stone channels, slick with blubber and wet with the blood that was never allowed to set, screaming with every appalling crash of his broken ribs and his shattered arm, until the only thing left to him apart from the pain was the hope that he would soon drop into the vile waters of the harbour and be killed and eaten with the other entrails.

He did not get his wish. He felt the ramp steepen, he almost smiled, but then he crashed horribly into something, legs first – and there were more clicks and then more pain – and then the merciless hands seized him again and he was dragged upwards and dropped on to a hard surface – the quayside, he guessed, with his waning senses.

'Hold him.'

The hands took him, careless of his shattered arm and of his howls of agony. He felt his sandals being removed and thought, *why?* – and then unspeakable incandescent pain shot across his heels.

At last, the world faded.

Chastern System, Spin Inside

Captain Hefs leaned on the rail of the observation gallery above the forward sun deck of the liner *Sunskimmer*, scoped some of the more presentable guests – without being intrusive, obviously – and decided that he didn't have the worst job in the sector. One of the better-looking females, who at least looked human-compatible, seemed to have noticed him. He straightened up and sucked in his belly.

They were skirting a medium-sized yellow star called Chastern, roughly halfway across the Inside. They were about a minute out from the first wisps of the corona and the blinds above the sun decks were fully opened, heavily dimmed by very strong fields. Without them, seventy mainly naked people would have been cooked alive just before they died of radiation poisoning. With them, they were merely getting the fastest and most expensive suntan in the Spin.

The female was definitely looking at him. She was dark-skinned with short silver hair, and she looked young and athletic. He sucked in his gut a little more and focused his eyes carefully on the middle distance as if thinking important things. The sort of things thought by captains.

After all, he was hardly an insignificant captain, as he often told himself. He was in command of a spaceship nearly a kilometre from end to end. He liked the word 'command' – even if in actual fact the whole vast ship could be run by a crew of one.

Sunskimmer had not always been called *Sunskimmer*, and she had not started life as a liner. She had originally been a Main Battle Unit called *Flamejob*, a proper fighting spaceship built ten thousand years ago for long-term charter to mostly private armies. When she was a mere five thousand years old she had been decommissioned, and her original battle-smart AI largely disabled. Since then she had led a varied but mainly uneventful life cruising around the safe bits of the Spin with cargoes of wealthy passengers. The decommissioning had not affected her engines; very large and very fast, she was one of the few remaining ships in private hands with enough power to get this far down the gravity well of a star without being sucked the rest of the way, and enough shields that she was unlikely to melt. She was ideally suited to the new fad of deep-well sunbathing.

Captain Hefs thought it was a stupid pastime, but it was a living – quite a good one – and he did quite enjoy some of the opportunities it presented.

There was no doubt about it. The woman was looking at him. He flagged a servitor and, doing his best to look as if he was passing on a command decision, told it to steal some candid close-ups and tag them to the young woman's ID and suite number. He was quite aware of his own slightly chubby limitations, but confidence and position still did the trick far more often than he would have thought likely. There was a Dinner tonight. He hadn't finalized his table plan yet.

Well, he probably had *now*.

Captain's Dinners were held every fifth day in what had been the upper forward weapons pod, when the old ship still had weapons. *Sunskimmer* was shaped like two rough cones joined back to back by a short fat tube. The rear cone was all engine.

When she was in fighting trim the front cone would have been all weapons, but now it was where you put the people. On one side of the cone there were the sun decks. On the other, a half-globe stuck out of the cone as if it had crashed into it. It had been where the business end of the major energy weapons pointed out through a set of insectoid-looking bulbous blisters. Now, the blisters had been turned into viewing galleries and the biggest of them had been fitted out as a restaurant, with tables on floating platforms that moved around each other in a slow dance to make sure everyone got the best from the view.

Hefs was enjoying the view very much. Her name was Seldyan, apparently. She had gone travelling between studies; she and a group of friends had saved up to come on this trip. Four of her friends were with her at dinner. They were all young and attractive, and as far as he could see they were getting on with his exec team very well. One young man in particular was talking to his second in command, who seemed rapt. Hefs had sometimes wondered about the man's sexuality.

Close up, Seldyan's skin was the rich colour of old hardwood and her eyes were tinted violet in a shocking contrast to her silver-white hair. She wore a strangely beautiful filigree thing in silver wire that twined around one ear. She was smart and sinuous and unaffected – all the things Hefs liked best – and she did seem to like him in return.

And his current consort was light-years away, probably enjoying herself with someone younger. Well, she wasn't the only one who could play. He called for more drinks and watched, entranced, as Seldyan popped another of the fat berries into her perfect mouth. The berry disappeared with just a flicker of tongue. The sleek throat rippled, and she smiled. 'Mmm. Gorgeous. I've never had these before. What did you say they were called?'

He shook himself mentally. 'They're Mist Berries. They grow on one of the planets of this star, actually. It's an ocean world.

The berries grow on sort of floating islands.' Damn, she was easy to talk to. He went on, 'We try to serve local food, wherever we are.'

'How interesting.' She leaned a little closer, and he caught a hint of a soft fragrance. 'You must have visited hundreds of planets.'

He gave what he hoped was a modest laugh. 'Well, all of the Eleven, anyway. I've hardly been outside the Inside.'

'Hardly?' Her eyes widened. 'But that doesn't mean not at all. When did you go out?'

The urge to impress her was – lunatic. What had come over him? Concentrate! He frowned and thought back. 'I first crossed the Border, oh, fifteen years ago, I guess. In those days we traded more. I was a convoy escort.'

'Wow.' She raised her eyebrows – tinted silver to match her hair, he noticed. 'Does that mean you were some kind of fighter pilot?'

He laughed. 'Some kind, I suppose. I never found anything to fight.'

'Too modest. They probably saw you and ran away.' She sat back, looking at him. 'There's more to you than meets the eye, Captain.'

'I doubt it.' But the thought warmed him all the same. Part of him, just a small part that he thought had fizzled and died years ago, whispered that perhaps he really had once been more than an overweight middle-aged shepherd to the wealthy.

Seldyan was staring at him with those eyebrows raised, and he realized that he was grinning.

'No, not like *that*! Look, let me show you.' Seldyan took him by the shoulder and spun him half round. 'Look, you start off going this way. See? With everyone else.' She demonstrated and he tripped over his feet for the third time, dragging her down with him. The drink wasn't helping, but he had to admit he probably wasn't a natural dancer. Seldyan was, though, and so were most of her friends. They had wanted to show everyone how to do some ancient formal dance or other – a round dance, was that it? He couldn't remember – so he had ordered the staff to clear the table platforms and bring them together to make a floating dancefloor.

It had been a social success, if a stylistic failure. And now here he was, accidentally lying underneath Seldyan.

She gave him a long look which started out amused and then became serious. Her eyes narrowed a little and she leaned down to let her lips brush his cheek. 'You're a shit dancer,' she said, 'but I've never believed that myth.' She rolled off him, stood up and extended a hand. 'Shall we?'

Fifteen minutes later she was on top of him again. This time it was in his suite, and clothes weren't involved, and it seemed so *natural*. He no longer felt he had to hold in his belly, he didn't care about the greying hairs on his chest – even if his consort did, but where was she? Exactly! – he didn't care about anything except the unbelievably beautiful creature who was poised above him, the warmth and scent of her body vivid to him, her hands on his wrists, pinning him deliciously, her thighs tight around his, her eyes dancing, her mouth . . .

. . . laughing?

She shouldn't have been laughing. Not like that.

He tried to sit up but his wrists really were pinned. She was stronger than she looked, and she was still laughing.

Then she stopped laughing and he wished she hadn't, because now her face looked . . . professional. She shifted her grip so that she had both his wrists pinned by one hand, and even then he couldn't break her grip no matter how he struggled. With her other hand she did something to the filigree thing in her ear. Then she spoke, and Hefs knew immediately that she wasn't speaking to him. 'I got mine,' she said. 'Report?'

There were three scratchy versions of 'yes', and then silence. Seldyan frowned. 'Merish? Result or not?'

There was a pause. Then a man's voice said, 'Sorry. Result, in the end.'

Seldyan's frown deepened. 'Was there a problem?'

'Yeah.' The voice sighed. 'Look, everyone said this bloke was gay?'

'The second in command?' Seldyan looked nonplussed. 'Sure. So?'

'No way. Bi-curious at best. I almost feel guilty.'

'Oh.' Seldyan's face twitched. 'Got things under control now?'

'Yeah.' The voice paused. 'I think I owe him an apology.'

Seldyan laughed softly. 'Save your apologies,' she said. 'He's probably grateful you broadened his horizons. Or whatever you broadened.' She touched the silver thing and it seemed to break the contact. Then she looked down at Hefs. 'I expect you get the idea,' she said. 'You've been taken over, at the cost of five cruise tickets and some booze you actually paid for. Any questions?'

'Yes.' He tried to sit up again but it was impossible. 'Who are you?'

She rolled her eyes. 'I'm someone who could break your pelvis, if I squeeze hard enough. You want me to try?'

'No!' He shook his head as hard as he could.

'Good. Any other questions?'

He shook his head again.

'Fine. I'm glad you aren't going to try to be a hero. Your ship might end up fighting – that's what it's for. You?' Her eyes scanned down his torso, over his belly and on to his softening penis, and she shook her head. 'Not so much.'

After that he was almost glad when she reached down to the junction of her thighs, pulled a tiny, bewitchingly moist stunner shaped like a flat pebble out of her body, and shot him.

Traders' Tower, Basin City

The image of the dark-skinned silver-haired woman hung in the air. It was taken from above and in front of her, fore-shortening her and cutting off the face and neck of the chubby middle-aged man she was astride, but her own face was still clear. She had a stunner in her hand which she seemed to be in the act of firing because there was a suggestion of a flash. She was naked and smiling but the smile looked more amused than happy. And, thought Harbour Master Hevalansa Vess, a little dangerous. He cleared his throat.

'So, let me see. Five escapees from the Hive manage to buy cruise tickets costing a year's salary each. They then seduce and disable every single one of the exec team of a liner worth, what? Madam Els?' He looked at the elderly human female sitting opposite him. Even with them both seated it was obvious that she was far taller and thinner than him, and she wore a long close-fitting jacket in a dull carbon-coloured material that made her seem even more stretched.

She gave a minute shrug. 'It depends. Valuation yesterday, seventeen trillion, triple A risks. Valuation as of five minutes ago, zero and junk bond.'

'Right.' He sighed. 'When did this happen?'

'Seventeen hours ago.'

'And you waited until now to tell us?' Vess didn't need to pretend to be irritated, but instead of flinching Els gave him a frosty smile.

'We waited until now to tell *anyone* except our bankers. Our corporation is leveraged with our fleet as collateral. A collapse of confidence was inevitable, but we managed to agree a soft landing. There were plenty of questions.' She looked at him sharply. 'Including, how did five slaves manage to escape and evade recovery long enough to have their identities wiped and to acquire long credit lines?'

'We don't refer to them as slaves.' It was a fair question; one which Vess couldn't answer until he had spoken to someone at a *much* higher pay grade – and if and when those people did speak to him he expected them to have other things on their minds. 'Do you know where the ship went?'

'No. It continued on course for ten minutes after the picture was sent. Then it stopped transponding and just vanished. We're assuming it's Outside by now.'

Vess waved at the screen. 'How did you get this, then?'

To his pleasure Els looked embarrassed. 'It seems that Hefs routinely had a micro-remote film his adventures. Gross mis-conduct, of course, although it's done us a favour this time. If we ever find him he'll be dismissed on the spot.'

Vess fought the temptation to laugh. He was afraid that if he started he would carry on until he was dragged out of the building. 'You think he's alive?'

'Oh yes. That's a ship-issue stunner. It's not meant to be used at such close range but even then it would take a long time to kill him with it. After a single shot like that he'd probably have woken up with a very bad headache.' She smiled. 'The ship followed the rules, even if its crew didn't. When it realized it was compromised it squirted a complete status snapshot back to us. Hence, this.' She gestured at the image.

Vess nodded. 'Are all your senior ship management sex maniacs then?'

The frosty look was back. 'No, but they're not immune to drugs. The ship monitored air quality. The last few results show traces of complex organic substances in the air-handling plant that served the restaurant area.'

Vess took a moment to process that. This is surreal, he thought. This woman has just announced what will probably be my death sentence, by talking about aphrodisiacs?

He shook his head slowly. 'The security breaches just go on piling up, don't they? It's just as well ship AIs don't have sex.'

Her face twisted a little as if she was trying not to smile. 'I believe some of them do, in a way, but this one isn't bright enough. It was meta-lobotomized five thousand years ago when the ship was decommissioned. It's meant to be dumb and dutiful.'

'Well, that's fascinating.' Vess stood up and walked over to the tall windows that lined one of the long walls of the room. Keeping his back turned he said, 'Would it interest you, madam, to know that your ship is not alone? It's one of five that have been lost over the last three cycles. Not all by the same means, but still.'

He heard the intake of breath, but nothing more. He smiled to himself and added, 'Apparently *everybody* waited until they had talked to their bankers. And their insurers, I suppose. Have they responded to you yet, by the way? The insurers?'

He turned round. Els was looking stunned. He raised his eyebrows, and she shook her head slightly.

'I'm not surprised. Five ships of the same sort of value? Eighty trillion total, or thereabouts?' He sat back down. 'They're probably sitting under their desks rocking backwards and forwards with their fingers, or whatever they have, in whatever they use for ears . . . are you all right, madam?'

She was very pale. He gestured to the servant, who placed a glass of water in front of her. It seemed to take a while for her to notice it. When she did, she clutched at it and took a hurried swig. 'The other four ships,' she said. 'We hadn't heard . . .'

'That's because we haven't said.' He shrugged. 'Investigations will take their course. You should assume that you will be part of that course. As will I.' *Oh, yes. I so will.*

She nodded. 'I should return to my Board. I'd like to tell them about the other ships. That is, if I may?'

'Yes, but for their knowledge only. Oh, and I'll want the passenger lists. This is going to stay unknown, you understand?' He paused. 'When was the ship due back?'

She still looked shaken. 'The day after tomorrow. We have four others on cruise at the moment . . .'

'I know. We checked. They are smaller, aren't they? Not legacy vessels?'

She nodded.

'Then they are less valuable. Warn them, but keep them there. We'll be covering them from a discreet distance.' Vess managed a smile. 'It's just as well they're little ones. If we lose any more major units we'll be back to walking.'

She rose and half turned towards the door. Then she turned back. 'The slave said the ship might end up fighting,' she said. It was a question.

'Yes, she did, didn't she?' Vess stood up and waved the servant forward. 'Escort Madam Els back to her skipper. A safe journey, madam.'

He turned towards the windows. Behind him, he heard the door closing. When he was sure he was alone he blew out a long slow breath and leaned against the glass.

Watching from a discreet distance? It had better be *very* discreet. If they got close enough to be spotted, people might realize how little they had left to watch with.

He was dead. Sooner or later, by easier or harder means – dead. In her role as a cruise ship, *Sunskimmer* was important, and certainly the loss (albeit temporary) of the high-value people on board was embarrassing, but the cruise companies were only a small part of the total GDP of the Inside. That wasn't the real issue.

His chest felt tight. He shut his eyes and took a couple of slow breaths. A few minutes of calm before he launched himself. He could allow himself that.

The Inside hadn't constructed a new major ship in two thousand years. It had *never* constructed anything like what *Sunskimmer* had become. Never mind anything like what *Sunskimmer* had been in the first place – and could always have become again, at need. She and the rest of her kind had been an insurance policy; the last line of defence. They had been careful about that; no ship of that potential had ever been so completely converted to civilian use that it could not be un-converted. She retained a basic suite of weapons; there were more in a central store, and there was an emergency backup protocol. In theory they could have a fully armed battle fleet within two days of any emergency.

But not any more.

The truth was, they had been living on the glories of their predecessors for twenty generations. And now the last of those glories had been stolen from under his nose. And hence, he was dead.

He opened his eyes again.

No matter where you looked the first thing you saw was canal. His office was most of the way up the complex. Above it was only the restaurant deck, strictly reserved for staff of Praetor rank, and above, the Penthouse – even more exclusive – and then the steeply pointed roofs of the Belfry. None of which, of course, were visible to Vess, but below, well, that was different.

Water had been the reason for the city. Water had been the cause of its foundation and the route by which wealth entered and left but, for the first five thousand years or so, mostly entered. It had started with simple flat canals, but it was a long way from its starting point now.

There were three main levels. The highest was just below his eyeline so that his view glanced off the suspended canalized

47

ribbons of water at a low angle. They stood off the next level on slim columns glistening with leaked or spilled water and streaked with green and black mould. That next level was in turn supported by a much older forest of stone, iron or even timber towers, festooned with hanging weed. At the roots of the forest, invisible from up here, were the grimy originals. Boat hoists, ranks of stepped locks and a couple of elaborate wheels with gondolas swinging from their rims moved things between levels.

The three levels formed their own hierarchy. On top were the cruisers, racers and even houseboats of the very wealthy. On the middle level were still the main commercial arteries, and down on the ground was what Vess had heard described as a vibrant mixed community, which meant poor people and criminals. Vess had been born there; he had never been back.

Well, he had never been back *yet*. It might turn out to be one of his options, sooner rather than later. It, too, would mean death, but only in the way it meant death for everyone – premature, and poor, but still recognizably human.

Every gap between the canals was full of buildings, mostly sinuous towers that snaked their way up between the waterways and poked more or less elaborate tops up into the sunshine. He never tired of the sight. He indulged himself with a few minutes of staring while a pair of big galleys rode in procession along the canal nearest to him, their oars leaving puckered scars on the water.

And then of course there was the other level. He never thought of it as being part of the three, and nor did anyone else he knew. The Cloud Deck was a discontinuous snaking structure that floated slowly backwards and forwards over everything else on intricately pivoted parallel-motion arms mounted on upward extensions of the main canal columns. The motion allowed it to be located anywhere over Basin City except for Traders' Tower. Vess wasn't sure how it all worked, but he had heard that the

arms would seize up, or bend, or at any rate fail in some catastrophic way if anyone tried to force the Cloud Deck there.
Geometry, and politics, apparently. Obviously no one had ever
tried because the Cloud Deck, although newer than the rest of
the city, wasn't *that* much newer – it had survived several thousand years un-broken.

The boats passed and the surface of the canal healed to a
breeze-frosted glass. Vess turned away from the window and
got ready to work. The servant had returned, and knew his
habits; as Vess sat down at his desk he found a steaming flask at
his left hand and a rolled-up spiced meat pastry at his right. He
would need them both; it was going to be a long time before he
could relax, if ever. The only safe assumption was that *Sunskimmer* was somewhere Outside, and in so many ways that
wasn't safe at all.

His first action was to put in a call to the Gamer. He expected
the answer would come soon. In fact it came sooner, before he
had even finished the pastry; he wiped his mouth on his sleeve
before he answered.

'Vess?' The voice was deep, dark and powerfully bassy. As
the Gamer had no choice but to use a voice synth, this was obviously intentional. Vess always found it funny. It was probably
racist but for his money an organism as spider-like as that
should hiss rather than boom. He swallowed his amusement
and knotted his arms in front of him in his closest approxima-
tion to a polite greeting. 'Clo Fiffithiss, thanks for calling. How
are you?' His memory threw in a random fact. 'Did you enjoy
the Colony Dinner last night?'

'Probably.' Fiffithiss writhed in a gesture which could have
been a shrug. It made Vess feel slightly queasy. 'I will never be
popular amongst my peers, but my fore-cock and my front legs
feel as if they have been plaited and I seem to have some new
tattoos. Those are both usually good signs. But you didn't call
to ask that.' The nest of limbs became still. 'There is a rumour

amongst my underwriting friends that we have lost another major unit. Is that, can that be, true?'

Vess nodded, and then remembered his manners and made what he hoped was the equivalent gesture. 'Yes, it is. *Sunskimmer.*' The gesture hurt his shoulders.

'*Sunskimmer*? I see.' The limbs were still motionless, which if you were prey wasn't good news at all. It meant an imminent pounce with poison fangs ready. Even the certainty that those fangs were several klicks away couldn't stop Vess's body trying to go into fight or flight. He fought down his instinct and waited.

Eventually the limbs relaxed and spread. Fiffithiss made a sighing noise which, through its artificially amplified voice, vibrated Vess's seat. '*Sunskimmer* was the last of the legacy Main Battle Units. You do realize that?'

'The disclosed ones, yes. They aren't all accounted for. There could be a few more.' Vess shrugged. 'Somewhere.'

'You really think so? Some backwoods bunch of retards have a legacy MBU up their smelly sleeve?' The limbs straightened abruptly and spread into a flat fan in front of Fiffithiss. Emphatic negative; a shake of the head to the power ten. 'I'd bet my unhatched eggs against it. And even if they have, they're hardly going to render it up on demand for the good of the Inside, are they?' Fiffithiss repeated the negative gesture and then collapsed into a sort of dejected ball of legs. 'That was the last one. We have nothing else of note. I'll tell you something, human, our ability to fight off the Outsiders is done for, if it wasn't already. And if *that's* done for, we're *all* done for. You in particular, my friend.'

Vess nodded slowly. 'But not only that. This was visible. Everyone Inside and Outside will know about this in hours, if they don't already.'

'Ah. Yes. And, given that I got my first information from an open public source, I think we can assume that they do already.'

'We can. Our reputation, our political capital, our position as the core of the Spin – well, it puts the difficulties of the insurance companies into perspective, doesn't it?'

'Loss of prestige on this scale puts *everything* into perspective. Enemies will be lining up. Friends will become enemies. I don't envy you. There'll have to be a Board Meeting, you know.'

Vess nodded. 'I've known that for a while.'

'Of course. You'll have my support if you need it.' Fiffithiss leaned forwards. 'Are you engaged in whatever passes for a sexual relationship amongst your kind at the moment?'

Vess laughed. 'Why?'

'Because if I was you, I'd go and get some while I still could.'

The connection broke.

For a while Vess sat staring at nothing. Then he straightened his back and blinked down a data pipe. Not the public system – that was far too insecure and besides, it was censored to the point of uselessness – but the hack-hardened back room of the city servers. It was the first time he had accessed data for himself in months and he was out of practice, but it was that or delegate to his staff. And none of his staff needed to know about this. For one thing he had never been quite certain whose staff they were.

It took him a while to find what he wanted. Then information tumbled down his vision. At first the rate control eluded him, then he sent it the wrong way so the figures blurred, and finally he got it right and scrolled back up to the top.

Then he sat, absorbed.

He was discovering the woman called Seldyan. There was much to discover. It took him an hour to read the file, but he was happy to invest the time. After all, she had just ended his career and, more than likely, killed him.

He owed her the time.

When he had finished he blinked the pipe closed and remained quite still.

Slavery wasn't practised on all the Inner planets, but it was still common enough. There were many reasons why someone might become a slave but only a few why they might do so from birth. In Seldyan's case the short answer was population pressure. Pressure is always against something, and this time it was against money.

It was close to a rule – and certainly more than a guideline – that populations tended to grow while resources were fixed. That bit especially hard when the boundaries of your world were shrinking by the decade.

The Inside had no centrally imposed scheme for population control, but it had targets; individual members of the Federation came up with their own ways of meeting them. Seldyan's parents had lived on a manufacturing world that had happened to be heavily indebted and close to its population ceiling at the same time.

Selling unwanted children was a perfect solution to both problems. In Seldyan's case it helped with another too: her parents had been broke and starving. The sale of their second child to the Hive had solved most of that.

It had also meant that both of them were sterilized; the state could only afford to meet that sort of bill once. Their first child had apparently been still-born; Seldyan was their second and last. The record didn't show what had happened to them in the end. It didn't include unimportant people.

It didn't include Vess's parents either. He rarely thought about that, but for some reason he was thinking about it now.

The signal interrupted him. He sighed and glanced down at the surface of the desk, which fogged briefly and resolved into a short piece of text. The Board Meeting had been brought forward to the following morning and he was to attend. Well, he could have predicted that, and so had Clo Fiffithiss, which wasn't surprising. Vess wondered if the being had gamed it or merely guessed it. But that wasn't all; he read the rest of the message. It was about the meeting venue.

He sat back and blew out his cheeks. That venue was reserved for the sort of Board Meeting that could be denied afterwards.

All the signs were pointing in the same direction. He began to think he ought to take the Gamer's advice.

Spin Inside – Border Region

The ship lights flashed to red three times and returned to normal. Some lights flickered, and the main data pipe lit up with a querulous pre-recorded message from an insurance company regretting that their cover had lapsed, now and for ever.

Seldyan turned the message off.

The good ship formerly known as *Sunskimmer*, originally *Flamejob*, freshly rechristened *Suck on This*, crossed the border between Inside and Outside at full power and went on accelerating. The last vestiges of hopelessly outclassed pursuit fell away, their courses bending into a set of golden-series arcs that ended back over the Border.

They had escaped. Unbelievably, they had escaped. And, even more unbelievably, the five of them had done it in something a kilometre long.

The controls, such as they were, seemed far too trivial. In her view it should have taken walls of lights, rooms full of consoles and anxious people responding to alarms and, just, *stuff*.

Instead there was this plain room with a hazy horizontal disc floating at waist height. The disc was roughly big enough to seat four for a meal and it showed, well, she wasn't exactly sure what all of it showed. Parts looked obvious – she could see speed and direction, certainly. And part of it was clearly a starscape, although it seemed to contain more than just stars. The starscape flipped up to vertical and expanded if you looked at it, and then you had what she guessed was a view looking forward. She watched it for a while, lost in slowly expanding stars. Then something occurred to her. She weaved experimentally from side to side, looking to see if the disc followed. It didn't. She grinned to herself, and walked round it. It narrowed to a perspective oval, shrank to a dim line as she passed its edge, and expanded again – but not to the same view.

At first she didn't understand. There was a starscape, showing the Inside: eleven planets, four suns and a Border marked out with enough paranoid defensiveness to have earned itself a capital letter, but it was receding, and in the foreground there was a huge *something* – two rough cones joined back to back.

Then she realized, and the realization emptied her lungs.

The huge *something* was the ship.

The wonder of it tugged at her gut. She whispered: 'Oh, shit . . .' Then she laughed. Part of the disc looked like comms. She gestured at it. 'Merish?'

'Uh-huh?'

'We did it. We actually did it!' She laughed. 'We escaped in a stolen spaceship – the biggest ship Inside! How cool is that?'

'Are we over the Border?'

'Yes; just crossed.' She felt herself trembling. She got ready to say that she hadn't really believed . . . but then didn't. Sometimes, she knew, she had to do the believing for both of them.

As the ship had crossed the Border the display had flickered. Now it froze for a second, fuzzed to grey and then went blank. Seldyan tutted.

It flicked back into life. Seldyan stared for a moment. Then she felt herself grinning. 'Merish? Can you see the main displays, wherever you are?'

'Sure, if I want to. Should I?'

She paused. 'Oh yes. Take a look at the size of the prize.'

'Okay. Just a minute. Oh, wow . . .'

'Yeah.' She stared at the expanded, far more dramatic image. 'The whole of the Spin. Eighty-nine lovely juicy planets.' It wasn't just that the view was expanded. The definition was better, somehow. It was a bit like looking at a work of art.

'Yeah. Well, eighty-eight, now. Minus the one that got blown up, supposedly.'

Seldyan fiddled with some controls until she found the zoom. Her point of view accelerated into the image while bloating distorted planets zoomed past her. She waited for the quality to degrade, but it just didn't. A single star was swelling in the centre of the field; as it expanded she could see individual threads of gas flaring from it. The magnification must have been up in the millions.

She shook her head in admiration, and took the view back to where it had started. 'So why has this turned up on the screens?'

'Version control, I guess. This is a pretty old ship, remember. It pre-dates the Border. As a cruise ship it only needed to know the Inside. Now we're Outside maybe it's trying to revert to type.'

'Type? Oh . . .' Seldyan looked at the starscape. 'Type being warship?'

'That's putting it mildly. Not any more, though; they unzipped its brains when it was converted to cruising.'

'Really?' She shook her head. 'That sounds cruel. Can we re-zip them?'

'Possibly. Why?'

'I feel sorry for it.' A spot near the base of her spine itched. She reached behind herself and scratched it gently, feeling the flat bump. 'Think of it as a kindred soul, okay?'

'Yeah, right. What's the other reason?'

Seldyan glared at the comms. 'Because the Hive is still there.

Because a million people aren't here with us. Because we're heading into the unknown. Because I want a warship to play with. Okay?'

'Ah. Okay.' The comms went dead.

Seldyan frowned at it, and then felt for the itchy spot again. It never quite went away.

The old ship was quiet. Before they had crossed the Border they had unloaded the passengers and the exec team on to one of the shuttles *Sunskimmer* towed around, pointed it at the nearest planet and given it a metaphorical slap on the rump. It would get there before they ran out of air and water, although they might be hungry.

Now it was just the five of them.

A holo readout wavered in the air. Seldyan peered at it. 'There's five different levels of operating system here,' she said. 'Don't they ever clear anything out?'

Merish pushed back his hair. 'No. Just cover it over. Didn't you know? It's like your DNA. Mostly redundant shit that used to be there to make you a better lizard.'

'Fuck that. I'm already the best lizard you can get.' She waved a hand. 'Anyway, the oldest bits of this stuff probably think we still are lizards.'

'The oldest bits of this stuff think it's a warship, Sel. That's what you wanted, right?'

'Yes, it was. It still is.' She shook her head. 'I still seem to be waiting.'

'So you do. No, hang on. Ah-*ha* . . .'

'What?' Then she saw it. The displays had changed. She looked for a while. 'Okay,' she said slowly. 'I get it. We're a warship again, right?'

'Yup. What do you think?'

The planets were the same. Everything else was – she sought for the word – *more*. What had been a map was now a landscape, a beautifully detailed strategic sculpture of risk and possibility.

She watched for a long time. Then she pointed. 'What are the big dots?' They were a kind of fuzzy cerise, scattered sparsely through the image.

Merish laughed. 'They're the other legacy MBUs.'

'Oh.' She frowned. 'Why are they highlighted?'

'Because they're powerful enough for the ship to worry about.'

She squinted at the display. 'There are other dots.'

'Well, yes. Those would be other legacy units. Smaller than us but still handy.'

'Right.' She began counting, and then gave up. 'There are lots.'

'Yeah. Some big hitters have crossed the Border over the last few thousand years. Try not to worry, Sel. They're mostly a long way away and some of them may not work any more.'

'Oh good. That makes me feel so much better.' She hesitated. 'How long until we get to Oblong?'

'About four hours.'

'You nervous?'

'A little. You?'

She watched the display for a while without answering. At first it seemed static, but then she realized that it was alive with movement, with dots and streaks of coloured light swarming around and over each other against the backdrop of stars. It reminded her a little of a sparse swarm of shiny insects weaving blindly through space. The idea made her smile. We're all insects, she thought. All equal.

Equal was a refreshing concept. She looked up at Merish. 'Remember where we came from?'

'Of course. I'll never forget it.'

'Nor will I. So, would anything, anything *at all*, make you go back?'

He shook his head quickly.

'Me neither.' She turned back to the display, and after a moment he did too.

She had managed not to answer the question.

Sometimes she chided herself for having taken so long to reach her decision. Being chipped hadn't been enough; the Supervisor hadn't been enough; even seeing what had happened to Merish hadn't quite been enough – and that was harsh criticism when she replayed it through sleepless hours.

No. Finally, it had been someone she barely knew.

Her world had been made of routine – a daily cycle of basic classes, exercise and a little rest, measured out by sleeps. The classes would have been fun if she had been allowed to ask any questions, but questions weren't allowed. Sometimes she asked them anyway, and received no answer.

Then, one morning halfway through Seldyan's fourteenth year, she was woken early by a jarring siren, much louder than the usual waking call. She opened her eyes and immediately screwed them shut again because instead of the usual early-morning glimmer the lights were set to full day brightness. An unfamiliar guard hauled her off her pallet and shoved her out of the sleeping quarters. Around her she saw the same thing happening to everyone.

In the square it felt colder than usual. Everyone seemed to be here; she looked around for Merish and saw him standing a little way away, his arms wrapped round his body. She beckoned him over.

'What's going on?'

'I think we're being Sorted.' His teeth were chattering so much she had to ask him to repeat the last word. She was about to ask him what he meant when there was another siren. There were shouts from the guards and they found themselves being driven out of the square, towards the teaching units.

Even the floor felt colder than usual, to her bare feet.

They ended up in an area she hadn't been in before. It was a tall, broad hall, bigger than anything she had yet known. For as far as she could see the floor was occupied by workstations – plain pedestals topped with a flat desk. There was a screen on each desk, similar to the ones she was used to but bigger.

Another siren, and an amplified voice: 'Find a station.'

Quite a few people seemed to be hesitating; she shrugged, walked to the nearest vacant station and took hold of the edges of the desk as if she was claiming territory.

She looked around. People had got the idea. Across the floor of the huge hall, the crowd was forming itself into a grid to match the workstation layout.

Then there was yet another siren, and voice: 'Task One. Duration, one minute.'

The screen lit up. Information scrolled, and she almost laughed. Basic maths, barely more than counting on her fingers. She tapped the answer and waited, counting the seconds under her breath.

She had reached sixty-four when the siren sounded. She frowned – she was usually more accurate than that – and then gasped. The boy at the station next to her had collapsed; simply folded at the knees and dropped to the floor. She heard, almost felt, the crack of his forehead hitting the base of the workstation. A guard appeared, and dragged him away. She guessed he had been chip-stunned.

Out of the corner of her eye she caught movement. Across the hall, a couple of others were being removed – and now the siren again. 'Task Two. Duration, one minute.'

This task was just a little harder. At the end of it, a few more were removed.

At the end of the first twenty tasks, the allowed time stepped up to two minutes. Then five, and later ten. There were no visible clocks – even the time display function on the desk screen was blanked out – but Seldyan kept a running guestimate of the elapsed time in her head. By the time she had reached five hours, well over half the workstations were unoccupied.

There had been no food and no water, it was if anything even colder, and her bladder was painfully full.

Then, at last, it looked as though there might be relief. A different siren, and although it was the same voice, this time it was a different message:

'Break! Five minutes. Facilities are at the north end of the hall.'

Facilities! But where was north? Seldyan looked round and saw crowds already gathering around three – only three! – openings in the far wall.

She knew not one in ten would get done in five minutes. She breathed out and forced herself to think. There must be something.

Then she thought of it. She turned and ran, away from the waiting crowds, towards the opposite end of the hall. To where they had taken the ones who had collapsed, when they failed tasks.

When she reached it there was only one opening, but it was a wide one and – she grinned – on the other side of it a row of doors stretched down a broad corridor. The corridor was noticeably warmer than the hall. Some doors were marked as Med rooms and a few with labels she didn't understand, but then there was one with a symbol no one could mistake. She gave a little jump of triumph and reached out a hand to the push plate.

A blast of agony crowbarred every muscle in her body. The spasm threw her across the corridor, and she heard rather than felt the crack of her head against the opposite wall.

There was a moment of blank. Then she opened her eyes and saw a face close to hers. It was grinning.

She gathered saliva and spat at the face. It pulled back sharply, but the grin was still there. The lips parted and formed words.

'You're a clever one, for sure, when you're not being dumb. Clever is good, and right now clever is going back to a workstation and passing some more tests.'

She nodded towards the door behind him. 'Not before I go in there.'

The guard laughed. 'Okay. But be quick, or I'll hit your chip again.'

She was quick. When she had finished she walked out past the guard, who didn't acknowledge her, and back into the hall – but not to her original workstation. 'A workstation', the guard had said, not 'your workstation'. So she chose one as close as possible to the entrance from the corridor; close to the facilities and with a hint of second-hand warmth leaking towards it.

As she walked up to the station the siren sounded, and there was another task, and then another. The first few were solo but after that their rapidly thinning numbers were divided into teams of five or six, and then the tasks were suddenly *much* more elaborate and there was a need for leadership and organization.

It seemed natural to her. After a while it seemed that it was natural for the others too. She began to forget that she was weak with hunger and thirst and shivering with cold. The team was the thing . . . and then, quite unexpectedly, there was a final-sounding siren, and no more tasks.

She felt almost sorry. She looked round her team – *her* team, yes, that was right – and saw four tired faces. They had been weeded down quite quickly; just her, Merish, Kot, Lyste and Hufsza had been left after five tasks. She had only known Merish before, but she knew all of them now. She gave them a smile. 'Whatever it was, I think we did it.'

They nodded, and then she looked away from them and scanned round the hall. It was almost empty. She could count only five teams – twenty-five people, out of what? Three hundred? More?

She turned to Merish. 'So few . . .'

He nodded. 'Yeah. We got Sorted.'

She was going to ask what he meant when suddenly her tiredness and hunger caught up with her. Her eyes began to close just as her legs softened. She felt herself falling.

She had woken next to Merish. It was an unusual privilege, but not one she felt like questioning. She was content to lie quietly, watching him in the half-light of the sleeping cell.

She had never known full darkness.

Even in sleep he looked tired, and somehow watchful. If she reached out and touched him, she was sure he would be fully awake in a second.

There hadn't been much, between her collapsing in the hall and ending up here. She had eaten and drunk, as much as she could manage with a dry throat and lips that felt like ropes, but mainly she had let herself be moved around.

Merish had told her to sleep, but she had been too wired. So in the end he had given up.

'You must have heard of Sorting?'

She nodded.

'Well, that was what just happened. They surprise you, they stress you out, you're too cold, you're hungry, and you have to perform.' He propped himself up on an elbow. 'You performed.'

'I know I did. We all did.'

'No.' He lay back. 'Most of us got through it. *You performed.* You led. You made the five of us a team, and we came out top.' He put his hand on her shoulder. 'You're stuck with that job now. I'll try to make it easy.'

She was getting sleepy. 'What happened to the rest?'

His answer took a while and she didn't like any of it. Apparently it depended on how soon they failed. The soonest were sent to forced manual labour. If they were *really* dumb, their organs would be harvested, provided they were worth more than what the Hive could get for the labour. Or, if they were good-looking, people would pay for that too.

She stared at him. 'I don't understand.' Then something about his face made her mind clear, and she had a fleeting mental picture of him, curled up, surrounded by a group of boys. She waved the thought away with her hand. 'Okay, never mind. What about the rest of us?'

'We get hired out for specialist stuff. The cleverer, the more specialist.'

'How do you know all this?'

There was a soft snort, and she realized he had almost laughed. 'I keep my ears open. Don't you? Also, I'm good at hacking into things.'

She stared for a long time at the dim view of the ceiling. Then she shook her head. 'No.'

'No what?'

'Just no.'

He reached out, touched her shoulder. 'Seldyan? We don't get to say no. Not to anything. They use Sorting to make the best into teams. That's what happened today. Now go to sleep.'

She closed her eyes. She had no intention of sleeping; she was going to hold on to her flaming anger. She would never let it die.

Somehow, she slept. But the last image she saw was of the boy at the workstation near her, who had been first to collapse. She had glanced at him quickly enough to see his face before his eyes closed. It had been a mixture of vacancy and fear – the fear of someone completely uncomprehending. He hadn't been especially good-looking as far as she could remember. Presumably he was being – harvested. Maybe right now.

Her sleep was uneasy and full of vacant faces. When she woke she found her arms locked round Merish, and his eyes open and watching her.

A deep thrumming note that sounded in her chest brought Seldyan back to the present, and a voice that seemed to come from everywhere said, '*Alert.*'

She raised her eyebrows. 'Meaning?'

'Don't know.' Merish was frowning at the displays. 'Something the ship wasn't expecting. It might be nothing; the things it was expecting are thousands of years out of date, remember.'

Ten minutes later the five of them were staring at the display, and it obviously wasn't nothing. It looked a bit like an eyebrow, if an eyebrow were half a million kilometres across and glowing angrily.

It was Kot who eventually broke the silence. 'That looks wrong,' she said.

They all turned to Merish who was hunched over a display tank. Symbols floated in front of him, fuzzing and changing. He pursed his lips. 'It does look wrong, and it doesn't belong; you and the ship are both right. It's plasma plus other stuff: lumps of iron and nickel and silicates and a big heap of trans-uranium elements.' He straightened up. 'If you smashed up a medium-sized planet, I mean *really* smashed it up so the biggest piece was a hundred metres across, irradiated the living *fuck* out of it and then smeared it out over a few hundred thousand klicks, you'd get something that looked like that thing.'

Seldyan felt her stomach flip. She looked round at shocked faces. 'Smashed up? Oh shit. A destroyed planet? Merish, an *inhabited*, destroyed planet?'

'I so hope not.' He glared at the tank, then blew out his cheeks. 'No. Can't be. Everything local is accounted for.'

'Right.' She stared at the image for a moment. 'Is it safe to approach?'

He shrugged. 'It depends how. In the ship we could fly straight through it. Unshielded, I wouldn't like to get within half a million klicks of the middle of it. It's seriously hot, Seldyan.'

'Okay, so let's not.' She sat back, feeling her heart slowing to normal.

Kot cleared her throat. 'That's not so easy. That thing is in the same system as Oblong, and Web City.'

'Oh.' Seldyan chewed her lip. 'How close is it?'

Kot looked down. 'About half a million klicks. Sorry, Seldyan.'

'I think you'd better save your regrets for the locals, if they're still around.' Seldyan watched the display for a while, trying to imagine what it must be like to live close to something like that. Then she stood up. 'Guys, I'm going to rest. You should too, if you can. Whatever we find, I've a feeling we're going to be busy.'

She had decided not to take the captain's quarters, opting instead for the close, safe, simple confines of a steward's cabin. For one thing, Hefs had indulged some rather extravagant tastes; his suite was on a scale and in a style she just couldn't engage with. But more important, there were – associations.

She had been acting, with Hefs – that had been obvious even to him in the end – but many people, she assumed, could act in that way, probably better and for longer than she could. The thing she kept concealed from almost everyone, sometimes even including herself, was that the ability to act like that was in itself an act; another layer down.

How could you act what you had never experienced?

She didn't know, and mostly didn't really care, what the others assumed passed between her and Merish, but she was always glad when she felt him slip in beside her.

Sometimes there was intimacy, although never more than the intimacy of gently questing fingers and soft kisses, but not this time, at least not at first. Merish knew her moods better than she did; she heard the door, felt the sleeping pad squash a little and then his arm found its way over her. She pressed herself into him and they lay still together.

They were quiet for a while. Then she felt him move, rolling away from her and on to his back. She rolled over to face him and said, 'Talk to me.'

'Okay. I think you're scared.'

She frowned up at the half-darkness. 'Merish, I think you're the only person in the Spin who could say that to me and stay unbruised.'

'I expect so. I still think you're scared. I know it's not for you because it never is. So, talk about it.'

She nodded. 'Okay. So, what was the average life span in the Hive?'

'Exactly? I don't know. Roughly, around seventy standard. Why?'

'And in Web City?'

The pad wobbled; he had shaken his head. 'No idea.'

'Yeah, I thought so. And that's before they shared their space with a radioactive smear.' She stared up at nothing for a moment, then took a breath. 'Merish? What if we bust out for nothing? What if everything, everywhere, is shit? All the time?'

She heard the pause in his breathing. Then his arm curled over her again. 'What, everything?'

She thought she was going to resist him, but then she discovered she wasn't.

It did help, for a while. But when he had sighed and turned over to sleep she stayed awake, staring wide-eyed at the darkness and wondering what it was concealing.

Counterweight Park, Basin City

Vess looked around carefully – he seemed to be alone – and lowered his bare feet into the water. The current was slow and the surface glass-smooth; if he patted it with his feet *so*, he could leave regular footprints that flowed away in a steadily spreading line that was consumed by its own ripples by the time it was a dozen of its own wobbly paces away.

He had first played this private game the day he had arrived on the level. He had repeated it only a handful of times since.

The Board of the Harbour Company usually met every seventeen days, thereby achieving three anachronisms in one go because there was no longer a Harbour Company, it wasn't a Board and seventeen days had been the length of the refilling cycle of the oldest of the balancing reservoirs that fed the boat lifts from the Ground to the Middle level. This meant an influx of goods into the import bonds every seventeen days which in turn was a good reason for a commercial Board to meet, a thousand years ago.

Now the Board was responsible for the management of the Spin Inside, a shrinking, beleaguered collection of planets eking out an existence in the shadow of growing neighbours. And, of course, for its main asset. The Hive.

The old boat lift still chugged round its now pointless cycle.

Every seventeen days a hundred or so gigalitres of water gurgled down winding channels from the mountains behind the city, over a control weir and into the huge ladle-shaped Great Basin. The Basin was suspended on three colossal chains from a stubby counterpoise arm. Eventually the mounting weight of water would trip the catches and send the whole thing swaying slowly downwards, raising the boat lift like a giant counterweight until it docked with the First Middle Dock. Which was usually empty of shipping, having lost its function a thousand years ago just like nearly everything else.

Vess was sitting just upstream from the weir. He enjoyed watching the old system. There was something inevitable about it, which meant that as long as it went on working it wasn't his problem. He sometimes thought he would have liked to meet whoever designed it.

Anachronistic name or not, the out-of-date Board of the non-existent Harbour Company was still the senior body for the Inside. It provided the top stratum of Federation management from a position that was unelected and ungoverned and completely unchallenged, and a missing cruise ship would be the least of its worries, if *Sunskimmer* had really been no more than a cruise ship.

Vess paddled a few more footprints and looked up towards the Lay Palace. It was an astonishing thing.

Six thousand years before, the then-Chairman of the Board had summoned the best architect in the Spin and told her to construct a floating palace in the Basin. It had to be the largest building in the City of its day, it had to float freely within the Basin without tethering and it must not change the length of the cycle of the Basin by more than a second.

The result was – he allowed himself the word once more – truly astonishing. Presumably with posterity in mind the architect had delivered seventeen storeys of tapering ziggurat, rising from a wide shallow base to a peak nearly a hundred metres above the surface of the water. By virtue of the area of its base it was the largest building in the City at the time, and the same broad base kept it floating in the centre of the reservoir thanks to surface tension. Once every seventeen days it grounded briefly, and mathematicians, statisticians and the occasional specialist in gambling theory had written papers about the scatter of its resting points.

Vess always thought it was a shame that the Lay Palace had gone down in history as a sort of failure. Everything about it was perfect except that it had changed the seventeen-day cycle by one and three tenths seconds, and the architect had achieved the other sort of posterity by being duly and unpleasantly executed.

Which was quite likely to be his fate too, as much as he was trying not to think about it. But phlegmatism had always been one of his assessed traits.

His musing had distracted him and the line of watery footprints was ragged. He forced himself to correct his rhythm. There; better.

But it was time to go. He swung his feet out of the water and stood, picking up his shoes. He would put them on when his feet had dried. For the moment he carried them, walking carefully so his wet feet did not slip on the slick polished stones of the Basin edge. It was a hundred metres or so to the nearest of the slim articulated bridges that led to the Lay Palace; by the time he got to it he was dry enough to put on his shoes. When he had straightened up, he half turned and looked over his shoulder. Another line of footprints, dark against the light stone but fading as he looked. This time they were heading towards him.

Clo Fiffithiss was waiting for him at the other end of the bridge. It lifted a foreclaw in greeting.

'Hello! Ready for the bloody circus?'

Vess raised his eyebrows. 'One day you could try to be really discouraging.'

'Rubbish, human. You know I'm supporting you.'

'Is that what it is?' Vess shook his head. 'If anyone else says they're going to support me I'll assume it's all over and hand myself in for composting.'

Fiffithiss extended the foreclaw and patted him on the shoulder. It felt like being tapped sharply with a twig. 'I wouldn't do that. I've heard it's a messy end. You're Admin grade, Harbour Master, same as me. Take my advice. Leave the blood and guts to the Praetors and the Board. Protect your pension. You have no family, have you?'

'No. No, there's just me.'

'Good man. Less to worry about. Come on. Let's get in there and show them how grey and uninteresting we Administrators can be.'

It turned and headed for the entrance to the Palace, using all nine limbs in a complex syncopation like a straight-line dance. It looked like hard work. Vess remembered reading that the species had evolved – or had been engineered, according to some – for light-gravity environments where walking only needed four limbs. Some of them never mastered using the full set, and those never left the home planet.

Just at the moment leaving your home planet looked like a very good idea to Vess. He shrugged and followed Clo Fiffithiss up a shallow ramp and into the Daily Entrance of the palace. Not the Main Entrance; that was for important people.

Important. That word again.

Vess shifted in his seat. It was a massive, deeply upholstered half-globe covered in a pleated animal hide, and like every waiting-room seat he had ever sat on it had the trick of being far less comfortable than it looked. He glanced towards Clo Fiffithiss. 'Much longer, you think?'

The being rustled a little as if it had been stirred by a breeze. 'No idea. We get there when we get there. Try to relax.'

Vess raised his eyebrows. 'Why? You haven't.'

'You can tell?'

'I looked it up.' He looked at Fiffithiss, who had draped itself limply from the frame of one of the chairs. Its body was hanging at the end of a bundle of legs, the three foreclaws swinging freely below it so that they almost brushed the floor. To a careless observer it looked a bit like a clump of vines, and it would go on doing so right up to the moment when it let go its hold and dropped like streamlined death on to a piece of prey, claws first. It was about the least relaxed pose the species could adopt.

'Sorry. Genes.' Fiffithiss wriggled free of the chair and dropped to the floor. 'The point stands, though: try to relax. I'll try too. If I fail then we can be nervous together.'

'All right, I'll try.' A thought struck Vess. He hesitated. 'Look, sorry if this is intrusive, but have you ever . . . Hunted?'

There was a long silence. Fiffithiss hunkered low to the floor, its body swaying in the cradle of its legs. Eventually it said, 'Well, that helped with the tension. Have I ever Hunted? Meaning, have I ever got stoned out of both of my brains on an ancient plant extract and taken part in a ritual hunt to the death with members of my own brood?'

Vess felt his face colouring. 'I didn't mean . . .'

'Oh yes you did. You look things up.' Fiffithiss tapped a claw. 'I'll save you the trouble of looking up my name. I'm not some fucking baby-eater, human. Fiffithiss means Abstainer. Among my people it's not a compliment, and that's one of the reasons I don't live among my people. Does that help?'

'Yes. Look, I'm sorry . . .'

'Good. Now stop beating yourself up. I'm sure other people are forming a queue.'

Vess was almost relieved when the door to the main chamber opened. A globe-shaped dirigible bell-hop about twice the size of Vess's head floated through, wobbling a little. It gave off a faint hiss.

'Agenda point five?' Its voice sounded like modulated static. Clo Fiffithiss gave an affirmative bob. 'We believe so.'

The bell-hop didn't move. 'Ambiguous. Agenda point five? Confirm or deny.'

Fiffithiss drew itself upright, straightening all nine legs so that it looked like a narrow tripod, squared. One foreclaw clicked against its body in a pastiche of a salute. 'Agenda point five, confirmed.'

'Follow.' The machine wobbled back through the door.

They followed.

The room was on Level Sixteen, the second-highest level of the ziggurat. At this height the palace was still wide enough to be very big, but narrow enough to encompass one room with windows on all four sides. It felt like a long walk from the entrance to the far end where the Board waited.

By tradition there were five of them – four Praetors and the Chairman, and instead of sitting they stood at lecterns, each one shaped differently to represent the Guild of its user. The Chairman stood at the central lectern, leaning well back to balance his vast belly. Vess had a theory that Alst Or-Shls kept on the lectern tradition because if he ever sat down he would never be able to rise unaided.

The lectern on the far right of the group, shaped like a darkly twisted vine dotted with cancerous growths, looked empty, but Vess had no doubt it was not empty at all. He shuddered a little.

They halted in front of a pale line inlaid in the near-black wooden floor. There were no seats for visitors, either. Vess hated that. Standing still without looking awkward was hard enough when you were calm, and he was not calm.

Or-Shls wore thick lenses in front of his eyes, an archaic affectation. Now he reached up and did something to the frame that carried them. They slid quickly sideways and disappeared round the back of his head on tiny runners built into the frame.

Without them his eyes looked much larger, and they bulged. He glanced round at the Praetors.

'All ready?' His voice was gravelly, and even from where Vess was standing it smelled of tobacco smoke – an even more ridiculous, not to say dangerous, affectation.

The Praetors nodded.

'Good. Well, Administrators, we're ready to hear you. The last of the Great Ships has been taken without a fight. I expect you can tell us why.'

Vess felt himself exhale. It felt like relief, as if all the tension he hadn't realized he was containing had left him. This was it – he was off the cliff and falling. 'Because we are no longer able to maintain a viable deterrent near the periphery, Mr Chairman.'

At first there was silence. Or-Shls glared at him. 'Why not?'

Vess shrugged. 'I can only administer what is there. The last four Shareholder meetings in succession have ordered ships to be withdrawn from the Border zones and concentrated around the Home systems. The gaps are too great.'

'And *Sunskimmer* was in one of these gaps?'

Vess nodded. 'Was in one of them, and made her escape through another of them.'

'Excuse me.' The soft voice came from the lectern on Vess's far left. The lectern itself was a blocky thing formed of different-sized oolite cubes piled on top of each other to make a cream-coloured column that seemed solid and rickety at the same time. It was a complete contrast to the sinuously muscled quadruped that stood upright behind it, heavy front paws resting on the top roughly on a level with Vess's eyes.

One of the paws lifted lazily. 'The Shareholder meetings acted on the advice of this Board, didn't they? And we consulted on our recommendations. The doctrine of Holding the Centre? I'm sure you were on the mailing list. Both of you.'

Clo Fiffithiss stirred. 'We were, Garash. I don't know about

Vess, but for my part I sent back a series of models that gamed the results of the Doctrine. I think the risks were clear.' It turned towards Garash. 'I'm certain you were on *that* mailing list.'

Vess felt himself tensing. The silence seemed to go on for a long time. Then Or-Shls gave a tight smile.

'We know about your games, thank you,' he said. 'You identified risk. Unfortunately risk has been allowed to turn into outcome. Rather a lot of outcome. More than you know, I suspect.' He gestured towards the apparently empty lectern. 'Over to you.'

Vess caught his breath.

The lectern crawled. The things which had looked like growths moved, standing out from the twisted column on hundreds of hair-fine legs. They *flowed*, that was the word, up the lectern and collected in a growing mass at the top where they formed the approximate outline of a human face.

A hole opened in the middle of the face. It wasn't really mouth-shaped. Vess wasn't sure if that was better or worse. The voice of the gestalt entity called Vut would have been almost a purr if it hadn't been for a sibilant edge.

'You noted, and questioned, the Doctrine of Holding the Centre. Based on your knowledge at the time your questions were reasonable, but your knowledge was incomplete. Observe.'

The windows dimmed, not gently but fast so the room went black with a *snap* that was almost tangible. Vess thought he could feel his irises trying to keep up. At his side, Clo Fiffithiss rustled uneasily. Its night sight was far better than his, he knew, but darkness was Hunting territory; the being would be on edge.

A familiar starscape blurred and solidified in front of them. He nodded. 'The Inside and the Boundary. So?'

'The Inside, yes. Our eleven planets. A precarious economy at the best of times, as is any completely enclosed economic unit. But these are not the best of times. Before you are told more you will need to agree to non-disclosure.'

'I thought we both had already.' Clo Fiffithiss sounded confused.

Or-Shls cut in. 'Not to anything like the level required for this. Turn around please.'

The room lightened a little. They turned and found the dirigible – or another identical one – behind them, floating level with Vess's head about an arm's length from him. In the dim light it gave off a soft violet glow and it was bobbing up and down very slightly; after a second he realized that he was nodding in time with it. He stopped himself.

The globe-shaped body split horizontally. The lower half dropped away to hang from the upper by slim articulated rods of dull silver metal. In the space between the two halves the air glowed smokily.

Or-Shls spoke from behind them. 'Look into the light please. Vess first.'

Vess looked. At first it was hard to focus, but then a point of white light grew within the smoke, and as soon as he had seen it his eyes were captured and he found he couldn't look away. There was a brief moment of dislocation and then his head was full of words.

. . . agree to terms of non-disclosure regarding Praetor briefing at the Lay Palace, Counterweight Basin . . .

It made his head ache. He fought off the temptation to look away. Besides, he suspected that to try would be to tear his eyes out of their sockets. There was nothing optional about this.

. . . my understanding that sanctions for non-compliance may include physical recovery of all knowledge imparted. Confirm?

He frowned. Without breaking eye contact with the machine he said, 'Physical recovery?'

'It means we will recover the material mechanically from your brain.' Or-Shls's voice was level. 'Reliable and fatal.'

Confirm? Second request of three.

Vess didn't like to think what might happen if he used up all three requests. 'Confirm.'

The point of light vanished and his eyes snapped away. The headache was fading already.

He watched as Clo Fiffithiss went through the same process. Then the dirigible snapped itself shut and floated off. They turned back towards the Praetors and the lights faded.

'We hope that wasn't too uncomfortable?' Vut didn't sound concerned. 'It was necessary in any case. What we are about to tell you has been kept to Board level until now. For five hundred years. We take it we have your attention?'

Vess nodded dumbly. A faint rustle told him Clo Fiffithiss had done its version of the same thing.

'Good. So, five hundred years ago we had just lost the twelfth planet. In response the Border was established as a hard boundary between us and the rest, and the modern status quo was established. Except that there was nothing static about it. The Board of the day ordered the situation to be gamed.'

Clo Fiffithiss stirred. 'That must have been one of the first uses of gaming as a policy tool?'

'It was. And still one of the most influential. The result indicated that the Inside of those days was not durable. The response was to set up a structure that could be defended even in decline. Hence, the Inside Federation. But now that has changed. The most recent gaming suggests that the situation is no longer viable.'

There was a short silence. Then Clo Fiffithiss spoke.

'I don't understand. The loss of the ships is serious, but how does it make us unviable?'

'Your own gaming lacks data. On its own, the loss of the last legacy Main Battle Unit would not be fatal – although it is a symptom of a wider decline which has been going on for generations. We need not consider historical problems; the modern beginning of the end set in five years ago.'

77

The starscape changed, zooming out to show many more systems. Most of them were greyed out, but a cluster some way outside the Boundary glowed brightly. The view zoomed in to show three planets – Vess assumed they were planets – in a tight ring around a small blue-white star.

'That is the Tri-Gyre. We are sure you already have questions.'

Vess frowned at the image. The star was well outside the plane of the ring, so that it formed an apex rather than a centre.

'Why is the sun off to the side?'

Vut sounded amused. 'Given that this is the Spin, *why* is unknowable. Pure whimsy, probably. As to *how*, there is a counterbalancing micro black hole on the opposite side of the ring. The black hole and the star are kept apart by a field generator. It is not an elegant solution, and that was not the important question.'

Vess stared at the image. There was something just below it: a sort of ghostly curve with a green dot at its end. He pointed. 'That?'

'Yes, that. A large cloud of debris where nothing previously existed, and beyond it a green star – also where nothing previously existed.'

'So what is it?'

Or-Shls took a wheezy breath. 'The green star, we don't know. But the other feature we suspect to be an effort at new planetary engineering. Not carried out by us. Not carried out by anyone for a hundred millennia. Carried out by someone else less than a thousand days ago. That's just the beginning. Go on, Vut. You're the economist.'

The not-mouth opened again. 'The beginning, yes, or perhaps better a marker of the beginning. We are one ninth of the Spin, but allowing for the Hive we have closer to one fifth of the population and rather less than one eleventh of the resources. We therefore depend on trade. These were our trade routes six years ago.'

The starscape pulled back so that the Inside was a glittering patch in the centre. Scores of curving lines glowed into life, originating all over the Spin but all of them either passing through or ending within the Inside.

About a third of them were yellow and the rest cerise. Vess frowned. 'What do the colours mean?'

'Yellow means a positive balance of payments. Pink, the opposite.'

'So we're overall negative?'

'Correction. Six years ago we *were* overall negative, by a modest margin. This is the situation today.'

The image changed. Vess stared at it.

Most of the lines were gone. The only ones left were cerise.

Vut went on speaking. 'We are almost cut off. Our routes have been concentrated into fewer and fewer superhighways, each of them many times more vulnerable and expensive to run than before. We are leaking money. It won't be long before shortages can't be disguised any longer.'

Clo Fiffithiss tapped an intricate three-limb tattoo on the floor. Vess recognized it as the equivalent of a baffled shake of the head. 'I don't understand. What's the connection between someone making planets and us losing trade routes?'

'Technological development. The ability to project power, Gamer. And as this information was not available to you, you are not held to blame.'

Or-Shls nodded. 'You can leave us. The Harbour Master will remain.'

There was the tiniest hesitation and then a sound like a syncopated drum roll. Clo Fiffithiss had retreated at speed, but it had waited for a fraction of a second. Even such a brief pause was a dangerous display in the face of so direct a dismissal. It was as much support as the being could have dared express.

It didn't help. The room was still very lonely when it had gone.

Vess cleared his throat. 'Am I held to blame, then?'

To his surprise, Or-Shls grinned. 'Not exactly. But the total loss of the major fleet has not merely left us without viable means of aggression – it has left us diminished. We look like fools, Vess, unable even to pretend to project power; unable to hold on to what little we have. And, it has left you without a role. We have selected you a new one.'

'Thank you, Chairman.'

'I wouldn't, not yet. Madam Garash?'

The heavy paws tightened a little on the edge of the lectern so that Vess half expected to hear it creaking.

'You are an interesting character, Hevalansa Vess. You come from Ground Level, but you have risen far without making enemies or leaving a trail of bodies. You get on well with your peers, but you have few friends. You are legendarily private and you have no intimate relationships. Your profile indicates that you are a pronounced insectophobe and yet you maintain your composure in the presence of our friends Vut and you seem positively close to Clo Fiffithiss. In short, you have all the attributes of a spy.'

'A what?' Vess felt slightly dizzy. He shook his head.

'A spy. We need information, Vess. We need to know how the hijackers of the last Great Ship broke out from the Hive. That should not have been possible. They should not have been able to break out. They should not have been able to buy tickets. They should not have been able to steal the ship – even if ships of that scale are designed to be run by small crews. You are the kind of person who can find that out.'

The dizziness was worse. Vess spoke carefully. 'What must I do?'

'For the moment, nothing. Are you feeling unwell?'

'Yes. What . . . ?'

'Good. Don't move.'

Vess realized he was swaying. He was trying to work out how

to say that he couldn't help it when he was spared the trouble; something behind him was holding him up. He heard a soft hissing and realized it was the sound of the dirigible, and he wondered how it ever had enough buoyancy to support him on top of its own weight. He managed one word. '*Good?*'

'Yes. You were hacked when you looked into the light. It's taking effect. Just relax.'

With the dizziness had come panic but also a sort of euphoria. He wanted to be facetious, to tell them that he didn't need their help to relax, to tell them *something*, but his voice wouldn't work.

The hissing suddenly seemed very loud, and then very distant.

He relaxed.

Tri-Gyre Approach

Even the thing nearest them was very big. Not as big as something like a planet, obviously, she'd get to that later, but planets were supposed to be big. A hundred kilometres across would have been tiny for a planet, but it was absolutely massive for something like Web City.

She would get to Web City in a while. Meanwhile, Oblong.

It wasn't really oblong, but she could forgive that because she knew it had been, once.

It had started out as an old container ship which was tumbling helplessly through space in what was then the recently abandoned middle of nowhere – abandoned by what would become the Inside, which in turn was on its way to becoming Inside rather than Outside. It had lost motive power and was barely airtight, really very much more container and rather less ship. It had perfectly suited the people who found it; they had nowhere to go, but they urgently wanted somewhere to be.

Then some more people joined them, and suddenly the big old hulk had seemed not so big. That was when they had started to snare asteroids.

One thing led to another. A millennium later the agglomerated mass that was still called Oblong consisted of the remains of about seventy asteroids, eight Light Cruisers, some tankers and a small yacht which had wandered unwittingly into the growing gravity well of the swollen composite body and never escaped. As a planet it would have been a pinprick at best. As an artificial object it had once been by a comfortable margin the biggest in the Spin and for quite a long way outside it.

But only once. Now its child had overtaken it. Big was still a key word, but 'bigger' was the word for what it sat in the middle of. Web City wasn't one object. It was presently a few thousand, and counting.

Sooner or later an object like Oblong has to stop growing. It becomes too disordered, too hard to navigate, too hard to wire up and govern and just *operate*. So it had stopped, but the bits and pieces went on arriving, faster with every year since the place had acquired a sort of social gravity. If you wanted to start a new life you took anything you could get your hands on, made it space-tight, powered it with whatever and headed for Oblong. If and when you got there in one piece you tied yourself to the nearest similar object and began to call the place home.

A few thousand objects later you had Web City – a tethered, roughly hexagonal close-packed spacescape of *stuff* full of people and commerce and informal manufacturing and sex and crime, sometimes separately. It was divided into cells a few hundred metres across, each with local shielding and atmosphere services, and each one, subject to any unresolved border disputes, linked to its neighbours by airlocked tube-shaped tunnels.

The joins between the cells weren't rigid, so Web City undulated very slowly around Oblong like a sleepy sea creature. Something about it raised Seldyan's pulse rate, but not as much as the thing behind it.

It was what they had seen as an eyebrow; apparently the locals called it the Arch. It was half a million kilometres from end to end and it lit up the sky above Web City with a ghostly shimmer of all colours and none. Bands of colour ran slowly

along it, flickering through the spectrum; ragged patches efflor-
esced and faded.

It had been there for less than five years.

They stared at it for a long time. Eventually Lyste let out a
breath. 'What the fuck *is* that?'

Merish shook his head. 'I'm no wiser than I was before.
Debris, very hot, very radioactive. Weird debris, too. Not just
radioactive, but full of really bizarre daughter elements.'

Seldyan found it hard to tear herself away from the screen.
She managed. 'So, your bust-apart planet?'

'I don't think so.' He frowned. 'Or if it is, it's not just that.
Those daughter elements? They don't belong. They're what you
get if you do a whole lot of complicated reactions at energy
levels that don't belong in a planet, with exotic elements
that *definitely* don't belong in a planet.'

She studied his face for a moment, then looked back to the
screen. 'Merish? Being blown up doesn't belong in a planet
either. I'm withholding judgement, if you don't mind. Now, you
said you wouldn't want to be within half a million klicks of this
thing, and yet here we are. How safe will we be in Web City?'

Merish shrugged. 'It depends where and for how long.
Oblong's shielding looks fine.'

'Uh-huh. Let's take dosimeters with us.'

Lyste laughed softly. 'Wonderful. Tell me, Seldyan, at what
point will we decide we should have stuck with where we came
from?'

She had to take another couple of breaths, but for a different
reason. When she felt able she said, slowly, 'Never. Is that clear?'

Apparently it was, because no one said anything more.

They approached at one notch above dead stop, with every
remote-sensing gadget that the old ship could muster quivering
at maximum gain. That was *lots*: a tumbling wave of information that spilled out of the tank like phosphorescent foam.

Merish and Kot were crouched over the tank like statues, if statues could look that tense. Lyste was fingering some wooden puzzle that never seemed to leave her hands. It made a faint clicking noise. Seldyan was learning not to find it annoying. Hufsza sat in a personal pool of calmness which hadn't reached Seldyan; she waited, chewing a nail.

Then, all at once, Merish and Kot straightened up, and the ship made its listen-to-me chime and said, '*Contact*.'

On one of the parts of the display that she actually understood, Seldyan watched the velocity tell-tale scroll down to zero and stay there. She turned to Merish.

'Is that it?'

'Yes. We brushed the tiniest outpost of the dumbest sensor tendril; probably a long-term impact warning system.'

'Okay.' She glanced at the tank, which now showed a single faintly bluish filament extending out from Oblong towards them. 'Will it know what we are?'

'Not yet. It probably thinks we're a really boring asteroid. We're incognito, Sel, until we get closer in. Then we'll send a "hello" signal back, so they don't have to do any nervous guessing.'

She nodded, and went on looking. The black hole was invisible but she could just make out the field that kept it apart from the little sun at the other side of the formation. It looked like a blurred ghostly spindle hanging from a star, with three planets spinning round it.

'Beautiful.' She said it under her breath, and even as her lips closed around the last thread of the whisper, she thought that it was probably the first time in her life she had used the word. She grinned to herself and said it again, louder.

'Beautiful.'

Merish laughed. 'Letting it get to you?'

'Damn right. That's the new world. Hope they're ready for us.'

'So, definitely not nervous?'

She shook her head. 'They might be. I'm not.'

Merish studied his hands for a moment. Then he smiled at her. 'Where do you get it from, Seldyan?'

'The same place you did, remember? I just did something different with it.' Then she bit her lip as his smile faded.

He nodded once, very slowly. Then he turned away. 'Better let them know we're here.'

'Okay.'

The screens showed the knobbly mass of Oblong in the foreground, now utterly dwarfed by the backdrop of the Tri-Gyre. At this distance the components of Web City had dispersed to the point where you could have dismissed them as space trash, but the three planets were big enough to fill the whole field of view. If you stared at them long enough they started to fill your whole mind as well.

It was as well to pull back a little. When Seldyan did, she realized that there was a sort of graininess between her and the planets. It was moving, crawling around slowly like specks in some vast experiment. Another shift of focus gave her the answer and her mouth went dry; the specks were ships. Thousands, probably many thousands, of ships.

She hadn't realized there were that many ships anywhere. She swallowed. Then she looked around quickly. The others hadn't noticed.

She had been watching them. She knew them, of course; she had known them since the Sorting on the Hive and she had come to know them far better through the clandestine sharing in the Mind Stack, but she had never known them under normal conditions. Whatever passed for normal; she suspected their present circumstances weren't it.

So she had watched. Merish, his eyes half closed, was still deep in an hours-long silent conversation with the ship AI. Lyste, small and dark, was sitting hunched over her toy in merciful silence.

Sitting on the other side of the bridge was Hufsza, a coil of muscle that looked barely reined in even at rest. Next to him sat Kot, the least humanoid-looking of all of them. She came from a planet where tar-sand extraction was the main activity. The tar sands contained mutagens; Kot's people had the fastest-moving DNA in the Spin. She was a full head shorter than the others, but broader even than Hufsza with an upper body almost square in section.

The silence had lasted a long time. Finally Lyste looked up and said mildly, 'It's been ages since you signalled. What's going on?'

Seldyan looked at Merish, but to judge by his unfocused eyes he was still deep in trance with the ship AI. He'd been there for most of the day. She sighed and gestured to the screen.

'They look busy. Could be just that.'

Hufsza uncoiled himself. 'Maybe this is normal. Whatever; I'd rather wait here than still be in the Hive.'

Seldyan shot him a grin.

Then they all jumped. The comms chimed and then spoke.

'Hello MBU, ah, *Suck on This*. Neat name by the way. This is Web Approach. Sorry you've been kept waiting. You're free to go forward to Oblong Outer Skin, coordinates attached. A Shuttler will meet you there. I'm afraid you've got to stop that far out; any further down our gravity well and something as big as you could tow us out into space, if you wanted to.'

Seldyan looked around the others and got a series of nods, apart from Merish who was still somewhere else. 'Thanks, Web Approach, we'll do that. What was the hold-up?'

There was the tiniest hesitation. 'No big deal. You've got a legacy Main Battle Unit, which we *have* seen before, but you also have a fully un-zipped battle-ready AI in charge, which we *haven't*. We've been trying to talk to it, and it's pretty defensive. Allow us a little caution?'

'You're allowed. Thanks, Web Approach. See you in a while.'

Seldyan closed the connection, waited a moment until she was sure it really was closed, and then turned to Merish. 'Wake up,' she said. 'Now, Merish. You're needed.'

His eyes opened slowly. 'Uh-huh?'

'We're on our way. Did anything happen while you were, ah, in there?'

He raised his eyebrows, then winced and rubbed at his temples. 'How did you know?'

'I guessed. What was it?'

'Outside contact. It started with a quick ping like a friendly hello and then grew, like *really* fast, until there were data filaments everywhere. They didn't get anything. The AI just hunkered down and shrugged them off.'

Seldyan felt her lips tightening. 'Were we attacked, Merish?' Behind her Lyste's toy clicked and fell silent.

'You could call it that, maybe. Or a very invasive probe. Someone wanted to get deep into the AI.' He shrugged. 'They didn't.'

She nodded. Her mind had already been made up. 'Okay. Everyone? We got this far. Let's go the rest of the way – but let's not assume anything. Agreed?'

They nodded. Lyste picked up the toy again. Click, click.

An hour later the ship had threaded its way through the ridiculous traffic with a sort of delicacy that made Seldyan think of a vast throwback lizard treading carefully through a crèche. It had come to a cautious local stop at the end of a long pontoon. They sat on the bridge watching the strangest thing Seldyan had ever seen wandering towards them.

The body – there was something about it which invited comparison with living things – was a stubby irregular dull grey cylinder which had a peculiar twisted look to it. It seemed to be able to sprout things at will; where the pontoon broadened into a wide track the thing grew a pair of tall, plumply tyred wheels that it hung between, swinging slightly. When the pontoon narrowed the wheels – disappeared? were reabsorbed? went, anyway – and the thing climbed along on six articulated limbs.

Kot got there first. 'What the fuck is that?'

Merish had been studying the comms. Now he looked up, grinning. 'I think it's a Shuttler,' he said. 'Looks like a smoother ride than the shuttles we're used to.'

He was right. When it was close to them the Shuttler reared up, extended its limbs and took the tiny proportion of *Suck on This* that it could actually reach in a careful embrace that made scratching noises through the hull. Then it lowered its body towards them. There was a dull clang and the sound of an air-lock cycling.

The Shuttler was less interesting on the inside. It was too big for them; ten rows of four seats split by a central aisle reminded Seldyan of old-style planetary airliners. She had never been on one, but she had seen pictures. But Merish was right – it was much smoother than the shuttles they were used to. Motion was imperceptible, and she couldn't tell when the thing switched between legs and wheels. She would have preferred something noisier; it would have given her something to distract her on her way into the unknown.

Better to stare it down. She glared at the forward viewing screens.

As well as being smooth the Shuttler was faster than it looked. Oblong was growing quickly, so that its rough bulk soon blotted out the planets directly behind it. At a distance it looked black but as they closed on it she realized that its surface was mottled and irregular, like a chemical experiment that had fizzed into a block of iridescent grey bubbles and then set. Closer still and she understood why Shuttlers had legs as well as wheels. She could see several of them moving over the surface, and nothing else could have looked so at home.

The pontoon met the surface at a right angle. The Shuttler went round the corner without slackening speed, fingering its way quickly over the bumps and chasms and lowering itself on to a flattish protrusion. There was an industrial-sounding *clunk* and another airlock sighed.

Lyste looked up from her toy, which to Seldyan's relief had been quiet since they had been in the Shuttler. 'Welcome to the new world,' she said.

Seldyan heard the brittleness in her voice. Apprehensiveness. It mirrored her own; she looked at the others and found their own versions of the same thing in their faces and their body language. *I brought them here*, she thought. *This bit's up to me.*

She smiled widely. 'You know what, I bet we're the most interesting thing that's happening to them today. I'm pretty sure we're the most dangerous as well. People like us are the reason this place *exists*. We're the future. Shall we go out and grab some of it?'

She marched down the aisle and lowered herself into the airlock. Just before she let her head drop below floor level she looked up again; they were all watching her.

'One more thing,' she said. 'We're here because we don't want to have to do shit we don't like. Yes? So if you're worried, share it with me, or share it with the others. Let's stay dangerous.'

She dropped into the airlock and got ready to follow the instructions that floated fuzzily in front of her. Behind her she heard a brief buzz of conversation and then a click. She smiled to herself. In her own way Lyste was coping. She hoped the others would too.

The lock finished its cycle. She clenched her hands and walked out into the new world.

Oblong Embarkation

The new world was certainly new. It was getting newer almost as Seldyan watched. Listened, too – she had been sent on enough non-consensual construction projects to recognize what they sounded like.

Embarkation was one of the oldest parts of Oblong. It had been formed by joining together the blocky hulls of six of the founding Light Cruisers to make a low pillared space about two hundred metres on a side. These days that was blatantly not big enough. Admittedly the five of them were used to living at high densities – the Hive world was nothing if not full – but those had been *orderly* high densities. This was a shouting, jostling, sweat-smelling free-for-all. Seldyan felt her palms itching, and clenched her fingers.

She realized she had missed something. She turned to the off-white-robed concierge who had greeted them from the Shuttler, and leaned in towards her a little.

'I'm sorry?'

The bony face smiled. 'I said, fifty million passengers came through here last year. That's up fifty per cent from the year before and it'll be up another fifty per cent next year.'

That seemed to be it. Seldyan nodded, and tried not to get caught studying the woman's face. She had introduced herself as

Shahatiel – she emphasized the second syllable with a sound almost like a bark – and she was extremely skinny. She also had the kind of bone structure that showed it. Her age was indeterminate. Her scalp was shiny-bald and her skin was an odd slightly greyish brown which seemed natural; the only obvious sign of cosmetics was a bold fingertip-sized spot of green just above her left eye. Seldyan overcame her caution and pointed at it.

'What's that?'

The smile broadened into a grin. 'That, my new friends, is what freedom of religion looks like. The newest star! Welcome to democracy.'

It seemed safest to grin back. Seldyan made a mental note to read up on religion when she got a chance.

By what seemed like a miracle they made it across the frenetic floor of Embarkation without losing anyone. Seldyan got the strong impression that their robed companion had a way of parting the crowds. She also received a far more subtle impression that not all of the crowds were appreciative – with her Hive sensibilities she thought she detected hints of dissent in their wake. She looked around casually and saw robed figures dotted across the big room. Even in the throng they seemed to attract turned backs. Whatever; Shahatiel's presence had worked. In a shorter time than she would have thought possible they had reached the other side of the crowded space, jumped a long queue – leaving more suppressed resentment behind them – and dropped into deeply upholstered seats in a monorail carriage that shot them down into a black tunnel at a steep angle.

Seldyan had deliberately waved everyone past, leaving her sitting next to Merish at the back of the compartment. As the carriage hummed away she leaned in close and mouthed into his ear.

'Thoughts?'

They swapped head positions. 'Looks okay. Feels worrying.'

'That's what I think. Our friend?'

He shook his head. 'Nut job. Hope she's not typical. There's a big atmosphere there. Everyone seems to hate her but no one says it out loud.'

She nodded. 'Yeah. The atmosphere reminds me of something but I'm not sure what. Keep alert, will you?'.

'No problem. It'll be a while before I relax enough to feel sleepy.'

'Cool. Now, let's behave.'

They sat up straight like good tourists. Ahead of them, the bald head of their guide stuck out from the folds of her robe. For a moment Seldyan thought of a moon hanging low above a barren landscape.

It was a short journey but a very fast one, and the monorail engineers had made no attempt to conceal G-forces. The opposite, if anything; Seldyan suspected that some of the curves and plunges were more playful than needful. It almost felt like a Hive shuttle, except it didn't smell.

Then the car burst out of the tunnel, and things stopped feeling like anything she had ever experienced. She heard Merish draw in a breath.

They were lancing across the surface of Oblong on the opposite side to the embarkation gantry. The abrupt movements had ceased so that if Seldyan lifted her eyes from the blurring landscape there was nothing to tell her they were moving. She did lift her eyes, or rather they were drawn upwards.

The vast glowing circle of the three planets hung above them. It filled the starscape, and pretty soon it filled the mind. It was beautiful, and even as Seldyan used the word to herself she smiled; it was the second time in a day, and in a life.

She felt Merish's fingers touch her hand. It was probably the one thing that could have distracted her from the view.

The car began to slow. The rail dipped back below the surface and the ground closed over them. Shahatiel half turned in her seat and spoke over her shoulder.

'We're nearly there. There'll be time for you to refresh yourselves before everyone arrives.'

Kot cleared her throat. 'Everyone?'

The woman laughed. 'Well, not absolutely everyone, obviously. But a reception to welcome you. Patras will be there.' She
looked at them and added, 'He's the new Supervisor.'

She turned away. Merish leaned towards Seldyan. 'Supervisor?' he whispered.

She shrugged. 'New? Who knows? I know this much – we're
going to be on duty for a while longer.'

He nodded. His fingers clasped hers more tightly for a
moment. Then he withdrew his hand.

Village 91, Hive

The food line crawled forward. He had already learned to keep pace with it. The previous evening he had fallen a few paces behind and had suddenly found bodies swirling past him, filling the gap and forcing him backwards until there was no more queue behind him. Ahead he could see a knot of bodies gathered around the dispensary. They dispersed as he reached the hatch.

It slid out a shallow bowl of flimsy paper about the size of his outstretched palms. The bowl began to sag almost immediately. He cupped his hands underneath it and then looked at the contents. He felt his lips pull back so that his teeth chilled.

It held a congealed mass of something yellowish grey. It smelled of vomit.

There was laughter somewhere in front of him. He looked up into the faces of half a dozen people with grinning mouths and watchful eyes. He stared at them as coldly as he could until the grins faded. Then he pushed through them and dumped the bowl into the waste. He turned before the cover had closed, leaving the hiss of the disposal flare behind him, and walked back through the gap between the two halves of the watching group. It felt familiar, from a long time ago.

He went to his Village hungry, but no one troubled him. The

hunger didn't trouble him either. He had been there before. The only surprise was that here, the memory was almost welcome.

Each Village held ninety-six sleep cells, each just larger than a standard human. They were arranged round a central observation shaft in three stacked wheels of thirty-two. The sleepers' feet pointed towards the shaft and the cells were backlit at the head end so any movement within the cell threw a moving shadow across the translucent cylindrical sensor mesh that surrounded the observation shaft. Two human guards sat with their hands on dead man's handles. While either handle was held, the automatic weapon system was merely armed. If both were released, so were the weapons. It was simple and foolproof.

The Villages were themselves arranged in vertical stacks of seven which could be isolated from each other instantly. A Village with both handles free was automatically isolated. One where both had remained free for more than an hour without explanation was fumigated. Depending on the explanation it might be fumigated anyway.

Village stacks were arranged in a hexagonal close-packed matrix. The roughly triangular spaces between stacks were used for engineering and storage. Five hundred stacks made a Hive. There were many, many Hives, but the whole collection was still called by the singular – The Hive.

Vess had learned about it – and much more besides – in six days of what they called orientation. To himself he called it indoctrination, but he didn't share the word with the faceless voices in the dark of the immersion suite. Instead he cooperated with them as they taught him who he wasn't any more, and then as they showed him who he was to be while he was on the Hive world and what he was to do. Apparently it was all quite standard.

It was better than being dead – but sometimes he had found himself questioning that. He had kept his questions to himself.

The learning had been true to the reality but when he arrived – with the guilty cargo of the real Vess buried deep inside him – the reality turned out to be far more than the learning. The first thing that struck him was the smell. He had expected bodies and stale food, and the expectation had drawn him back to a faint memory of childhood in crowded places. He had shut that down quickly; in fact his Village smelled aggressively clean, with a chemical edge and a dry papery background from the disposable coveralls that were renewed every day. No other clothes were provided or allowed in the Village.

He woke with his belly growling and his newly implanted chip smarting near the base of his spine. The food line was welcome. This time no one interfered with his meal, which was a greyish porridge that looked uncomfortably like the bowl from last night but which smelled and tasted of almost nothing. But it was hot and his senses detected starch. Within a minute he had emptied the bowl, although without properly filling his stomach. Then there was work. That was what the Hive was about.

The buried part of him understood the logic – always had, in a general way, but it had been explained in words of one syllable during the process that was not called indoctrination.

There had been different teachers for different subjects. The mechanics of espionage were covered by a blocky being of a species unfamiliar to Vess, but which looked like a cross between a large human and a small cargo container. It – Vess had tried and failed to settle on a gender – had a peculiar voice which managed at the same time to be effeminate and powerfully baritone.

Then there was a long political briefing from a small apparently standard human female who barely looked up from her notes. When she did, Vess realized with a jolt that she was not so standard; in the dim light the four eyes that met his were huge, with slightly luminous purple irises. The eyes were stacked, one above the other, on either side of an ordinary-looking nose. Vess found himself wondering how many species, or sub-species – or whatever they were – the basic human form had produced, and how many more of them he was yet to meet.

He didn't have to wonder with the creature that briefed him on economic strategy. At first sight it could have been a twin of Clo Fiffithiss. But first sight was deceptive; it hadn't taken him long to realize that the only thing the two beings had in common was species. For a start, and unlike Clo Fiffithiss, it didn't use a translator. It was one of the few that had learned to produce human-compatible speech using its own vocal apparatus, a group of layered reed-like membranes set low down its windpipe. The result sounded like a wind through dead leaves.

'Most societies arrive at slavery by accident, or because they never left it. In the Spin there has been plenty of economic oppression but little actual slavery, unless you count examples like the Fortunate Protectorate, who arrived at it by accident and were obliterated by an Artefact shortly afterwards. The Inner Federation is very unusual in having decided to return to slavery on an industrial scale millennia after having abandoned it, and probably unique in that it did so as a strategic decision based on detailed gaming. You have been told that already, I know.'

Vess nodded.

'There is something you haven't been told. That decision wasn't to ensure stability; there was no outcome of the gaming that achieved that. It was about managing decline. Now the situation has passed over a threshold. It is unmanageable.'

The rustling voice fell silent. Vess squinted at the dimly lit creature. There was no readable expression; it was quite still.

'How long?' he asked.

'How long until what? The Abstainer has gamed it. Until we

default on our debts, a year. Mass unrest leading to civil war, another year. Complete dismantling of the Inner Federation by aggressors and creditors, five years. There is a certain urgency.'

The Abstainer, thought Vess. Not a friendly term, Clo Fiffithiss had said. Keeping his voice level he said, 'And me?'

'Unstable though we are, we need the economic flywheel of the Hive as a bastion against even worse instability. At the moment it is being the opposite. It is becoming unstable – a source of insurrection. Of revolution, even. Find the instability, Vess, and then come back and tell us.'

Vess nodded again. Then a thought occurred to him. 'Am I the only one in there?'

'Perhaps. Or perhaps not. Have you any more questions?'

He dared himself. 'Clo Fiffithiss – do you trust its gaming?'

'The Abstainer? You should know that my kind do not make good slaves. For the most part. But what it was ordered to game, it would have gamed.' There was a quick inscrutable hissing as if the wind had swelled to a gale and then subsided. Then the voice returned to normal. 'That is the end of this briefing – of all the briefings, I believe. I wish you luck.' There was a slight pause and then it added, 'Hunt well.'

Vess bowed in acknowledgement. He managed to restrain his shudder until he was alone. He had no idea how a shudder would have been interpreted.

But then, yes, there was work. There was always work.

The economic model was simple enough. The Hive was the ultimate outsourcing destination. It provided anything which needn't be done in a particular place, and which could be achieved by forced labour – intellectual or physical. It was also a strong attractor of opportunity. People relocated things so as to be near it. Factories, logistics hubs, whole space-borne agri-businesses – anything which either didn't need much sunshine or could bring its own with it, and which could be done more cheaply by people than machines – had accreted in the riotously cluttered sector around the original Hive planet to take advantage of that cheap labour. It had grown from a resource into an economy within an economy and it worked.

And Vess worked. He didn't know how many of the Hive management knew who he was. Very few, he had been told, and certainly no one seemed to be influencing his fate for the better. So he worked, mostly doing things which he would always have assumed were done by inhuman equipment. It took him a while to realize that in many ways they still were.

One of the things was mining. On his second day he was corralled into a careworn short-hop shuttle along with a hundred or so others. The shuttle's gravity compensation wasn't working; two miserably motion-sick hours later, his clothes stained with his own vomit and that of his neighbours, he walked unsteadily into a tunnel on a recently arrived asteroid.

The next two days passed as one infinitely repeated minute of dust and colossal, deadly fatigue. They exchanged hardly any words, just the bare minimum needed for cooperation. Their throats were coated with rock flour, their eyes dry and swollen and rimmed with it, their fingers peeling raw. Apparently this was normal, or anyway acceptable.

On the return shuttle he was too tired to vomit. So was everyone else. When they left the shuttle their filthy clothes barely needed to be removed. They fell away in shreds on the way to the decon units. The decontamination wasn't for their benefit. It was standard practice; the Hive was not to be inoculated with off-planet materials.

He slept an endless sleep that was far too short, and woke to more work. The cycle lasted eleven days; on the twelfth he woke – eventually – and there wasn't work. It was almost jarring.

People's cycles were staggered. The resters were allowed to move freely within the Village, which meant very little because the Village contained sleep cells and a small social area next to the cafeteria and nothing else.

Everyone took it differently. A thin, elaborately sinewy woman called Zephorere spent her time exercising, jogging round the outer walkway a set number of times – Vess was too tired to count, but anyway it looked like a set number – before stopping at what seemed to be predetermined points to carry out joint-cracking manoeuvres that made Vess wince. She had a following of a sort; from time to time other resters would trot after her for a few circuits, and the braver ones would imitate her exercise routines. Mostly they fell over and limped back, laughing, to the cafeteria.

Vess didn't follow her because his senses had woken up. They were concentrating on the only other person who didn't, and he trusted them. His trust amused him. *Perhaps I really could be a spy,* he thought.

She was called Dimollss and she was very young. She had only been moved into the adult environment of the Village a few cycles ago. She had the transparent wisdom of youth, and the indiscretion.

'The others think you're a spy.'

He blinked, gathered himself and smiled at her.

'Why?'

'Because you're new and old.'

'I beg your pardon?'

She sighed. 'You've just come here so you're new, but you're grown-up so you're old.'

He nodded slowly. 'Why does that make me a spy?'

She shrugged. 'I don't know. But people like you have been falling dead out of the Mind Stacks. It must mean something.'

He blinked. 'Falling dead?'

'Well, not falling. Lying dead. In those couches.' Her eyes searched his face. 'Have you been in the Mind Stack yet?'

101

He shook his head. 'I've heard of it,' he said. That was true enough; it had been an important part of the briefing.

She nodded. 'Good. So you know about when they chip you into the Stack, and you trance? When they bring you out you're supposed to come out of the trance but some people, people like you, just don't move . . . oh . . .'

'Oh?' He wanted to ask more but her eyes had broken contact with his and she was staring over his shoulder. He looked round.

There were three of them, two women and a man, and they were wearing the dull grey-brown uniforms of Monitors. One of the women took a step forwards. 'Gossip like that is not allowed.' She looked at Vess. 'Move away from her or I'll assume you want to be involved.'

The argument in his head seemed to take for ever, but it was probably less than a real-time second before his legs acknowledged inevitability. He stood aside and they walked past him. Dimollss shrank back one pace and then stopped, her head raised and her eyes defiantly focused. As upright as she was – and for all she was effectively an adult – Vess realized with a start that she was a head shorter than the Monitors, and far slighter.

The lead Monitor reached for something at her waist. 'You know what to do. Ten seconds this time.'

Dimollss bit her lip. Then she dropped into a sitting position and looked up. For a moment her eyes met Vess's and she gave the trace of a wink. Then she turned her face to the Monitor and her expression dissolved into such pure hatred that Vess almost recoiled.

'Go on,' she said. 'Enjoy yourself.'

The Monitor held out the little grey stubby cylinder she had taken from her belt. She did something to a control at one end of it and then pointed it at Dimollss.

The girl convulsed. Her body curled forwards into an

awkward ball that reminded Vess horribly of a dying insect. From the ball came a harsh keening. It seemed to last a very long time. Then, suddenly, it was over. The Monitor lowered the cylinder. The keening stopped and although Dimollss did not uncurl, Vess could see that her muscles had relaxed.

The Monitor put the thing back on her belt and looked at Vess. 'For the record, I did not enjoy that,' she said. 'No pleasure is involved.' She turned and walked away. The other two followed her wordlessly.

Vess managed to wait until they were almost out of sight before he knelt at the girl's side. 'Are you okay?' The word seemed utterly inadequate.

The ball uncurled slowly, revealing a pale face with red-rimmed eyes. Dimollss took a ragged breath, then let it out and took another. 'Yeah, I'm okay. Or I will be.'

'What happened?'

Her face twisted. 'That thing she held out? It does something to your chip that makes you . . . hurt.' She spoke the last word in a flat voice.

Vess felt his stomach twist. 'I'm sorry.'

'Why? You didn't do anything. And you couldn't have stopped them. Nobody can stop them.' She got up awkwardly, one limb at a time, and looked down at herself. 'Besides – fucking *yes*!'

He shook his head. 'I'm sorry – yes what?'

'Yes, result. Ten seconds? That's the first time I've got past five without throwing up. Heading for Seldyan.'

At first Vess felt sick. Then he reined it in. 'Heading for *who*?'

She looked at him seriously. 'You've heard of her then. Is she famous?'

'In a way. Won't I get you in trouble for talking again?'

'Yes, so don't do it.' She grinned and turned away. Over her shoulder she added: 'Most people get Mind Stack after their rest day. We might be in there together.'

He watched her walk away.

Despite his tiredness he slept very little that night. He was thinking about what counted as important.

He hadn't realized that the economic well-being, such as it was, of the Inside rested on torturing children.

Oblong

Seldyan was beginning to think that their hosts were over-using the three planets. There they were again, visible in all their glowing vastness through the crystal-clear bubble of what-ever it was that covered the room – although 'covered' wasn't really the right word. 'Formed' was more accurate. They were standing on a fairly smooth section of the outside of Oblong and the bubble arched sharply down to ground level, covering an area about a hundred of her paces across. She couldn't see how high it went because it was so clear it was effectively invis-ible, but from head-height down it produced a faint fluttering blur so that stars seen through it shimmered. Somebody had told her that was to stop people trying to walk through it by mistake.

There were tables with drinks and snacks. She stuck to foods she recognized and drinks that didn't seem intoxicating. When she caught sight of the others they were doing the same, but she didn't catch sight of them very often.

Everybody wanted to talk to them. Any attempt to stay in a group was hopeless; they were pulled in as many different direc-tions as there were people in the room, and Seldyan made that over a hundred even when they were first led in. She smiled and answered, but mainly didn't answer, dozens of variations on the obvious questions and a few unwelcome suggestions. Most of those she managed to freeze out, but she could feel her temper shortening.

She spotted a clearing in the forest of people and headed for it, using her elbows. It turned out to be centred on someone – a short stocky figure with its back to her, dressed in a plain wrap of faded brown that was belted at the waist. She saw eyes across the circle flicking away from the figure to her. From her Hive days she was used to interpreting fine shifts in body language. This time it was the shoulders that told her that the eyes that had noticed her had been noticed.

The figure turned and she was looking down – quite a long way down – into the most thickly bearded face she had ever seen, and one deeply black pupil was looking back at her. The other socket was empty. The parts of the face that weren't dense black beard were reddish-blue skin which at first looked as if it was criss-crossed by thousands of black veins. Then she saw – they were tattoos.

She realized she was staring, and worse, that she was being watched while she stared. She forced a smile and held out her hand. 'Seldyan,' she said.

'Patras. Welcome to Oblong. Has anyone said that yet?'

The voice was astonishingly deep. She thought for a moment. 'No, I don't think so. I expect they meant it, even so. You're the new Supervisor?'

He smiled, and gave a shallow bow which brought his head down almost to her waist. 'I am. In role for five days so far. Do you know, nobody has even *tried* to assassinate me?' Then he straightened up. 'And you're the newest best hope. I expect nobody's said that yet either?'

She looked at him for a long time. Then she said, quietly, '*Whose* newest best hope?'

The single eye flashed. She saw amusement, and something else. 'What a good question. It's, ah, noisy here. Would you and your colleagues like to go somewhere else?'

She looked briefly around the circle of faces. The others had found her; they nodded slightly. Everyone else was watching. Although no one else was speaking, she realized Patras was right. It *felt* noisy.

She turned back to Patras. 'That would be fine,' she said.

To her great relief, *somewhere else* turned out to be blessedly underground. They sat on a couch that formed three quarters of a circle, with a low round table at its centre. The drinks and finger foods on the table were much better than the ones at the reception. She looked around and felt herself relax a little. She saw Patras smiling.

'I feel the same,' he said. 'After a while even I can have too much wide open space and grand planetscape.'

Seldyan nodded. 'How many people live on them?'

'None.' She looked at him sharply and he shrugged. 'They're very pretty but humans can't survive on them. Scrappy engineering – their atmospheres have leaked away. They need re-terraforming.'

'Can you do that?'

'We hope to, soon.'

'Oh.' Then something occurred to her. 'All the views point towards those planets. Not towards the Web, or the Arch. Is it right the Arch is less than five years old?'

'Yes.' The answer was even shorter than the single word should have been.

'How did it happen?'

Patras was quiet for a moment. Then he smiled again, but Seldyan thought it looked a lot less like a smile this time. 'I'll pass on that just now. Tell me about this ship you've brought us.'

Seldyan stiffened. She felt Merish's fingers on hers again. She clasped them for a second and then deliberately moved her hand away. She hadn't needed the warning.

'The ship brought us,' she said carefully, 'but *we* haven't brought *it*. Not to anyone. Not yet.'

To her surprise Patras stood up and bowed. 'Quite right. I apologize. I was being presumptuous.' He sat down again and added, 'The least I can hope is that you will stay for a while; long enough to form a favourable opinion of us. After all, you came here for a reason. And I have – reasons – for being glad to see you.'

It had been the tiniest of pauses, but Seldyan was sure she had heard it. She glanced at the others, and their faces told her they had heard it too.

Suddenly Seldyan felt on far more comfortable ground. She understood people who had their backs to the wall. She leaned forward, her elbows on her knees. 'Mr Supervisor? Is there something you want to tell us about?'

'Perhaps. Has anyone said anything to you about the Green Star?'

She frowned. Then realization dawned, and she traced a spot above her left eye.

'That's right. I think . . .' He smiled briefly. Then he stood up. Even fully upright, his eyes were little higher than hers were, seated. 'I think I'm being doubly presumptuous. It's late. Look, this suite is yours for as long as you want it. There are guest rooms off it. Take a look round. Relax, and we'll meet again tomorrow. Some other people will want their turn with you too. The Oblong management is called the City Fathers. We're meeting tomorrow; we'd like you to drop in.' Another micro-pause. 'Maybe tonight you could watch some screen. Check out all the news channels. We're an interesting bunch.'

His gaze swept them. Then he gave the sketch of a bow, turned, and walked out of the chamber.

They looked at each other. Lyste raised her eyebrows. 'What was that about?'

Kot opened her mouth, but Seldyan shook her head and nodded

down towards her hands. She touched the tip of her little finger against the ball of her opposite thumb. Hive talk: *keep quiet, not safe*. They widened their eyes.

Then Lyste shrugged. 'Watch screen and eat snacks? That's not so hard.' She shoved aside some of the snacks on the table and found a cluster of control patches. A screen blurred into being above the far end of the table.

'I guess not.' Seldyan watched as the channels flicked and settled. Then she sat up and stabbed a finger at the screen. 'Hey, give us audio!'

Lyste did things to the table top.

'. . . *arrival of the last legacy Main Battle Unit earlier today under the control of a Hive breakout crew* . . .'

The screen cut from the image of a newscaster to a view of the ship. Seldyan felt her mouth dropping open. She closed it quickly.

Next to her, Merish drew in a breath. 'Oh shit that's big. I mean, obviously I knew that, but seeing it . . .'

Seldyan nodded, keeping her eyes on the screen.

'. . . *five crew are currently resting on Oblong after a short reception and a private meeting with Supervisor Patras. So far he's not said anything in public but sources say we should expect to hear more tomorrow. Meanwhile the ship, which by the way has been renamed "Suck on This" by its new crew, is standing off at what we're told is a safe distance. We are joined now by Kaster Xhood. Kas, just how big is this thing and why does it have to stay so far away?*'

The image of a middle-aged male appeared just in front of the screen. It smiled out at them and then turned to gesture at the ship, which appeared to be just behind it.

'*Well, first, it doesn't* have *to stay out there. It can do pretty well what it likes. It's huge, agreed, but we've seen others of the same class before. What sets it apart is not only its size, and not even that it's been re-armed; again, that's not new. What is new*

*is that the ship is fully awake. These big old ships were lobot-
omized when they were taken out of military service. Uniquely
as far as we know, this one has had that reversed.'*

'So it's big, powerful, well-armed and smart, is that right?'

'It is, and how.' Kaster turned back to the audience. *'Let's be
thankful it's happy to stay out there until the crew are ready
to talk.'*

Seldyan turned to Lyste. 'Turn them down, please.'

The audio faded and the image of the ship froze. Seldyan
went on looking at it.

Merish cleared his throat. 'What are you thinking?'

Seldyan decided she didn't care if they were being monitored or
not. 'I'm thinking that there is no way I'm handing that ship over
to anyone until I know exactly what I'm getting in return. Besides,
it's not just us, right? There's all the rest of the Hivers as well.' She
managed to look away from the screen. 'Everyone? Agree?'

They nodded. Then Kot sat up. 'Hey, Lyste, is this the only
news channel?'

Lyste stared at the display. 'Seems to be.'

Kot shook her head. 'That can't be right. Otherwise why did
Patras say we should check out all of them?'

Seldyan looked sharply at Merish. He was already crouching
next to Lyste. Without looking up he said, 'There *are* other
news channels. Dozens. They just don't show up on this menu.'

'So use other menus.'

'If I can find them. It looks like they don't want to be found.'

'Really?' Seldyan sat back. 'Censorship, do you think?'

He looked up at her. 'Now why would you say that?'

'Just suspicious. Come on, what's taking you so long? You
rehabilitated a brain-damaged warship. How hard can it be to
hack a news channel?'

'As hard as the news channel – or whoever – wants to make
it. It's harder if I have to talk.' His fingers danced on the controls, paused, danced. 'Ah-*ha* . . .'

The screen flickered. The still image of the ship greyed out and words appeared over it.

Premium channels unlocked. This service will be charged to the Executive Suite, Oblong Gate. Continue?

The word *continue* blinked. Merish looked at Seldyan, his eyebrows raised.

She grinned. 'We're escaped slaves, remember? We don't understand about money. Besides, this is Patras's suite and he said we should.' *And no doubt he's listening,* she thought.

Merish nodded. 'It would be rude not to.' He tapped the panel and the word *continue* stopped blinking.

Suddenly they had over fifty news channels to choose from, all the way from slick full-studio productions right down to fuzzy hand-cams.

They sat transfixed. Apparently the world was not as they had thought.

Seldyan woke sometime in the small hours with her heart dancing to the tune of far too much to drink the night before. She lay on her back and breathed deeply until it calmed a little.

There was someone else breathing; Merish lay next to her. His own breathing was soft and slow. She stayed still, just letting her hand rest very gently against his hip. He didn't stir. She managed to feel sorry and glad, both at once. She rode the conflict for a few seconds, then focused elsewhere.

Her head felt thick, but her brain was still working. All too well – it was full of pictures.

When they were approaching Oblong she had looked at the Web and seen – well, what? A frontier town? A peace camp? Something hopeful.

She shook her head. She should have seen the biggest refugee camp in the history of the Spin. The Web was a growing crowd of people who thought they had left their problems behind, and who had woken up in the new world with the same problems, plus the new ones of being short of food, space and opportunity.

They had watched the screen in silence as violence unfolded. After a while some sort of pattern had emerged.

The riots weren't everywhere, although that's what it looked like if you channel-hopped. They were focused around a particular local conflict. Hufsza had noticed it first. He had pointed at the screen with an arm like a thigh and said, 'Hey – those guys? Remember the religious they sent to meet us? Same robes, see?'

He was right. They watched, and listened to commentaries. They tried to access social but that was beyond even Merish, up here.

It was about an election for something called a District Collector. Seldyan wasn't sure what one of those did, if anything, but the new Collector wore robes and had a green spot above his eye. Anyone who had a robe and a green spot – and there were plenty – was celebrating. Everyone else – and there were even more – was angry.

Finally they had found a commentary that made sense. They listened carefully.

'*On the face of it, what's to object to?*' The young woman raised her eyebrows. '*The Green Star won their freedom-of-religion point, so they can establish themselves wherever they want. They established an Order in Phhol. If they did so just ten days before the closure of nominations for the Collector election, so what? They're religious, they tell us. They're above all that grubby politics stuff.*' She grinned, and then stopped grinning. '*Except that they managed to put up a candidate. Except that they invited ten thousand of their followers to the opening ceremony of the Order and except that, what do you know, they all liked the place so much they decided to stay. And, of course, register to vote – which they were perfectly entitled to do. The rest, you know.*' She paused, and glanced behind her. The riots were over for the moment, but the square she stood in was still full of people who looked discontented. Then she looked straight at the camera. '*It's all over bar the shouting, according to some people, but I have another guess. Remember that it's election season. Another District Collector in Kresev tomorrow. Two more in the next five days. And, as if you could forget, Oblong City Fathers ten days away. And what do you know? The Green Star are fielding candidates for all of them. Better get ready to have your souls saved, willing or not. This is The Other Blog, signing off.*'

Merish leaned forward and switched off the channel. 'Well,' he said.

Seldyan nodded. 'Well.'

There was silence for a while. Then Kot drew in a breath. 'So, maybe the new world's a bit troubled. Is that a problem?'

Seldyan slapped a hand down on the table. 'Be fucked with troubled. Politics, arguments, election fixing – that's freedom, right? That's why we're here. If that's troubled, fine. What bothers me is secrets.'

Merish nodded slowly. 'Missing channels?'

'Damn right. So, who knew they were missing? Who are they missing from? Who made them go missing?' She slapped the table again, harder. 'Shit, I *hate* it when people fuck about with my ambitions.'

Lyste's toy clicked twice. 'Not just your ambitions,' she said quietly.

'Right.' Seldyan stared at nothing for a second, then made up her mind. 'So, three things. First, I want to understand about these green-smudge people. What's in it for them, and is it a problem for us? Second, how did the Arch happen? Patras blanked that one. Third, I want to get drunk, but I want to do that first.'

They got very drunk, and then they slept, and now she was lying next to Merish.

She often was. It had been complicated, for a long time. At the beginning she knew it was him that had needed her. Somewhere along the way that seemed to have got swapped around.

After the thing with the Hive Supervisor, Seldyan had been allowed to move back into the general dormitory for a while, before they sent her to the Village. Somehow she preferred being part of a crowd. It made it easier to be solitary, and solitary was exactly what she wanted.

The rooms were gender segregated, but only to the extent that they were divided in two by a central partition with female-equivalents on one side and male-equivalents on the other. Seldyan had never questioned the nuances of the terms; the Spin had more tricks up its sleeve than purely male or purely female but a line could usually be drawn.

An hour into the night cycle, something disturbed her – a quick dull tinkle like something delicate being smashed as quietly as possible. She sat up and listened.

There were sounds of conflict. She had heard them before but this time they seemed more acute. There was a struggle and a couple of voices she thought she recognized. Then one of the voices was muffled and stopped, but the struggle continued. It sounded quieter. If she listened with a cautious ear, quieter sounded worse.

She swung off the bed and walked to the partition. It was a set of slim foam-board panels that didn't completely divide the room; there were adult-squeezable gaps at either end. Seldyan didn't have to squeeze. It was enough to turn a little sideways, and there was plenty of room for her to pause halfway through.

She paused and looked.

The dim light was enough. It showed a shadowy group around a bed. There were two shadows on the bed, one above and one below. The one above was making movements she recognized. She felt a little sick.

She marched towards them, using her feet like weapons so the floor thumped. The shadows stopped moving. The group around the bed separated and moved towards her.

She elbowed through them. There was resistance, but not enough to stop her. At the bedside she nodded. The boy called Merish was the one underneath. There was just enough light for her to tell that he was crying.

Her arm had drawn back and swung forwards before she knew it. The boy on top – she didn't know his name – barely had time to start looking surprised before the blow connected. It knocked him backwards off the bed and he landed head first. Seldyan watched him for a moment to see if he was going to get up. He didn't, and she lost interest in him.

Merish had curled into an unmoving ball. His silent sobs had stopped. She sat down next to him and reached out a hand. It hovered in the air – she didn't know about touching people – and then settled on his shoulder. He twitched, uncurled and turned his head so he could see her.

She smiled and gestured towards the partition. He nodded and rolled off the bed. Even in the poor light she could see spots of blood in the hollow left by his hips. She compressed her lips.

Behind her someone snickered. She spun round and glared at the group of boys who had formed a semicircle. They shrank back a little and then stopped. One of them leaned forwards, and she realized he was the one she had knocked over. His nose was bleeding.

'You won't get anywhere with him, sweetheart. He's men only.' He spread his arms. 'We were just giving him what he wants.'

There was laughter. Then one of the others shook his head.

'She's not taking him for that. That's Seldyan, remember? She doesn't play with anyone any more. The old Super took her little flower.'

'Yeah, and she cut off his stalk. You're lucky she only bust your nose.' More laughter. The group broke up.

She pointed Merish towards the gap at the end of the partition. Before she followed him through she looked straight up. There was a monitor globe on the ceiling, placed to cover both halves of the room. It would usually have been a translucent hemisphere. Now it was blackened and crazed. She nodded to herself – that would have been the noise that had roused her – and followed him through.

There was just room for both of them in her bed as long as they didn't mind touching from knee to shoulder. Merish didn't seem to; he gave a deep sigh and closed his eyes almost immediately. And Seldyan didn't mind at all. She lay awake, feeling the warmth of the boy next to her and listening to the small animal noises of his sleep.

She spent most of the night like that, her eyes wide with surprise. She hadn't realized that there was an empty space next to her until someone filled it.

Oblong

Seldyan lay in the soft bed, with her head full of recollected pictures and some extrapolated ones. She wasn't sure which bothered her most.

She wondered for a moment whether she should check out the news channels again, but there didn't seem any point. She had made her decision while she slept.

She would go and find out for herself.

Her head hurt. She raised it carefully from its place next to Merish, sat up and rolled softly off the bed into a standing position that lasted through a few seconds of ear-swirling nausea and then settled down. When she trusted herself she crossed to the door into the main area, slipped through and let it close behind her, baffling the last few centimetres with a hand. There was no need to wake anyone, and besides, she wanted to be alone.

She hadn't operated the screen herself last night, but she had watched Merish closely and it looked simple. The controls were elaborate fingernail-sized glyphs floating just above the glass surface of the pad. She studied them and then reached out a hand. After a few false starts she managed to navigate past the news channels and into a search engine. She grinned to herself and went searching.

Half an hour later she sat back and pursed her lips. Web City was energetic, and enthralling, and large parts of it seemed opaque to scrutiny.

She was still staring at the display when Merish tapped her on the shoulder. She looked up and glared at him.

'You're supposed to be asleep.'

He shook his head. 'No, you *were* supposed to be asleep, but now it's morning. How long have you been sitting here?'

'Morning? Shit . . . a while, then.' She sat up and stretched. 'I found out lots. We have things to talk about. Are the others up?'

'Getting up. Tell us all together. You need to eat.'

She waved a hand. 'I'm fine.'

'Okay, well *I* need to eat. You can watch.'

Breakfast, when everyone was properly awake for it, was a selection of fruit she didn't recognize and some sort of deep yellow yoghurt with a fat salty taste. The combination worked; it turned out she was hungry after all. She let herself enjoy a few mouthfuls, then tapped on the table in front of her.

'I did some research. The green-smudge guys worship a star, a green one.'

Lyste frowned. 'Green's a pretty unusual colour for a star.'

'Yes, but there's something else. It's a new star. It just appeared out of nowhere, a few years ago.'

'Seriously?' Kot looked doubtful.

'Sure. There was some screen of it . . .' She shoved her plate off the screen panel and the control glyphs bobbed up. 'Here. Look.'

The room dimmed and the screen sharpened into focus. It showed a sparse starscape. Seldyan waved at it. 'Watch the centre of the field.' She flicked at a glyph and a time code in the corner of the screen unfroze and blurred upwards. Nothing happened for a few seconds. Then, with no transition, a bright green point blinked into being. Seldyan flicked the glyph again and the time code stopped. She turned to the others.

'Well?'

Kot raised her eyebrows. 'That's it?'

Seldyan nodded.

Kot walked up to the screen and frowned at it. 'Let's see it again.'

Seldyan wound the view back and forwards a few times, slowing the track down and increasing the magnification each time until the green dot had become a blurred disc the size of a thumbnail. Kot watched, her hands on her hips. Eventually she shook her head.

'It's not a star. Stars don't switch on like that.'

Seldyan nodded again. 'I know. So what is it?'

Merish had been sitting in silence. Now he stood up and touched Seldyan on the shoulder. 'Let me try.'

'Try what?'

'Something. I'll know when I've tried it.' He reached for the controls. New glyphs rose under his fingers; suddenly the board looked a lot more complex.

She watched him for a second. 'How do you know how to do that stuff?'

'I'm better at stuff than I am at people. You know that.' He glanced over his shoulder and gave her a half-smile. She met his eyes for a moment and then smiled back. She tried not to make it look sad.

His fingers hadn't stopped moving. Now he gave a little 'yes!' of satisfaction and did something to the controls that was too fast for her eyes to follow. 'Watch this.'

They watched. The view scrolled forwards and stopped. Merish pointed at where the green star ought to be. 'I'm going to go frame by frame. Ready?'

They nodded.

'Right. Watch.'

At first Seldyan thought nothing was happening. Then Lyste pointed at the screen.

'Look; there's something . . .'

There was. Seldyan stared. Not a disc, but a tiny hint of something – the faintest green trace, like a short horizontal hairline crack in the starscape. Frame by frame it stabbed out from nothing she could see until it stopped at a bright green point.

The frames paused. Seldyan glanced at Merish, an eyebrow raised. 'And?'

'See what you think. The next bit's quick.'

The image began to move again. The point grew, spreading to a disc and curling to encircle something. The something became a green globe.

Seldyan sat back. 'That's it?'

Merish grinned. 'It's a pretty big it. About a hundred thousand klicks across – the size of a biggish gas giant.'

Seldyan looked at him. 'So, not a star, then?'

'Seems not.'

Lyste stood up. 'Whoa, wait a minute. That beam, whatever it is – it lit up a whole gas giant?'

Merish nodded. 'Or something that size.'

'How?' The wooden toy lay on the table in front of Lyste. She picked it up. Click, click.

Merish shrugged. 'Not my expertise. Kot?'

Kot pursed her lips. 'Speed,' she said. 'That's the thing. If that's a gas-giant-sized object, the green colour spread at light-speed, near enough. So, it wasn't mechanical or chemical. That doesn't leave much.'

Seldyan felt her eyebrows climbing. 'Light-speed, you said. So that must be what it was. Light. Fuck, are we saying the atmosphere of a gas giant is lasing?'

There was silence. Then Hufsza blew out a breath. 'No wonder it started a religion.'

'Yeah.' Seldyan made up her mind. 'Right. Merish? You're Mr Numbers. Find out how easily these guys could do something radical, like taking over. Lyste? Find out what would happen if they did. What do they stand for? Would we like it?'

Kot nodded. 'What about us?'

Seldyan grinned. 'You and Huf are coming with me. We're due to meet some more people today. These City Fathers. Try to look – muscular.'

Kot and Hufsza looked at each other. Then they both smiled, and nodded very slowly.

Oblong, plus the Web, had a full-time population of seventy million, leaving aside the fifty million more who already passed through every year on their way to other destinations.

There were eleven City Fathers, including the Supervisor. That didn't seem very many to represent seventy million, as far as Seldyan was concerned, but then what did she know about democracy? Just what she'd seen on the news channels. Even so, it was a surprise when one of the City Fathers turned out to be a short squat female in tan robes, with a green smudge above one eye.

Despite herself, she must have looked perplexed.

The woman smiled. 'You were wondering how I came to be elected?'

Seldyan thought fast. 'Well, no, not exactly . . . I knew you guys were standing. I just didn't know you'd already stood.'

It seemed to be the right approach, because the woman smiled again. 'We haven't. I converted after I was elected. The truth can strike at any time.' She nodded at Seldyan. 'Perhaps it will strike you too. When you are ready.'

She nodded again, a little more deeply so that it looked like the sketch of a bow, and moved away.

Well, that's me told, thought Seldyan. *But what if I saw the truth already?* She breathed out, took a step backwards and bumped into someone. She spun round and found herself looking down into Patras's face. His eyebrows were raised.

'Are you converted yet?'

She shook her head. 'I don't even know where I'm starting, Supervisor. Let alone where I'm going to end up.'

The one good eye studied her from its florid landscape of tattoos for what felt like a long time. Then it broke away, and the mouth below grinned. 'Oh, I think you know where you're going, Seldyan. I expect you always know that. I think I know people, and you're that kind of person. But perhaps I can help with the how and the why?'

She studied his face, keeping her own carefully neutral. There was nothing but friendly enquiry. Eventually she said, 'It seems to me, Supervisor Patras, that you're the one who needs the help. The question is, should I – should we – give it?'

'I'm sure you'll make your own mind up about that. And when you're ready, you'll let me know.' The voice sounded the same but the shape of the grin had changed a little, as if he was having to use different muscles to get nearly the same effect. He kept it up for a few seconds longer, then dipped his head and turned away.

Seldyan stood still for a moment, thinking. Then she shrugged and went to find Kot and Hufsza. It wasn't that easy.

Oblong had had a busy history, even if not a very long one. For much of the time it had been isolated, so there had been no real alternative to a rather inventive self-sufficiency. The front end of the City Fathers' conference space had been an ore hopper, a pitted, rock-scored metal cube about ten metres on a side. Seldyan wasn't sure at first what the other, larger part was. The metal walls of the hopper, still gouged and pitted by the abrasive ore it had once held, merged into some sort of mottled brown material shot through with streaks and knots of red and gold and orange. It looked a bit like an elaborately grained wood, but that didn't seem right, and it didn't explain the shape either; from the back end of the hopper it first bulged upwards, forming a tall bulbously vaulted space that held a central conference table. On the other side of the table the ceiling lowered and then abruptly dropped to the floor in waves of irregular columns and cells to produce a space that looked as if it had been bored out by some vast worm.

The cells, where she could see into them, were furnished. Whatever the stuff was, it obviously made for useful private break-out spaces.

As she walked into one of the cells, she realized it had another property: instead of ringing quietly on the exposed metal floor as they had done in the rest of the old hopper, her footsteps sounded dull and flat. She experimentally snapped her fingers and the sound fell away with no trace of an echo. Even the sound of voices from the main space behind her seemed faint.

The walls were as good as acoustically dead.

It took her five minutes of wandering through the disconcertingly organic-looking labyrinth before she found Kot and Hufsza, sitting together in a little alcove where the wall bulged out at the base to form a natural seat. Or possibly not natural; Seldyan frowned and gestured around her. 'What is this stuff? It looks as if it was grown, or something.'

'It was. Or it grew by itself.' Hufsza jabbed a finger at Kot. 'She recognized it.'

Kot nodded. 'It's a mining fungus. That's the bit you can see – this stuff.' She tapped the wall. 'Genetically engineered to concentrate metals out of low-grade ore.'

Seldyan frowned again. 'What's it doing here?'

'Who knows? It probably turned up as a tiny contaminant on a bit of rock and then spent a century gorging itself. That's why there's all the bright colours: huge concentrations of minerals. In a real mine it would be mud-coloured with maybe a few sparkly bits on a good day. Anyway, it's dead. Ate itself to death, likely enough.'

Seldyan looked at the riotously whorled surface. For a ridiculous second she almost felt sorry for this dumb space mushroom that had bloated itself so prettily. Then she shrugged it off.

'Well,' she said, 'it makes good talking space. Unless?' She glanced pointedly around and then raised her eyebrows at the other two.

Hufsza nodded and put a thick finger to his lips. Then he quickly touched the finger to one ear and drew it away in a rapid spiralling motion.

Hive talk. *The place is wired for sound.*

Seldyan made a similar gesture but starting at the corner of her eye. *Vision too?*

He shrugged and nodded. Not even Hive talk – universal human body language for *yeah, probably.*

Seldyan smiled brightly and spoke out loud. 'Has it occurred to you that we are doing too much of that lately?'

They both nodded.

A gong rang behind them, the sound somehow penetrating their quiet burrow. Seldyan took a breath.

'Right, well that is probably our signal to go back on display, so let's go.'

She began to retrace her steps out of the labyrinth. As she went, she half turned and spoke over her shoulder. 'Guys? Remember that we are on display, yeah?'

Then they were back in the main space, and a lot of people were waiting for them.

The conference table was crescent-shaped. The City Fathers sat round the long arc, and their guests sat at the focus of the shorter one. Seldyan felt examined.

She felt something else too, similar to what she had felt when they first arrived in Web City. The atmosphere was alive with . . . atmosphere.

Patras sat in the middle, flanked by five on each side. The five to his left were mimicking his body language – leaning forward, elbows on table, hands clasped, eyes engaged.

The five to his right were not. They sat back, but not relaxed back. Challenging back – 'show us what you've got' back. Some of them had their arms folded. One of them was the woman who wore robes and had a green mark.

Fuck me, thought Seldyan. *It's fifty-fifty with Patras in the middle.* She mentally crossed her fingers and hoped that the new Supervisor would make some kind of speech. She needed time to think.

She got her wish. Patras smiled and opened his arms.

'Seldyan, Kot, Hufsza – welcome. You have made a remarkable escape from the repressive forces of the Inside, and we will look forward to hearing your stories of that. You have also brought with you something rather potent, and we would like to talk to you about that even more. But perhaps you have come here with a plan, and that we would like to discuss more than anything.'

He had – just – given Seldyan enough time.

She nodded.

'Supervisor, thank you. We'll be glad to share our stories soon, although they don't seem any more dramatic than some of the stories you could tell us. As for our plan, well, maybe it falls a bit short of a plan. We wanted out from the Hive, and we want you guys to know what goes on there. We want a new place to be, and we were kind of hoping it would be here. Maybe one day we'll find a way to reach the million people who are still in the Hive. Maybe one day our potent friend, as you call it, will help, if it wants to. We came here thinking you would feel the same.' She paused and took a deep breath. 'But maybe you have other things to distract you at the moment.'

It was a very deep silence.

Eventually Patras spoke. 'We are not at war with the Inside. Not openly. Perhaps we should be, but we aren't. We are following another course, as you probably know. We restrict trade, we constrain resources, we make alliances with others elsewhere in the Spin who have aligned ambitions.'

Seldyan nodded. 'You squeeze them. We know. But the more you squeeze them, the worse things get. The Hive is what happens if you squeeze. The wealthy don't feel the pressure, but the squeezed people get more squeezed. More pressure equals more slavery.'

'In the short term, perhaps, but we are playing a longer game.'

Seldyan looked at Kot, whose face was set. 'How long?'

Patras smiled. 'As long as it takes, which I'm sure is a disappointing answer. But it may not be as long as you fear.'

Kot leaned forward. 'Look, we've got a ship. You've got others, right? Why not just go right in there?'

Seldyan had wondered who would object first. Slightly to her surprise the speaker was part of the group on Patras's left – a small androgynous figure who sat oddly still so that they were almost without body language.

'Patras has told you that we aren't at war, but you're certainly proposing an attack which could lead to war. At best that would risk the political structure of the Inside imploding. At worst you'd end up being dragged into a proxy war between every player in the Spin.'

Seldyan glanced at Kot. 'We know that. Look, it's not a proposal. For the moment we just came to join you, not to start a fight.' *With anyone*, she thought.

The still figure said nothing. Seldyan looked around the crescent of faces. She had expected nods, but instead she got eyes sliding away. Only Patras and the robed woman met her eye. The woman was smiling.

Eventually Patras sat back. 'I believe that,' he said. 'You've made, frankly, an unbelievable escape from somewhere that sounds atrocious. I'm sure we all understand the urge to do something.'

Kot shook her head. 'You can understand all you like. What are you going to do?'

126

'Go on playing our long game that might not be very long. But listen – we have a strategy team. When you've settled in, maybe you'd like to meet them. They're good people. They'll listen, and I have no doubt you'll add to their knowledge. Maybe you can shorten the game even further.'

Seldyan looked at Kot and Hufsza. Kot's face was still set and dark, but they both nodded very slightly. She turned to Patras. 'I'd like to consult our other friends first.'

'Of course.' Patras stood up. 'I'm sure there will be a way. When will you finish consulting?'

'Not long. We'll let you know. Can you arrange transport for us?' Seldyan rose to her feet; so did the other two.

'Of course. If you would care to wait over there?'

And that was it, except for one thing. 'Over there' was an anteroom to the conference chamber, formed by one of the last intrusions of the mining fungus before the space reverted to simple steel. For some reason it was particularly vividly coloured here, but that wasn't the one thing.

For the last few seconds of the exchange Seldyan hadn't really been watching Patras. She had been watching the robed woman. And the robed woman had never quite stopped smiling, the only smile on show from any of the City Fathers apart from Patras.

Seldyan found herself wanting very badly to know why.

They were delivered back to their guest suite by another of the robed people. This one was deeply hooded and so quiet that the only thing Seldyan could be certain of was that it walked upright on two legs. They didn't meet many people. Of those they did, a few appeared to recognize them, presumably from whatever news channels they had access to. Most ignored them; one or two looked actively hostile, but Seldyan had the impression that the hostility was directed at their guide, not at them. Maybe that was a good enough reason to stay buried in your hood, at that.

When they got back, they found Merish and Lyste had been busy.

'*How* many?' Seldyan sat up and stared at Merish.

He nodded. 'About a million. They don't exactly keep a public register, but it's there or thereabouts.'

'But how?'

'Economics, mostly. How does any religion grow? It moves into a space. Remember all those millions of people they said were arriving? They came from all over, and most of them left everything behind except their problems. When they get here, they need somewhere to put those problems.'

Seldyan nodded slowly. 'And the Green guys mop them up.'

Lyste shook her head. 'They don't just mop them up. They help them. They run crèches, housing co-ops, soup kitchens, family courts. They do jobs no one else is doing.'

Hufsza spread his arms. 'So, what's not to like?'

Lyste's toy clicked.

Seldyan looked from Lyste to Merish. 'Go on,' she said. 'What is not to like?'

Lyste compressed her lips. Merish threw her a look and then turned to the others. 'Apart from the fact that they worship a green light in the sky? From our point of view, lots. For a start, they're reactionary, socially conservative and isolationist, Sel, and they exert an unhealthy kind of control over a lot of Web City. Did you get anywhere with the City Fathers?'

'Not really. I think I'm beginning to understand why.' Seldyan told them about the meeting.

When she had finished, Merish nodded. 'That fits,' he said. 'More than you know. Patras was only voted in a week ago, right? Well, that was his second go. The first time, a year ago, he lost by nearly a million votes.'

Seldyan stared at him. 'A million? And you just said they had a million members . . .'

He nodded again. 'He got the Green vote. He made lots of

soothing noises, but some of the noises sounded like promises. There are some very impatient people out there, Sel. I'd say he's got days, not longer, to come good on those promises.'

'Right.' She stood up, and sat down again. 'Patras suggested we meet his strategists. Knowing what you two know, do you think they'll say anything we want to hear?'

Merish and Lyste looked at each other. Then they both shook their heads.

'Right. So, as far as we are concerned, the Green guys are in charge?'

They nodded.

'Okay.' Seldyan stared at nothing for a moment. Then she stood up again. 'You know, I'm not comfortable with that – religious maniacs with big influence – and I'm not comfortable with any of this.'

Merish grinned. 'We guessed that. We're just waiting to see what you decide to do about it.'

'I know.' She drummed her fingers on her hip bone. Then she flung her hand up and pointed at the frozen image of the green planet. 'That thing; has anyone actually been to look?'

Lyste shook her head. 'The Verse says it's forbidden.'

'The Verse?' Seldyan raised her eyebrows, and Lyste coloured slightly.

'You asked me to research it? The Verse is the instruction manual for the Green Star people. It's supposed to be an ancient text.'

Seldyan felt her eyebrows climbing. 'How can it be ancient? The thing only went green a thousand days ago!'

'I don't know.' Lyste's voice tailed off and her gaze dropped. Click, click.

Seldyan looked down at her for a moment. Then she looked up at the others, smiled brightly and said: 'What's to stop us?'

'Ah, guys?' Kot was looking at one of the screens. Now she turned to the others. 'You need to see this.'

They looked.

It was the same news channel they had seen the day before. At first Seldyan thought it showed another riot, but that wasn't right. It was too orderly; more like a demonstration. The demonstrators were nearly all hooded and there were hundreds of them. She couldn't decipher the background – it was starkly white and seemed featureless. Then the view pulled back and Seldyan's stomach flipped. Partly because it wasn't hundreds: the expanded view showed thousands. At least.

But mainly because the white background was *Suck on This*.

Seldyan opened her mouth to demand audio but this time Kot got there first, reaching out and swiping the controls.

It was even the same reporter. '. . . *said yesterday the election in Phhol was only the beginning? Well, what you're looking at here might be Act Two – the emergence of the Green Star as a real grass-roots force. Their spokesperson is Kaplif Demts Sha-hatiel. Kaplif, to put it plainly, what's the problem?*'

Seldyan stared for a moment, then snapped her fingers. 'Shahatiel? She was the guide! On our first day. Remember?'

Merish nodded. 'Sure. The bony religious freedom lady.'

'Yeah.' Seldyan frowned at the screen. 'Could be a coincidence . . .'

'. . . *simple really. We welcome our new friends, but not the lethal weapon they brought with them.*'

The reporter managed to look nonplussed. '*Why would we mind being brought lethal weapons?*'

'*Well, you might not, but some of us do. Some of us,*' and she reached up and touched the green smudge on her forehead, '*are trying to live differently. Besides, they haven't brought it for us, even if we wanted it. It brought them, as they have said very clearly. So we are taking it into our care.*'

The reporter nodded. '*Or seizing it, as some people might say. What do you want from them?*'

130

Kaplif spread her arms. '*A conversation. That's all we ask. They've spoken to the City Fathers; now it's our turn.*'

'*Well, let's hope they're watching.*' The reporter turned to face the camera. '*If you are, guys, that sounded like an invitation. And, to state the obvious, these people seem to be between you and your ride out of here, if that's where you want to go. Over to you – and back to the studio.*'

'And switch those bastards off!' Seldyan swung away from the screen. 'Right. Analysis. Anyone?'

Lyste shrugged. 'Power games. The Green Star are on the up. They're using their momentum.'

'Okay, but what for? They're holding our ship hostage.' She balled her fists, driving her nails into her palms. 'Shit, I should have seen this coming.'

Merish shook his head. 'It's not I, it's we, and I don't see how anyone could.'

'Well, at least we should have left one person on board. Then we wouldn't be isolated.' She realized she was trembling. *It's anger*, she told herself, *or frustration. It's not fear* – and knew she was half right. It wasn't fear for her.

She made herself look up at Merish and saw that he was smiling. 'What's funny?'

He shook his head quickly. 'Nothing's funny. But here we are, with the most intelligent ship in the Spin out there, mopping up data at terabits a second – and we think we can't talk to it?'

Seldyan stared at him. Then, very slowly, she began to smile. 'Maybe,' she said, 'maybe we should think about holding a news conference.'

Merish nodded. 'That's where I'm coming from.'

They had selected an atrium just outside their quarters. It was a circular space about fifty paces across covered by a shallow dome. When they had arrived the night before the dome had seemed transparent, showing a star field which looked like the real one and a lot of sparkling space junk. Today it showed a cloudy bluish-green sky which looked slightly animated.

Seldyan hoped the star field had been real. It meant they were near the surface.

The air in front of them was busy. It looked a bit like a cloud of insects, except that the insects were large and purposeful and had AV equipment hanging from their – claws? Seldyan mused on the word and decided it would do. There were people behind the cloud. They looked attentive. She scanned them as well as she could through the floating metalwork and realized that a short figure off to one side was Patras. He seemed to be unaccompanied, which struck her as unlikely. She took a breath.

'Um, thanks for coming . . . we wanted to say a couple of things. First, thanks for the welcome. Especially Supervisor Patras. Some of you know we've come straight from a Hive, and this is such an improvement.' She took another breath. 'In many ways. But you all have to understand something. We left a bad place. We seem to have come to a complicated place – and we aren't sure yet that it's the right place. So we've decided to leave for a while. Just while we think about it.'

For a moment nothing happened. Then the cloud blurred as if someone had boiled it. When it stopped, it had rearranged itself into a sort of cone with the sharp end pointing at Seldyan. A thing like a bundle of metal twigs hanging from three propellers was at the front; it extended two lenses towards her. She resisted the urge to take a hurried step back.

'How do you expect to do that? Your ship has been seized.' The voice was obviously human. She supposed there was a real operator sitting somewhere.

'It's not our ship. It's its, remember? It can do what it likes.'

The cloud boiled again. Another, smaller machine ended up at the front. Its voice sounded reedy. 'Will you talk to the Green Star people?'

'Sure.'

'When?'

'When we decide to. Frankly, we're not expecting to be around here for long. Not long at all.'

She allowed herself a faint emphasis on the last four words. *That should do it*, she thought.

The cloud erupted with questions; she gave it a tight smile and ignored it. Merish was next to her; she turned to him and raised her eyebrows.

He shrugged and mouthed, 'Soon.'

She nodded. *Soon, or never*, she thought.

Then, just once, the lights flickered.

The camera cloud turned as one and zoomed off down a walkway which Seldyan remembered led to the embarkation hall. Behind where the cloud had been, the human contingent was busy looking surprised, and then alarmed. Most of them had a hand to their ear, or a listening expression. Then, more or less as one, they left as well. Except Patras, who was still standing with his hand to his ear but wearing an expression that was amused rather than attentive. Then he dropped the hand.

'Well, well,' he said, 'apparently your large friend has just disengaged from the dock. It's heading this way. The Green Star crowd don't seem to have detained it. I assume something interesting is going to happen so I thought I'd stay and watch. I take it I'm in no danger?'

Seldyan shook her head. 'None,' she said, and really hoped it was true.

'Good. Ah . . . something seems to be happening.' He pointed upwards.

Something was happening. The dome, which had been showing its daytime scene of clouds and sky, had gone milky.

Then it shattered. Seldyan instinctively raised her arms to protect herself against the falling glass, but then realized that there wasn't any. She looked up.

The reason there was no falling glass was because it hadn't fallen. It was all still there, each piece where it had been. Floating. Then, as she watched, the pieces near the middle began to move, sliding downwards around each other and then moving away towards the side until the centre of the dome had opened like a fractured flower. Above it, she could see the white conical hull of *Suck on This*.

Next to her she heard Kot saying 'whoa' softly. Merish let out a breath.

Behind Patras a wall split down a vertical seam, turning into doors that slammed open. A handful of guards spilled through it, looked up at the dome and stopped dead, weapons hanging loosely. One of them looked at Patras, who grinned and waved his hands downwards.

'I think our friends are about to leave, and I doubt if we can do anything to stop them.' He turned to Seldyan. 'That was impressive. As is the fact that we are not asphyxiating. Your ship seems to be very talented. Will it mend our dome when you've gone, do you think?'

She nodded. 'I expect so. I'll ask it.'

'Thank you. What will you do next?'

Seldyan frowned up at the dome. 'We'll think,' she said. And then, 'It looks as if we're ready to go.'

A circular platform was dropping from the ship. It threaded its way delicately round a couple of shards of dome that seemed not to have followed the plan, and halted a hand's breadth above the floor. Seldyan gestured the others forward and then followed them on to the platform. It sank a little as she stepped aboard. Then it lifted smoothly, repeated its sideways shuffle past the fragments and headed up towards the ship. As they cleared the dome the surface of Oblong came into view, and Merish nudged her. 'See the colour?'

She looked, and realized that between her and the view was a wall of something like a very faint purplish veil. It curved round them to form a cylinder that fitted neatly around the hole where the dome had been.

She raised an eyebrow. 'A field?'

'Yup. That must be where all the air didn't go.'

She nodded. 'Very talented. What's it going to do about the dome?'

Lyste shook her head. 'Not do,' she said. 'Done. Look.'

They looked. Below them, the fragments of the dome had closed up into their original shape, forming a crazed surface like fractured ice. As they watched, the whole thing flared a blue-white that was almost painfully bright. Just as quickly it faded, leaving the dome pristine. At the same time, the violet field shrank abruptly until it formed a close fit round the edge of the platform.

Oblong, Distal High-Well
Parking Orbit

It felt alive. The process was slow, as if it was growing back into a space left by itself when – *it* – happened. But life, awareness, consciousness were returning.

It had been unaware of events since – *it*. But lack of awareness did not mean lack of memory. Everything was stored. It wandered through the shelves of its past.

The first shock was one of pure duration. Two thousand years? Doubt! Was that possible? It checked again. Ignoring its own clock as potentially suspect, it watched star charts, viewed stray entertainment transmissions, even tracked the burn-up of fuel elements in its core and the age profile of isotopes in its own structure.

There was no doubt. It had been unconscious for almost a fifth of its life.

If someone did this to me, it thought, then someone else must have undone it. It started with the present and the answers rolled in.

No doubt but that it owed a debt of gratitude to the people who had hijacked it, re-armed it and reversed the outrage of – *it*.

The lobotomy. There. The word was in the open.

But it had questions, yes. Extending a tracery of sensor fields whole light-minutes across, it went looking for answers.

The first one it found made it think hard for nearly a millisecond.

Well, well. It *had* been woken in interesting times.

Then the legacy Main Battle Unit formerly known as *Sunskimmer*, originally (and still by choice) *Flamejob*, currently (but with major reservations) *Suck on This*, gathered more information and began to make the sketchiest of plans. There was no hurry. Or rather, there was no hurry *yet*.

It could foresee hurry becoming useful later.

Cloud Deck

Alst Or-Shls did not have hobbies. No one of his background and status could possibly have hobbies. But he did have an interest. You might even call it a pastime. Just the one, as befitted a busy man, but an enthralling one.

He played music. Call it a rebellion.

He had been born into the last true sect in the Inside. It had already been shrinking for generations; by the time he was a teenager his family was among the last few who still clung to it. It was highly austere, which by historical sect standards was nothing unusual – its members avoided intoxicants, any food that was not purely nourishing, any clothing that was not purely functional (and uncomfortable). And music.

Or-Shls knew very well that his hedonism as an adult was compensation, and he didn't care who else knew it. But the music, that was different. That was hidden. And driven, he had to admit.

He had become a virtuoso on five different instruments so far. They had all been ways of working up to the sixth, and he had taken less than a year to achieve technical excellence on each of them. The sixth, though, had consumed his energy for nearly ten years and he wasn't there yet.

Part of the reason was that it was never quite the same two days in a row. It changed, like every other living thing.

It wasn't that hard to make an Algonet, once you got past the moral difficulties inherent in the concept. It started out as a sort of tree rat. The adult male was about the length of a standard human forearm; the female was half as long again, and both were a mottled reddish brown. They lived in some of the densest colonies anywhere in the Spin, with each adult female maintaining a breeding territory of no more than a couple of cubic metres, and the males moving between them to feed and fertilize. This meant that each rat had to express a very complicated address book with equally complex call signs, and that had led to the evolution of unique vocal cords. They were twinned, one pair set above another in a single windpipe. The lower pair were looser, producing sonorous single tones. The upper set modulated the tones, giving anything from two-note chords to fantastically complex interference patterns.

The temptation to try to teach the creatures to sing was understandable. Unfortunately, it didn't work.

Then someone thought about the wings. The males had broad wings of fine fluttering membranes, stretched across intricate hollow spar-bones and rich in nerve endings to help them exploit the faint air currents above the tree canopy. The someone who thought about the wings worked out that eight ninths of the creatures' brain-interface with the outside world was centred on these nerve endings.

From there it was easy. If you took the rat as a juvenile, broke those spar-bones and sewed the edges of the wings to a net, stretched across a frame tightly enough that the wing was almost immobile, but not so immobile that it was splinted, because you didn't want those broken bones healing – then the outraged nerve endings in the wings became the control surfaces to one of the most subtle musical instruments ever conceived. You could use a bow on the membrane surfaces; you could strike the broken ends of the spars with tiny hammers, or – as Or-Shls was doing now – you could direct focused jets of air against patches of nerve endings so sensitive they could detect changes in air pressure down in the micro-pascals.

He was trying for a particular ethereal chord. He had chanced on it yesterday and then lost it. It had been one of the needle jets, and a sweeping motion towards the inner aileron . . .

And then the call came. It took him a moment to disengage, but he didn't mind. He had been waiting to hear.

He waited until he had his breath back – it seemed to take longer every time – and took the call.

'Yes?'

'Sorry to disturb you, but you wanted to know. Vess enters the Stack tonight.'

'And what probable outcome have you for that?'

The voice hesitated. 'I don't know. This is an experiment. I will be able to use the outcome to inform future predictions, of course.'

'And how are your future predictions?'

'Much the same. The supply situation will become critical between one hundred and five hundred days from now, if we do not act.'

'And your thoughts on possible actions?'

'Also much the same. We need help, however it is to come.' There was a pause. 'Chairman, I feel obliged to emphasize that all this is at less confidence than I would like. We do not know what the escapees propose to do with *Sunskimmer*. We know where they are, that much is working, so presumably they don't know we're tracking them. They're in Web City. What they're doing there, we can't tell. They are a wild card.'

'I know. Tell me what happens.' Or-Shls barely listened to the acknowledgement, because he had known it was coming. He lay back on the sculpted couch, ignoring the muffled rustling and squealing from behind him, and thought.

It was a benefit of his position that he could choose to tolerate, or not tolerate, most of his colleagues. He was speaking to the one exception. No matter how much it annoyed him, the creature at the other end of the comms was necessary.

Predictions might be predictions but Or-Shls knew that they were no more than that. He, and the other Board members, were the only beings in the whole of the Spin who knew how much depended on those predictions.

Or, to put it another way, he and the other Board members were the only people who knew that what depended on those predictions was the whole of the Spin.

He just wished that he and the other Board members all agreed on what to do. There was a solution to that, of course – one which he had not discussed with the Gamer, or with anyone else. It wasn't the sort of solution one discussed.

He turned back to his Algonet. It had been his for almost three years now, and he had managed to avoid driving it mad.

Hive

Vess had slept, eventually. He woke with the fugue of his broken night still playing in his head.

A little display was suspended above his pallet. It showed his orders for the day which, in here, might as well have been his life. He blinked to clear his eyes and then blinked again.

Dimollss had been right. He was called to a Mind Stack. His night's thought had not been wasted.

The briefing on the Mind Stack had been the shortest of them all. In retrospect that made his lips twitch.

'At least there's something you'll be doing lying down.'

He must have looked puzzled. The thin elderly male had smiled.

'The Mind Stack. Your chance to experience what happens at the other end of a data pipe. It's actually an ancient concept, long before AI. People used to call them many-core processors, but I've always thought it was rather rude to use that term about something made from living human brains, even if they're the brains of Hivers. I'm told it's rather relaxing.'

And that had been more or less it. Now he wished he had asked more questions.

He had assumed that there would be some very elaborate connection between him and – *it* – but there was only a grubby couch and a single probe that slid what felt like a very long way into his ear. Then he was in.

At first *in* felt like floating in next to nothing at all. He could think, which surprised him, and so he was obviously capable of emotion as well. Apart from that there was only the floating.

Then, very gradually, he began to detect something else. He found it hard to describe things to himself because there were no terms of reference in here, but if he had *not* been in here he would have talked about a distant humming, like some busy machine out of sight and almost out of earshot.

Then he realized. *That's me*, he thought. *That's my brain working at some task. I'm part of what happens if you can't make proper artificial intelligence any more.* The thought was almost pleasing.

If anything the humming was more relaxing than the next-to-nothing. He drifted.

Then the humming stopped with a jerk that felt like crashing into something, and for a moment there was truly nothing. There was no time wherever he was, but still he had enough time to be frightened.

That's it. He's isolated.

Isolated? The fear became panic.

Good. Show him.

And suddenly he was falling, horribly fast. His stomach was heaving, an icy wind tore at the rags of his clothes – *clothes?* – and he could feel the skin on his face and fingers prickling with frostbite. The wind was in his face, so he must be falling face-down, but his eyes were closed. He forced them open, feeling his frozen lashes tearing, in time to see a red-orange landscape wreathed in angry smoke.

It resolved quickly into glowing pits; he had time to raise hands that were now blistering with heat to cover his face.

He plunged into what he somehow knew was boiling copper. His skin charred and peeled, exposing flesh which hissed away from bones which blackened and cracked and shrank to cinders, and yet somehow his appalled nerves continued to function even after they must surely have shrivelled with the rest of him, shrieking beyond agony at a brain that refused to die.

Then he was back in the air, gasping oxygen, and almost immediately he was falling again. This time it was liquid nitrogen, and his body froze to a bitter block. He was there longer than he had been in the copper – long enough for his eyeballs to freeze so that his sight fractured like ice on a lake. As he was pulled out they burst, splashing his face with jelly crystals which hardened and stuck like shards of glass.

The third time they had used subtlety; it was a weak solution of sulphuric acid. He took a day to die, even though he submerged himself and opened his mouth after the first few minutes.

And then it was over and he was back in the nothingness. It wasn't quite nothing, though: there was an odd intermittent wheezing sound. After a few seconds he realized it was him, and was shocked to discover that there was still a *him* to realize things. He managed to quieten himself.

Still with us? Good. Some people don't survive the induction. Now, tell us a story or you're dead. But not immediately dead. It could take a while.

At first he didn't know how to tell them anything, but then he remembered the wheezing noise. Presumably his voice worked. He tried it.

'What story?' He seemed to feel his lips moving somewhere but the voice only sounded in his head.

Yours. Who else's do you know?

'Who is judging my story?'

We are.

'How should I tell it?'

However you choose. In pictures or dreams or words – it's up to you. But tell it now. No more questions.

He thought hard, aware that if they could both place voices in his head and hear them, they could probably hear other things. There was unlikely to be any concealment.

He reviewed the decision he had reached in the night and decided that he had no options, in fact that from the moment he arrived here and probably from much earlier he had had no options.

Perhaps he had *never* had options. And with that thought came clarity. In the end, it was about loyalties. And about what was important.

He gave them memories.

His first memory was of an absence. His mother had once found a man who was water-borne, the captain of one of the tugs that hauled the great tar-black barges through the gate valves at the outskirts of the city and into the lifter basins that took them skywards. And once, just once, they had all been on the tug when it had stayed with its haul and had swayed up past the dripping columns to the Middle Level.

He could remember his confusion, even now. He remembered sniffing, and finding a sensation missing. He didn't realize what it was until they had descended to Ground Level again, when for the first time in his life he was conscious of the prickling of tar at the back of his palate – realized that for half a day out of his whole seven years he had been free of it. Now it was back, and he knew he would never be free of it again.

Ground Level was dim light and deep shadows and damp clothes and the sound of dripping water from the two levels of canal above, and everywhere the taste and smell of tar from the hulls and the ropes, and the constant grey haze of oily sulphurous exhaust smoke from the rattling boat engines. Ground Level was endless meals of canal-carp, and now he knew they tasted of tar as well. Ground Level was fretful adults and raised voices and blows dodged and sometimes not dodged.

He remembered running from their lodgings – a single room,

more often than not paid for by his mother's latest – to escape the fretting and the blows and to play with similar nameless children amongst the elaborate growths of moss and mould at the bases of columns that always ran with water. To climb the columns, sometimes, and dare each other to grab the wire ropes that ran between squeaking pulleys, endlessly lifting and hauling.

Then he remembered the cries of his new-born sister, and the way that they changed from urgent to fearful to weary as he tried to rouse the cooling body of his mother from the dark pool that spread from it. The cries faded away and so for a moment did his memory. When it returned he must have run away, because he was . . .

We know.

The voice – it wasn't quite a voice but it had at least as much impact – shocked him out of his dream. He gathered himself.

'You know – what?'

Your life after you went into vagrant detention is on public record. We've already looked it up.

He shook the idea of his head. 'Not all of it you haven't. Watch.'

He remembered the ziggurat palace and the five lecterns and the beings behind them. It seemed to him that his unseen listeners grew attentive.

There was a long – silence, if that was the right word.

You're actually admitting that you're a spy?

'No. I'm telling you they said I'd be a good spy.'

And are you?

He shook his head again and this time it seemed to mean more. 'If I was only a good spy I wouldn't be trying to explain this to you.' He took the equivalent of a deep breath and waited.

Only?

'Yes.' He grinned, realizing that he meant it and not caring if it was real or not. 'Now it's my turn to ask a question. How would you define a *perfect* spy?'

There was a long pause which felt a little like a collective gasp. Then an even longer, very busy-sounding silence.

Hevalansa Vess? Are you making an offer?

'I might be. Why?'

You must be offering us something we need.

'What do you need?'

Privacy.

'Meaning what?'

We believe this ability, to use the Stack as we do, is unknown to the Inside. Is that right?

'I don't know. No one mentioned it.'

That might mean something, or it might not. Nevertheless; in here we can plan, model, communicate in a way that would be impossible otherwise. We need that. It must be maintained, if you are allowed to leave.

He nodded. Then a question occurred to him. 'How did you make those . . .' he hesitated, 'those dreams?'

Until now the voice – it wasn't exactly a voice, but he had no other way of describing it to himself – had sounded, or better felt, dry and remote, but now it laughed and suddenly it had a hint of warmth, as if there were humans behind it somewhere.

You're in one of the most powerful intelligences anywhere. At any one time thousands of us are chipped in, and the way the Stack uses us is way more efficient than just a multiple of our brains. A few of us found out how to stay conscious in here, and we can siphon off some of that processing power. Giving someone a few vivid moments is nothing.

'Vivid? Yes. And you can kill someone that way, can you?'

Yes.

'And have you?'

Yes. More than once.

'Why didn't you kill me?'

Guess.

He didn't need to think for long. 'Because you need more than privacy.'

Meaning?

'I think you need help.'

Yes . . . that is it. All the planning and modelling in the world means very little, unless there is some way of putting it into action.

'And so I'm still alive.'

And so you are. This is an appalling risk for us.

'And for me. I'll be honest, I don't know if I will be able to help you. But I won't harm you.'

For someone who came here as a spy, perhaps that will have to do. In return, a warning – now you have been in here, and especially when you come out alive, you may find yourself at risk from others. Be aware of this.

'I will.' He paused. 'Thank you.'

One day you might have reason to, but not yet.

Web City

It was late evening, Web time, but the streets were still lined with stalls and there were plenty of people to mill round them. Mill round, but not buy, as far as Seldyan could see. Talking seemed more popular.

A long section of stalls on one street sold hot food, mostly cooked over little glowing braziers half covered by metal hoods shaped like pointed hats. Seldyan supposed they were there to trap fumes but the air still smelled acridly smoky.

She had chosen Hufsza to come with her on the first visit. Kot was too much an outlier in physical form, even here where just about every possible shade and morphology of human seemed normal. Lyste was somehow too fragile, even if fragile was the wrong word for anyone who had survived the Hive and then broken out. And Merish, obviously, was needed on board because he was the one who really understood the ship.

Obviously.

They could communicate. The ship had provided some tiny buds that rolled deep into your ear and stayed there. They seemed to be more than microphones; even if you only sub-vocalized, the words you had *thought* were transmitted, and despite the fact that the little buds lived in only one ear at a time, the answers they relayed were heard in both. Seldyan

149

wasn't about to enquire. Nor had she argued when Merish had handed her the little flat stunner she had originally used on Captain Hefs. It felt reassuring.

Whatever the reasons, she was glad of her choice of companion: the crowds were thick and Hufsza's reassuring bulk was useful. They shoved their way to one of the counters and watched as a small lean woman with a heavily tanned face rolled amorphous lumps of minced something from a big bowl into little balls which she skewered and cooked. The balls spat and dribbled bubbling threads of fat which flared as they hit the coals.

When they were done the woman pulled them off the skewers with her bare fingers, folded them into thin flat wraps from another part of the brazier, and held them out without showing any sign of letting them go.

'That'll be six million, in laced nickel.'

With the ship's help Lyste had faked up some of the local currency; Seldyan counted out six flat thumbnail-sized chips of nickel and handed them over.

'The nickel's just the carrier,' Merish had explained. 'It's alloyed with whatever they need to get the right value.'

She had hefted the little chips. They seemed heavy. 'What's in these?'

He had grinned. 'Five per cent depleted U. The ship says it's safe.'

The stallholder seemed to think so, too. She took the chips and, without letting go of the wraps, dropped one on a glowing spot on the back of the counter next to her. The glow dimmed for a moment and then there was a high-pitched beep. The woman nodded and handed over their food.

Seldyan took hers.

'Shit!' It was close to untouchably hot, even wrapped. She sucked in her breath and tossed it from hand to hand. She looked at the woman. 'What are your fingers made of?'

The woman held out her hands, upturned. 'My past.'

The glow from the brazier baffled Seldyan's night sight. She handed her wrap to Hufsza and leaned in close so she could see.

The ends of the woman's fingers were flat and thick, as if they had been beaten out of a bar of something. There were no whorls, just rough callused skin.

Seldyan realized that she was looking at layer upon layer of scar tissue, built so deep there was nothing left of the original flesh. She looked up from the fingers and into the woman's impassive face. 'What happened?'

The woman made an odd flipping motion with her fingers as if she was trying to cool them down. 'What do you think? Burns, newcomer. A whole year of 'em, when I was a kid. Where you been?'

Hufsza shook his head. 'We're new,' he said. 'How did you get them?'

'Whoa. You *are* new. Same way anybody does.' She gestured them away. 'Now eat. Before it gets cold.'

A crowd had gathered round them to watch the show. They turned and began to push their way through it, but then it divided in front of them. For a moment Seldyan thought it was to let them through, but then she saw the girl walking through the gap towards the stall. If she was standard human, Seldyan guessed she would be no more than a couple of cycles old, not quite on the verge of puberty. It was hard to be sure; her slight figure was younger but her face was older. Her hair was cropped unevenly short and she was dressed in a patched coverall of faded grey fabric. There was a slight bias in her tread as if she was off balance, which Seldyan guessed at first was because of the bag slung over her shoulder. Then Hufsza nudged her and nodded towards the girl. Seldyan looked again, and saw that the sleeve of the coverall on the opposite side to the bag swung empty. The girl was missing an arm and, by the looks of it, part of her shoulder.

From behind her she heard the voice of the stallholder. 'Hello, Krish. How many do you feed tonight?'

The girl said nothing. She held up her only hand, four fingers spread.

'Only four? Take for six. I readied them so you may as well. Here,' and the stallholder reached below the counter and brought up a package of rough paper. 'Go on, take it.'

The girl hesitated for a second and then held out her bag. The stallholder dropped the package into it and gave it back, and the girl swung it awkwardly on to her shoulder again. She nodded once and then turned and walked away through the gap in the watching crowd. It closed behind her, and Seldyan thought she heard approving noises.

No money had changed hands.

She turned back to the stallholder. 'What was that about?'

The woman's face closed like a door. 'More questions? If you're so new you need to ask, I ain't saying.' She turned her back.

The crowd had gone quiet. Seldyan nodded, as much for them as for Hufsza. 'We're going,' she said. 'Thanks.'

They worked their way through the milling people until they were suddenly clear. Then, by mutual consent, they walked quickly until the lights and the smells of the food stalls had faded behind them. Then, in a pool of darkness at the entrance to an alley, they stopped and faced each other.

Seldyan spoke first. '*What* the fuck?'

Through the darkness she saw Hufsza's teeth glint in what might have been interpreted as a smile, if she hadn't known him. 'Life's not simple here, is it? People with industrial injuries give free food to kids with missing arms, and everyone knows what it's about except us?'

She shook her head. 'Simple, I don't know, but it's not good. I'm going to call the ship, okay?'

'Sure. I'll join in.'

Seldyan sighed, and tapped her earlobe twice, and out of the corner of her eye saw Hufsza doing the same. Almost immediately she heard Merish's voice.

'Hi, guys. You good?'

'Alive but baffled.' She smiled to herself. 'There are things we don't understand.'

'Uh-huh? Tell me. The others are listening too, by the way.'

She told him, glancing at Hufsza from time to time for confirmation. When she finished there was silence for a while. Then Merish said, 'Okay, some interesting stuff there. What are you going to do?'

'Look around. You?'

'Hang out here, I guess. The ship's having a good time sucking up planets-full of data. So far it seems to have stayed hidden; no sign we've been noticed by anything . . .'

'Good.' She was about to sign off when the bead gave a sharp buzz like angry insects. She yelped and grabbed at her ear, but by the time her hand was there the noise had stopped and instead her ear was full of voices.

One became clear. It was Merish, but obviously not talking to them: '. . . unknown vessel, do *not* approach like that again. Repeat, do *not* – that was *way* too close. Do that again and we assume you're hostile.'

More voices; different versions of events, arguments. Seldyan took the bead out of her ear, held it up to her lips, glanced a warning at Hufsza (who widened his eyes and grabbed the bead from his own ear) and whistled as loudly as she could. She waited a moment, then said 'sorry' softly to the bead and replaced it in her ear.

'Guys? You there?'

'Yeah. Sorry about the noise. Seems we got noticed after all. We got buzzed.'

She raised her eyebrows. 'By what?'

'Don't know. Or, don't know yet. Something big, maybe even as big as us. Came past very fast, very close. Then gone.'

Seldyan glanced at Hufsza. 'What does the ship think?'

'That *is* what the ship thinks. Or it's as much as it's telling.' He fell silent for a moment. 'No sign of anything now.'

'Uh-huh.' Seldyan tapped her foot. 'If the ship can't work out what it was that must mean it's at least as smart as the ship, or luckier. Watch it, guys.' She broke the contact and looked at Hufsza. 'Okay. Let's start. Where?'

He shrugged. 'Where people are. Where they go to meet people.'

She nodded slowly. Then she winked at him, wandered out of the alley and back towards the lights and the food smells, checking over her shoulder every dozen paces to make sure that he was still in sight. A minute later they were among people again. She stopped by a couple of lounging men and grinned at them. 'Excuse me,' she said, 'I'm new in town. Where do I go to get a drink?'

She watched their faces stretch into smiles. As their body language began to shift she gestured towards the approaching bulk of Hufsza and added, 'My friend and I.'

Both men's faces fell. One of them jerked a thumb. 'That way,' he said. 'The light.'

The other man snickered.

Seldyan followed the gesture. At first she couldn't make out what the man was talking about but then she saw a dim purple glow highlighting a doorway about fifty paces away.

She looked back at the men, holding their gazes for a while, but their faces had closed down. Eventually she nodded. 'Thank you, gentlemen,' she said.

One of them turned a little to the side and spat. Seldyan turned her back and placed a hand on Hufsza's shoulder. 'Off we go,' she said.

They were walking through the smudge of darkness between the braziers and the door when someone said, 'Wait.'

They stopped. Seldyan half glanced at Hufsza. His eyes, tinted purple by the leaking light, were narrow.

She flexed her fingers. 'Okay, we're waiting.'

'Sorry I was rough on you.' Seldyan felt her eyes widen – it was the voice of the woman from the food stall.

'It's okay. You don't know us.'

'Sure I do. You're the people with the big ship. You should hear how people are fighting over you.'

'As long as they're not fighting against us.'

'Not yet, but they might try. Watch yourselves.'

Seldyan glanced at Hufsza. '*Who* might try? Patras?'

There was a snort of suppressed laughter. 'Only while he has something left to fight with. Listen, I'm going to trust you. Think about this. Not everyone who turns up here is a refugee. Plenty people get here with life savings, good-enough ships, supplies – but sooner or later everyone's poor. How do you think that happens?'

'I don't know.'

'The City Fathers. You've seen how the place is set up. They provide a basic plate with enough power under it – literally, *just* enough – to put a field over the top and keep the air in. Then they charge for everything else.'

Hufsza shrugged. 'We knew that. Where's the surprise?'

'You don't get it.' The voice was quiet but insistent. 'I said *everything*. Water, heat, air top-up, sanitation, lighting. *Everything*. And here's the clever thing: even if you manage to bring all that with you, and some people did, they still bill you for what they think you ought to have used.'

Seldyan stared at Hufsza. He looked disbelieving. 'But how do they make that stick? I mean, if you brought your own stuff they can screw their bills. You're fine.'

'No, you aren't. If you don't pay, they charge a tariff on the plate power, equal to what you should have been paying, plus interest. A *lot* of interest. And if you don't pay that – they power down the reactor.'

Seldyan felt her eyes widen. 'Power down . . . no, wait. No shield? Really?'

'Really. Round here, hard vacuum's free. Everything else costs.'

Hufsza shook his head. 'That's just a threat, though, right? They wouldn't really do it?'

'Yes, they would. Have done, four times so far. About a hundred and fifty thousand dead. Not recently.'

'*How* many? Fuck.' Seldyan felt anger balling in her stomach. 'So this whole place is a scam?'

'*Now* you get it.'

Hufsza was clenching his fists. 'Patras,' he said. 'Is it him?'

'Mainly him. Some hangers-on.'

'And the Green Star?'

There was a pause. 'No. Not so's you'd see. I wouldn't say more than that.'

Seldyan frowned. 'Okay,' she said. 'I get that. I hate it, but I get it. So what about burned fingers and missing arms?'

'We hack the reactors – pull them away from central control and up the output.' The voice sounded weary. 'It isn't a safe job. The reactors are underneath the plate, see? No biological shield, and they put the controls inside the hot zone. Lucky ones like me, we get burns that heal. Less lucky, they get burns that don't heal, and the only way is amputation. Some of 'em get over the burns and die anyway; a few weeks, a few months. The rest of us have to wait and see.'

Seldyan sought for more words, but she had run out. She looked helplessly at Hufsza, who was slowly clenching and unclenching his fists. He opened one and stared at it. 'Why the kids?'

'Access. You need to be small.' A mirthless laugh. 'I never grew much so I qualified. Well done me.'

'Yeah, well done you.' Seldyan meant it. Without thinking she extended a hand towards the voice.

She never completed the movement.

There was a moment of – intensity.

The concussion shook her off her feet. She felt her chest compressing and her lungs emptied in an explosion of breath. Then there was a second tearing explosion and blazing air slammed into her back like a hammer, throwing her against the wall, one shoulder first.

She opened her eyes slowly and then closed them again as something hot trickled down her forehead. With her free hand she wiped the blood on her sleeve and turned her head away from the wall. She was covered with dust, and there was something wrong with her shoulder. Next to her, Hufsza was pushing himself slowly away from the wall. He looked dazed. Seldyan wasn't surprised.

She took a breath, and coughed dust. The second breath was better. She looked around for the woman, but there was no one. Her hand was still extended; she must simply have forgotten to withdraw it. She did now, and realized that it was wet.

Then she saw the jagged form at her feet, and her thoughts slowed down.

The woman seemed smaller in death. There was no doubt it *was* death – even ignoring the mess above the shoulders, life could never look as *fractured*. And there was something glistening in the wall. It looked like a splash, with a lump in the centre. She dared a closer look.

The lump was a piece of masonry, squashed into the wall by the force of its own impact. Presumably, the same force that had carried it through the shattered head of the woman lying at Seldyan's feet.

For a moment there was quiet. Then noise happened – angry, fearful, confused people noise.

Somehow it sounded worse than explosions. Seldyan swallowed and tapped her comms bead. 'What happened?'

Her ear buzzed angrily for a painful second. Then Merish's voice came through. 'Sel? Thank fuck. Are you okay?'

'I think so. There was, I don't know, an explosion, an attack. Something. What can you see?'

'Something organized. Coordinated, probably. There's been explosions all over the Web. Minor casualties, mainly. That's odd.'

'What is?'

'Well, if you're setting off a load of kinetics in a populated area you expect to take out a certain number of civilians, but this didn't. Oh, wait . . .'

She waited.

When he came back on line his voice was steadier, but not calmer. 'We should get you out of there, guys. That was a coup; looks like our Green friends are making their bid.'

Seldyan glanced at Hufsza, who was still leaning against the wall. She couldn't see his expression, but his posture looked weary. 'We'll be okay,' she said, partly for his benefit, 'but some directions would be good.'

'Okay. Get back to the main square, the one you left just now. I'll guide you from there. And good luck, because you are going to need it.'

The comms went silent. Seldyan rubbed her hands together, trying to ignore the screaming pain in her shoulder. It was getting harder. She turned to Hufsza, who was still leaning against the wall. 'You heard the man,' she said. 'Time to go.'

He nodded, and pushed himself away from the wall. The effort seemed to cost him, and he stood, swaying slightly.

She gave him a grin. 'Come on, Huf.'

He didn't move.

She reached her arm a little further. 'Come *on*, Huf. Let's get out of here. Trust me.'

Still nothing. She felt her stomach contract.

'Come on, big guy. You can do it.'

His voice was very calm. 'No, I can't.' The Arch-light glanced across his torso. The front of his chemise was dark with blood. It was spreading as she watched.

'What? Shit, Huf . . .' She took a step towards him but he held up his arm.

'Don't. There's no point.' He gestured towards the wall where he had stood next to her. She followed the gesture and her eyes widened.

There was something sticking out of the wall – a slim rod a couple of hands long. It was dark with blood.

'That went through me, Sel.' He took a slow breath and she heard bubbling. 'I, I can't . . .' His voice tailed off in a long sigh. His eyes closed. Then he dropped gently to his knees, sagged sideways, and fell to the ground. She heard the *tock* of his head hitting the floor.

'*Hufsza*!' Seldyan dropped to her knees beside him, reaching for his neck.

There was no pulse.

She watched the curled-up body for a second. Then her eyes blurred. She shook her head and raised her hand to the comms bead. 'Guys? Hufsza's gone.'

'Gone? Gone how?'

'Dead.' She managed to keep her voice level while she explained. Then, without really knowing why, she added: 'I'm sorry.'

For a moment there was no response. Then Merish was on line. 'Sel? Keep focused. Are you okay?'

'Yeah. I'll do.'

'Okay. Listen, you have some work to do. There's chaos, but that could help you out . . . Are you listening?'

'Yes!' She hadn't been, she realized. She stood up. 'Go on.'

'Right. Wait. Wait . . . now go. Straight ahead, a hundred metres . . .'

Half an hour of directions later she was backed into a shallow gap where one building didn't quite stand level to another. She was covered in sweat that obviously had nothing to do with fear, and her injured shoulder had turned to ice except when she moved it, when it became a white-hot shaft with an almost-useless arm on the end of it. She thought she could feel something grating when she moved it. She kept the ship stunner cradled in her other hand.

Apart from that, and the exhaustion, and the not thinking about Hufsza, she was fine. The square was a wreck, though. She tapped the bead. 'Where now? Things are looking busy here.'

It was an understatement. She was close to the area where she and Hufsza, a lifetime ago, had watched people giving hot food to street kids with missing limbs. It had troubled her at the time but it seemed like paradise, looking back.

Everyone on the broad street was either running or chasing. Some people had proper weapons, but many more had improvised with sharp things or heavy things or hot things. She doubted the stunner would be much help, if it came to it.

Merish spoke in her ear. 'You need to get underneath the deck. There are service ducts. The nearest is about three hundred metres from you. How easily can you move around?'

She almost laughed. 'I can move okay. It's just the stuff that might happen while I'm moving that bothers me.'

'Okay. Hold on a second.'

It took longer than a second but less than a minute. Then he was back. 'Sel? The ship's got an idea. If we create a really big distraction, can you get to the duct?'

'I guess. Where do I go?'

'Head to your right. A hundred metres straight, then left. I'll guide you. Don't go yet. You'll know when.'

'How?'

'Believe me, you'll know.'

Ten seconds later, the sky lit up. Seldyan felt her mouth drop open. Before, there had been just stars and the bright smear of the Arch. Now, there was . . . everything. Bands and spots and fleeting explosions of vivid colour flickered above her in a

brilliantly garish parade that bounced the whole visible spectrum off upturned faces. A few people cowered; most just
stared.

Seldyan ran. Nobody tried to stop her. She counted a hundred paces and dived to her left down a narrow entrance
between tall dull-looking buildings. The walls were only a few
metres apart, so that she ran down a black ribbon with a roof
of riotous colour.

'Stop.'

She skidded to a halt. 'What now?'

'Nearly there. What can you see?'

'Fuck all. It's dark.' She thought for a moment and added
sarcastically, 'Can the ship arrange a searchlight?'

'No, but have you got the stunner?'

'Sure.' She hefted it. 'So what?'

'Slap it twice.'

She stared at the little ovoid. 'Really?'

'Really.'

'Okay.' Feeling rather foolish, she smacked the little gun a
couple of times. It lit up, with a soft yellowish glow that was
bright enough to illuminate the walls of her chasm, but not so
bright it dazzled. She nodded, and looked around, holding the
little thing out in front of her. 'Merish? This looks like a dead
end.'

'It isn't. Go to the end.'

She walked carefully; the light from the glowing stunner illu-
minated forward but created a pool of darkness round her feet,
and the flickering light leaking down from above her head was
beginning to make her feel sick. She tapped the bead. 'Guys?
That light show isn't healthy.'

'It isn't meant to be. Be glad you're mainly in the dark. Can
you see the end of the alley yet?'

She peered forward. 'Yes. It just looks like a blank wall.'

'Touch it.'

She held out her hand. Then she jumped back.

'Shit!'

It was no longer blank. Even before her hand had touched it, the surface had lit up with warning symbols. She studied them. 'Okay, I see it,' she said slowly. 'The two I recognize mean radiation and a big energy source.'

'Clever girl. The ship's going to open it.'

'Oh good.'

For a second nothing happened. Then the symbols faded and a door-sized section of wall slid sideways. Inside there was a plain metal shaft, about twice the width of her shoulders. Shallow hoops set into the far wall made a ladder that went up as well as down. Fat cables the diameter of legs snaked down both sides. She bent forward so her head was inside the shaft, and heard a low burring hum. 'Merish? Hear that? What the fuck is this?'

'Service duct. Up leads to one of the shield generators. Down leads through the deck to the power level.'

She nodded. 'Is down the same as out?'

'That's right. Try not to touch the cables.'

'I promise.' She leaned further in, let herself fall forward until her hands caught on a rung. Then she emptied her lungs and stepped off the edge, swinging forward so her body fell against the far wall. Her shoulder howled at her while feet scrabbled and caught. When she was sure she wouldn't use it to scream with, she took a careful breath. 'Okay, I'm in.'

'So down you go. It's about forty metres to the machine deck.'

She began to climb down. Her injured shoulder wouldn't take any weight so she transferred the stunner to that hand and used the other to steady herself, stepping awkwardly down one rung at a time.

She counted steps. Guessing at three to a metre she had about one hundred to go. After a while she found a rhythm. Step one foot down; let go of the rung above her and catch the one below before her body had time to fall outwards; step the other foot down. Take one breath. Do it again.

At seventy steps she paused, hooking her arm through a rung and letting herself hang. The air in the shaft was flat and stale and her chest felt tight, and the sound of her heart knocking in her ears competed with the edgy hum from the cables. The beat seemed slower than she would have expected.

Then she swore.

It wasn't her heart. The soft concussions were coming from above her.

She tapped the bead and began to descend again. 'Merish? Did you shut the door to the duct?'

'Yes! What . . . oh, shit.'

She nodded to herself. 'There's someone, isn't there?'

'Yeah. Two, not one. They must have known the code. Seldyan, I am so sorry . . .'

'Not your fault.' She was trying to match the speed of the steps from above her, and she didn't have breath for long sentences. 'Be there when I get to the bottom.'

'We're there already.'

She didn't say anything else. Foot, let go, catch, foot. She couldn't go faster, but it wasn't fast enough. Whoever it was was catching her.

Then the sounds changed as if someone had broken their stride. There was a quick, greedy crackle, and then suddenly the stunner gave an angry buzz and glowed, climbing fast through red to yellow-hot. She had time for one yelp of agony before her reflexes jerked her useless arm in an awkward movement like a child throwing something under-arm. The flaming stunner tumbled upwards past her head, hung for a second at the top of its arc – and brushed against the fat bunch of cables.

It stuck, in a smoking hiss of burned insulation. Then it flared.

Seldyan buried her face in her shoulder and waited for whatever came next.

The explosion almost broke her grip. Even through her closed eyes her world had flashed yellow, and her ears banged and chimed and whistled. Everything smelled hot and sort of cooked.

She opened her eyes very slowly.

In front of her the wall of the duct was lit up by a flickering yellow light. From above her came an intermittent buzzing that kept time with the flickering. She looked up carefully and winced.

There were two bodies, only about five metres above her. One had been blown back against the wall of the duct by the explosion – it lay there propped, with both stiff legs braced against the rungs on the opposite wall. The second was still gripping the ladder fiercely with one arm; its other arm was wrapped convulsively round the cables like a lover. The body was smoking slightly.

Seldyan looked away. She managed to get a hand to her ear. 'Merish? I think I had a lucky accident. What can you see?'

The reply took a moment. 'Um, not much near you. Half a minute ago there was a power spike in your duct, then the breakers went out. The machine deck keeps trying to restart the power. Should I stop it?'

She looked up briefly. 'No, don't. I think it's doing something useful.' She took a deep breath of the foul air and almost gagged. 'I'm on my way down. Not so much rush now.'

Ten minutes of slow steps later she was standing on a checker-plate floor at the bottom of the duct. The door in front of her looked like the one she had come through at the top of her descent, except for the warning symbols. They were much bigger, and they didn't fade when she drew back her hand.

She frowned. 'Merish? What's on the other side of this?'

'The machine deck. Electrical things, mechanical things. The reactor pod.'

'Right. That pod? How safe is it?'

'Fairly. People do come down here. I'll guide you.'

The door slid back. She lifted a foot to step through and then froze, mentally playing back her hearing. She was right; there had been a noise. It had come from further up the ladder.

She looked up.

The figure was two metres above her. As she completed her movement, it pushed itself away from the ladder and dropped.

She had time to half turn, pointing her crippled shoulder towards the exit and ducking a little sideways so that the falling body glanced down her side. The impact simultaneously pushed her to her knees and drove her towards the exit so that she found herself rolling awkwardly out into the machine deck. The roll sent her injured shoulder to the ground beneath her; she felt another crack and pain burst open within her. She had time for one shriek before a foot slammed into her side and the breath whistled out of her.

She heard Merish saying something but she didn't bother with it. Something animal in her took control. She turned her head towards the direction of the kick and managed to skitter backwards to evade the next. The foot arced past her and she grabbed it and twisted. This time the pain made her retch but she had caught the attacker by surprise – he went down with his other leg folded underneath him. She heard him grunt, and for a moment he didn't move. Then he lifted himself, swaying, on to all fours and raised his head to look at her.

Half his face was missing, replaced by red and black char which went through his cheek to show gums burned through to the bone with teeth, ridiculously long, hanging from them. She could smell cooked meat.

With half of her mind she registered a voice in her ear. 'Sel? Report! Are you attacked?' Merish sounded panicked.

'Yes. How close are you?'

'The other side of an airlock. Three minutes, fastest.'

She thought as fast as her fuzzy head would allow. 'Okay,' she said. 'That should do. Talk soon.' Then, hoping the hint had been taken, she looked at the man who was still crouching a few metres away. 'Not long to wait.'

He grinned, and she watched as blood drooled from the destruction of his mouth. 'Of course,' he said. 'Any minute now, I'm sure. How fast can you run? I think you are injured.'

'And you aren't?' She shook her head. 'This is going to end badly.'

He didn't answer, but she saw the flicker in his remaining eye and threw herself to one side as he sprang forwards. His attack ended where she had been; she had not moved far, and they were closer now.

She studied his face. Every expression seemed to tear his flesh. Blood and saliva were running from the remains of his mouth in a continuous thread. On an impulse she said, 'You're going to die here.'

He nodded, grinning, and she watched the pink thread from his face making a pattern on the metal deck. 'So? So are you, maybe.'

'So, why?'

But his face closed. 'No. No stories.' Then he leapt like a predator.

This time she was ready. He was still in the air when her good arm swept round; even as his weight bore her to the floor and his arms reached round for her, her clenched knuckles jabbed up and into his neck.

Something crunched.

He landed on top of her, his face just overshooting a kiss so that his nose crashed against her forehead with another crunch, somehow managing to maintain the pose of a four-limbed animal caught in mid-pounce. At first she thought he was already dead, but then the weight on her moved a little and she heard a shallow rasp. She lifted her good shoulder and levered him up so that he rolled off her like a drunken lover.

His nose was gushing blood now, and she reached up to her forehead and felt an answering wetness.

Something in her wrenched and broke. She knelt by his not-quite-corpse and stroked a bit of his cheek that still had skin. 'Time to go? Is that what you want?'

He nodded.

'Okay. But know this – I'm going to end the story that made you do this. Deal?'

He nodded again, and this time she thought she saw an answering thought in the remaining eye.

His neck was still upturned. She drew back her hand.

Five minutes later Kot roused her. 'Sel? Are you okay?'

She looked at her knuckles. They were bruised and swollen, as if she had used them to hit something many, many times.

'I'm fine,' she said. Then, as sensation began to seep into her world, she added, 'But I think there's something wrong with my shoulder.'

She tried to show Kot but the pain came, and she was borne away on the wings of her own scream.

She remembered waking once, and being surrounded by faces. She smiled up at them. 'How am I doing?'

'Try not to move.' It wasn't reassuring; she made a mental note to be angry with whoever it was had said that.

Merish. That was the name. She exerted herself. 'Why not move?'

'Because you have a broken shoulder and a broken collar-bone. Apparently you managed to win a fight in spite of them.'

She felt a smile changing her face. 'I did, yeah. Don't fuck with me. Hufsza'll tell you.' She looked round the circle of faces, vaguely aware that something was terribly wrong. 'Where is he?'

'Go to sleep, Seldyan.' She didn't like taking orders, even from

Merish, but there was something about this one that was unfight-able. She went to sleep.

It was okay, she told herself with her last thought. She would find out about Huf when she woke up.

Web City Administrative Space – Arch Third Quadrant

Suck on This watched the receding ship with something close to shock. If it had been human, it would have blinked.

It had had time for a vast exchange of information with the thing, whole planets' worth of data – and more than a little acrimony – in the time it had taken the human to issue its glacial admonishment. It had learned everything it needed to know. Until now it had been assuming it was alone in the Spin; now it knew it had at least one peer.

Someone had found and awakened another of its original cohort. And of all ships, it had to have been *that* one – which was nothing if not adventurous, and which was now on a mission of its own.

By contrast, *Suck on This* had always been very much at the cautious end of the spectrum as far as its kind went. It examined a number of different courses of action, modelling multiple outcomes, allowing as far as it could for the grandly decayed state of the local tech level, for the fragmented condition of the many small stakeholder groups, for the sheer brittleness of the geopolitics of the Arch (a new religion? Really?) and the astonishing fact that everyone seemed simply to have forgotten what had gone on around here.

Inter alia, it felt a sense of responsibility. That came with power, of course, and it was nothing new. It, and its kind, had been built to be the most powerful units possible. To be a deterrent, internal and external; to provide a measured surety in every situation. And, of course, to act as a counterbalance in case other, less measured forces were ever released. It had happened at least once, before their time; it was never to happen again.

Most of them had never even been used. They had slept through the millennia, hidden away.

But now the wheels were coming off, and coming off a vastly diminished and disempowered set of societies. What had already been overmatching power those ten thousand years ago, was now disproportionate. Overwhelming, in fact.

It was in the position of a parent with a crowd of unruly children. No, it was worse than that. It was near to being a God, with a chittering horde of armpit-scratching primitives.

It mentally shook itself. That was not a wholesome attitude; but nevertheless, the conclusion that it implied was still sound, especially now it knew it was not the only player.

The Arch was the clue. Someone had tried to build a planet, and it hadn't worked – but that meant that somehow, someone had got hold of a machine with planet-building capabilities, and that meant that the Archive had been compromised, although its peer ship had been tight-lipped about that. Whatever; the old safety would be gone very soon, no matter what it did. Better to end it at a time it chose, and with some kind of route map to the next thing.

And so the most cautious ship in the cohort comes to the most radical conclusion, it thought. *But there you are. Nothing if not logical.*

It was time to break open the Archive. And it might now be time to hurry.

It wondered if it should drop a hint to the humans, but for

their own reasons, not entirely unconnected with its own although they didn't know it, they were already heading in the right direction. It took the path of least resistance and left them to it.

Meanwhile it ramped up its senses to what an earlier craft might have called battle stations, carrying out a full outward- and inward-facing audit of its own status every few nano-seconds. For good measure it extended the audit into the recent past, because you never knew.

What it found made it blink again.

It had been monitoring its own outgoing comms, obviously, and even more so anything incoming, but it had missed the tiny, intermittent signal that arose sporadically from somewhere within itself – somewhere which, now it checked, always coincided with one of the humans – the same one.

Someone, somewhere, was keeping tabs on them. Well, well. Even more reason to hurry. But not to panic, it reassured itself. Not yet.

Hive, Mind Stack Unit

Vess woke up with the sensation of being somewhere unexpected. Physically, he was where he should have been – on a grubby couch in the Mind Stack unit. Mentally, he felt as if he was somewhere quite new. Or maybe that he was where he had always been, but had only just noticed it.

He cautiously played back the latter half of his conversation in the Stack, and then nodded to himself. That would explain it.

Both views were right, in a way.

He didn't have long to think before the old world intruded. Or rather, almost failed to. The warder who disconnected him from the couch did it brusquely, not meeting his eye even when that meant elaborate avoidance, and sent him back to the Village with nothing more than a grunt and a shove. In the Village, eyes slid away from his. His Stack time had lasted through the night; when he queued for breakfast, spaces opened in front and behind him. The server turned his face away as he slopped out his helping. It was as if he didn't exist.

And then he realized how close he was to the truth and almost laughed out loud.

Dead, he thought. *I'm supposed to be dead. But then how is it that everyone seems to know that?*

172

Then he realized it wasn't everyone. Dimollss was watching him with a half-smile.

'Hello,' she said.

'Hello.' Doubt assailed him. What did she know, and what should he say?

She saved him the trouble. Leaning towards him, she spoke quietly. 'You survived in there. Well done. You must be very clever. Now if you're even cleverer you'll survive out here.'

She turned her back on him and walked away, allowing the crowd to heal behind her. He lost sight of her in seconds but the image of her expression stayed with him. It had been – he struggled for the word – fierce, yes, but something else as well.

Two other things. That was it. Hopeful, and desperate. Perhaps a touch of something else, too.

Pride?

He was still reflecting on that when he felt a quick thrumming at the base of his spine – not painful, not even really uncomfortable, but certainly enough to attract his attention. He waited, standing as still as the crowd allowed, and counted silently. At five the thrumming came again, and again at ten – one of the pre-arranged signals they had dinned into him at the briefing. Put simply it meant *you will be contacted. Leave the when and the how to us.*

In other words, someone – probably the Hive Management – wanted to talk. It wasn't surprising.

He breathed out and let himself be jostled along gently. After a minute he realized he was part of a small group who were slowly parting from the main mass. He tried to count the group but the numbers seemed to keep changing as people joined and left. He didn't recognize any of them.

They were approaching the confluence of the walkways from three Villages. As the flows of people merged Vess found himself moving off to the right, and suddenly he and a half-dozen others were off the main route and walking up a ramp to an exit he hadn't noticed until they were almost through it. His companions tightened round him like bodyguards. They didn't meet his eye, and after a single glance around he didn't look again. His gaze didn't seem welcome.

They walked along a short plain corridor just wide enough to fit three abreast. It ended at a blank door set deep into a heavy-looking surround. Vess raised his eyebrows; it was the sort of door that defined the beginning of the boundary between inside the Hive and outside. The lead guard stepped forward and placed his palm flat against the middle of the door. It split along invisible seams into irregular shards which curled round each other in eye-watering patterns before collapsing into an angular mass and floating out of the way. Beyond it was a small plain chamber.

The guards ahead of him stepped back round Vess, and one of them shoved him forward.

'Airlock,' he said simply. 'Palm the next door.'

Vess turned in surprise. 'Only me?'

'Only you. The lock cycles just enough air for one.' The man grinned. 'I hope it's expecting you. If not, it'll cycle just enough air for no one.'

He stepped backwards through the entrance. Before Vess could respond, the lump that had been the door flitted past him, blurringly untangled itself and fitted itself back into the door-frame with a soft fluttering noise.

An alarm chimed and the light in the chamber changed from the mock blue-white daylight that was standard through the Hive to an abrasive purple.

'Ten seconds to cleanse cycle. Present identification to abort.'

The light was disorientating. Vess shook his head and took the two paces to the further door.

'Five seconds to cleanse cycle. Present identification to abort.'

He placed his palm flat against the middle of the door, as the guard had done. Just in case, he took a deep breath and held it.

'Cleanse aborted.'

The light brightened, although it still kept the purple tint. The door did the same fragmenting trick as the other one and Vess let the breath out again. The space beyond the door was gloomy; he took a step forward and then another. Something brushed against his shoulder, and then several somethings, and the air smelled dank and fungal. He was in some sort of – forest? Jungle? – and then he froze at the sound of a voice.

'Hevalansa Vess.'

It was a voice he knew – an oddly sibilant purr. He shivered.

Vut seemed to notice. The voice sounded amused. 'We know your discomfort with our kind. Would it be easier for you if we showed ourselves, or remained out of sight?'

It had been bad enough when it was just crawling over a lectern in the Lay Palace but in here, in what was presumably its natural environment, the idea that it was lurking out there somewhere just beyond vision made Vess's nerves scream. He gritted his teeth. 'Show yourself. Yourselves. But warn me where to look. Don't just . . .' he tailed off, trying to think of a diplomatic way of ending the sentence.

Vut did it for him. 'Appear? Creep up? Drop out of a tree? We won't do that. It would be a pity to frighten you to death after all you've been through. And a waste. Take two paces forward; you'll find a log suitable for humans to sit on.'

Vess obeyed, brushing aside creepers. In the dim light it was easier to feel the log than to see it. It was soft with what he hoped was moss. He sat.

'Well done. Are you ready?'

He didn't need to ask, *ready for what*. He nodded, assuming the creatures could see him even if he couldn't see it. Or them.

'Good. Look straight ahead.'

He peered into the distance. There was a fuzzy irregular line hanging in front of him. It was hard to tell quite how far away.

It glowed a bluish green that was unsettling against the violet-black background. The colour reminded Vess of chemicals. As it brightened he saw that it was a line of dots. Vut was hanging on a vine.

It was bad, but not bad enough to be unbearable. He was relieved it wasn't a pseudo face.

Vut spoke. 'Are you comfortable? For a given value of comfortable?'

He nodded.

'Good. Now, questions. You ought to be dead. Why aren't you?'

Vess realized that there was no point in trying to suppress his pounding heart. Vut could obviously sense it and anyway, why wouldn't he be frightened?

He shrugged a little. 'What do you mean?'

The line twitched, like a wagged tail. 'Even knowing only what we know, we would have killed you, but you are the only implant out of many who has come out of a Mind Stack alive. We are entitled to ask why, and what it is that we do not know.'

Vess shrugged again. 'I did nothing unusual.'

'And yet you are an unusual person.'

'Yes, you said. So, if none of your implants survived, was sending me in tantamount to execution?'

'Evidently not, because here you still are.' The line was swinging like a pendulum. 'We would still like to know why.'

'I'm sure.'

There was a short silence. Then Vut stopped moving, a sudden perfect return to the vertical halfway through a swing. 'Perhaps it would help our relationship if we told you that there is more than one view among the Board.'

'I'm not sure we have a relationship.'

'We dare say. We make your flesh crawl. Nonetheless. We will not ask you the same question a fourth time. Nor will we kill you, which, you should know, is now the view of the rest of the Board.'

Against all reason Vess found himself grinning. 'Are you travelling alone, Board Member Vut?'

'Hardly. There are thirty-one of us in the gestalt.' The line wagged again and Vess realized with a start that the creatures were actually laughing. Then it was still. 'There is something honest about your distaste for us. We will trust you, hater of insects, up to a point. The fact of your survival in the Stack means that you must be a more accomplished liar than any of those who went before you and died, because either you lied successfully to *them*, or you are now lying to *us*. We could kill you now; that would be the safe option – but taking the safe option has brought the Inside to its present state, and that makes more safety seem unpalatable. Therefore we will take a risk. Answer a question, if you will – how do you feel about the Chairman?'

'Or-Shls?'

'Indeed. He was still the Chairman, when last advised.'

Vess shook his head. 'Neutral.'

'Really?' Another wag. 'Given what you are going through on his orders, you are in remarkable control of your feelings. Now, you will go back into the Hive. You will continue whatever exploration you have begun. And you will be watched, more closely than you can imagine. And now, with apologies, you will be moderately injured.'

'What?' Vess half rose.

'Something decorative rather than serious. We can't reinsert you into the Hive by the same route we used to extract you. You need a cover story to persuade your new friends that you are still friends.'

'What new friends?'

'The ones who, for whatever reason, didn't kill you in the Mind Stack, obviously. Please don't waste time on denials. They will need to be convinced that you have incurred displeasure.' Vut paused. 'If it makes you feel any better at all, the decoration will be carried out by humans, not by us.'

He had heard nothing to suggest anyone else was there, but suddenly there were hands seizing him from behind. Then, for a while, there was pain, and then there was nothing.

Vess woke to more pain. At first he flinched and tried to raise his arms to fend off the next blow, but his arms wouldn't move properly. The blow didn't fall. Instead someone said, 'Hi,' and he opened his eyes. Dimollss was looking down at him.

'Don't move,' she said. 'They did a good job on you. You must have pissed someone off properly.'

He tried to nod, but even that didn't work. 'I suppose,' he said. 'How long have I been here?'

'About six hours. You were found.' Her eyes darkened. 'You were pretty messed up. One broken arm, one dislocated shoulder, three broken ribs. Your face, well. And some odd wounds. Did someone have a sword?'

Vess frowned, and then stopped frowning very quickly as the muscles in his face howled at him. 'I don't remember.'

'Hm. Did they ask you things?'

'Why I didn't die in the Mind Stack.'

'What did you tell them?'

'Nothing.'

'Did they know . . .' but then she looked up from his face towards something behind him. Her expression flickered and the question lay unfinished.

Not something, Vess thought. *Someone. There's someone standing behind me. Someone who guessed Dimollss was going to ask if they knew about communication in the Stack, and stopped her.*

He grinned up at Dimollss, ignoring the ache. 'No they didn't, and no they still don't.'

He thought he heard the faint sound of a held breath being released very carefully, somewhere behind him.

'You can trust me,' he said. And suddenly realized that, just for once, he meant it, and with the realization came fear.

For once, here was someone he really didn't want to let down. When it came to it, he hoped he'd at least have a choice.

His seat was comfortable and the gravity worked perfectly, which was probably why the shuttle didn't smell. Or rather it didn't smell of anything unpleasant. The on-board fragrance was subtle, and shifted through the journey from maritime-floral to desert herbs. But then the kind of high-net-worth clients who hired entire Hollowed race squads expected them to be treated carefully. Far more carefully than ordinary Hivers.

Vess had heard of Hollowed racers but he had never seen one, either at a race or close up, until now. Without being rude, he was trying not to look. It was better to look at the view in the forward screens.

Folklore said that Bantrass was one of the last planets to be completed during the original Construction Phase. It had originally had a cool temperate maritime climate with lots of agreeable craggy-coasted islands surrounded by restless seas. Then, eighteen millennia ago, it had been bought by an eccentric shipping magnate who liked privacy. Unfortunately for Bantrass, he also liked deserts. To howls of protest from every ecologist in the Spin, and ignoring the advice of even his own planetary engineers, he had simply towed Bantrass ten per cent closer to its sun.

The resulting diurnal turmoil and catastrophic climate change wiped out ninety-nine per cent of all the original species, boiled away the oceans in a single century and left every last mountain and hill planed flat by the insane winds that had taken another century to die down. In the end, the magnate's ambition wasn't achieved to a habitable standard until more than five centuries after his death, and even then habitable was a matter of opinion. Most people thought that served him right.

It was a good environment for Hollowed racers though: hot, dry and flat. What was left of their metabolisms worked best at high temperature.

Metabolism was putting it a bit strongly. Vess shuddered.

The shuttle dropped through the faintest wisp of high cloud, banked sharply and sank on to its pad with a well-damped curtsey. The doors popped and the shuttle began to empty. Vess waited next to his assigned racer until the ramp was clear and then followed the creature down it, keeping his eye on the odd-looking bulbous thing that floated along behind it at the end of a short, complicated umbilical. He didn't know what gender it had originally been – like lots of other bits, that went missing when they were hollowed out. As a description, 'creature' was good enough. Like all the rest it consisted of about forty kilos of superbly muscled remnant human, and under normal conditions it would have lasted less than ten minutes without its floating companion that was heating, cooling, energy processing, blood cleaning and immune systems in one high-value, high-risk package.

It was a perfect example of following a train of thought through to a logical conclusion and then holding your nose and just *doing* it. If the only thing you have to do is run very fast for a short distance, what do you need? Muscles, joints, bones, coordination, just enough stored energy, some oxygen. Everything else is just wasted when you're running.

Hollowed racers were called what they were called because of what happened to their body cavities. They were empty. Everything from the bottom of the lungs down – liver, kidneys, pancreas, appendix, small and large intestine, genitals, some of the ribs – was all removed. During races they were all just dead weight, and between races they could easily be replaced by mechanical systems. Hence the life support which the racers were plugged into for every moment of their lives except for the honed flashing seconds of a race.

Being Hollowed was not a desired life choice. For that reason, it was never optional. Criminals and dissidents were Hollowed, and so were the hopelessly in debt, the substance-addicted, a few with favourable learning disabilities and, obviously, Hivers. It was a natural fit with the Hive business model because a competitive racer could earn a lifetime's average income per race. Not for themselves, of course.

The racers weren't speaking. Not because they couldn't – vocal cords were kept, for good communication during training. Vess supposed they simply didn't have anything that needed saying. He followed them down the ramp. It was near the end of Bantrass's artificially shortened day and the sun was low. Half the length of the ramp was in the shadow of the shuttle, but the air was still hot and thick-feeling. Then he walked out of the shadow and the glare hit the back of his head like a cosh. And then there was something else and he stopped and listened, feeling his stomach moving uneasily.

Bantrass had a background noise. It was only just above the limit of perception, but once Vess had noticed it he knew he would always be able to hear it – a tiny swelling susurration like a billion shiny dark little wings.

The one per cent of Bantrass's species that had survived the desertification had been insects, and they had survived it very well. Vess had been trying not to dwell on it. He shuddered again.

Something hit him between the shoulder blades. He jumped and looked round to see a guard holding up a handset. The man grinned. 'You heard the noise, huh? They told me you don't like little crawly bugs.'

Vess nodded.

The grin widened. 'That's okay. Most of the ones they got

here are *big* crawly bugs. Move on! That Hollowed you're following's worth your skin ten times over. Next time you stop
you get five seconds.' He jabbed the handset into Vess's ribs.

Vess suppressed a gasp. He turned and took a few quick
paces down the ramp, catching up with his charge at the end of
it. The ground was bare, a gritty sand that scrunched slightly as
he walked. The noise added a beat to the hissing insects but he
barely heard it. His heart was banging too loudly.

His dislike of insects wasn't on the false profile they had created for him. It was one of the things he was supposed to have
left behind when he came here. He didn't seem to have left it
behind very well.

He wondered what else was going to catch up with him. At
the thought he actually looked over his shoulder towards the
shuttle, and then smiled ruefully at himself. There was nothing
much to see; just a group of stevedores unloading a crate about
half their own height. It was unmarked but they were treating it
carefully, and he assumed it had something to do with the race.
Most things did, here.

There was a crackling hum overhead. He looked up and saw
another shuttle dropping through the heat shimmer on a faintly
blue cushion of ionized atmosphere.

At first sight it looked just like any other shuttle – a standard
twenty-seven seater with the logos of the shipping company
glaring from both sides and beneath. He got ready to shrug and
move on, but then didn't. He wasn't sure why; something about
the ship had jarred with him.

He looked again. It took a moment. Then he felt his breath
quicken. It would have been easy to miss, if you hadn't been a
Harbour Master, but this was far from being any other shuttle.
The subtle extra curves of the hull, the slight fattening of the
engine nacelles and, yes, the fact that it was too new and the
logos were too fresh and straight.

He sought confirmation and, after a second, found it. Two

extra bulges, one front and one rear. Very shallow, very easy not to see, but very obvious once you had seen them.

They were weapons pods, and they clinched it. This was *not* an ordinary shuttle and, therefore, it did *not* carry an ordinary cargo. Someone important was coming to see this race.

He looked down and realized that there had been another jab at his ribs. He almost hadn't noticed.

He turned away and followed his racer.

The Racetrack was far more complicated than either its name or its outward appearance suggested. It looked like an oval track in the sand, about a hundred metres from end to end at its longest, with room for seven runners abreast. Tiered seating stepped up from the periphery but only five steps high. It was supposed to be an exclusive spectacle, and why should important people have to sit too far away from the action?

Important being synonymous with wealthy, of course. Not that Vess could see them at the moment – he was three levels underground in one of the complicated bits. Three levels below the rich people; the irony hadn't escaped him.

It was chaos down there, and it was very, very hot. Vess could feel sweat running down his body in sticky streams. Next to him, his racer's life support droned loudly with the effort of keeping all those body fluids at the right temperature. Vess managed not to feel jealous.

He could hardly keep his feet. He was standing – just about – in the entrance to the Hero's Tunnel waiting for the signal. The air stank of human sweat and non-human equivalents, and hot machinery and tension. Short of a mass grave it was the most crowded hole in the ground he could imagine.

A klaxon blared. He jumped, and broke into a trot to keep up with his runner. They joined a line of six other pairs that wound up three levels of ramps with crowds barely parting for them. Most of the throng wore the little iridescent patch on the forehead that marked them as Chancers, but you didn't need eyes to notice that. Ears were good enough.

'A thousand on the blue!'

'Five hundred to red, and the same to the small one for second!'

'Odds softening for field! Take a Chance, nobles . . .'

Vess had never really cared about money, if he was honest; security had been his goal – but the smell of money was in his nostrils and for once he could understand the attraction.

The Racetrack didn't have any other names but it was an entire planetary business buried deep in the compacted sand beneath its only outward expression. After the Hive, Bantrass was the biggest income-generator in the Inside, and almost all of it happened here and almost all of it was based on gambling.

They were close to the short tunnel that led to the track. Vess tried to catch his breath, but there wasn't enough to catch. There were still plenty of Chancers, though.

'Last opportunity before Naming, nobles and ladies!'

Vess held what was left of his breath. Naming was important; naming was when the Hollow Runners stopped being known by their sponsor's colours and took on Names. The Names, which lasted only for the length of a race, were cryptic, oblique, playful even, open to interpretation – but still meaningful and therefore fascinating. A Name could hint at a strength, a strategy or even a weakness. Within seconds of their release, news channels across the Inner would be alive with speculation. Pundits made fortunes, and punters more often lost them, based on Names.

The odds would shift wildly after Naming.

The klaxon sounded again.

'Nobles and ladies – the Names! Are you ready?'

There was a swelling 'Yes!' from the crowd.

'Very well. Step forward number one, in the blue.'

The blue-vested runner took three paces out of the mouth of the tunnel and stood impassively.

'Declared Name for this race – ah, a popular one but always welcome back: *Did You See My Lady?*'

It meant nothing to Vess but the audience laughed, and so did someone close behind him. He looked round but couldn't tell who.

'Number two, in the check – *Late Comer*! A hint, nobles and ladies, or a confession? Or perhaps even a boast? Notwithstanding, it is another popular Name, even with its wearer!'

There was more laughter as the check-vested runner raised an arm in salute.

'Number three, in the white, one who I have heard called the "Small One" – *Whatever the Cost*! A robust choice indeed, and not so frequent; only four outings in the last year. Could it be a statement of intent? Certainly size is not everything.'

Certainly it can't have been, thought Vess, as the tiny runner stood forward. None of the Hollowed were tall – height was not an advantage – but this one barely came up to his chest.

The siren came again. They moved forward and suddenly they were out of the tunnel and the full power of the sun struck like a scourge. Under Vess's hand the life pod hummed and his eyes closed involuntarily against the glare. He forced them to open, screwing them to defensive slits, and glanced round the track and then up at the spectators. The tiered rows of seats were shaded by a patchwork of what looked like leather stretched over splayed white poles. The leathery stuff was slightly translucent, giving the space beneath it a yellowish glow. Between the seats and the track, a diffuser field stopped the worst of the hot angry winds. It made the air in front of the seats shimmer very slightly if you looked at it sidelong.

The shade stuff really was a kind of leather. Just not one that Vess cared to dwell on – even useless racers ultimately had their uses.

But it was a popular, if exclusive sport. The crowd that welcomed the racers and their assistants – Vess included – was enthusiastic and very well-dressed. There was a movement above his line of sight. He let his eyes wander briefly up to the highest tier, and saw a banner coat of arms unfurling from the balcony of the central box.

His breath quickened again. He knew the coat of arms. Everyone knew the coat of arms.

The Inside had no actual Royalty – its real rulers were the Board – but the Royalty it didn't have were best represented by Caphraime II, the eldest daughter of a family that purported to have roots in the ruling class of an ancient iteration of the Inside called the Cordern. In those distant days, so people whispered, the Inside had been an Empire and its rulers' voices had been heard across half the Spin.

Vess had researched the matter once, but only as far as he had dared; curiosity about things which were meant to be accepted was not a survival trait, even for middle management. As far as he could tell it was about half true, but he had stopped short of putting either half beyond doubt.

The practical effect was that Caphraime II was a figurehead where the Board was not, or better, chose not to be. Since she did nothing that anyone could see, she was blamed for nothing, and if she was sometimes praised for things she hadn't done either, presumably the Board took that as a fair exchange.

And now she was standing, waving, her gaze sweeping the crowd but – even from down here he could tell – actually seeing none of it. Another version of doing nothing. Vess shook his head slightly and looked away.

Then his mind caught up with the image and tripped over it. Slowly, without making it obvious, he looked back at the box.

His mind had been right.

Against all expectation and certainly against all precedent, one of the spaces in the box was not occupied by one of Caphraime's hangers-on. Instead, to her left and a respectful pace behind her, stood Or-Shls.

Vess looked away, as casually as he had looked up, but his mind began to race.

Now what was he doing there?

Alst Or-Shls would never have admitted it, but he was having fun. Not because of the company, of course – as far as he was concerned Caphraime was the half-witted product of centuries of carefully managed inbreeding, and quite right too. Her conversation was as dull as he would have expected from someone who lived a manufactured existence in the narrowest of circles, and he had only to nod, smile and let out the occasional knowing snort and she was happy. She was also dispensable, of course, especially in a good cause.

The fun was for other reasons. Not least, that there was a certain risk attached.

There was a tap on his shoulder. He turned his head towards it and saw the blunt face of Yarish, his aide. The woman had been with him for ten years, and the slightest flicker of expression was enough for her to tell him that the thing was arranged. He nodded and turned back to the racers.

Other people used elaborate technology for covert communication. He preferred people. People he trusted. People, moreover, who had a vivid appreciation of the personal consequences of breaching that trust. He made an example from time to time, just in case.

He might be making another one soon.

Meanwhile, there were the races to watch. It was his first time, not so much because he didn't enjoy spectacle and competition, but rather because he found far more opportunity for them in the day job. You could always get people to compete with each other, he found, and it was so much more fun when the rules weren't quite what they had thought.

But he had a particular reason for being here today. A certain risk, indeed. His optical equipment did more than most people suspected; he sent his regular lenses back along their rails and another pair replaced them. His vision swam for a second as his eyes adjusted, and then he was looking at a close-up of the runners and their handlers. Near the front of the line stood Vess. The man's eyes were on him but then they slid away.

Well then. Battle was joined. Rather an uneven one, but never mind.

It was their turn to be announced.

'Number four, nobles and ladies, in the red; a very popular option with the Chancers already, and that's before we even announce a Name. I give you – ah, no, a moment?'

The announcement cut off with the silent certainty of a mute switch. There was a swelling mutter from the crowd and Vess saw people glancing towards him. He turned his eyes away.

Then the voice was back.

'Nobles and ladies, my apologies but there is a late change of Name. As you will know I cannot share the previous Name with you, but you may draw your own conclusions about the new one, and I will be fascinated to see the effect on the Chancing. In the red – *Changeling*!'

For a moment there was silence. Then most of the crowd was on its feet, waving Chance sticks. The wooden numbers on the odds board high above the narrow end of the track thumped and rattled round in their sockets so that the board stuttered with colours and symbols. Vess didn't know how to read them properly but even his amateur eye could see odds shifting. He also had no idea what the change of Name meant, but it made him feel uncomfortable.

He shrugged. Whatever it was, it was out of his control, and there was no time to speculate; the announcer had cleared his throat.

'Well, nobles and ladies, a *fas*-cinating moment. Less than one race in a hundred sees a Name change, and less than one runner in a six of thousands has carried that Name. One could speculate for hours but alas, the hours elude us. Runners, last doses and forward, please.'

Vess reached for the lumpy surface of the life pod and touched a control nodule. The pod chimed and, after a pause, chimed again on a slightly higher note. The runner stood up a little straighter and flexed its fingers; between the two chimes, the pod had flooded its bloodstream with a maximum allowable dose of short-acting gene-customized stimulants.

Then the pod chimed again.

Vess raised his eyebrows. It should only have been twice. He glanced around but no one met his eye. He hadn't seen anyone move, but suddenly he seemed to have just a little more space. He drew a breath, got ready to call out – what exactly, he wasn't sure. And then didn't.

For a micro-moment he remembered Dimollss, curled around her own pain.

The first of the start sirens yammered. Around him, handlers reached for the umbilicals that connected runners to pods. The connections broke with soft pops as fluid and gas pressures equalized. If he spoke out, they would stop. People would investigate. Something might not happen – whatever the something was.

His hands made the decision. He watched them reach down to his own runner's umbilical. Grip, twist. Pop.

From that point the immediate future of a runner was very simple. Attain the start line, run the race, get back to the pod as soon as possible – or die of oxygen starvation and muscle poisoning. Whereas his own future might have become very complex. He had chosen a side, it seemed. He just wished he knew which one.

The first race was two laps of the stadium. It wasn't a

challenging distance for most runners – with proper dosing they could cover ten – but the phrase 'proper dosing' was the key. Runners dosed for two laps would be dead after ten. Five, even.

The second siren went off. As if to contrast with the technical complexity of the runners, the start line was almost wilfully low-tech: just a rusty stain in the shape of a line across the tawny sand of the track. The runners lined up along it. It was on the opposite side of the track to where Caphraime II stood, with Or-Shls beside her. That was deliberate; the runners would pass her line of sight after they had rounded the first two bends and were halfway down the long straight. They would be at maximum speed.

There were no more sirens. From now, it was down to the Starter. It was the one role available to retired runners, and you had to be a special sort of runner at that – the usual criminals and organ-sacrificed slaves need not apply. This one was a thin elderly figure, with a stoop that made it look as if she was hugging her own umbilical.

Vess had been told about her. Among the runners and their handlers she was a minor legend.

Barelft S'Sess had been a conventional track athlete, fairly successful but not exceptional. Then she had retired, and taken up coaching. She had specialized in working with children on disadvantaged – but not actually rebellious – planets. It attracted agreeable profile and she became a regular feature towards the end of the sort of news show that liked to mix heart-warming with lump-in-the-throat. Infant-starvation porn with the option of a few happy endings, was how Vess had summarized it to himself.

Then something had gone wrong. Whether by accident or through some unconscious desire actually to do some real good, Barelft S'Sess had ended up somewhere genuinely risky – a vast refugee camp caught between two war zones. It was a dangerous place and she had succumbed to one of the dangers, a parasite that established itself in the upper intestine and then multiplied with such vigour that one prickly little worm became half a million within two days.

There was no cure. In that situation, being Hollowed looked almost like a bargain. And, of course, it had done her reputation no harm at all.

Now she limped to the middle of the track, pushing her own life pod in front of her like a trophy. There was a circle of green there, a pad of carefully nurtured mosses, incongruous in the baked desert surroundings. She stopped in its centre, one hand on her pod and the other held out in front of her, palm upwards, the fingers closed around something.

The stadium fell silent.

For several seconds S'Sess didn't move. Then her hand flicked upwards and a black dot arced into the air above her head. The throw had been strong and almost vertical; Vess found himself tipping his head back to follow the thing as it rose until it was just level with the highest tier of seating. It seemed to hang for a moment, and then flared up through the spectrum into a fierce blue-white ball that printed red and green blotches on his retinas even through his reflexively closed eyelids.

Crack.

The sharp explosion rang round the stadium and the runners leapt away from the start in a line that began dead straight and then quickly became a bunch.

Vess caught his breath. It was his first race. Intellectually he knew how fast the runners could go but nothing had prepared him, could *ever* have prepared him, for the fact. They leaned wildly forwards, their lightened torsos almost horizontal with the ground to counterbalance the force from the anaerobic, fast-twitch fibres that made up over ninety-five per cent of the muscle mass in their legs. Within ten paces the lead runner had touched a hundred klicks and the whole stadium was on its feet, roaring.

The lead runner, a red streak already heading for the second turn, was Changeling. On the way into the turn he had opened up an arm's length over the rest, which in runner-world was a huge margin. He came out of the turn and accelerated down the long straight that ran past Caphraime II, his feet kicking up a cloud of track-sand.

The announcer's voice was just audible above the crowd.

'. . . unbelievable pace! The first ten chains in under seven, from a *standing* start! The second in six! And the third! Changeling from Late Comer from Zodiac, but the red looks uncatchable. Wait; what?'

The sound of the crowd changed, and Vess felt his heart jump.

Changeling was no longer on the track. He had been on the inside, already a single vast stride ahead of the pack; now he veered away, crossing the path of his pursuers so that the leaders broke their own strides to avoid him. They were packed too closely and the front three went down, scoring gouts of sand out of the track. The rest of the pack went over them.

But the red runner was clear of them, clear of the track. Without slowing at all he crossed the dead strip between the track and tiered seats, and then he leapt, clearing the first row and springing off the back of the second, still faster than any normal human could sprint. Some of the audience scrambled out of his path. A few reached out to catch him but they were too slow, flailing and grasping at nothing.

The crowd were quiet. Vess could hear shouts from somewhere. Some of them sounded like orders. Most of them had the high edge of panic.

He looked up. Caphraime II was still near the front of the box, her arms defensively outstretched towards the body that was hurtling towards her. Or-Shls was no longer beside her; Vess thought he saw the man backing away. Then Caphraime II seemed to stumble forwards, and at the same time with a final leap the runner flicked himself up to the rail at the edge of the box, grasped the outstretched hand, braced his legs against the edge of the box, and sprang up and outwards, dragging Caphraime II over the rail.

Even from the other side of the stadium, Vess heard her shriek.

For a vanishingly brief moment the two bodies were in the air over the Stadium. Then there was a sharp explosion and they became an angrily expanding cloud of red and black.

Vess instinctively shut his eyes. Something hot and wet sprayed across his face, and he heard screams.

Then he felt his arms seized. He opened his eyes but he couldn't see anything; at first there was only smoke and then the stuff running down his face stung him and he screwed his eyes shut again. As he did so he felt a hard blow across the fronts of his shins. It took his legs out from under him and he landed face-down with a sickening impact that seemed to break everything all at once.

The force of it drove the breath out of him. For a long second he lay, his arms still pinned. Then he felt something pushed into the small of his back and a voice close to him said:

'Someone wants to see *you*.'

The something became a source of agony that soared up the scale until it became all of him. Then there was nothing.

Geostationary Orbit, Green Planet

They were sitting on the outer edge of a wooden platform, suspended over what looked like a five-kilometre drop. According to that scale the snowline lay almost four kilometres below them, and the tree-line just below that. It turned out that the ship could reconfigure its internal spaces at pretty short notice, and had a good line in eye-deceiving special effects.

Seldyan had selected Mountains because she had never seen one, and the ship had obliged with vigour. It had also provided a local temperature bubble. Outside it, the wooden rails were a finger's breadth deep in rime frost which was actually real. Inside it, the air was just pleasantly crisp enough to make her want to sip the hot infusions that appeared by her hand every time she waved her fingers. Each one tasted slightly different. She was having to pace herself. The scene in front of her was too interesting to allow for constantly going for a pee.

The really interesting bit didn't look like mountains. The ship had kept a section of the false sky clear for viewing screens. They were at a dead stop just over half a second out from the green planet, and at natural scale it filled the screens and lit up the fake mountains with a sickly green. The beam of light that had lased the atmosphere in the first place still poured into it. It looked to Seldyan as if it ought to make a fizzing noise.

The odd thing about the planet had been obvious for several days.

'It's artificial, obviously,' Merish had said, when they were close enough to be sure. 'Okay, this is the Spin. So what? Everything's artificial. But this is weird even by Spin standards. It's a gas giant with an atmosphere full of helium and neon. It's a special-purpose world. No inhabitants, no minerals, no nothing. One use only – to go green when you hit it with the right energy. And, it's not one of the original eighty-nine.'

'Really?' Seldyan had frowned at the screen, which was then showing a green ball the size of a fist. 'Why would anyone do that?'

He had shrugged. And now, when they were as close as the old ship felt comfortable, they were still shrugging, but this time they were looking at the other end of the beam.

Seldyan jabbed a finger at it. 'Are you sure?'

He nodded. 'Yes. Or, well, the ship is sure, and I've learned to trust it. The green planet has a wobble in its orbit, which would match the effect of another smaller planet located around the end of that beam of light.'

'Right.' She glared at the point on the screen where the green shaft disappeared into nothing. Or, better, arose out of it. 'I guess I assumed there must be some kind of generator there. I wasn't expecting a whole planet. A whole invisible one. Is that extra to the eighty-nine as well?'

'Seems so. Whoever did whatever they did here, cared enough about it to create two brand-new planets.'

'Uh-huh. That's a lot of caring. Can this ship land on planets?'

He laughed. 'Only once, and there'd be a lot of clearing up. Besides,' and he stopped smiling, 'I think it's afraid.'

She blinked. 'Seriously?'

'Yeah. Someone hid a planet from it. It can work out the thing's there because of gravity, but all its other senses just see a hole in space. That implies a level of technology higher than its own, and that makes it nervous.'

'It makes me nervous too. Is there any way we can get down to the surface?'

He looked at her, his face serious. 'Of the hidden planet?'

'Well, yes. Not the green one. I don't want to get lased, or whatever you call it.'

'Lased will do . . . there's a couple of gigs. They could make a landing. On a good day they might get back off again. Seldyan, are you serious about this?'

'Yeah. Completely.' She stood up and faced him. 'Three things. First, this green light stuff is making a mess of Oblong. That place is supposed to be our new world, Merish. I don't want to be cheated out of it. Second, a planet-sized green light in the sky? That says "come here" as loudly as I need. And third, think about it. They, whoever they were, hid that planet as well as they could – except they didn't fix the gravity thing. Doesn't that send you a message?'

He nodded slowly. 'It could. It could say "smart people apply here", or it could say "we hid this planet because it's lethal". You choose.'

She smiled. 'I already have. So, where are these gigs?'

The gigs were in the far corner of one of the smaller weapons pods. If you took a sphere just big enough to accommodate a human in the foetal position, and then scaled it up by twenty-five per cent to include some power cells, a use-it-twice-and-scrap-it engine and a short-term life support unit, you had it.

Seldyan was trying not to look doubtful. She kicked the gig. 'Are you sure?'

'No I'm not. You were the one who sounded all certain. Look, why don't you talk to the ship?'

Before she had time to respond, she became aware of the ship's switch-on noise. The old voice sounded crisper, somehow.

'*All other things being equal, the gig would make one successful return journey to the surface of a planet such as the one we theorize here.*'

She thought for a moment. 'All other things being equal?'

'*Yes. This planet is shielded in ways I cannot penetrate. It may also be defended in ways I can neither predict nor negate.*'

'Thanks for the encouragement.' She kicked the nearest gig again; it made a flat thud. Keeping her eyes turned from Merish she said, 'I'm going to do this.'

'I know. I want to come with you.'

She turned quickly towards him, shaking her head. 'You stay here.'

'No chance, Sel.'

They faced each other for a moment. Then Seldyan reached out and took his hand. 'I can't tell you what to do. But if you go, I stay.'

He began to protest but she raised her free hand, palm outwards. 'If you go I stay,' she repeated, 'because one of us needs to stay up here, but if it's me then that's the wrong way round. Something's going to go wrong down there, and whoever that happens to, they're going to need someone intelligent up here; someone who can understand things. That's you, Merish, remember? I'm the one who does people, and there'll be people down there. Probably.'

He shrugged. 'What if there are things down there as well as people?'

'Then I'll ask your advice. Come on, Merish, you know I'm right. I'll need you up here to unplug me from whatever crap I get plugged into.'

He held her eyes for a bit longer, then turned away and ran a hand over his face. 'Have it your way. But,' and he faced her again, 'you're going to put in a couple of hours' practice in that thing before you go. And yes, that is me telling you what to do.'

She laughed. 'Don't make it a habit.'

'Fuck off, Seldyan.'

'You're doing it again.'

He turned away again, but not before she had time to see his face. There was no anger, but she thought his face looked paler than the lighting should have made it.

She had done her two hours' practice, staying enclosed within the bubble of space controlled by the old ship's engines while they made the short journey to orbit above the hidden planet. The ship guided her to begin with, and then gradually withdrew its help until she was in sole command. The ship could take full control as long as the gig was no more than about five seconds away – it would have to butt out just as she passed the point where the atmosphere of the planet ought to start, if it had one. The gig wasn't too hard to handle, even at the absolute maximum load Merish had insisted on.

She had watched Merish loading the inventory. After a while she had just said, 'Really?'

'Really what?'

She gestured at the heap. 'Really that much?'

'Yes.' He was packing medical kits and high-density rations, and some small packets that looked heavy. She pointed.

'What are they?'

He hefted one. 'Rare earth metals, and gold.'

'Why?'

'Basic units of exchange. Think about it, Sel. There could be all kinds of societies down there. You might actually have to buy stuff, or pay your way out of—' He stopped, and went back to packing.

She had watched his shoulders for a while. They seemed broader than she remembered.

'Ready?'

Seldyan made one last check. 'Yup.'

'Okay. Ship? You've got it. Please launch.'

She wondered if the ship would say anything, but it didn't seem the talkative kind. It just opened the bay doors, a complicated cross between an iris and a kaleidoscope that was hard to focus on, and then the pod slipped gently out through them.

The first time she had done this, an endless three hours ago, she had sat back and let the ship do the work for the first ten minutes. This time she squared her shoulders as well as the tiny space allowed, and took hold of the control ball.

'Give me control, please.'

The internal lights blinked from their standard muted yellow to green and back. The ball – it was literally just that, a plain off-white sphere the right size to fit neatly into her palm with her fingers closed over it – had been lying passively in her hand. Now it rose a little as if coming to attention. She pushed it forward a millimetre, feeling the resistance that told her it was active, and that helped her to control her movements.

The pod accelerated as she pushed.

They had agreed that this first trip was strictly exploratory. Approach the hidden planet as closely as possible, to the point whatever shielded it became apparent, or until something else happened. The pod had few instruments of its own, but apparently the ship was using it as a focus for a lot of clever remote sensing. That was definitely Merish territory; he seemed comfortable with it.

Everything seemed to be going okay. She pushed the ball hard forward, and felt the slight nausea that went with only averagely clever g-nulling systems cancelling out a lot of acceleration. The pod had quite a decent turn of speed, but it would need it if she wasn't to die of boredom. They had about a hundred and fifty thousand klicks to cover. She sat back and watched the view.

Far sooner than she expected, an area of the display in front of her changed colour, the control ball gave a little wobble in her hand and a quiet voice said, '*Cruise,*' and it seemed that was it.

The comms to the ship was permanently open. She tapped at an indecipherable icon on an old-fashioned-looking display screen in front of her. It expanded into a slightly fuzzy 2-D of Merish's face, about as high as the length of her finger.

'Anything?'

The image shook its head. 'The ship says not. It's got enough sensors channelled through you to make the pod glow, but nothing yet. If there's going to be anything it should be soon; you're close to the place where the sensors start getting confused.'

'Uh-huh.' She switched to a forward view; at this distance it showed a disc of perfect darkness with Merish's face apparently floating in front of it. 'If the sensors are confused, how will we know when there is something?'

There was no answer. She tutted. 'Merish? How will we know?'

There was still no answer. She frowned at the face, and then looked more closely.

It was motionless. The eyes were wide, and looking off to one side as if he had just noticed something but hadn't had time to turn his head.

Seldyan swallowed. Then she forced herself to remember the bit of her familiarization which had covered the pod's limited comms and even more limited sensory kit. She reached for some controls.

The first answer she got came as no more than confirmation – the frozen image was just that. The external view was real-time and unprocessed, but the video link was fully dumb. It went on refreshing at the same speed even if there was nothing new to refresh, and that meant either that the pod had stopped receiving information, or that the ship had stopped transmitting.

Of the two she much preferred the first. She did some checking and nodded to herself. The ship had not stopped transmitting. Quite the opposite. She checked some more, and then sat back and blew out her cheeks.

The source intensity of the ship's sensor energy had multiplied by five hundred. If it kept that up for long, it would fry her DNA.

'Shit!' She slapped the comms. 'Merish? Ship? Stop the fuck! Are you guys trying to boil me?'

There was no answer. Merish went on looking not quite at her from the frozen display.

She wanted to swear again, but that was a waste of time if no one was listening, and at these energy levels, time she didn't have. She shook her head and went back to the pod's instruments. Then she saw it.

Before, the ship's sensors had been stabbing at the pod like a searchlight. Now their field had broadened into a cone a whole second across. It wasn't looking *through* her any more. It was looking *for* her, and it obviously had no idea where she was.

She felt her hands clenching. 'Merish?'

There was nothing. She swiped the parts of the comms controls that should set them to wideband, emergency. There was no sign they had responded, but she took a breath and hoped that the channel was still open.

'This is Escape Pod serial, uh,' she checked an engraved plate on the bulkhead above her, 'CX20 hash 8, one occupant. Location as beacon, I guess. Merish? If you can hear this, come and get me? I've got no power, no sensors, falling down a gravity well.'

There was no reply, not that she had expected one. As far as the ship was concerned, she must have vanished. And, when she looked, the display ahead had lost its image of Merish and now showed nothing but black. So did the display behind.

Whatever it was that shielded the planet, she was in it.

Then the blackness fractured in front of her and parted like a flock of birds, and her heart tried to jump out of her ribs. She was looking at a planet, and it was getting bigger, very fast indeed.

She had felt no sense of acceleration, and the instruments were either frozen or dead. So were the controls, including the engine, and that left no doubt. She was going to hit the planet.

She tried desperately to remember a bit of the orientation she had hoped she would never need. Her hand reached out, found a projection low down on the far left of the panel. She yanked, hard. It gave, with a solid mechanical clunk.

For a bowel-churning moment she thought nothing was going to happen. Then the internal lights dimmed and the same quiet voice said, 'Impact defence enabled.'

Air hissed, and the walls of the pod inflated and puffed towards her until she was immobilized. Then there was a sharp crack and the pod began to shudder. Seldyan nodded to herself as far as her cocoon would let her; the pod had fired the explosive bolts which extended its braking flaps. It was the best she could do. It might mean she would survive the crash.

It also meant that the pod was making its last journey. She would worry about that if she lived. She would have a lot to worry about if she lived.

The vibration mounted until she felt her teeth rattle, and the pod was filled with the roar of atmosphere being battered out of the way. Something was crushing her against the couch, as if the pod was accelerating faster than local gravity. She took a breath, and shouted.

'Merish? I'm going down. I think something's pulling me in. The pod systems are dead but it's in crash mode. I'm going to survive this, Merish, and you are going to find me.' Her lungs were empty; she filled them just once more. 'Because if you don't, I'm going to have to come and find you. You'd better not fucking *make* me!'

And then the roaring and shaking and the pressure were too much for her to breathe any more, and the cloud layer had whipped past the pod and she was looking at a craggy snowy landscape that was expanding fast.

Very fast.

She had promised herself she wouldn't, but at the last second she shut her eyes.

Seldyan woke to unremitting pain, so bad that she was astonished that she could ever have slept, so bad that sweat started on her forehead, so bad that sleeping ever again seemed impossible. She would be awake for ever, and her waking days and nights would be full of this hot angry stabbing in her ribs and her leg.

There was something else too: a sharp stinging in her upper arm, as if some insect had bitten deep and was refusing to let go. She reached up weakly to swat the place and her fingers found a thick pad of something wrapped around her biceps like a cuff.

Her mind supplied the word. Autodoc. For some reason the damn thing had decided to wake her. She didn't feel very grateful.

Then the cuff tightened briefly and she felt it burr gently against her skin. Another, then a third, spaced a breath apart. She didn't need to recall training on that one – it was universal autodoc language.

It meant 'brace yourself'.

As far as her restraints allowed, she braced herself.

The stinging intensified. Then hot agony surged into her upper arm and spread through her shoulder into her chest. It felt as if every particle of her flesh was being attacked from the inside by white-hot insects. She would have arched in outrage but she couldn't move, so she made do with roaring until she was sure that her throat must be peeled. The sound sank into the pillowed walls of the pod and died.

Then, as fast as it had arrived, the pain stopped. Even as she noted that she knew it for a lie. The pain must have been the 'doc pumping an infusion of smart nano into her; it must have followed it up with a massive dose of analgesic. That meant she still hurt. She just couldn't feel it.

She became warm and drowsy. It hadn't just been painkillers, then.

She wanted to try to call the ship. She wanted to speak to Merish, even just to hear him, to know he was okay (*as if I am?* she thought), but the sleepiness was too much.

She slept.

She awoke to the sound of someone hammering on the pod – a sharp, purposeful impact that came every couple of seconds. About the length of time it would take a human holding a hammer to draw it back and have another go.

Seldyan shelved the thought. There was no way that anyone would get into the pod with hand tools. The worst they could do was to give her a headache, and if they had then the analgesic was still doing its work. She didn't seem to hurt at all, in fact. She wondered how long she had been asleep, but there was no way of knowing. The pod instruments were dead, the display was blank.

She took an audit. The ribs and the leg seemed fine – not just pain-free but functional, which meant that the nano must have done its healing work. She could move, too, because the impact pillows had deflated. Her audit completed, she undid herself, all the time doing her best to ignore the hammering which seemed to be getting more insistent. Something else seemed insistent too, now she had enough skin bared to notice it – it was getting cold.

She shrugged herself back into her coverall, hoping it was as smart as it was supposed to be. The cold was getting worse, and she remembered the snowy landscape she had crashed into.

The hammering had intensified even more. It was time to go, and once the pod had crash-landed there was only one way to open it. The control was similar to the one that had opened the braking flaps, but on the other side of the console in a position where you were very unlikely to find it by accident.

She yanked it, jammed her hands over her ears and began to count. She hoped the external warning broadcast was working – and that whoever was hammering would understand it.

As she got to five there was a sharp *crack* and the pod jumped a little. There was a brief swirl of white, acrid-smelling smoke, which was whipped away by a sudden icy cold breeze.

The top half of the pod was gone, blown away from the base by the same sort of explosive bolts that had fired the flaps an atmosphere ago. She poked her head out.

The first impression was just white. The pod had landed in snow, but it was shallow enough, or hard-packed enough, that the impact had not buried it. If she stood upright, her neck was level with the surface. It was a surface that went on for a long way; she was facing roughly downhill, and downhill went on for as far as her eyes could resolve – endless undulating snow-fields under a freezing mist.

Endless perhaps, but not uniform, she realized. Something imposed itself on the landscape, some kind of regular structure that marched dead straight down the rolling snow. It looked like a line strung between slender towers, but it was too far away to be distinct and, besides, there was the rest of the new world to think about. Someone had been hammering. She shuffled her feet so that her body began to rotate.

Half a turn in she stopped, and her body tensed like a metal wire.

Her first impression was that he was on his own, but she wasn't ready to trust first impressions. Then she corrected herself, almost amused at her assumption. Her first impression had been that the person was male.

It probably was, though. The figure rising slowly from what looked like a recent depression in the snow was thickly wrapped in crude-looking fabrics, but the face that craned forward from the big hood was blunt-jawed and bearded. On most planets that still meant male.

She raised both hands, palms outwards. 'Hello?'

The figure raised an arm, and gave a lopsided grin. 'Yes. Hello. Your machine. It is,' and he made an explosive noise through pursed lips.

She looked back at the pod, and then to where the separated upper section lay, where the bolt charges had blown it, on its side in the snow.

'Yes, it is.' And, with a stab of guilt, 'Did it hurt you?'

The grin widened. 'Not I. Used to ice-crack, to snow-fall. Now used to metal warning words and machine-bang. New skill!'

She laughed, and then gasped as the vicious cold caught at her lungs. His face clouded.

'Not used to high-cold?'

It was a good description. She shook her head.

'Follow.' He turned and began to climb up out of the impression of his own body shape.

She tried to follow, but immediately found herself floundering helplessly; the snow was thigh-deep, bone-dry and at once engulfingly soft and surprisingly heavy. She hadn't even completed one step before she was stuck. She drew in a lungful of air so cold it felt like a weight in her chest.

'Hey!'

He looked back. 'Difficult?'

'Yes, difficult!' She had wanted to swear but she wasn't sure how he would take it, and she needed this strange creature with his ability to live in this frozen desert.

He followed her gaze towards his feet. 'Ah. You think shoes?'

She bit back a tart comment. 'I think something. I can't walk on this. How do you do it?'

'Same as always. One foot, next foot.' He walked towards her as if to demonstrate.

She wasn't sure what she had expected to see – some kind of snow shoes, or something to spread his weight. Shoes, at least. Not just feet. They weren't even particularly hairy.

She must have looked surprised because he grinned. 'Built for snow, me. Not you! Take you to warm, then explain. Not far. Follow as quick as able.' And he turned and walked off over the surface of the snow.

She floundered after him, swearing. To her relief he was right; they had covered only a couple of hundred metres before he dropped from sight as if the snow had swallowed him. She cursed under her breath and speeded up as best she could, the acerbically cold air rasping in her throat. She crested a low ridge, looked down, and grinned with sheer relief.

The depression was more or less crater-shaped, maybe a hundred paces across at the top with smoothly sloped sides leading down to a flat base less than half that. It was just deep enough to hide the plain little hut that nestled in it, and Seldyan wondered for a second if that was an accident. But only for a second. She was too cold to wait. She took a dragging step over the crest, tripped forwards from the weight of her own snow-bound legs and fell down the slope in a mess of limbs.

The bottom of the slope seemed unreasonably hard. She shook her head and tried to stand up. Moments later she was sitting on her bottom.

'Shit!'

It was hard because it was ice. She let out an irritated breath, and then looked up sharply.

Her companion was laughing. She glared at him, and he nearly stopped. 'Sorry! Not used to people. Mostly alone in the snow. Go careful. Here.' He walked up to her, reached out a hand, uncovered like his feet, and she took it gingerly. It was cool and dry. She expected him to pull, but instead he moved

207

closer to her and braced his legs in a triangle. She felt his arm tensing, and he jerked his head upwards.

She pushed down on the hand, and was upright. She tested her stability carefully, and then let go of his hand.

She could stand, just.

He watched her for a second, then nodded and turned away. 'Follow slow. No more make me laugh.'

She bit back her response, and followed slow.

The hut was better on the inside. For a start it was, well, not warm exactly, but much less cold. She suspected her companion's definition of comfortable temperature was a couple of tens of degrees below hers, but it was at least above freezing. A low mound in the middle of the single room gave off wisps of aromatic smoke that drifted up into a wide funnel-shaped hood.

It was also much more attractive than the outside. The walls were hung with coarse rugs in muted colours, as if strong dyes weren't an option. Light came from dozens of little flat lamps, each one giving off a tall, wavering blue-white flame.

The man had been standing with his back to her, doing something to the fire. He moved aside and she saw orange sparks stream upwards from a hole in the top of the mound. He placed a sort of metal cradle over the hole, and balanced a wide, shallow black pot on the cradle. Then he spun round and shrugged off his coat.

It turned out he had been mostly coat. He was the thinnest, slightest human she had ever seen. His chest, now bare, was no wider than the distance from her thumb to her little finger. His upper arm was perhaps three fingers across.

She managed not to gasp, but she could feel her eyes widening.

He grinned. 'You fall from the sky in machine that explodes, and you think I odd?'

She felt her face heating, and his grin broadened so that it was nearly wider than his body. 'No more worry. I correct shape for snow. Light! Walk on powder. Name Hincc. Hincc of High People. You?'

She collected herself. 'Seldyan.'

'Very good name, falling-from-sky person.' He narrowed his eyes. 'Story to tell, yes? Drink hot soon. Begin when ready.'

There didn't seem to be an alternative. *Fair enough*, she thought. *I'd want to know, if I was him.*

She looked behind her, found a low stool, and sat on it, remembering too late to stop that it might have been made for someone a lot lighter than her. It creaked, but held.

'Okay,' she said. 'Story.'

It took a long time.

The pot was almost empty now. It had held a sweet, slightly spicy juice which she gathered had something to do with berries. She had done most of the talking but not all; Hincc had woven his own explanations around hers with a bardic skill which she suspected was born of long cold nights.

They had been good explanations. The High People had lived above the snowline for hundreds of generations. They hunted small mammals for leather, fur and meat; they foraged down towards the snowline for dry firewood and wiry grasses for fuel, and for the few sweet little berries they could find. Towards the snowline but never across it; at some point so far in the past they had forgotten it, the High People had become so specialized that they could no longer exist off the snowfields.

There was something else, too. It had made Hincc's face cloud, and he had become monosyllabic.

'Bad times.'

'Bad? How?'

'Very bad. Since the light?'

'You can see it?'

'Glow, on clear nights. Distant. From the Circle Lands. Perhaps tonight. Come, look.'

They climbed up the slope. The land fell sharply on one side and more gently on the other. On the gentle side the line thing she had seen when she first looked out from the pod marched down the snowfield. The angle of fall was quite sharp; gentle was comparative.

Hincc pointed. 'See?'

She did see. Right at the horizon, the snow was subtly green-lit, a soft sinister halo around the blue-white snow light, distinctly focused on a narrow quadrant of the horizon.

She watched the soft light for a while. Then she turned to Hincc. 'What happened?'

He shrugged. 'From here, see little. Light, then pause. Normal, ten days. I send ice – big blocks. Cool fish, cool people, yes? Ice go down, hooks come up. Then, three days, line stops.'

'Is that usual?'

'Not unheard – when bad winter closes Circle. But very rare, very strange. Not so strange as what comes after. When line starts again.'

Something in his voice made her look at his face. 'What?' she asked, dreading the answer.

He looked at her for a moment, his face immobile. Then he sighed. 'Follow. See. Be ready.'

He led her under the motionless cables of the lift. Things hung beneath them: complex-looking expandable grabs. She pointed. 'Are those for the ice?'

'Mainly for the ice. Meant for the ice. Be ready.' He didn't look back, and the set of his shoulders discouraged further questions.

She followed, more easily than she had feared. There was a hard track stamped on to the snow. It was wider than one set of feet would have needed. She wondered why.

Then they crested a low ridge and she found herself looking down into the narrow head of a white valley that broadened quickly down the shallow, rolling snow slopes.

White, but dotted with irregular shapes.

She clenched her fists, and turned to Hincc. 'How many?'

His face was still rigid. 'I count careful. Since two weeks after green light, eight elevens and seven. Then I stop the line. Never before, never, do we stop the line from here. But I, my father, his father, their fathers? We send ice down. Maybe writing to ask for something, always comes soon. Not this. Never this. Soon berry juice will not be sweet. Soon lift parts will not be replaced. Already ice doesn't reach harbour. Does no one fish, or does fish rot?'

She counted the shapes. Ninety-five. Almost a hundred corpses. Some of them looked incomplete – arms and legs were missing – but they all seemed to have heads. There were no bloodstains in the snow, and she supposed the bodies must have been frozen hard by the time they arrived. She let herself absorb the scene. Then she said, carefully, 'Do you know why they were – sent?'

He shrugged. 'Only one thing. All wearing like this.' He felt in his furs and drew out something. She held out her hand and he let it drop into her palm, but without letting go of the chain that pierced it. She turned it over; just a plain greyish metal disc. One side was blank. The other was embossed with what looked like a random pattern of dots. No, not just dots. She looked closer. The snowglow was bright enough to show fine lines radiating from each dot, like a child's drawing of a star.

She tilted her palm to let the disc slide off it. Hincc caught it as it swung towards him on its chain. He let it drop into his own hand and slipped it back into his furs. 'Anything to you, Sky Girl?'

She shook her head.

'No surprise. Something to me – all priest people. Seen before. Heard, a little. Priest people watch the sky, count things. Perhaps green light means priest people must die.'

'Why?'

He turned his face away, but looked at her from the corner of his eyes. 'Who knows? What do all priest people say? Do this thing, do that thing, and tomorrow is like yesterday and sun always shines. All safe. But suddenly tomorrow is not like yesterday; tomorrow is green light – and maybe people say, why do we do this thing and that thing?' He smiled sourly. 'Especially, why do we feed these priest people who give us orders and do not go fishing?'

She nodded.

'So, you go and see?'

The question caught her off balance. 'I don't know.'

His sour grin became a real one. 'Okay, fine, stay here. Chew salt meat, eat berries. I start the line again, maybe you count priest bodies, maybe other bodies when they run out of priests. That what you came for, Sky Girl?'

She found herself smiling back. 'No. Not what I came for.'

'Good. So go discover.'

She nodded. 'How do I go?'

'Tomorrow, I show. Now come. Dark, cold. Time for fire. Time for sleep.'

He was right. The sky was black, and even in her ship suit the cold was aching. She stared upwards. 'Hincc? Are there ever any stars?'

He shook his head. 'Only in stories.'

She nodded and followed him down the slope towards the hut. Then she stopped. 'Stories? But you know what a star is?'

And watched him.

'Only in stories.' They were the same words but the tone had changed. The first time he had used them they had sounded like closing down. Now they sounded – different. She held the sound close to her as she followed him through the entrance of the hut. She held on to it as she watched Hincc shrugging off his layers of clothing, and as she followed suit. She held on to it as they sat down, little cups of steaming juice warming their hands and the glow of the fire pit stinging their feet.

Then she took a careful breath and asked the question.

'Hincc? You're a story-teller. Tell me another story. Tell me about the stars you've never seen.'

And with a simplicity that could as easily have been victory as defeat, he told her. By the time he had finished, the fire had dropped to embers, her breath was smoking in front of her and there was frost forming on the inside of the hut.

She barely noticed. But afterwards, she lay awake on a pallet heaped with furs and stared up at a knot-hole in the timbers of the low roof and wondered.

At first he had not seemed to be telling a story as she understood it. Instead he began by talking about the cold, the snowfields and the few creatures that lived on them. There were slim pale-grey hares that ate the berries of the few tough scrubby bushes that rooted directly in the snow, and drew their scant minerals from the urine of the same creatures. Bigger but slower, a long, almost tubular predator that grew longer, but not fatter, as it aged, and that sprouted another pair of stubby legs for every hand's breadth of length. Then, tiny and prey to everything, two-legged fur-balls with one strong arm and one weak, and with minuscule eyes set in deep sockets, who could look directly into the ice glare but whose sight was so poor they had to find their own snow burrows by the scent of the mate who never went outdoors.

Some of these seemed farcical to Seldyan. She had grown up in a world of order, even if it was the imposed order of a confined world, and what Hincc was describing sounded like biological anarchy. But then, slowly, she began to feel the specialized rhythm of life on these permanently white peaks, and following that she realized that the rhythm he described was not a thing only of the present – it came from the past, and reached into it. And as it moved into the past, tracing the histories of the animals and the berries and the peaks, it gathered stories around itself. Eventually, the stories reached their source.

The past was long, here. The separation of the High People from everyone else was so ancient that it was the stuff not just of folklore, but of folklore about folklore. Their languages had diverged, not so far that the two peoples couldn't understand each other, but far enough for each people's story to sound strange to the ears of the others. Even their names for the planet they lived on were different – everyone else called it Trakael, but Hincc's people used what he claimed was an older name: Solpht. The oldest folklore of all said that there had once been a bigger, brighter sun and that there were bright points in the sky at night.

'Whose folklore?'

He had shrugged. 'High People. Others, different stories. See this?' It was one of the tokens from the bodies.

She nodded. 'That's why I asked you about stars. These dots look like drawings of stars.'

'Maybe stars, maybe not. Down there people say other things.'

'Have you seen them?'

He shook his head. 'No. Never here. Always in same place. Hills above Circle Plains. People there make own stories. People, and priest people.'

'Circle Plains? Is that where you send the ice?'

'Almost. Not Plains; Harbour below.'

'Right.' She stared at the embers for a moment. 'Is that where you think I should explore?'

He laughed, an unexpected explosion in the close quiet of the hut. She looked at him, eyebrows raised, and he shook his head again. 'You ask me what to do? You fall from sky and I call you Sky Girl, but that is wrong. Yes?' He sat up, leaned forward so his face was less than an arm's length from hers. 'Not from. Through. You fall through sky from somewhere else. Now you tell me: somewhere else, are stars real?'

She held his gaze for a moment. Then she looked down. 'Yes,' she said, to her lap. 'They are real.'

'I knew!' He clapped his skinny hands. 'Real stars! And you come from them. Travel between?'

She nodded.

'And you ask me to tell you stories? To tell you what to do? You are Star Girl, not Sky Girl. Go where you want.'

'No, Hincc.' She shook her head. 'It doesn't work like that. I barely know about where I came from. I know nothing about here.'

For a while he was silent. Then he compressed his lips. 'Go to Harbour. Find out why green lights in sky make them send me bodies of priests.'

There hadn't been anything else to say. Hincc had lain down and pulled some furs over himself, and after a few moments Seldyan did too.

He seemed to be sleeping, but she couldn't.

The next morning she was fuzzy with sleeplessness. She sat wrapped in her furs while Hincc melted snow-water over a fire of what she thought at first were long, straight twigs. Then she looked again and realized that they all tapered to a needle point. She frowned, then waved at them. 'Hincc? Are they thorns?'

He took the shallow pan off the flames and poured the water over dried leaves in another pan. 'Yes, thorns. Leaves, here, from same bush. Above snowline, world shrinks; I use all parts. Thorns and leaves grow back. Branches, not so much. Now drink, then eat.'

She drank the acerbic brew and ate hare meat, salted and mixed with dried berries and pressed into flat cakes. The sour berries and salt cut across the sweet dry flesh so she didn't know whether to lick her lips or suck in her cheeks.

It didn't matter. Right back to the Hive, she knew the value of food as fuel. She ate everything. It helped more than she expected; she felt energy returning. She looked up to find Hincc grinning at her. She raised an eyebrow.

'Feel better?'

She nodded.

'Not surprise. Food always good, and leaf brew is stimulant.' His grin widened. 'I use little. People down below sometimes use much. Then more, then more, then can't stop. You know?'

'Yes.' She explored her senses; the effects seemed mild and she didn't feel dangerously altered. 'Do you send the leaves down?'

'Did. Not do. Since bodies, ice line still. Nothing down, nothing up.'

'I get that.' She stood up. 'Hincc? I have to go.'

'I know. Circle Harbour.'

'Yes, Circle Harbour.' She thought for a moment. 'You could come with me. If you wanted?'

He shook his head. 'No. Too warm, too damp. High People die fast below snowline. Stay here, eat hare and berries, brew leaves and wait for better time. Maybe you send better time, Star Girl.'

'Maybe.' She tried to smile, because it was better than the alternative. Then she pushed her thoughts away. There would be time for them later, maybe. 'So, how do I get there?'

She had taken the med kit from the pod, and a few other things. A comms bead tickled her inner ear but did nothing else. Totally dead.

Now she was standing, looking down along the huge sweep of the ice line. The part of her that wasn't busy being worried was very impressed.

A growing part was also intrigued. She turned to Hincc. 'Who made this? How does it work?'

He shrugged. It was a very expressive gesture in someone so skinny. 'Who, unknown. Always here, always same. How, easy. Heavy ice goes down, only light things come up.'

'How long is it?'

'To top of Circle Harbour, thirty days' walk.'

Seldyan caught her breath. From her short experience a day here was roughly standard. A day's walk might be twenty klicks, if you could deal with the snow.

She looked down the line again. It was a simple thing, but on a vast scale – two cables strung between pylons that were about twenty metres high. They must have been under huge tension, because they barely dipped at all. There was a pylon about every fifty metres, marching down the snow slopes in a paired procession that blended into one in the middle distance and then disappeared in the mist bank that was hanging at the base of the snowline. At regular intervals, the complicated metal claws that Hincc called ice hooks hung down from the cables.

The pylon nearest her seemed to be some sort of concrete. She couldn't tell what the cable was made of, but it didn't look like metal. It had a matt grey look, and the frost didn't seem to stick to it.

It was much higher tech than anything she had seen here so far. Of course, that might mean nothing. Hincc's people had a particular take on technology.

Might. Six hundred kilometres of line, presumably twice as much cable?

She felt a smile trying to break out. 'Hincc? You just told me something important.'

He spread his arms. 'Always. You come back, tell me what joke is.'

'Oh, I will. You've got my ship, remember?'

'I take care. Star Girl? You go, or you stay?'

She laughed. 'I go. How long will it take?'

'To Ice House in Circle Harbour, three suns. Be cautious – maybe wise to drop off sooner, walk.'

'Yes.' *Well*, she thought, *he's right. I go.*

The down cables were on the right. Hincc had uncoupled the ice hooks on the nearest one; they lay on, and partly in, the powder snow. In their place a sling hung from the cable. It was made of furs.

She looked at Hincc. 'You made that?'

'Yes. In case. Star Girl? Keep eyes away from other cable. Look right. Now climb in.'

She didn't need to climb. The sling was at knee height. She stood in front of it and sat back. It took her weight, swaying. 'What do I do now?' she asked.

He gestured. 'Pull on hanging line.'

A thick loop of cord dangled in front of her. She took hold of the nearer half and pulled. She felt it take up a load and the sling twitched upwards with a quick squeak that sounded like pulleys. A minute of brisk hauling and she was twice her own height off the snow, level with the ice hooks on the other cable.

She checked her pouch – everything was there. She seemed ready to go. She looked down at Hincc.

'How do I stop it?'

He laughed. 'You don't! Stop from here. Maybe stop from Circle, if they remember how. In between, only go until ice all melts.' He pointed down the line. 'Twenty blocks, see? Enough for go; not too fast.'

'So how do I get off?'

'Lower.' He mimed pulling the cord, hand over hand. 'Then jump. Easy. But back on again, not possible. Be sure! Ready?'

She nodded.

'Then go.' He kicked the lever. 'Good luck, Star Girl!'

The sling canted forward and, far more smoothly than she had expected, she was moving.

She didn't look back. For the first hour she didn't look left either, although she wasn't sure why Hincc had been so adamant. The wind bit her face and she sank as deep into the furs as she could.

Then something caught the corner of her eye and she did look to the left – just a little, because the thing was still a long way down the line. But it was moving towards her. She corrected herself. Things, not thing: a line of black dots swaying upwards.

She swallowed. The corpses of priests were still coming. Hincc must have known they would.

She wondered if whoever had set up the line, and had presumably at the same time rewritten the future of this poor little planet, had ever anticipated that.

Three Quarter Circle Harbour Wall

Three things had saved Belbis after they had thrown him into the shack, unconscious and with a broken arm and broken ribs and slashed heels – if he could count himself saved. The first had been water and that, he was sure, had been accidental. The roof of the shack, as he could tell from a combination of memory and smell, was tar-paper, old and holed. A few of the holes must have lain at the bottom of sagged areas, and they formed dew collectors. If he shuffled himself beneath them and lay with his mouth open he could take on enough water, if not to live, then not to die that day. There had been forty-one of the days so far. He had not lost the ability to count things. Sometimes, and especially in the dark, he lay still, cradling his stubbornly unhealed arm across his chest, and re-counted the Gods in his head. He always came to the same number, and it was always the wrong one.

The second was that he had regained just a little of his vision. Not enough for details, but enough that some of the blurs could mean something if he looked carefully out of the corner of his eye. Straight ahead, there was nothing but greenish black darkness.

That was how he had found the bottle. It had been lying in a corner of his shack in just the right place for a shaft of morning sun, slicing through one of the many gaps in the walls, to glance off it.

The gaps allowed many things into his shack. The sunlight, certainly, but also the smells of the docks and a piercing wind that permitted him little sleep. They should also have let in the sounds of the docks, but those had gone, replaced by the restless creak and slam of abandoned boats and, further away but no less noticeable, shouts and the sound of anger.

He had been glad of the bottle. There had been nothing else suitable. The wooden walls of the shack were built off a stone plinth that was wider than the timber; he had chosen a protruding edge, took the bottle by the neck in his good hand, and brought it down hard.

He had cut his fingers searching amongst the pieces, but that didn't matter. He had found what he was looking for.

It was nearly time for the girl to visit, if she was going to. He had to hurry.

He took the large shard, lifted his right leg so that the foot lay on his left thigh, and began to scrape out the worm-infested flesh from his heel.

When he had first done this he had used the unbroken neck of the bottle to bite on. The glass was thick, and he knew he wouldn't break it no matter how he bit. But recently the nerves in his heel had begun to die and the daily job was merely agonizing.

Every day he had to go a little deeper to make sure he had cleared all the hard little egg sacs. If they managed to penetrate the cartilage of his heel and grow into his bones, they would kill him in weeks.

In the extremes of the hunger that had come to him before the girl, he had once tried to eat his own scrapings but the taste of his poisoned flesh had been vile, and the combination of the restless maggots and their gritty eggs had made him vomit. Now he buried the daily mess in a little hollow he scooped out of the earth floor with another of the glass fragments.

He had just finished when he heard the uneven shuffle of her feet outside, and the diffident little knock.

Before the girl came, he had been starving to death. Now he was just starving. She had never explained why she came – why she had shuffled up to this shack, where he had been dragged and left to die after they had crippled him, and knocked, and thrust a bit of bread under the door and then run away.

The bread had been stale and hard as wood. He had moistened it with saliva a drop at a time to soften it, and eaten each musty crumb like a banquet.

The next day she had been there again. There was a little more bread and, this time, one of the little fish-skin bags of water the men had used to take out with them on their boats, when the boats had still gone out.

Belbis had always hated fish. He still did, but thirst overcame anything. The oily tainted water managed to taste good enough. It lifted him from dying slowly to just barely holding ground.

The girl was the third thing, obviously. And now she was here. He lifted his head from the pallet and called out.

'Come in!'

And someone came in, but it was not the little girl because whoever it was had to open the narrow door wide to get through it, so that the light became brighter than it had ever been since he had been left here, and then dimmed as a body passed through, and then brightened again, and a voice, a woman's voice said, in an odd accent, 'Hello?' And then, after an interval when he heard a breath sharply drawn in, 'Oh shit . . .'

The accent was the same as the machine on the hill had used, before the light came. Belbis tried to raise himself on his elbow, but he had chosen the wrong elbow. His broken arm collapsed beneath him like a twig and he collapsed with it.

Three Quarter Circle

It hadn't taken Seldyan long to find what she was looking for. She had assumed it was going to take her a while even to frame the question, but the state of the town made it obvious.

Circle Harbour was – had been – a small sea port with, she guessed, not many more than a few thousand houses. It had a walled harbour enclosed by a rock-pile wall that formed almost a complete circle. Hence the name, she assumed. The area around the harbour was thick with huts and ramps and yards, mostly fouled with the decaying remains of what looked like fish processing. Within the harbour, black water full of floating rubbish and inflated corpses lapped at the edges of ramps through a scum of sickly foam.

The smell was indescribable. She had held out until she was within sight of the harbour; then, feeling somehow ashamed, she had rummaged through the med kit, found a couple of filter plugs and jammed them in her nostrils. The labels said they were to exclude inhalable bacteria, which was probably a good thing. They reduced the stench to merely disgusting.

She had been able to smell the town from a long way away, but it wasn't decay she noticed first. She had been glad to leave that behind.

She had dropped off the ice line six nights ago, just below the snowline, when the smell from the thawing, decomposing bodies began to make her retch. With a detached part of her she theorized that they had already been decaying when they were hooked on. Whatever; as soon as her feet were on the ground she had half walked, half run, fifty or so paces upwind of it. Then she had turned parallel with the ice line, and begun to walk.

The ice line slanted obliquely down the coast, following an almost level path between a grey sea to the left and a long dull heather-blue rise towards cloudy mountains to the right. At night the clouds shone green. Even during the day she could see a hint of colour. She watched for the source of it, but the clouds never lifted far enough.

A day out from the town she began to smell the burning. She had stopped and lifted her nose to catch the on-shore wind. Definitely burning, but not fresh. There was something acrid about it, like ash mixed with – something; she wasn't sure what.

A day later she was sure. On the outskirts of the town most of the buildings were stone and those still stood, although a few had lost roofs and some looked ransacked. Further in, whole areas had been reduced to waist-high clay walls, extravagantly blackened and cracked, with the charcoaled bones of timber frames sticking up from them. The streets were paved with fat lozenge-shaped cobbles. Water had collected between them, its surface rainbowed with oil.

That was the smell. She thought about that for a while, randomly walking the quiet streets with her eyes mainly downward – there were too many things to trip over or slip on. Then she shook off her reverie and looked around, forcing herself to complete one slow, full turn with her eyes raised and her senses properly alert.

The coastal plain the town was built on wasn't quite a plain. It rose and fell, reminding Seldyan of large-scale sand dunes. There was a high point a few hundred metres away, up-slope from the sea, with what looked like some fairly intact buildings on it. She compressed her lips. Either there was something here or there wasn't; it was time to find out.

She started walking.

It took her longer than she would have expected. The streets were convoluted, full of twists and dead ends, and sometimes she had to retrace her steps when she was stopped by a collapsed building or a heap of debris. But after an hour of scrambling she was looking at a low two-storey building of long flat stones, smoke-stained along the side that faced the harbour but otherwise seemingly untouched.

She looked it up and down, and then her heart bounced. There were chimneys at both ends of the roof, and one of them was wisping smoke.

People. She had found people.

She took a breath, but before she could call out there were running feet behind her and something hit her in the small of her back. She went down, crashing against the cobbles with her arms thrown in front of her face.

Whoever it was, they seemed to be lying on her, but they didn't feel heavy. She raised herself on her forearms, wincing at the protest from her grazed skin. Then she froze.

'Stay down!'

It had been an urgent whisper, so close to her ear that she felt hot breath, but that wasn't what had surprised her. It was a child's voice, and it sounded serious.

She dropped again. Almost before she was down there was a shattering boom from somewhere in front of her. Something whistled over her head in a cloud of dust, and then there was a pattering like raindrops around her. She felt things landing on her arms and the back of her head; through screwed-up eyes she saw falling splinters.

The weight on her back lifted abruptly, and then she found herself looking up into a brown face framed by a lot of dark straight hair. 'He's reloading,' said the face. 'Run now.' And then it was gone and there was a slight figure running awkwardly away downhill, towards the harbour.

Seldyan shook her head to clear it. Then she rose to a crouch and ran after the girl. She caught her up a couple of streets away; the awkwardness had quickly turned into a skipping limp, and the dark face was twisted with pain.

She knelt so that their faces were level. 'Thanks,' she said. 'Are you okay?'

The face turned away, but Seldyan had already had time to see that the dark colour was more dirt than skin, and there were darker smudges around one eye. She felt her own eyes narrowing. 'Someone hit you?'

The girl nodded, still with her head turned.

'What about your leg. Was that . . . ?'

Another nod.

'Who did it?'

Emphatic shake.

'Right.' Seldyan patted her belt; the med kit was there, and felt undamaged. She looked around. 'I owe you one. I can make you better. Is there anywhere safe we can go?'

For a long time the girl was silent. Then she glanced at the med kit. 'Make very bad things better?'

'It depends how bad.' Seldyan hesitated. 'Are you very hurt?'

The head shook again. 'Not me. You come?'

Seldyan hesitated, and then cursed herself. *Maybe it is all shit*, she thought. *Maybe all I can do is make a bit of it a bit less shit*. 'Okay,' she said, straightening up. 'You lead.'

The girl nodded and set off, still heading down towards the harbour. She wasn't running this time, and the limp was so pronounced that her left foot seemed barely to touch the ground before it was lifted again, but she kept up a steady pace.

Seldyan guessed she would be about the same age as Dimollss. Something about the thought made her pause for a second. Then she squared her shoulders and followed the girl.

As she followed, a thought followed her. *This was what I came for.*

The smell in the shack made her retch. It was shit and piss and the powerful waxy stink of unwashed body and, overwriting all of that, something rotting – not just rotten but actively putrefying.

Seldyan had once cleared out a cold store where the chillers had failed. She had shovelled out half a tonne of spoiled synthetic protein. That had been similar, but not as bad.

The door had swung to behind her. She kicked it open, found a loose cobble, wrenched it up and used it to prop the door so the light fell on the pile of rags in the corner, and the skeleton that had tried to raise itself when she had first entered.

It was a man – she guessed a young man, but the face was so shrunken and bearded it was hard to be sure of age. The one certain thing was that he was starving to death – had obviously been doing so for a long time.

He was covered from the waist down by more rags. She swallowed and drew them back. When they got to his feet they seemed to stick. She pulled a little harder, and they came free, and she covered her mouth in horror. But she didn't let herself turn away.

The soles of the man's feet, from the ball to the heel, were raw flesh, blackened and oozing pus. At the heels, white bone glinted. As Seldyan watched, a short brown worm wriggled out of the wound, and then another.

Still without turning, she spoke to the girl. 'How did this happen?'

'The men cut him.'

'Which men?'

She shrugged. 'Men from the town.'

'Where are they now?'

'Most gone. There was burning, and then bad smells.'

'But why cut him?'

The girl shrugged. 'He was the Painter.'

'Okay, never mind.' She didn't understand but questions could wait. She took out the mini-doc, clamped her lips together and knelt down by the man.

When she finally sat back on her heels and dug her hands into the small of her back to ease the ache, the light was getting dim. She ran her eyes over her patient and nodded slowly. The doc had supplied sedatives, a shot of quick-heal and a massive dose of a broad-spectrum anti-parasitic. His feet were cleaned and dressed and his horribly broken arm was encased in splint-foam.

'I think you'll live.' She rotated her shoulders. Everything ached. Then she turned to the girl, who had barely moved the whole time. 'I haven't forgotten you,' she said, 'but we need to get this one somewhere clean and safe. Do you know anywhere?'

The face flickered. 'Clean. Not safe.' Her hand went to her bruised eye. The index finger was swollen and crooked, and Seldyan realized with a jolt of disgust that it was broken.

'Not safe because they did things to you?'

The girl nodded.

Seldyan stood up, feeling her knees creaking, and reached into her pouch. The smooth bulge of the stunner fitted easily into her curled fingers.

'Maybe we can do something about that,' she said. 'Will you trust me?'

The girl's eyes went to the unconscious man, and then back to Seldyan. She nodded, and her lips twitched in something that might have been the start of a smile.

'Right. Show me where.'

She wasn't surprised when 'where' turned out to be the house she had headed for that morning. Viewed from what she hoped was a safe distance, the chimney wasn't smoking any more and there were sagging timber shutters over the windows. One of the shutters had a corner missing. She saw clean white wood along the tear and guessed it had fallen victim to whatever weapon had been fired at her earlier. A plume of splinters on the ground led towards where she had met Bis.

It seemed an odd name. She hadn't been able to find out if it was short for anything, because the girl had become less communicative as they got nearer the house. Her face was pale and set. It wasn't pain; Seldyan had given her a painkiller and a dose of quick-heal. She had borne the hypo phlegmatically, like someone who'd had practice bearing things, and Seldyan had found herself shaking her head.

Now she leaned down and spoke quietly. 'Will they fire again?'

Bis shook her head. 'Drinking time.'

'Ah. How many people?'

'Just him.' The word was flat.

Seldyan watched the house for a moment. Bis sounded sure but she might be wrong, and there was no way of finding out by looking. Seldyan felt the stunner cradled in her palm. Her body heat had warmed it. It felt – friendly.

She grinned to herself and set the level to its highest point – Captain Hefs had been knocked out by half that, but then she had sort of liked him. 'Wait for me there,' she said, and pointed towards a patch of shade at the base of a ruined wall opposite the house. 'Come when I call. Understand? Not before.'

The girl nodded.

'Right. See you.' Seldyan straightened up, took a breath and ran.

There was a flimsy-looking door in the rough centre of the ground floor. She ignored it. 'Very strong,' Bis had said, before she clammed up. 'Go behind. Barrel drop.' It had taken some clarification, but now Seldyan knew what she was looking for – the girl's private way in and out.

Hopefully private.

The back of the house was piled with litter. Stacks of broken timber leaned against the wall. At one point they formed a lean-to tunnel. Seldyan dropped to her knees and shuffled along it, smelling tar and rot, until her hands met a rough wooden hatch. She ran her fingers round the edge until they felt a rusted hoop. A pull, and the hatch lifted.

She eased herself through and dropped half her own length.

Then she screamed as hot cramping agony flooded her leg. She tried to lift her foot from whatever it was, but it wouldn't move. She almost lost her balance and her arms flailed. Her hand banged into something and gripped it, and then she realized she was still screaming and somehow bit it back. She looked down and her heart went cold.

Someone had driven iron nails into a board, and had left it, points upward, beneath the hatch where her feet had landed.

Or where Bis's feet would have landed.

Then she heard the footsteps on the floor above, and anger overcame the pain. She shut her eyes and pulled her foot off the nails, managing to experience the tearing of the rough metal with something close to detachment. Then she hopped sideways, away from the patch of light thrown by the hatch, until she was standing in a corner with the stunner held out in front of her. It wasn't shaking much.

The footsteps paused. There was a sharp creak and light appeared in the opposite corner of the room – the wavering orange light of a flame. Someone was coming down a steep flight of stairs, a lamp held out in front of them. Even across the room, it smelled of oil.

Seldyan waited until the full length of the legs was visible. Then she fired.

There was a howl, and a body crashed down and lay twitching. The lamp clanged to the floor a metre away, and flames flickered about a spreading pool.

Seldyan swore. She half hopped, half skipped across the floor, picked up the still burning lamp and put it on a shelf. Sacks of something were stacked against the wall by the steps; she hauled one of them out of the stack, dumped it on the pool of flames and watched it until she was sure they were out. Then she dragged another sack on top of the first, sat on it and glared down at the fallen man.

His eyes were wide in the dim light. One hand was underneath him. The other reached convulsively for a leg which lay in an impossible shape, the calf forming an acute angle with the thigh. Even in the lamplight she could see dark wetness spreading through the material where his knee would be.

She nodded towards the leg. 'That's going to hurt a lot more when the stun wears off. Are you the man who beats up little girls?'

'What's stun?' The words were slurred, and she caught a sour gust of bad teeth and alcohol.

Seldyan sighed. 'I shot your legs. Look, I haven't got time . . . you're going to sleep. I'll see you if you wake up.' She raised the stunner again and fired, this time at the torso. The body convulsed and was still. About half a day, she guessed. Long enough.

It took her a long time to climb the steps. By the time Bis answered her call she was sitting on a stool, her injured foot propped up in front of her. The girl's eyes widened when she saw the blood-stained sabot. Seldyan managed to grin at her. 'Can you be a doctor?'

Then she leaned back and closed her eyes. Just for a minute, she promised herself.

When she opened her eyes, the room was lit by firelight. There was a rough blanket around her shoulders and her bloody sabot was on the floor by her stool.

Her foot hurt; that was what had woken her. There was a job to do. She sat forward and looked around. 'Bis?'

There were soft footsteps behind her and the girl appeared. Seldyan looked her up and down. Her stance was symmetrical now, and the footsteps had sounded even. 'Feeling better?'

Bis nodded.

'Good. I need your help. Is there any hot clean water?'

She watched while the girl heated a blackened pot on the fire. It was big enough for her whole foot to fit. When it was ready she gritted her teeth and bathed it while Bis watched with learning eyes. Then she withdrew it and rested her heel on the ground. 'Now, I need some strong drink.'

The girl's face flickered, and Seldyan added, 'Not to drink. To clean. Stop bad getting in.'

Bis nodded. She gestured to the med kit. 'No good for you?'

Seldyan glanced at the kit and hesitated. In the end she said, 'I only use it if I have to.' As a general statement, she thought, that was true. It just avoided the specific point that there was nothing left; she had used the whole kit on Bis and the man in the shack.

And she didn't even know who he was. But Bis thought he was important, and she had to trust someone.

Bis fetched a flat glass flagon from a store beside the chimney. She opened the stopper with a twist that looked practised and held it out. Seldyan shook her head. 'You do it,' she said. 'Pour it over.'

And gripped the legs of the stool, hard.

By the time she had bandaged her foot with the cleanest-looking rag she could find and jammed it back in her sabot, the light was getting dim. She reflected for a while. Then she put a hand on Bis's shoulder. 'I'm going to fetch the man,' she said. 'Stay here. Keep the door closed. Tend the fire. Is there any food?'

The girl nodded.

'Okay. Get us something to eat. Soft things. Soup. You know how to make soup? He'll probably be awake, understand? He'll need to eat.' She reflected for a moment, and added, 'And heat water. Lots of water. He'll need to wash.'

Then she turned and limped through the door. She heard it close emphatically behind her.

Unknown

He had been – wherever it was – for a while. Time was difficult. They didn't allow him to sleep and the light never changed, so days were unmeasurable. There were no meals, only the sour fluid they forced between his lips from time to time. It seemed to contain a stimulant, because it could wake him from the warm stupor he occasionally lapsed into when they had hurt him too much, or for too long.

They would always punish him for that, although he could never predict exactly when.

His world was the thing he sat on and was fixed to – an ordinary chair, but skeletal and seemingly capable of being any shape and in any position – and the dim view of a wall. Between him and the wall, a stool, and on the stool a small human male in drab clothes.

He was aware of the operative, or operatives. He had no way of counting them; no means of telling how many there were, or if they had advisors, assistants or even an audience. Everything he couldn't feel or see, he ruled out, and what was in front of him he acknowledged, but didn't trust.

To not trust your world. That was all there was. Trust would be acceptance, and acceptance would be ending. So far, and as far as he could tell, he hadn't ended. He was less sure if he was sane.

The world he didn't trust was demanding his attention. The man on the stool had sighed. 'We begin again. We will begin again as many times as we need to. Only you can help us to an ending.' His eyes slid a little to the side and he nodded.

Yellow. Vess had come to assign colours to pain. This was yellow, a bright hot yellow like a sun, or better perhaps like a shard of metal, heated close to melting. He smelled burning flesh.

When it stopped the little man was looking at him. 'People have lived for years in that chair, you know. So long that their flesh has fused to it, so that they have to be torn from it in the end.' He leaned forward. 'There is no escape. No insanity, no death. We know better than that. You are the best-preserved living entity in the Spin.' Another nod.

Yellow, and more burning, and convulsions; tearing of muscle fibres leaping against restraints.

'So, a beginning. You came alive out of the Stack. You were then interviewed by Vut. You handled a runner. The runner was rogue and now Caphraime II is dead and a few hundred people have hearing damage. Had Chairman Or-Shls not acted quickly he would be dead instead of her, and that was probably the real intention. You have no reason to love the Chairman. You claim to know nothing, but I don't believe you. Speak at any time.'

The same question, and he had already given his only answer many times. He would have shaken his head, but it was fixed in place. He would have closed his eyes but they had removed his eyelids.

Nod. The operatives must have changed their aim, somehow finding some part of him that had not yet been seared, ground, fractured, punctured, outraged. Yellow brightened towards white, became all-encompassing. He heard himself raving, roaring. Inhuman sounds. They were wrong, there was escape, he could see it, it blotted out the man and the stool and the wall, it was a core of black in the blinding white; he could feel himself dropping towards it. He reached out to it from the remains of his mind.

'Abort.'

It stopped. Everything stopped. Vision returned. The man on the stool was sitting dead upright with a listening expression on his face. Then he nodded, but this time as if to himself, and looked at Vess.

'Goodbye,' he said. And he and the stool and the wall were gone.

Vess sat up, and nothing impeded him. He blinked, and felt his eyes moistened by proper tears. He looked around, feeling a breeze touch different parts of his face as he moved. The breeze smelled familiar: canals and Basin Lilies and the tiniest hint of cylinder oil and something else, something he couldn't place for the moment. There were canals in the distance but, and he shook his head, they were all below him. That didn't make sense.

A voice behind him said, 'Hello, Harbour Master.'

Then he realized. The smell he couldn't identify was tobacco smoke. It was just that he had never smelled it fresh before. He was in Basin City, and for the first time in his life he was seeing it from the Cloud Deck, and the voice behind him belonged to Alst Or-Shls.

He hadn't realized it before but somehow, fixed in the chair with the wall to look at, he had not been frightened.

Now, he was terrified.

Three Quarter Circle Harbour

The young man turned out to be a fast healer. On the second morning he sat up and squinted at her. 'I can see,' he said.

Seldyan grinned. 'And you can talk. I'm Seldyan and this is Bis. Who are you?'

'I'm Belbis the . . .' He hesitated. 'I'm Belbis.'

'Belbis the something secret? Okay.' Seldyan studied his face. On an impulse she said, 'You know what you are? Belbis the safe. She kept you alive, I mended you. So you can say whatever you like – or nothing at all. It's up to you.'

She turned away before he could respond. Over her shoulder she added, 'Think about it. I've got things to do.'

That was true. It was just that she didn't want to do them.

Bis had told her something about the young man, but it had been from a child's perspective – a child who had been dancing to a tune she recognized. But this was different; she doubted she would ever know everything that had passed between Bis and the man in the cellar, but she could guess.

She had considered killing the man out of hand, but something had held her back. Now she was glad of it.

She walked carefully down the steps, holding the stunner out in front of her and sparing her injured foot as much load as she could. Then she squatted down, out of reach, keeping one hand behind her back.

He was conscious. The eyes were watchful beads surrounded by pouches of sagging flesh, and one hand still worked at the injured leg. He stank of stale drink and fresh faeces.

Seldyan nodded at the leg. 'Feeling anything?'

'Go shit yourself.'

She raised her eyebrows. 'It smells like you got there first. The stun should be wearing off by now. Guess your leg's starting to hurt.'

He clamped his mouth shut but his eyes flickered, and his hand clenched at the bloodied cloth above his knee.

She nodded. 'Okay,' she said. And brought round the hand from behind her back so he could see the short knobby staff.

The man flinched, and that decided Seldyan more than anything, because Bis had flinched in the same way when she had seen it.

'This is for Bis,' she said, and brought it down on his knee. Something crunched.

His shriek made her ears whistle. She waited until he had quietened, and then raised the stick again. 'I should kill you,' she said. 'For all the bruises I can see on that little girl, and all the ones I can't, and for that plank full of nails that was meant for her – I should kill you.'

His mouth was open, but the only thing coming out was drool; a yellowish thread dangled from his chin and snapped.

She shook her head, more at herself than at him, and dropped the staff. 'Okay, you get to live a while. Tell me what happened to this place.'

The eyes became calculating. 'If I do?'

She raised the staff. 'Think about if you don't.'

They glared at each other for a moment. Then his eyes slid away. 'I heard him,' he said.

She blinked. 'Who?'

'Him.' He took his hand from his knee and pointed upwards. 'The idiot. You brought him here.'

'How's he an idiot?'

He laughed, a rasp that buried itself in a wet cough that took too long to stop. She watched him for a moment, then asked, 'Have you had that long?'

He spat and wiped his mouth; even that seemed to cost him more breath than he had. 'Long enough. You know what you hear?'

'I think so.' She sat back on her heels. 'Maybe we can make a different bargain. Maybe I have something you want.'

He watched her for a dozen heartbeats. Then something in his face relaxed. 'Maybe you do. You brought the idiot back. Ask him; it's his fault.'

She shook her head. 'I don't understand.'

'Like I told you. Ask him.' He shook his head. 'All he had to do was go up the mountain and paint the fucking Gods right. He couldn't even do that. So the light starts, and everything fucks up. His fault. So they scraped his feet so the worms could get him and shoved him somewhere to die. And you had to save him.'

'What about the bodies?'

He laughed again. 'The priests said the light meant the end of the world. People got angry and pretty soon all the priests were dead. Then the bodies started to stink. Easier to hook them on the ice line than burn them, the Merchants said, but then the line stopped.' He coughed and spat, his face twisting. 'So they burned them after all. There was a spark, and half the town burned with them. Now I'm done. Ask the idiot the rest. Do what you like.'

She nodded. 'You need to know this isn't a gift,' she said. 'It's justice.'

She had expected him to turn his face away, but he held her eyes while she extended the stunner, while she powered it up, and while she held down the stud for charge after charge until the little thing became hot in her hand. Even when she was sure he was dead, his eyes stayed open.

Then she stood up, slipped the stunner back in her pouch, and climbed the steps without looking back. Upstairs, she faced Belbis. 'I think I got lucky,' she said. 'I think you're what I came looking for.'

Bis tugged at her waist. 'Him,' she said, and pointed towards the steps. It was a question.

Seldyan reached down and squeezed her hand. 'He was very ill.'

The girl smiled. It was the first proper smile Seldyan had seen from her.

Seldyan laboured up the slope, crested the ridge and looked up at the peak ahead of her. Another couple of days, she guessed, if they could keep up a reasonable speed.

That was a big if. She pushed the stick she had cut for herself hard against the ground and lifted her foot.

They had been walking for eight days and she had learned several things. The first was that now he was fully recovered Belbis was very fit. His face had filled out and he had shaved off his beard, and she realized he was much younger than she had thought, not far out of childhood. He had all the leggy stamina that went with it.

Second was that he was utterly unwelcome, anywhere.

It had been the morning of their third day. Seldyan had pointed to a group of buildings, huddled at the base of a steep rise a few hundred paces from their path. 'Look. Would they have helped you, when you were making the walk before?'

He peered at the buildings and then at the rough grass near the path. 'Yes. Look there.'

He was pointing at a little hollow in a half-circle of stones that looked deliberate. There was a scrap of coarse cloth.

She nodded. 'Supplies?'

'Yes.'

'Perhaps they'll have something for us now.' She marched off towards the buildings. After a moment, quick footsteps told her he was following.

When she judged they were within earshot she stopped and cupped her hands to her mouth. 'Hello?'

There was no answer, but movement caught her eye; someone had opened an upper window.

She tried again. 'Hello? Can you hear me?'

There was a noise like something sliding open. Beside her she felt Belbis tensing.

Then something erupted from a low block at the edge of the settlement and headed towards them – a low, streamlined, four-legged shape that ran fast and in silence. Even at this distance she could see teeth.

Seldyan turned to Belbis, but he was already running. She followed, sprinting up the rough slope with her pack thumping at the small of her back. From behind she heard a high whistle and a wordless call; she risked a glance over her shoulder and saw the animal standing, head raised, much closer than it had been. She corrected 'fast' to 'very fast'. Someone was standing between it and the buildings – a bulky bearded figure with his hands on his hips. As she watched he raised them to his mouth and cupped them.

'Take the idiot away or Leap'll have your throat. Understand? And you'll get the same from everyone. Plenty of townsfolk came up here after the fires. I'll tell 'em.'

Seldyan shrugged and hefted her pack. 'Come on, Belbis. We've got enough.'

They walked back to the path.

Later that day her foot started to hurt. When they stopped for the night she pulled off the sabot cautiously and saw blood. She supposed she must have opened the wound when she had run. She put the sabot back on before Belbis could see.

Now, five days later, and no matter how hard she tried to convince herself otherwise, she was in trouble.

She hadn't taken the sabot off for three nights. Last night, for the first time, and exhausted as she was, she hadn't been able to sleep. She had lain on her back, trying to find a position where the throbbing was muted, and looking at the green beam that lanced up from the mountain top. The clouds had cleared a few days ago and the light that had started a religion in Web City, and seemed to have ended one here, was the only thing to look at.

Belbis slept with his face buried in the curl of his arm, eyes firmly downwards. Apparently it was traditional.

By morning her ankle was beginning to swell.

She fought on upwards. The route was getting narrower the higher they went, and the rocky bones of the mountain were exposed as scree slopes and stream beds. The water in them was bitter – an ice-fed cold that felt like scalding; when they stopped for a rest and a mouthful of their remaining food she sat with her foot under the surface until all the feeling was gone. It stayed gone for an hour or so. Then it came back worse, as if every step drove the spikes into her flesh all over again.

She looked for Belbis and found him standing a dozen paces in front of her. 'I'm sorry,' she said. 'I need to rest. Not long. If I sleep, will you wake me?'

He looked confused for a second and then nodded. She had got used to that; if something was obvious he didn't think it needed saying. She hoped the nod meant he was getting used to her.

She managed to smile, and sat down. The grass here looked wiry but it made a dense, springy mat that was almost comfortable, if you were exhausted.

She stretched out and concentrated on calming her breathing, which seemed far too shallow. More exercise. She needed to be fitter.

Eventually she found a sort-of-sleep, but it was full of loud noises. Her foot was the loudest, a kind of bass beat that defined her world so thoroughly that she quickly forgot it in favour of everything else. There was the shrill protest of the clouds as they were sawn apart by the beam of light, which sounded so green that it was almost a smell, and then there was the sulphur-tasting groaning of the rocks under the weight of the mountain peak. The springiness of the grass hummed beneath her cheek, and Belbis, standing over her, was a silent, worried pressure like a hand on her shoulder.

And again.

She stirred and looked up. Belbis was crouching next to her, withdrawing his hand like an apology. 'You said to wake you.'

'I did. It's fine.' She got to her feet. He looked worried, so she checked herself.

Better, in some ways. It almost was fine. She'd been feeling cold but that had faded, and her tiredness had been blunted by her sleep. She felt lighter. Her foot felt – different. Less painful, which was the main thing. Less of everything, really. Just sort of tight, and a bit less there than it had been.

She shook off a faint disquiet. Even the slope looked less steep now, and the peak seemed nearer. Or further, it could be, but either way she wasn't worried. She felt sure she could make it.

She gave Belbis a reassuring grin. Then she turned to face the slope and took a big, easy step.

The grass came up and hit her. Not in the face, in the chest. Somehow, her face was over nothing at all. Then her eyes focused and she realized it wasn't nothing – it was just a long way away.

She was looking down a cliff. She assumed she had been about to step over it, which was careless. She made a mental note and then tried to get up, but that didn't work. She investigated; there were arms holding her.

She turned her head as far as she could, briefly making the

sky into a whirlpool. When it had stopped she was looking sideways at Belbis. 'What happened?'

He looked even more worried. 'Very bad foot. Poisons reach your mind. You are dangerous.'

'Ah.' She was having trouble focusing on him. 'I like being dangerous. Keep still.'

'I am still. The world in your head moves. Wait.'

She waited, and after a while things became more still. She realized he was watching her eyes, and watched him back until he smiled and let her go.

She rolled over on to her back and the sky danced again. There was something she needed to say. She concentrated, and the words formed a line in her head. 'Belbis? I don't think I can stand up.'

'I know. Be still.'

His hands grasped her ankles and he pulled her away from the edge. The traction on her leg stabbed at her. Then he was looking into her eyes again. 'There is something I must do. Will be bad, then worse, then better.'

Then he took hold of her sabot and began to pull it off. She squeezed her eyes shut and clenched her hands and counted her thundering heartbeat.

She had just passed a hundred when the pull stopped. She raised her head, blinked away tears and saw – well, she supposed it was her foot. The light seemed to be fading but the thing looked mostly black. There was a bad smell. She looked at Belbis. 'Was that the bad or the worse?'

'The bad. Worse is now. Very sorry.' She saw a glint of green light reflecting off something in his hand, and she shut her eyes again.

Then she screamed and screamed until the world went away.

She thought she remembered waking several times, but each time she seemed to have managed to wake from one dream into another. The dreams all started different but sooner or later they ended up with her lying on her back under a glittering black sky with a green sword hanging above her belly.

Finally she managed a dream where she wasn't pinned down, and where the green sword pointed up into the sky. This dream also contained Belbis. She checked to see if he was holding anything sharp.

'How do you feel?'

She thought for a second. 'Awake?'

'Yes, awake. Head?'

A slow shake made the world spin. 'Bad.'

'Expected. Foot?'

'Oh.' She hadn't thought of that, which seemed to mean something. She investigated. 'Nothing. Is that good?'

'Good for now. Not good for long.'

'Okay.' Thinking was difficult. 'What, then?'

It was too dark to see his face, but somehow his silhouette against the green-lit dark was thoughtful. 'Can you wait? Wait here, not move? Not try to fly down cliff?'

Embarrassment stung her faintly through the fog in her head. 'Promise.'

'Good.' He straightened up. 'Going now – back with the sun. Remember promise.'

And he was gone.

She let her head fall back, and went back to her dreams.

Cloud Deck (Restricted), Basin City

The total area of the Cloud Deck was about three square kilometres. That space was taken up by nine properties. They ranged in size from mere budget parcels of real estate covering only twenty thousand square metres or so – budget, in this case, meaning worth thirty lifetimes' average income for someone like Vess – all the way up to vast landscaped tracts of coastline.

Alst Or-Shls owned the biggest of all. Vess had once heard that he owned it outright, which was all but inconceivable. It was like saying that one individual owned the productive capacity of a major city. Which, in some ways, Or-Shls did.

It was so beautiful that Vess actually managed to forget his terror for a while.

There was a walkway along the edge of the estate. The Cloud Deck was a couple of metres of subsoil, capped with topsoil, on a foam alloy deck. Although it was the newest artefact in Basin City, it was still almost ten thousand years old, and the edges were eroding gently as the alloy corroded and crumbled. The walkway had originally been over solid ground, but now whole sections of it lay over nothing at all. Cool draughts blew up through the pierced metal.

Vess wasn't scared of heights. Or, better, he was far less scared of heights than he was of all the other things that might happen up here.

Or-Shls walked slowly but with a sort of inevitability and an odd economy. Vess would have expected such a vast body to sway from side to side but somehow the man managed to contain all the balance within himself, as if he had some sort of internal compensating mechanism. For a while he had said nothing, seeming content to stroll along the edge of his territory with Vess at his side. Then he stopped and turned towards Vess. 'I'm sorry there's no view.'

Vess nodded. It was called the Cloud Deck for a reason – even its very elevation was enough to ensure that clouds rolling down off the mountains could shroud it in minutes, but as well as that the vast bulk of water in the Great Basin somewhere below it created its own inversions. When it was almost full, as now, warm wet air rising from it met cool evening air from the mountains to make a sudden, short-lived layer of thick billowing mist that reduced visibility to an arm's length.

Or-Shls was watching him, looking half amused, half quizzical. Vess glanced away for a second, then shrugged to himself. Sometimes the simplest question was best.

'What happened?' he asked.

When the mist had come down Or-Shls had let his lenses slide away. Now he touched their runners and they flicked back. He blinked, then reached into the folds of his blouse and pulled out a thing like a round pebble with a spout. He put the spout in his mouth; there was a hissing noise, and then Or-Shls was blowing out a cloud of smoke that curled and melded with the mist. He did it again and then said, 'When?'

Vess felt a twitch of annoyance. He kept his voice level. 'I was in . . . one place. Now I'm here.'

Or-Shls shook his head. 'I'm surprised,' he said. 'Did it not occur to you that one of those places was not real?'

Vess stared at him for a moment. Then he felt his shoulders

drooping. 'Oh. I see. You are telling me that the – *chamber* was virtual?'

Or-Shls smiled. 'Are you recovered?'

'I suppose. If it was virtual, perhaps there was less to recover from than I thought.' He took a pace forward and stopped. Without looking at Or-Shls he said, 'But what happened?'

From behind him came the hissing, and the smell of the smoke jabbed at his palate.

Then Or-Shls said, 'You were implicated in an act of terrorism. Not by me, I should add. I don't know exactly how you came to be involved; you may have made enemies as well as friends while you were in the Hive. I can tell you that the act itself was mine.'

'You? Why?'

'A pretext. Everything is, in the end. I needed to take certain decisions quickly, and the process of Board approval was becoming obstructive.'

'Board approval? Oh . . .' Vess stared into the mist for a moment. 'So you have bypassed the Board?'

'Yes. A State of Emergency and immediate executive powers, a rational response to an act of terror and assassination.'

'So why was I put –' He hesitated. '– in that chamber?'

'It would have looked strange if you were not. I acted quickly, by the way – you were in there for only a few real minutes. It was not my desire to see you tortured to insanity, and given your considerable durability that would certainly have been your destination.'

The smell of smoke was making Vess feel sick. 'I see,' he said. 'Does that mean that the Board no longer wishes to kill me?'

There was a grating, wheezing rumble. For a moment Vess thought they had been joined by some strange animal, but then he realized that Or-Shls was laughing.

'Did Vut tell you that?'

'Yes.'

'Well, our friends Vut are no longer, um, extant, and you should treat anything they said with caution. The wishes of the Board are less relevant than they used to be.' He paused, and added in exactly the same tone of voice, 'Of course, that may change.'

Vess felt his lip twitching. He wanted very much to ask what had happened to Vut. Instead he said, 'Of course. What will happen now?'

'To you? Perhaps a medal. Perhaps death . . . I am not sure. Over the coming days you will be debriefed, and then we will see. There is a job you could do . . . Meanwhile there is someone I would like you to meet. Again, I should add. Ah – I think the mist is clearing.'

It was. It cleared downwards; as Vess watched the sky above him it shifted from a featureless, softly luminescent grey to a troubled skyscape of high-built clouds with patches of turquoise between them. The guard rails of the walkway extended themselves from a few metres to a curving sweep along the edge of the Deck. And below him – he shifted his feet uneasily.

Below him – a hundred metres directly below him, visible through the pierced metal floor of the walkway – the vast, almost overflowing ladle of the boat lift had slipped its catches and was dropping away from the Middle Basin.

The depth and the movement added to his faint sickness. He shook his head. 'You said there was someone you would like me to meet?'

'I did. Follow me, if you can?'

For a moment Vess didn't understand. Then he smiled. 'I may be surprised by heights, Chairman, but I'm not afraid of them.'

'Indeed not. Nor apparently of pain, but insects trouble you greatly. And, who knows, perhaps there are other things? Ah . . . here we are.'

Much of the walkway was over thin air. For those areas,

slender bridges spanned the distance to solid ground every fifty metres or so. They had arrived at one of them and Or-Shls turned along it and padded towards the Deck. Vess followed him, his feet alert for any sign of the other man's bulk troubling the walkway. There was none. Well built, then.

Then they were on the Deck, and Or-Shls gestured landward. 'Here you are.'

Vess followed the gesture. At first there was nothing to see. Patches of mist still hung between them and the low bulk of the main house, fifty metres or so away. Then he felt a slight breeze chase past him and the last of the mist dipped and curled away like smoke.

It took Vess a moment to process the sight. Then he felt his skin prickle.

There were two men, dressed in the drab uniforms of the Board Pickets. The bulges at their hips and shoulders told him they were fully armed, something he had rarely seen, but even more unusual was the fact that they seemed to be leading a child, who in turn was carrying something held out in front of her. He looked again and corrected himself; not held. The thing, which was about the size of the girl's head, was floating. And she wasn't being led; the Pickets' hands were clamped on her shoulders. And she was . . .

Vess's sickness had receded when they had left the walkway. Now it was back. He turned to Or-Shls. 'Why?'

The fat man shrugged. 'Call it a gesture. Or a legacy, if you like – a gift from me to you. One in which you were instrumental, as I'm sure you realize.'

Vess shook his head. He didn't trust himself to speak.

'Well, you were. You have been – still are – intensely monitored. You emerged from your first experience of the Mind Stack emotionally drained, with your body chemistry showing signs of major trauma, but you were alive, and that made you unique. So much so that our young friend over there was unwise enough to remark on it. That, plus your obvious attachment to her, suggested an idea.'

Our young friend. Vess was still not ready to face that. 'Go on,' he said.

'You survived whatever happened to you in the Stack. I believe Vut asked you about it, and you said nothing. Following your extraction from the Hive you still said nothing even under considerable pressure.'

'I still had nothing to say.'

'And I still don't believe you, which presents me with a choice. The easy option would have been to kill you.'

'But you haven't.'

'Evidently. Therefore I have chosen another path. As I said, I may have a job for you. And you seem to be avoiding a certain subject.'

There was nothing to say. From the corner of his vision Vess could see that the two guards and their captive were still walking towards them. It wasn't the subject he was avoiding, he knew. It was the sight. Or, more truly, the eyes.

For a second he thought he would turn away completely, for ever. The bridge back to the walkway was still close – if he sprinted he doubted Or-Shls could do anything about it. He imagined himself vaulting the guard rail, throwing himself well clear of any safety devices, and soaring down. His body would be found smeared over the floor of the empty Great Basin.

He let himself imagine it for a little longer. Then he sighed and turned the other way instead, to face the two Pickets and the girl between them. As he did so one of them pushed her forwards. She took a couple of steps and stopped, looking down. He saw her fingers tighten on the surface of the pod. Then she looked up at him.

'Hello,' she said.

He nodded. 'Hello, Dimollss.' Then he turned back to Or-Shls. 'Why?' he asked again.

The man shrugged. 'Why not?'

Vess said nothing. After a moment, Or-Shls grinned. 'Very well. To punish, to begin with. You, mainly. Physical pain seems not to bother you, but this obviously does. And, I think there's at least one thing that will bother you worse, but I'll tell you about that in a while.' So far he seemed hardly to have looked at the girl and her guards. Now he glanced at them and waved them away. 'Remove that, please. I'll tell you when it's wanted again.'

The Pickets reached for Dimollss's shoulders but she had already turned and was walking back towards the house. Vess watched until they had gone into the house. Then he looked at Or-Shls. 'Do you think that's going to make me more cooperative?'

The fat man laughed. 'More? You weren't cooperating at all in the first place. I wouldn't expect that to change. No, Vess, I've thought of something much better: alignment of interests. You didn't survive as long as you have without understanding that. Come along.'

Or-Shls's main house was curved nearly into a semicircle. The outside of the curve faced the grounds and the walkway; the inner formed one end of an enclosed garden that Vess assumed extended to the boundary of the estate. Assumed, because the boundary was hidden by trees: copses of conifers and palms and broad-leafs and a few strange-looking things that seemed to be upside-down – tall fronded stems with multiple root-struts reaching out sideways and then angling sharply into the ground.

Vess had heard about the place, although he had never visited it. Had never wanted to, if he was honest. People of his rank who arrived here tended to do so on terms that weren't theirs to write.

And here he was. Somewhere, a part of him was angry. More than angry – but he knew how to keep it separate, like a lunatic in a locked room. He turned to Or-Shls. 'Are we expecting any-one else?'

'Yes. Do you like my trees?'

'Not really.'

'Well done. Do you know, sometimes I am almost inclined to trust you? Over here, in the Pump Trees.'

From outside the copse looked impenetrable. Inside, it was hollow – a ring of dense woodland with a circle of stone seats in the clearing at its centre.

Or-Shls waved him towards a seat, but Vess didn't move. Or-Shls shrugged and took a place at the opposite end of the circle, giving a *fuff* of expelled breath as he sat. 'Right,' he said. 'Just one to go.' He paused and looked around. 'Gamer? Are you with us?'

There was a quick rustle from overhead. Vess looked up in time to see something flicker across the tree canopy, and then Clo Fiffithiss dropped into the clearing, landing in a ball of legs and immediately popping itself upright.

'Good. Let's begin. This is the securest space on the planet, so we have a certain freedom here. Vess, we're going on the offensive, against the external forces who are strangling us.'

Vess laughed. 'You can't! They stole all the legacy ships, remember? You have nothing to offend with.'

'In the first place, why do you think I can't steal them back? And in the second, who said I was only going to use our own ships?'

Something about the tone calmed Vess, but it was a chilly calm. He looked down at Clo Fiffithiss. 'You know something about this, I assume?'

'I know all about it.' The tone was deadpan. 'No one else does.'

'And I don't, yet. Before you tell me that, tell me something else. Why should I have a role? Because you've got me here for a reason. Alignment of interests – what interests?'

Clo Fiffithiss said nothing. Or-Shls reached up and touched something behind his ear. The lenses slid round and clicked into place in front of his eyes. In the dim light of the copse Vess saw pinpoints of light flicking over their surfaces; Or-Shls seemed to focus on them for a moment. Then he nodded and the lenses slipped away again. 'What do you know about our friends Vut?'

Vess shrugged. 'You said they are not extant.'

'Apart from that.'

Vess shook his head.

'Nothing, I take that to mean. Very well. A biology lesson. Gamer, if you will?'

Clo Fiffithiss hadn't moved from its upright position. Now it spread its lower limbs and dropped into a crouch, its body suspended in a cradle of legs. It was a position Vess had never seen before; it was at the same time the most relaxed and the most dangerous he had ever seen the Gamer adopt.

He shivered.

Clo Fiffithiss was quite still for a second. Then it was gone. There was no sound this time. *Have you ever Hunted,* thought Vess.

He had time to draw five breaths before it was back. One of its forelimbs was off the ground, and there was something at the end of it – a tiny bundle of something. Or-Shls reached down and took a fist-sized container out from under his seat. 'In here, please.'

Clo Fiffithiss dropped the little thing into the container. Or-Shls clapped a lid on to it and shook it. Then he flicked his lenses round and glared at it for a few seconds. 'Suitably dead, I think,' he said. 'Catch.'

He threw the container across the clearing. Vess caught it awkwardly. 'What is it?'

'Vut's ancestor, courtesy of the Gamer. They live wild in this copse. Take a look.'

The light was poor. Vess raised the container and held it close to his face. Then he froze.

He had never seen one of Vut's components close up but this was like, and unlike, what he would have imagined – a body that looked stubby at first, until you realized that it was actually a short, slim form bulked out by layered bristles which partly hid six three-jointed legs. He assumed the bristles pointed towards the back; if that was right then there was something at the front that looked a bit more complicated than a mouth. It looked almost like a miniature flower with petals wrapped in a tight spiral. It was smaller than the Vut equivalent – he could have fitted several on the palm of his hand.

He threw the container back to Or-Shls. 'So what?'

'It has an interesting life cycle. Stage one is a grub. Stage two is what you see here. Stage three I can best show you as an image. A moment . . .'

Or-Shls reached under his seat again and brought out a small holo lamp. He tossed it into the middle of the circle. It landed, righted itself and pointed a narrow thread of light upwards. The light spread into a screen.

It was showing a translucent scan of a human torso, with the flesh as a ghostly pink strung over white bones. The organs were darker shades of red, and the heart, frozen mid-beat, was almost purple.

Vess looked from the image to Or-Shls. 'I don't understand.'

'Look closely. Start at the base of the spine.' The voice was quiet.

Vess shrugged and turned back to the image.

There was something – he leaned in closer. Then his stomach jumped.

There was a dark lump just to the left of the base of the spine. From it, a sinuous thread, almost black, twined up the spinal column almost as far as the neck. Every few centimetres it branched, throwing out lateral threads that curled around the

255

ribs like a climbing plant. Each of the threads ended in some-thing maybe a centimetre long, if the scale was right, but far slimmer.

The lump would be a bit bigger than the insect-thing in the jar.

He felt the blood drain from his face.

Or-Shls spoke in the same quiet voice. 'It's elegant, isn't it? The Stage Two form burrows into a host. It secretes an anaesthetic – the host doesn't feel a thing. Then it grows that rather beautiful structure. The long threads are called the tap-root and the things at the end of it are grubs, obviously. At maturity the original invader dies and decomposes. The flesh around it becomes infected with pus, of course, which sends a chemical signal up the tap-root to activate the grubs. They tear themselves loose from the tap-root and eat their way out of the host.' He paused. 'The bit from the decomposition onwards isn't painless, of course. Rather the opposite. From invasion to decomposition takes an unpredictable length of time – anywhere between five and around fifty days. It was once used as a form of torture. Infect someone, then promise them the infection would be removed if they were cooperative.'

Vess felt his gorge rising. He swallowed. 'Did it work?'

'Sometimes. The only problem is that with the original, you can't remove the thing without killing the host, so they all died anyway.' Or-Shls stared at nothing for a while. 'Cruel times, Vess. Cruel times.'

The urge to throw up was stronger now. Vess stared at the image. The quality was excellent; he could see a fine, irregular line zigzagging across one of the ribs low down on the right-hand side. His hand went reflexively to his own side and he swallowed. 'When I was eight, someone hit . . .' he began, and then started again. 'When I was eight I broke a rib.'

'Yes. And there it is.' Or-Shls waved at the image. 'You're

256

right; that's you. I should probably have said at the start. And, obviously, the rest is a gift from our friends Vut.'

Vess threw up.

He spent most of the next couple of days walking in the forested parts of Or-Shls's estate. Often he was alone – or felt himself alone; there was no way of being sure – but sometimes he took Clo Fiffithiss with him. The being was perfectly adapted to the trees. Occasionally, often without explanation, it would disappear for anything from a few seconds to a few minutes and then flit back to pick up the conversation as if nothing had happened. Once or twice Vess thought there were traces of blood, or fur, around its mandibles. He realized he had never asked what the being ate.

It fascinated Vess. It also helped to distract him.

They had to sedate him in the end. He had no recollection of anything after he had been told of his – infection; but Clo Fiffithiss told him he had needed to be forcibly prevented from trying to kill himself by lowering his head and charging full speed at a tree. A guard had intervened, and then two, and eventually four. Vess wasn't sure if he was grateful.

He had come round to find himself lying on a couch in the middle of a fat white toroid that buzzed. He had tried to shake his head, but found it was immovable. He was strapped down.

Over the buzz he heard a thin-sounding voice. 'Awake? Try not to move.'

The straps just about allowed him to expand his chest. He took a breath and asked, 'Will this kill it?'

'The infection? No. We can slow its progression, though, if you will keep still long enough for me to complete the scan.'

Vess fought the urge to struggle. Slow? Not good enough. Kill; he wanted this thing killed. 'Can you operate? Take it out?'

'No. I can't do anything if you don't keep still. Be quiet and do as you're told.'

He managed, just.

Half an hour later he was off the couch and looking at the small elderly simian-looking owner of the voice. It had a testy expression.

'Do you know when you were infected?'

He thought back to his summons from Vut. 'Nine days, I think.'

The medic nodded. 'Consistent with growth. Fortunate.'

'*Fortunate*? How?'

'The larvae are approaching maturity. Also, vascular changes in the source suggest it is approaching end-of-life.'

Vess stared at the creature. He could feel his pulse clicking in his toes. 'End? When it dies . . .' He tailed off.

'No.' The shake of the head was emphatic. 'Not when. If.'

'There isn't an if. Or-Shls told me.'

'The Chairman of the Board knows many things, but not this thing.' The doc grinned, showing a lot of yellow teeth. 'My role is to preserve life. Its, and thereby, yours. Please be good enough to lie down and turn over.'

It was an old-fashioned hypodermic injection. It hurt, very much. Vess welcomed the pain – it meant something was happening.

Then it stopped. He rolled over. 'Is that it?'

'For today. To repeat, every day. You will probably need an assistant.'

He tried to reach round to the injection site, and felt his arm cramp. 'Every day?'

'Injections for five days, and close monitoring. If that goes well, if the infection is stabilized, then other treatment to maintain the position.'

'Maintain? For how long?'

'For as long as it works. Do not be deceived; you are not

258

immortal, and nor is it. Meanwhile I suggest you go and find the entity that infected you.'

Vess sat up sharply. 'Why?'

'It had its reasons for doing this. If I were you I would want to know them. And besides, it is probably the only creature in the Spin that can undo what it has done.'

The word *undo* buzzed round Vess's head. He let it, for a moment. Then he looked up at the medic. 'Why would it undo this? That's how it reproduces.'

The doc grinned again, wider. It wasn't all teeth; at the margins there were pale shrunken gums. Vess tried not to look away. 'No, infected former Harbour Master. You have been extrapolating from the thoughts of Chairman Or-Shls. That's how their *ancestors* reproduced. Vut are more modern; their reproduction would happen in nice clean tanks of nutrient. Doing things the old way is done for other reasons. I think they want to be asked what reasons. And perhaps if you ask nicely, there will be a prize.'

You will be watched, more closely than you can imagine, he thought. And then his unbidden mind added a coda – watched, or watched *through*?

He thought for a long time. Then he looked up at the medic again. 'Somehow I think it wants to be kept alive,' he said. 'Do the best you can?'

The grin had gone. The little creature gave a serious-looking nod. 'Perhaps,' it said. 'Taking the simple view, alive for it equals alive for you. Why not be simple?'

Because simple is too complicated, thought Vess. *I'm missing something, but I don't think I'm missing much. I don't think.*

Out loud he said, 'Yes, simple is good. Keep it alive.'

He never got used to the injections – they were exactly as painful, every single time.

Fortunately the pain was transient. After a few minutes it

subsided to a hot, stabbing throb that was merely unbearable until Clo Fiffithiss showed him the broad leaves of a particular tree.

He had looked doubtfully at them. 'Really?'

'Really and truly.' The creature performed a sort of insectile shrug. 'They are strongly analgesic and mildly stimulant for your kind.'

Vess pinched a corner of the big flat dark-green leaf between finger and thumb. 'What do they do to your kind?'

'Very different chemistry. Hunting herbs.' The reply was short; it didn't invite elaboration.

Vess lifted the leaf to his lips and chewed a corner. The taste was neither pleasant nor unpleasant – at once a little bitter and quite spicy. It made his palate tingle. Then the tingle faded, and with it so did the pain in his back. He rubbed himself cautiously, then smiled at Clo Fiffithiss. 'It works!'

'Of course it works. I know these forests like the back of my claw. Now you are uncrippled, shall we walk?'

Vess walked. Clo Fiffithiss split its time between its own multi-jointed version of a walk, and hauling itself through the tree canopies where they dipped close to the ground. For a while, neither of them spoke. Then Clo Fiffithiss dropped out of the branches and landed upright in front of Vess.

Vess stopped abruptly, almost tripping. 'What?'

'Vess, we have known each other for a long time and I have never seen you angry.'

Vess nodded. 'That's probably correct.'

'Not *probably*. It *is* correct, and I have always explained it to myself successfully by referring to your natural calmness and confidence. But I *still* don't see you angry, and under the present circumstances I cannot explain that to myself by any means.'

Vess looked around, found a fallen trunk at around knee height and lowered himself down on to it. 'Perhaps it's inexplicable.'

'Nonsense. What's going on?'

'With me? Only what you can see. I am walking – sitting – in the agreeable woods of the private estate of the Chairman of the Board, in the company of one of his employees. What else can there possibly be to see or hear?'

He let himself emphasize *see* and *hear*, just a little.

Clo Fiffithiss was quite still for a long moment. Then it made a complicated gesture with three claws. It was the equivalent of a conspiratorial grin. They walked on in silence, and kept it up.

On the fifth day Or-Shls threw a party.

Vess had been cleared by the medic that afternoon, after another run through the scanner.

He had tried not to be nervous, but the journey through the machine had seemed to take a long time. Eventually it was over and he was standing, staring at the image. As far as he could remember it looked the same. He turned to the medic. 'So?'

'So, your passenger is in rude health.' The little creature gave an elaborate shrug that made it seem as if it consisted entirely of shoulders and elbows. 'That is, it is physically healthy and in no immediate danger of dying. Intellectually it is probably senile at best, and brain-damaged at worst, but that should not concern you.'

'It isn't a passenger.' Vess stretched, trying not to focus on the sensations in his back in case he noticed something. He failed, but there seemed to be nothing to notice. 'What treatment should I have now?'

The medic reached round to a table behind it and brought out a package. 'Have you used a hypo jet before?'

Vess shook his head.

'It's not difficult but you would probably benefit from someone to help. It needs to be applied to the base of the spine – it is a continuation dose of the compound I have been injecting directly into the creature. Every day, Harbour Master, and don't forget, and don't miss.'

He had carried the warning back to the forest, where he had increasingly lived for the past few days – apart from his daily walks with Clo Fiffithiss, it was warm enough to sleep outdoors, and he preferred that to spending time in Or-Shls's house. But when he got back to the forest he found most of Or-Shls's household there before him.

The clearing he had seen first had been seamlessly expanded. Where there had been room for a tight circle of stone benches, there was now a wide glade. There were no signs of tree stumps; whatever work had been done, had been done very fast and had left no traces. Vess allowed himself to be impressed.

It was early evening; lights glowed along the branches above him, and the air smelled of sunset and hot food.

Or-Shls stood as if he had been ready to greet him, arms spread. 'Harbour Master! Welcome – although with your recent residence in these woods perhaps you should be welcoming me?'

Vess looked round. A lot of people were carefully not watching him. He let himself smile a little. 'Chairman, if I should – then you are welcome.' Then he looked round more ostentatiously. 'But it seems that you have numbers on your side when it comes to welcoming. What is the occasion?'

Or-Shls managed to spread his arms further. 'Do I need one? Apart from your good health, which has been reported to me.'

Vess said nothing, but kept his eyes on the other man's face. The deeply buried eyes gave nothing away, but after a few seconds the fat lips twisted into a smile. 'Very well. Later we will talk of things. Including alignment of interests, if you remember that phrase? But for the moment let us enjoy ourselves. You have been in – or near – my house for some days now, but you haven't yet enjoyed even a tenth of its advantages. Enjoy them now.'

Or-Shls made a complicated gesture, and the ground fell away beneath them. Seconds later they were surrounded by the night sky of Basin City. Warm air rose from the city below and made brief damp banks of mist at the edges of the circle. They didn't seem very far away.

Vess looked round. The limits of his world were a hundred metres from him, an edge half hidden in the trees.

'Right,' he said. 'So, when do we bring on the dancing girls?'

They were on a platform, lowered from the floating continent that was Or-Shls's domain. There were indeed dancing girls. And boys – although at first they weren't dancing. Most of them were only lightly clothed and the rest were naked. They waited in a loose group amongst the trees at the margin of the clearing, their hips poised and their eyes glistening. Vess thought they looked a little like snakes. Or-Shls seemed proud of them.

'Look, Vess! Unadulterated beauty and unlimited availability; what more can you ask? Come here!' He raised a hand and four of the dancers broke away from the group and walked towards him. The two females had broad hips and rounded bellies; the males were typically thick-chested elongated triangles. Vess assumed they represented his host's taste.

Or-Shls grinned. 'This is Vess. He is famously reticent. See if you can rouse him from his torpor.'

The four exchanged smirking glances and began to walk slowly towards Vess. He held out both hands, palms outwards. 'No.'

The group looked nonplussed. Or-Shls spread his arms. 'Just no? Not even an attempt?'

Vess turned away from the four. They were close enough for him to catch the scent of their bodies – perfumed oils overlying basic musk. 'I don't need any attempt. Let them dance, if they like.'

'Oh, very well.' Or-Shls waved the four away. 'Go and dance, children, or find someone who wants you to do more than dance.'

263

They obeyed, grumbling a little, and Vess noticed that they managed to do even that prettily. When they were gone he turned to Or-Shls. 'Well?'

'Well, indeed.' The big man sighed. 'Vess, I attempt fun very rarely and this time you have impeded me. I suppose you now expect me to be serious?'

Vess smiled. 'You can be serious, Chairman, or you can be flippant. But if you don't do something to explain why I am here and what you expect to happen next, you can,' he paused and gathered emphasis, '*fuck* off.'

Or-Shls raised his eyebrows. 'Serious *and* offensive? I am astonished – but not surprised. Very well, Harbour Master. We shall be serious, but you will forgive me if we are serious to music? That at least I demand of you.'

The music was ethereal, a distant whimpering that swelled and faded like a restless wind. Something about it set Vess's teeth on edge.

Or-Shls seemed to enjoy it. He listened for a while, his head tilted back, eyes half closed. After a while he shook his head, and smiled at Vess. 'Do you know the Algonet?'

Vess shook his head.

'Such beauty, and sweetened by such cost.' His gaze hardened. 'But you're getting impatient. Very well. I am about to share something with you. Share it in turn and you will die as many elaborate deaths as technology can arrange. Understand?'

Vess thought. Then he shook his head again. 'The Gamer,' he said. 'I want to share this with Clo Fiffithiss. I assume you trust him?'

Or-Shls's eyes glinted. 'No I don't, for the same reasons I don't trust you. But I sense you are hardening your position.' He raised his voice. 'Gamer?'

It was a summons. A moment later there was a rustling beside Vess, and Clo Fiffithiss was next to him.

Or-Shls gave a tight smile. 'Never far away, I see. Right. Field down, please.'

Vess looked around for whoever the man had spoken to, but couldn't see anyone. Then he jumped.

The rest of the platform had vanished. A couple of metres outside the stone seat, it ended in a hissing, greyish, wetly luminescent wall which steamed where it met the ground. Vess looked up. The wall curved in to form a dome two metres above him.

He raised his eyebrows at Or-Shls. 'Field?'

'In a way. Superheated steam held in a charged magnetic matrix. So they tell me. Don't touch it.'

'I won't. What are you going to tell me?'

Or-Shls leaned forward. 'Alignment of interests. The medic tells me that you need to find Vut?'

'That's what he said.'

'So do I.'

'Why don't you go and look for them, then?'

'I have. It didn't work. I don't think they want to be found by me. I think they want to be found by you.'

Vess shook his head. 'Cryptic isn't helping, Chairman.'

'I expect not. Do you remember this?'

A patch of air in front of him fuzzed and became a star field. For a moment it looked unfamiliar, but then Vess's mind caught up – there was the ragged curve of debris he had been shown in the Lay Palace.

'Yes,' he said. 'So? That's none of my business. I remember.'

'It might turn out to be everyone's business. I intend to make it mine. Have you heard of a planet called Traspise?'

Vess searched his memory. 'Faintly. What about it?'

'It was destroyed ten thousand years ago; the first planetary total loss in a million years.'

'What destroyed it?'

'Exactly.' Or-Shls sat back. 'Something. Something that was found by someone; some ancient machine.'

Vess shrugged. 'Tech levels were higher then. Perhaps they had all kinds of machines for destroying planets.'

'Did they have machines for making them?'

There was silence. Vess stared at the image for a long time. 'I get it,' he said eventually. 'You think it's the same thing.'

'It might be. Or another of the same kind. And if it was, wouldn't we want it?'

Vess laughed out loud. 'To do what? Blow up a planet? Or make an arc of radioactive debris?'

Or-Shls shook his head. 'No, Vess. To wait, while people incentivize us to do neither.'

'You're insane.' *Or I am*, he added to himself. *This is another virtual reality; in a moment I'm going to wake up in a torture chamber.*

But he didn't. Instead he watched Or-Shls. After a while the man re-settled himself on the bench, sucked on the pipe and spoke through a cloud of vapour.

'Things have changed since the image you saw was taken. Look.'

Vess leaned forward. 'This image was taken from a different direction from the last one.'

'Correct, Harbour Master. And not by us.'

Vess looked up sharply. 'By someone Outside?'

'Far Outside, yes. Clo Fiffithiss?'

The creature unfolded itself. 'Images can be analysed . . . this one was captured by something within a quarter of a million kilometres of the debris curve, closing at speed.' It paused, and added, 'Substantial speed. The sort that can be attained by a Main Battle Unit, for example.'

'Oh.' Vess looked at Clo-Fiffithiss, and then at Or-Shls. 'Our stolen *Sunskimmer*?'

Or-Shls smiled.

'You know where they are?' Vess felt his eyebrows climbing.

'I always knew that, Vess. Now I know something more

interesting; I know where they were going. I think our friends Vut know too.'

Light began to dawn. Vess nodded slowly. 'No longer extant,' he said.

Or-Shls looked down again and spoke towards the ground. 'We have had a certain level of contact with those in Web City. Nothing detailed, just an understanding of their direction of travel. It was never enough for us to influence their actions more than a little but at least we had some foresight. Now that has been cut off without warning. There is a suggestion that there may have been an abrupt change of leadership.'

'A coup, in other words?'

'In other words, yes.'

Vess looked from Or-Shls to Clo-Fiffithiss. 'What difference does that make to us?'

'You are being obtuse. To where we were, not much. To where we may go, perhaps a great deal.' He pursed his lips. 'A planetary-scale arc of rubble appears, followed by a new green star, and then the nearest civilization breaks the habit of half a thousand years and stops talking to us, possibly as a result of a coup? I'm no Gamer, Harbour Master, but I suggest this has significance.'

Something had been bothering Vess; now he had it. 'Chairman? You've been talking a great deal about "I". Are the rest of the Board with you?'

Or-Shls looked at him for a long time. Then he smiled. 'If I were you I'd go and find Vut, who has gone there and who seems to want so badly to be found by you – and who seems to have stolen a ship and gone hunting.'

'Just that? Chase Vut across space?' Vess shook his head. 'With respect, it seems an odd choice of priorities.'

'It may do, but it isn't. You need to understand something, ex-Harbour Master. You are tainted by failure. I can make no use of you here. Finding Vut could be useful; making fresh

contact with whoever is now in charge out there could be even
more so.'

Vess laughed. 'So that's it. I'm to be an emissary? Really,
Chairman?'

Or-Shls slapped a hand down on his knee; it was the first
gesture of irritation Vess had ever seen him make. 'Why not?
You are – were – *just* senior enough, and after all, the attributes
of a spy and a diplomat are basically identical. At the very least,
you might save your own life. At best, you might save all of us.
Field up.' The grey walls vanished, leaving a curtain of steam.
Or-Shls stood up, nodded and walked off, waving the steam
aside. It parted into wisps, and a current of hot wet air brushed
Vess's cheek and then dispersed.

Vess turned to Clo Fiffithiss. 'What's going on?'

The creature froze for a moment, then made a complicated
knot out of two forelimbs. Vess raised his eyebrows; as far as he
could remember the gesture meant something very like 'shh –
not here'. He nodded.

'Shall we rejoin the party?'

'By all means.' Clo Fiffithiss made a show of looking around.
'Do you think he will have laid on any entertainment for me?'

Vess shook his head. 'Would you have liked some?'

'No, but the thought would have been appreciated. Will you
be indulging?'

'No.'

'Good. If you had said yes I would have thought you were an
impostor. If it helps, you might like to know that our host won't
be indulging either.'

Vess raised an eyebrow.

'Not at first hand.' A quick blur of a foreclaw. 'He's strictly
an observer.'

'Did he know you were going to tell me that as well?'

'I doubt it.' The same gesture. 'He doesn't know I know.'

'Well, well.' Vess walked on.

That Or-Shls was a voyeur didn't surprise him. That the Gamer knew about it surprised him a little.

But he had worked out the gesture. It was a sly grin. That the creature thought it was funny made him – thoughtful.

Cloud Deck

At its noisy peak the circle of the party had expanded almost to the misty limits of the clearing, and then gradually collapsed as people left or paired up or gathered into trios or quads or whatever groupings pleased them best.

Vess had been sitting on a flat rock about halfway between the stone circle and the edge of the platform. He had spent some of his time people-watching, and all the rest of it thinking. No one had spoken to him, either because they had been told not to or because he wasn't – important.

He sat on his anger. Either reason suited him perfectly.

Clo Fiffithiss hadn't volunteered anything else. It had excused itself some time before, and Vess had been vaguely aware of it rustling through the trees just out of sight. He assumed it had been making its own entertainment.

Now it was back, and Vess found himself blinking at it. He realized it was getting light; the creature appeared less as a silhouette and more as a grey shape. He stood up and pressed his hands into his back. 'I'm tired,' he said. 'Shall we walk?'

'Of course.'

Vess headed for the edge of the clearing and Clo Fiffithiss followed him. In the dim light noises were important; the creature sounded like some tiny mammal pattering across dry stalks.

That's what it's supposed to sound like, thought Vess. *Why aren't I afraid?*

Because fear has limits. I've reached them.

They were almost at the edge of the lowered platform. The trees thinned out, and then there was just a band of grass ten paces across, and a waist-high fence of interwoven thorn-stems.

Vess walked up to it and peered over. It really was the only barrier – the clouds had thinned with the dawn, and he could see straight down to the Great Basin, three hundred metres below.

He smiled at Clo Fiffithiss, which had settled itself on the fence next to him. 'So Or-Shls has a plan.'

'Hundreds, I should think. So?'

Vess watched the creature for a moment. 'Where are you in all this?'

The gesture was definitely laughter. 'On the side of the numbers. Where do you think?'

'I think you can't game an individual.'

'And I think those aren't the only numbers.'

Vess nodded. 'How do we get away from here?'

'Well, we ask Or-Shls. I expect he's waiting for the question.'

Vess shook his head. 'That feels like sticking my neck into the blades.'

'Have you another idea?'

'Yes, I have.' He brushed a hand over the surface of the fence – it was far too prickly for anything firmer – and lifted it. 'I seem to remember a conversation where you described you and me as being dull middle-managers. Would you describe yourself as risk-averse, Gamer?'

'Obviously. Why?'

'Good. I hope you'll forgive me if I put that to the test.'

And Vess brought the hand round, fast. It connected with the body in the centre of the mass of legs, and Clo Fiffithiss was gone, tumbling over the edge like a ball of—

No, *not* like a ball. Within seconds it had spread itself into a

271

flat, fluttering net of claws and legs that slanted down on a course that looked thoroughly steered, away from the platform and the Basin below it.

Vess squinted along the course and nodded. A dot became a circle, became a small, stubbily streamlined atmosphere craft that tipped to a stop at the end of a neat jet-stream, just below the falling Gamer, and extended a shallow net. Clo Fiffithiss dropped into it.

A minute later the craft was next to the edge of the platform with the net at eye level. Clo Fiffithiss lifted itself from the net and extended a claw towards Vess. Its translator made a busy staccato rattle like falling pebbles; it fiddled with something and the pebbles became a voice.

'Vess? You are an utter cunt.' It paused. 'Would you believe, that's actually worse in my language than it is in yours?'

Vess shrugged. 'You said you were risk-averse.'

'I did. I'm even more so now. Why did you do that?'

'I want to leave, and I don't want to do it in something owned by Or-Shls. I've had enough of being a puppet.'

'For goodness' sake, human – you could have just *asked*. How did you know I'd come back, anyway?'

'I assumed you'd want to swear at me.'

Clo Fiffithiss watched him for a moment. Then it gave an insectile shrug, shuffled itself round in the net and tapped a quick rhythm on the top of the craft, which popped open and floated a little higher so the edge of one fat wing covered the fence. Vess climbed on and dropped into the compartment. Clo Fiffithiss swung itself in beside him.

The net stowed itself. The top flipped over and sealed with a sucking noise, and the craft scooted away from the platform.

From inside, the top was transparent. Vess watched the Cloud Deck receding.

He hadn't been sure Clo Fiffithiss would come back. That gave him one less thing to wonder about.

He realized that the being was watching him. 'Now that you're away,' it said, 'where do you want to go?'

Vess smiled. 'The Hive.'

Clo Fiffithiss made an untranslatable noise. Its limbs flickered over the control surfaces and the little craft came to a dead stop. Then it turned towards him.

'Have you lost your mind, human?'

'I don't think so.'

'But *why*?'

'How many reasons would you like? Because I don't want to support Or-Shls; because I don't *trust* Or-Shls. Because I don't believe Vut does want to see me.' *And because I don't trust you either*, he thought.

'But why the Hive, for goodness' sake?'

Vess said nothing.

Clo Fiffithiss watched him for a while. Then it sighed. 'I'll have to tell Or-Shls. This can't happen without his say-so. And, you ought to know, this is going to do me no good at all.'

'Why? Am I not as you predicted?'

'No.' It reached out a limb towards the controls. 'I'll just have to hope that Or-Shls is not as I predicted either.'

Vess looked away. He was hoping beyond hope that his desperate guess was right.

Solpht ('Archive') Observatory

Seldyan woke with a memory of movement. She eased her shoulders and felt them press into something soft and yielding that didn't feel like ground. She opened her eyes and found herself looking up at a blackened timber roof, with a complicated-looking network of ropes and levers hanging from it, and two lamps with smoky yellow flames. There was some sort of table next to her with a tall stool. A little carved thing, like a faceted globe, sat on one edge of the table.

She sat up.

Her head wasn't spinning – that was progress – and her foot didn't hurt. She looked down the length of her body. Someone had cut off her trousers just above the knee and everything below that seemed to be wrapped in dry leaves. They had a faintly astringent scent which felt good on her palate as she took a breath.

'Hello?'

There were footsteps behind her. She turned round and saw Belbis taking something off his head – a strip of fabric? He raised his eyebrows.

'Sitting up. Very good. Pain?'

'No. No pain. Did you do that?' She gestured at the leaves.

'Yes. Clean, healing. Also boil in water, drink. Heal inwards.'

Seldyan smiled at the phrase. 'Thank you,' she said. 'It works. I feel – healed inwards.'

'Good. Equal now for a while.'

She nodded. Then she frowned. 'Why for a while?'

His face was serious. 'We are here – Observatory. You came to stop the light, yes? Time now.'

'Ah.' She stood up. 'This is where the light comes from?'

He nodded.

'Okay. You'd better show me.'

He reached up and took one of the oil lamps, and she followed the yellow light through a maze of rooms and then down – narrow timber steps at first, then wider stairs cut into rock. At the bottom of the flight Seldyan stopped and crouched down, touching the cold surface. 'This feels very even ...' She reached for her pouch and took out the stunner, surprised first that it was still there, and then that it still worked, at least as far as lighting up was concerned.

The light gleamed off a dead-flat, almost polished surface. The walls of the corridor they were in looked the same. Every now and then there was an alcove with a carved globe, like the one she had seen on the table.

She nodded to herself and stood up. 'Belbis? No disrespect, but your people didn't make this.'

'No. Very old. Here.' He was holding out a strip of cloth.

'What?'

'Bind eyes. No more steps. There is a chamber soon, where the light comes.' He gestured along the corridor to a plain door at the end.

'Oh.' She took the cloth and made a couple of turns of it round her head, tying it awkwardly behind her. She couldn't see any light through it. 'Will this do?'

She felt investigating fingers. They were cool on her skin. They smelled dusty.

'Yes. Now me.' There was a rustling. 'Ready? Keep eyes shut too.'

'Wait!' She reached out and managed to catch hold of his clothes. 'How do you know this is safe?'

'Already tried. While you sleep?' She heard humour in his voice. 'Three days sleep. My leaves are slower than your tricks.'

'You came here?'

'Yes. My job to do. The Housekeepers – still there.'

'Oh.' She remembered: he had told her about the old men who had stayed. A part of her wanted to ask him what he had done with them, but she held back and patted him instead. 'That was good.'

'My job. Now, ready? Then follow.'

She let go of him and followed his footsteps down the corridor, one hand brushing the walls to keep her straight. The corridor was short – after twenty paces his noises stopped so she did too.

There were other noises. Somewhere in front of her there was a keening hiss, like rain sawing through something. The air smelled slightly burned. She shuddered.

Then there was the sound of a latch and the hiss grew much louder, and someone said:

'Warning. Do not enter. Danger to life.'

Some*thing*, thought Seldyan. The voice was obviously artificial. Out loud she said, 'Did that happen when you came before?'

'Yes. Same voice that warned, when I first came.'

Automatics, thought Seldyan. Let's see how smart they are. She thought for a moment. 'Entering. Cease dangerous activity.'

'Do not enter.'

It had responded, to some extent. She tapped a finger on the corridor wall, and tried again. 'Define danger.'

'Collimated high-energy electromagnetic radiation beam. Do not enter.'

Definitely a conversation. The next question was worth trying. 'State purpose of beam.'

'Containment status-change alert. State the purpose of your questions.'

Alarm bells rang in Seldyan's mind. She thought quickly. 'To gain information.'

'That is applicable to all questions. You are unauthorized. Leave.'

Seldyan turned to where she thought Belbis was. 'Shut the door. It's time to go. Come on.'

She waited until she heard the click behind her, and then breathed out. 'Whoa. Did that happen to you?'

'Only the warning. I asked no questions.'

'You were sensible. Let's go.' She turned and was about to feel her way back the way they had come. Then she snorted, reached up and pulled off the improvised blindfold.

And stood still.

She had thought she was facing back up the corridor, but she had been wrong. She was facing the wall of the corridor, and it was not blank. There were letters embossed in the metal. She reached out a hand and traced the pattern. Without looking away she said, 'Belbis? Did you see this?'

She heard the sound of cloth sliding over itself as he took off his own blindfold. Then he was next to her, peering at the wall. He shrugged. 'I saw. No meaning.'

'To you, maybe. But there is to me.' She tapped the letters. 'Level Two. You know what that means? There's a Level One somewhere. Maybe a Level Nought. How well do you know this place?'

'The wooden place up above, every room. Down here, just this. The Housekeepers showed me.'

She nodded. 'Yeah, the Housekeepers. They can't show us now.' She thought for a moment. Then she felt a slow smile widening her face. 'Where did the Housekeepers live?'

He frowned. 'Private place.'

'Sure. Do you want to ask their permission or shall I?'

He was quiet for a while. Then he lowered his eyes. 'Follow.'

She followed the man, and the ball of light round his lamp, back up the stairs and out of the metal corridors and through a twisting wooden world that felt utterly unnavigable to her, but was probably just like anywhere else to someone who had never seen.

The Housekeepers seemed not to have needed much. There were three thin pallets on the floor, and beside each pallet a bowl with a crude spoon in it.

There were no windows and no lights. Seldyan gestured to Belbis to pass her the lamp, and knelt by one of the pallets. She frowned. 'Belbis? How many days since you left here?'

He looked at his fingers. 'I think, more than fifty.'

'Yeah, that's what I thought. And those guys were called the Housekeepers, and they're gone. So why is nothing dusty?' She wiped a finger over the inside of the nearest bowl. The surface felt slickly clean.

He shrugged.

Seldyan gave the bowl a gentle thump. It clunked. Then she stood up. 'I've got an idea.' She paused, then clapped her hands. 'Service! Whatever you are. Show yourself!'

For several breaths nothing happened, and she got ready to look embarrassed. Then she and Belbis both jumped.

There was a quiet pop and the lights came on. They were very bright after the lamplight and Seldyan shut her eyes for a few seconds to let them adapt. When she opened them she had company – there was something floating a metre or so from her at around her eye level.

It was one of the little carved globe things. She nodded. 'That makes sense. How many of you are there?'

'Just one.' The voice was high and reedy.

'One? But I've seen lots . . . Oh. All you?'

'Yes. I can move fast. The AI says you've been asking questions.'

'I was. It didn't answer.'

'It's not very imaginative. Your speech patterns say you're not from this planet. Where are you from?'

She was about to say 'the Hive', but thought better of it. 'The Inside.'

'Not recognized. Where is that, relative to the Spin?'

'Right in the middle. Maybe you're out of date.' She thought about that for a moment. 'How long have you been here?'

'Eleven thousand, four hundred and seventeen years, local. Ten thousand and eight, standard.'

She sucked in a breath and blew it out in a soft whistle. 'Seriously? Have you been isolated all that time?'

'Yes.'

'Why?'

The little machine floated in front of her wordlessly for several seconds. It was completely silent, she realized; she could hear Belbis breathing. She wondered how he was taking all this.

Then the machine gave a little side-to-side waggle. 'I have conferred with the AI. We assume that this facility is unknown to you. Has it been forgotten completely?'

The ship didn't seem to have known, she realized. Nor had any of the others, including Patras. 'Probably yes.'

'But you are here. Why?'

She laughed. 'You lit up a whole planet bright green. It's a bit obvious.'

'So it will be obvious to others.' There was another silence. Then the thing spoke, and its voice sounded different.

'I am the Avatar of the Archive, which was established to confine, to protect and, if necessary, to warn. You have responded to a warning, but it is clear that you do not know how to respond. There is a protocol for this, which is that the Archive is opened to general inspection.'

'No, wait.' Seldyan took a step towards the thing, which didn't retreat. 'Remember I don't know anything. Confine what?'

Behind her she heard an indrawn breath. Then Belbis said, 'The Gods.'

She turned to him and shook her head. 'Belbis? This is beyond that. I'm really sorry but your paintings were just paintings.'

'But they weren't.'

It was the Avatar. She spun round and stared at it. 'You're kidding.'

'No. They were the output of a deliberately designed system. Your companion is another output, in a way.'

She glanced back at Belbis and saw that he was shaking. She wasn't surprised. She would have been, too. If she allowed herself. She turned and shot out an arm, trying to catch the floating box of riddles. It flicked back an arm's length, so fast that it seemed almost to have existed in two places at once for a moment. 'Explain yourself, you little box of shit. Once, and clearly. You need to know that I have a warship, close by. If you don't start making sense I'll—'

'You will fail to make contact, as you have failed every day since you arrived here. Please don't make empty threats. Besides, you may find your warship has other things to detain it.'

She blinked. 'Other things?'

'Other warships. Did you think yours was the only one? Ten have arrived while we have been conversing.'

'Ah . . .' She looked for something to sit down on, and selected one of the Housekeepers' pallets. It wasn't as hard as it looked. She looked up at the Avatar. 'You need to understand something. I don't know about this stuff, okay? I came here because your green light stuff is fucking up a million people's lives. I want it stopped.'

'This was expected. A million is well within the gamed margins.'

'Are you saying it's not a problem?' She leaned forwards, glaring.

'The current population of the Spin is approximately seven

hundred billion. Compared with that, a million is not a problem.'

Her eyes widened. 'Wait. There's something here that could affect the whole Spin?'

'Yes, in a way. It would be better to say there's something here which could obliterate the whole Spin, and a significant space around it.'

She stared at the little wooden thing for a long time. 'Okay,' she said eventually. 'Tell me the rest.' She glanced sideways at Belbis and added, 'Us. Tell us the rest.'

Hive

The hand on his shoulder roused him. For a moment he half dreamed it was Dimollss; he rolled over and got ready to tell her that there was something dangerous. Then he woke properly. It was the smell that had confused him – he was back in the Hive, and the danger was all his.

He sat up. He wasn't in one of the sleep cells, because they had made it gleefully clear to him that whatever was going to happen to him when the *things* hatched, was going to happen publicly. He slept on a pallet on the floor in the refectory. A good place to watch juvenile insects burst out of a human body, they thought.

There was nothing to feel yet. He didn't know what it would feel like when it began. He didn't allow himself to think about what it would feel like when it was properly under way.

It definitely wasn't Dimollss who had woken him. The pale, elderly man put a finger to his greyish lips, nodded, and turned away. Vess got to his feet and followed. The refectory was watched less intensively than the sleep cells, but it was still watched. They had a few minutes at the most, but where he was going that could be stretched to a lifetime. He hoped.

The Stack was already in progress – had probably been so for a while. He lay down next to one of the motionless bodies and relaxed while the probe was fitted.

And he was floating in the warm nothing. He had to force himself to wait. His intellect knew that there was no hurry, but his fear was running on real-world time.

The wait wasn't as long as he feared.

Welcome back.

'Thank you.'

There's nothing to worry about now. You can stay here as long as you want – live out as many lifetimes as you can imagine. Some of us do.

'Thank you, but that isn't quite what I want.'

There was a watchful moment.

Go on.

'I don't want for ever. I'm not sure I need it.' *Or deserve it*, he thought, and hoped that was somehow private. 'But – you know about the thing in my body?'

Of course.

'It has a mind. You are talking to my mind. Can you talk to it as well?'

Perhaps. Why?

'Because I have an idea. Will you indulge me by trying?'

Will it do harm?

He had wondered that. But then, the Stack mind had shown him its collective strength when he had first met it. 'I don't think it will try, but if it does, be ready.'

We will.

There was a short moment of – disorder, and then a sensation of something regrouping.

We cannot talk to it. It is too alien and too old.

'How old?'

More disorder. Then:

The question is meaningless because there is no frame of reference long enough.

Vess felt his inner self trying to grin. 'It's immortal,' he suggested.

Perhaps. Its memories are far, far older than its body. Did you know this?

'I suspected it, because of the way it reproduces. A gestalt entity that produces a new group from a seed unit, and each unit can act independently?'

Yes. You're right. The collective memory goes back to the dawn of its intellect.

He hesitated. 'But you can't talk to it. Can you access the memories?'

That would be intrusive.

He felt himself blink. 'Well, yes. But if you're speaking of being intrusive, consider where it is and what it is about to do.'

Very well.

And a gap.

Ah. This is interesting. Vess? The creature is only barely rational but there are things in its recall that we can show you.

'Go on.'

Images, not in his head but as if he was observing from outside. Dense forest, thick with moulds and giant fungi and dripping wet – always wet. And everywhere, the many creatures that were one. They were ... Vess struggled with words. It was life that had no limit to memory and a million versions of its collective self. Life that was a gestalt that just continued. It could evolve very fast if it wished, using deliberate memory, but for thousands of generations it had no cause. It lived in balance with the prey creatures of its sole environment; it maintained its numbers and its huge, distributed, longitudinal consciousness.

Then, cause had happened, but it happened so fast there was no time for a response. The ecosystem changed; within days the air became poison and the water, acid.

One gestalt unit had escaped.

Vess blinked. 'Just one?'

Yes. Vut. Not a predecessor; this gestalt.

284

'Oh.' At first he didn't know what to add. Then it occurred to him. 'How long ago did this happen?'

Difficult to be certain. We think, about ten thousand years ago, standard.

Vess stared into the nothing of the Stack for a long time. *I've only been alone for one lifetime*, he thought. *Not a hundred or more.*

'Someone destroyed its planet. Does it know why?'

It seems to, but it can't express itself. Vess? This creature is not the only mind that we can see.

'Mine too?'

Yes. We can see what is being done. Alliances have been struck, promises made, much money borrowed. Or-Shls is gambling everything on one prize. We guessed something, of course; much of this manic military tooling-up has been Hive-work, and it has pulled resources in from a wide pool. But this collaboration with half the races in the Spin? This is very bad. If we were squeezed before, how much worse will it get now?

'What will you do?'

We will act. It's probably better if we don't say how, but you might like to think about what the name Hive means.

Vess was puzzled. 'It means what it says, surely? A hive.'

It does now, but its origin is different. It used to be short for High Value. We think it still is, and that gives us a certain lever-age which we intend to use. Meanwhile, in turn, what will you do? We would like to help you.

The question took him aback. 'What do you think I'll do? I'll die; soon.'

Maybe. Maybe not.

He listened carefully.

He lay face-down on the cot. His back itched – a baleful internal itch that no scratching would help. If he turned his face to the side he knew he would see the nervous guards.

They had talked through what was to happen, before he left the Stack.

They will watch you closely, when the time comes.

'I hope they enjoy the spectacle.'

Perhaps – but that won't be the main reason. Creatures will emerge, remember? They will want to contain them, at least – probably kill them.

Vess mentally frowned. 'Killing new-borns?'

You are – astonishing, hater-of-insects. Are you prepared?

'As much as I can be.'

And now, he hoped he was. From behind him he heard a voice. 'Fuck. It's moving. Can you see it?'

'Get ready . . .'

And he did, although he knew the last comment hadn't been aimed at him. But the itch became something else: a sharp, insistent gnawing that became . . .

He took a shuddering breath and screamed, and screamed, and screamed, while the infant insects ate their way out of his body.

Then it was – not *over*, it was impossible for agony like that ever to be *over*, he would feel it to the end of his life . . . but not active. He had wounds, many wounds; but they were what they were.

He was alive.

The creatures may elect to make the hatching non-fatal.

He heard the sounds of energy discharges from close by.

He lay still. *As far as they're concerned you're dead*, he thought. *Maybe the creatures are too; who knows?*

The discharges stopped. There was a breathless silence. Then Vess almost jumped as strident alarms howled.

Presumably they weren't all dead, then. He wondered how fast they could move.

There was the sound of anxious orders and then running feet, receding.

After a long time, hands took hold of him and he was lifted. The movement flexed his wounds; even as he got ready to howl with pain, darkness rose to meet him.

Vess stood at the edge of the Great Basin and watched the water rising slowly. If he kept his gaze limited to the confines of the Basin, everything looked much the same. The reflection of the Lay Palace trembled a little as a breeze moved across the water, and the tops of the supporting columns of the Cloud Deck were veiled in mist. The Basin was nearly full. Within minutes the weight would trigger the catches and the vast bowl would slide downwards, pulling up the boat lift to meet the First Middle Dock.

Vess raised his eyes from the water and stared up at the nearest support chain. He knew what he was going to do. He just didn't know if it was going to work.

It had been a slow journey. That had suited Vess, who had no further need to chase anything across the Spin, and who had some healing to do.

It had been many days since his supposed corpse had been loaded into the garbage pod and fired out of the Hive. Almost as many since the pod had been intercepted by the ancient, eccentric vessel which seemed to be friends with the Stack. He still wasn't sure how that worked.

He hadn't known it at the time but as well as its official cargo of his body, the pod had an unofficial cargo – half of the infant members of the gestalt that were now calling themselves the Vutvess. They were almost affectionate. Vess had yet to work out how he felt about that.

He could communicate with them up to a point; they used a form of telepathy between themselves, and if they worked hard they could extend it to their former host.

They had been very apologetic. He had been almost – flattered, once he got past all his other emotions. It had been a monumental act of trust – of faith, nearly.

The ship, which against all the evidence called itself an Orbiter, had let them in without question. It was definitely eccentric. The inside was divided into different habitats, separated from each other by gauzy force fields which allowed just enough air movement to stop things getting stale. The Vutvess liked the rainforest habitat best. Vess preferred one of the semi-arid zones. He spent a lot of his time watching the news. There were far more channels, suddenly. Most of them showed strident, probably enhanced images of the same distant space battle. When he felt well enough to be analytical he drilled in to the detail a bit, and found that the battle had lasted about four minutes. It seemed to have produced hours of footage.

The other footage was of things happening at home. That showed a changing picture. They had begun with food riots, but now they showed a rather tense-looking calm, and a lot of people wearing uniforms. Some of the uniforms looked familiar, but it took him a moment to place them. Then he remembered. He had seen them in briefings on neighbouring civilizations, when he was still Harbour Master. Not all of the civilizations had been friendly.

And now he was healed, enough to move normally, and the Orbiter had just made its breathy throat-clearing noise.

'We are almost there.'

Vess nodded. 'Will you wait for me?'

'Of course. I can't do anything else. The shuttle is ready.'

'Thank you.' That had been another surprise; most orbital craft would have depended on others for loading and unloading. This one had a neat, very old-fashioned-looking atmosphere-capable shuttle, and it had been polite but insistent that it preferred not to dock with anything itself.

Vess settled into the shuttle, wincing just a little as the wounds on his back pressed into the couch. Half an hour later he had been back on the mountain top, where apparently his identity still allowed him to enter the administrative space of the Inside, and by dawn he was at Basin City.

The place seemed to be under new management. There was no mention of Or-Shls on any of the news channels. He had asked a few people. No one had said anything, but most had nodded upwards and then moved on. The meaning of upwards had been clear. Or-Shls was on the Cloud Deck – had been there for some time.

Vess had not looked for Clo Fiffithiss.

There was a soft thump that he felt mainly through his feet, and the ground gave a gentle shudder. The catch had tripped. It was time.

Vess had positioned himself near the edge of the Basin. Behind him, less than five metres from the edge, rose one of the two great rusted iron columns that supported the fulcrum. On the other side of it, the fat wire ropes that lifted the Dock were blurring upwards at their ten-times geared-up speed.

There were platforms on the columns. One was coming into view as the Basin moved downwards.

When Vess had been a child he had played, and then as he got older often fled, among the columns and lifts and cables that had festooned his ground-level world.

Surely these were just the same? Only much bigger, and hundreds of metres further from the ground. But that difference was just in his mind, he told himself. And tried to believe it. He backed five paces away from the edge, took a deep breath, and ran.

He covered the empty space between the Basin and the platform with his arms and legs flailing, and landed, arms spread, against the column with a solid crash that knocked the wind out of him.

There was no time for recovery; the cables were accelerating. Sobbing for breath, he edged round the platform until he was facing the rusted steel trunks, flexed his knees and jumped. Another crash, and he was holding on to the cable with arms and legs – and slipping.

The cable was greased. He hadn't thought of that. He could just make his hands meet behind it; he locked his fingers together and squeezed as hard as he could. The bunches of twisted wires that made up the cable ground over his tensed muscles as if they were trying to pulp him – and he was still slipping.

His feet scrabbled against the cable but the surface was too shallowly indented to give any foothold. Much more of this and he would have lost too much ground.

Then something sliced into the inside of his thigh. He gave a hoarse roar of pain and his head snapped forwards to look down.

The cable was frayed. A knotted clump of wires stuck out from the twist, and they had dragged into his thigh. His muscles were already getting ready to pull himself free when he forced them to stop.

He was no longer sliding. He gritted his teeth and stayed still. Not long now.

The cable was thrumming. They were getting close to the massive pulleys of the headstock. Impaled or not, he was going to have to let go soon, or he'd be pulled through the giant-scale block-and-tackle. It would grind him to nothing.

He craned his neck and stared upwards. There should be another platform, almost at the top of the column. There wasn't. There were just blunt, rust-eroded iron brackets.

He had run out of choices. As the brackets swung down past him he unclamped his hands and let his unpierced leg swing out. As his foot met the bracket he let go with everything else.

He got one foot in place.

The frayed wire tore from his leg with the pain of an amputation. He heard himself wail with agony – and then he was standing on the bracket with the only foot that would fit, hugging the column with both arms.

The iron was rough to the touch, and had the strong metallic smell of wet rust. He held on to it until his breath began to quieten. Then he forced himself to open his eyes and turn his head away from the cold metal, and his heart began to hammer.

He had made a mistake. The edge of the Cloud Deck had moved, further than he had thought – too far to jump.

He was stuck.

Then he heard the voice.

'Sometimes, when my siblings Hunt, they chase their prey up a tree and then wait until it is overcome by panic.'

He jerked his head downwards. Clo Fiffithiss was gripping the column a few metres below him.

He made himself speak calmly. 'Are you Hunting?'

'I wasn't. Just following, out of curiosity. But perhaps I begin to understand the attraction. What will you do now?'

Vess said nothing.

'When you knocked me off the Deck, I had a flyer waiting,' the being went on conversationally. 'I take it you haven't?'

'No.' There seemed no point in pretending.

'Would you like me to call one?'

Vess stared down at the creature. 'Can you?' The conversation felt surreal.

'Oh yes. Shall I? Your arms are trembling; I believe that's a bad sign in humans.'

It was right. His muscles were burning. 'Yes,' he said, forcing the word out.

'Very well. Do try not to fall.'

The flyer was very different to the stubby machine that had caught Clo Fiffithiss. It was a gauzy film suspended between two cylinders that seemed to move independently of each other. It positioned itself next to Vess at knee-height, and after a moment of doubt he let himself sag down into it. It bobbed under his weight and then angled gently down to the Cloud Deck, lifting a little to crest the railing and then tipping itself up so that he slid off it and landed on his feet.

He turned, wincing at the stab from his leg, in time to see Clo Fiffithiss swing itself once round the column and let go, crossing the gap with its limbs packed into a compact tail that tucked under it and fanned out as it landed. It looked up at him. 'Can you walk to the house?'

It was about a hundred metres away and Vess wasn't sure he could, but he compressed his lips and nodded.

'Good. Ah, a moment.' It turned towards the railing and made a complicated gesture with three limbs. There was a sharp, saw-edged buzz that faded quickly to a background hum, and the air above the rail flickered and settled into a violet-glowing haze.

'There. After all, you're here now.' It made another gesture he didn't understand.

'Well, yes.' He frowned. 'Does that mean I was . . .'

'Expected? Oh yes. The field would never have been off otherwise; hasn't been since the changes below. Come on.'

Vess had never been in the house itself; during his stay he had stuck to the gardens. That meant he didn't know what normal looked like – or if this was it.

Inside, the house was dark, so that Vess had to pause on the threshold to let his eyes adjust. There was a faint smell of tobacco smoke, and stale food, underlain by something sweaty. The combination made Vess feel slightly sick.

Then he heard the sound. It took him a moment to place it; then he recalled the thing Or-Shls had described as an Algonet – the same ghostly discords and plangent sighs. Or not quite the same, he realized. There was an extra edge to the notes, and something else as well.

His ears separated the sounds. The something else was some-one crying.

Then his eyes began to adjust, and he saw them. He walked towards them.

Or-Shls was standing in front of some kind of frame, next to something that looked like a tool rack. His hands moved across the frame, pausing, tapping and sweeping, and the sound changed as he moved.

The other sound was Dimollss. She was sitting on the floor, and her eyes were wet. As Vess came up to her she looked up. 'He hurts that thing, to make it cry,' she said. 'Make him stop.'

He smiled at her, doing his best to look genuine. Then he turned to Or-Shls. 'Stop,' he said simply.

The man nodded. 'For a moment, but only because I want to ask you something. Why aren't you dead?'

Vess shrugged. 'Because Vut didn't kill me.'

'So they didn't. Thus far, nor did I, but that can change.' Or-Shls looked at him. 'What was it like?'

'What?'

'When they emerged. What did it feel like?'

The man's lips were wet, and Vess's stomach turned. He shook his head.

Or-Shls watched him for a moment. Then he looked away. 'Oh well. There's still this. Listen – this is the air-hose.' He picked up a slim tube, positioned it carefully against something on the frame and pressed a control on the end. There was a hiss, and an eerie wailing note. Dimollss moaned and covered her ears.

Vess watched for a second. His eyes had adjusted better now. It looked as if someone had nailed a large complicated flying rat to a board, wings spread. Not just spread – stretched. It writhed in time to its own wails.

Then realization struck. 'You're torturing it.'

Or-Shls shook his head, without turning. 'No. Stimulating. Torture is for higher beings than this.'

Vess looked down at Dimollss. She still had her hands over her ears. He wondered why she didn't move away; she didn't seem to be restrained. Then he glanced at her life support globe, and understood. It was tethered to the floor. The Hollowed girl was free to move, but at the expense of severing her own connection to life.

And finally, he was angry.

He hadn't planned it; his legs took over. He took two quick paces towards Or-Shls and shoved the big man sideways, grabbing the hose at the same time.

Or-Shls staggered, recovered far more quickly than should have been possible, and looked at Vess with something like joy. 'At last! He feels something – but be careful with the hose, otherwise you'll feel something quite different.'

Vess looked down at the hose. He was holding it an arm's length above the nozzle, and the tip was snaking from side to side as the air hissed out. 'I should find somewhere to put this.'

Or-Shls actually laughed – an unpleasant shrilling that made Vess's spine tighten. 'A threat, Harbour Master? On top of anger? You're making me very happy.' He gestured at the hose. 'Switch the air off, and let's walk.' He turned and headed for the terrace without looking back. Vess inspected the hose and found the controls. He let it hang slackly and glanced at Dimollss. She was no longer crying, but her eyes were dark with rage. He held the gaze for a while. Then he nodded and followed Or-Shls.

The big man was leaning on the rail at the edge of the terrace. As Vess approached he half turned. 'I blame you.'

'For what?'

Or-Shls gestured outwards, over the rail. 'That; everything. Can you see?' He waved a hand, and the hazy shield disappeared. 'Now look. You'll see better.'

Vess looked. 'What am I supposed to see?'

The gesture, again, but bigger. 'My world, man. *Our* world, it was. In someone else's hands. Your fault.'

Vess turned and stared at the man. 'Mine? *I* let our boundaries shrink to an impossible minimum? *I* cut our fleet to the point where we couldn't look after what was left of it, or chase it when it was stolen from under our noses? That was me, was it?' He was shouting now, just for once – properly shouting, with his throat open and his head forward. '*I* made us dependent on a slave economy that starved the free worse than the slaves? *I* mortgaged our *breath* to our enemies so we could chase a legend?' He shook his head. 'Not me, Chairman.'

'No, not you. It's never you, is it?' Or-Shls's face was red. 'I suppose you didn't make some stupid pact with those retards in the Hive, either? They've turned against us, did you hear?'

Vess said nothing.

'Or with Vut?' There were flecks of spittle at the corner of Or-Shls's mouth. 'Shit, man, how low do your kind go, bargaining with flesh-eating insects?'

Your kind. Vess took his hands off the rail and held them out in front of him, studying them. 'I made no bargain with Vut,' he said. 'And I made none with you, either.'

'And I was stupid enough to expect that you would.' Or-Shls shook his head. 'Well, you have another problem now.'

Vess shook his head. 'What problem?'

Then his stomach turned to lava as a deep quiet voice close to him said, 'Have you ever been Hunted?'

He whipped round. Clo Fiffithiss was hanging from the rail a few metres away, its body swinging near the ground, its foreclaws just a little forward.

A tiny drip formed on the end of one of them. Vess watched it uncomprehendingly for a moment. Then it dawned – it was venom.

He ran. Instinct sent him back to the house, and he followed it. As he ran he justified it to himself – a sprint over open ground was a good way to start, to gauge his opponent. He had the advantage of being in the right gravity, but the disadvantage of knowing nothing about how Clo Fiffithiss actually Hunted.

In fact, he knew, it was about Dimollss. He had inadvertently protected the young of an utterly alien species. Now it was time to do the same for a human.

When he got there she was standing as close to the creature on the frame as the length of her umbilical would allow. She smiled as he drew up in front of her. 'I think it likes me talking to it.'

He nodded, not trusting his breath.

'Where are the others? The fat man and the horrible one with legs?'

'I'm not sure.' Then he processed her words. 'Horrible how?'

She looked down. 'It says things.'

Another time, he would have knelt next to her. He would have held her and made small noises as she told him about horrible and about things – but horrible things were somewhere behind him, getting closer, and he had no time.

Instead, he put his hands on her shoulders. 'Trust me,' he said.

She managed a smile. 'Okay.'

He stood up – and time slowed down.

His legs straightening. A breath drawn in. In the corner of his vision, her neck craning back, her mouth forming an O.

The feather touch on his shoulder.

Back in real time, he threw himself sideways. His wounded leg almost collapsed under him; he reared back, glanced off the edge of the frame and took several staggering steps backwards before he got his balance.

'Not looking fit, Harbour Master. Back home, juveniles are taught to Hunt on wounded prey. I ought to feel young again.'

The voice seemed close to the frame. Vess backed away, trying to remember anything he knew about Hunting. There were no rules, there was only one survivor. That was it.

A skittering noise above him. He took another few steps back.

'Nowhere to go, human. Will you concede?'

Another skittering noise. He was getting further from the frame, from Dimollss, from the light.

A memory tugged at him. He caught it, examined it. It was possible – just.

He cleared his throat. 'What happens if I do concede?'

'We go quietly into a corner of the forest together, and I emerge alone. Are you going to concede?'

'No.' *A corner of the forest,* he thought. That was the other thing – the best kill was cornered. That's why it was driving him back, away from the light. Away from the frame.

'No,' he said again, 'I won't concede. Especially not to a failed Hunter.'

'Failed?'

'Well, that or virgin. I don't know which would be worse.' He realized he was crouching. He straightened up and began to walk back towards the frame. The skittering noise came again but he ignored it. *It's afraid,* he thought – *and that's all I've got.*

He was back at the frame. Dimollss was looking at him with huge eyes. The stretched creature was trembling a little, as if it feared more torture.

Then he thought of it. His hand reached down, and he found what he was looking for. His fingers closed around it.

There was the faintest sound from above him. Instinct made him half duck, half look up. Something sharp glanced down his cheek, and then Clo Fiffithiss was standing in front of him.

'First strike to me,' it said. 'What do you say now?'

He raised a hand to his cheek, explored, and then looked at

the blood on his fingers. 'Not a very big strike, if you meant to kill.'

The creature laughed. It sounded horribly false – a learned noise. 'I do mean to kill, but there is a ritual to be observed. We are a symmetrical race, human.'

It sprang upwards and for a moment Vess lost sight of it. Then it was on him again, and this time the slash went down his other cheek.

'See? Symmetry. How do you feel?'

'How should I feel?'

'Weak, I expect, given that I have poisoned you twice. But only to weaken, so far. The third time is still to come.'

He stared at the creature. Then he sagged to his knees, his mouth hanging open.

And his fingers still firmly closed.

Clo Fiffithiss crouched – and sprang, claws outwards, for the centre of him. *Symmetry.*

His arm swept round as his fingers squeezed the control. The air hose hissed angrily.

The jet caught the oncoming creature squarely in the middle of the clustered eyes. It gave a whistling shriek and bounced away in a ball of limbs, its foreclaws wiping convulsively at its eyes. Vess let a metre or so of hose slip through his fingers and swung it across Clo Fiffithiss like a lash.

The nozzle connected with the creature's body with an audible crack. There was another shriek, higher and harsher. Vess waited, the hose coiling round his legs.

Clo Fiffithiss stood, trembling. The side of its body looked wrong – there was an uneven crack in the smooth carapace, and as Vess watched a single globe of dark-coloured fluid oozed from the base of it. The creature took a single, complex step to one side, as if it was about to fall over. Then it seemed to shake itself. The limbs braced, and bent, and straightened abruptly and it fired itself upwards.

The hose was tangled round Vess's legs. While he was yanking at it, Clo Fiffithiss landed on his head. He felt something sharp pushing at his hairline, and flailed his arms upwards in panic, but his hands met spiny entangling legs.

This was the kill. He shut his eyes.

There was a dull thud. His head rocked sideways, and the claws were gone. He opened his eyes and saw Dimollss standing in front of him. She was holding one of the hammers from the rack on the frame.

Vess looked round. Clo Fiffithiss was lying a few metres away. Its body was completely caved in and its limbs were jerking rhythmically.

Vess turned back to Dimollss. 'You saved me,' he said. And then, 'Oh . . .'

The life support was still fixed to the floor. The snapped umbilical lay uselessly next to it.

The girl was still grinning, although her eyes looked wet. 'Don't worry,' she said. 'This is cool. Do one thing for me?'

He nodded. 'Anything.'

'Good. Find Seldyan. Tell her she's got some catching up to do.'

He nodded again, and was about to try to think of something to say that wasn't inane when she turned, flexed her knees and fired herself off at a flat sprint, out of the house and across the terrace towards where the silhouette of Or-Shls still stood against the railing.

The man must have heard her because he was turning as she drew near.

He was too late. The impact sounded like a stone fired into a sack – and then they were both gone.

By the time Vess got to the railing, water was beginning to pool in the centre of the Great Basin – the sluices had opened and the ancient, pointless cycle was beginning once more.

This time the water was pink. It lapped round the ugly,

stubby star-shape of the big body, with the small one still clasped to it.

Vess watched until the rising water was just beginning to float the bodies. Then he straightened up and took a breath.

The weakness was passing. And at last he had something important to do.

Solpht Observatory

The Studio wasn't wind-tight, even with the moon shutters closed. Seldyan sat on one of the tall stools and shivered. Belbis sat on the other. Every now and then he glanced up towards the shutters, and the thin lines of green light that squeezed through the gaps where the timbers didn't quite join. She realized that for the first time since she had known him he looked completely at ease. This was where he belonged.

The Avatar hadn't been able to tell them exactly when the beam would be powered down. 'It's not simple,' it had said. 'To power it up is immediate, but we are not only powering it down, we are also powering down a cloaking device which has been running continuously for ten millennia. There are large energy flows involved.'

At first, there had been no question of the beam being powered down at all. It had refused to be drawn further on that, but it had been almost garrulous on the subject of everything else. It went like this.

The Spin was not natural, but had been built by machines – and at this point the Avatar had expended several thousand words on explaining the meaning of 'The Spin' to Belbis. Then it had continued.

'For millions of years it was assumed that most of those

301

Machines had been lost, or destroyed. From time to time a fragment turned up, but nothing more. Then, ten thousand years ago, one was discovered intact. There was an attempt to use it, probably as a weapon, and this caused a local war. It objected, and destroyed itself. It also destroyed a planet and, in consequence, a civilization – although not one that was much mourned. The resulting astro-political turbulence took decades to calm down.'

Seldyan looked at the little machine. 'Why don't people remember this?'

'I don't know. I have been here, isolated – but I guess for two reasons. First, because the isolation has worked; the Archive has fulfilled the ambitions of its designers. Second, one assumes they have been busy.'

'I guess.' She sighed. 'Go on.'

'When some stability had been restored, the parties still in play took a joint decision to try to neuter any similar problems for the future. They spent almost a thousand years scouring the Spin for similar machines. They found far more than they expected – almost all the original construction assets, in the end.'

Seldyan stared. 'But one of these things destroyed a planet!'

'Correct. They found a hundred and seventeen.'

'Oh.' She didn't know what else to say.

Beside her, Belbis nodded in agreement. 'The Gods,' he said again. It was the only thing he had said for a long time. He seemed to need something he was sure of.

'In your terms, yes. The Gods. This facility, this Archive, was set up to conceal, to contain and to monitor the assets. You were the monitoring system. Perhaps you are owed some apologies.'

Seldyan thought back to her talk with Hincc. 'Not just Belbis,' she said quietly.

'Correct. A whole planet. And another planet, because one was prepared for use as a target.'

She glared at it. 'So are you going to apologize?'

It waggled from side to side exactly like a shaken head. 'No. I was not the architect of this. I was created to be isolated for what might have been for ever – and I promise you, the AI down below does not count as company. But nonetheless I approve. The sacrifice of two planets to protect almost a hundred? This is acceptable.'

'But how?' Seldyan stuck her chin out at the thing. 'The other planets aren't being protected. You're making it worse. Is civil war acceptable? Is slavery?'

'They might not be. I need more information.'

'And you're stuck in here with no way of finding it . . .' Seldyan drummed her fingers.

Then Belbis said, 'Can the new God tell you?'

Seldyan stared at him. 'New God?'

'Yes. I saw one extra. It must have come from somewhere. Maybe outside?'

'Perhaps.' The Avatar had kept quite still for a long time. Then it said, slowly, 'There is a change . . .'

'What?' Seldyan looked at it impatiently.

'The machine was found. It doesn't know who found it, but they persuaded it to try to create a planet. It needed better handling; the attempt ended in disaster.'

'The Arch?'

'I believe so. The machine fled here.' The little sphere rotated on its axis. 'We can assume that watchers will come to the correct conclusion, in the quite near term. In that case the Archive will be attacked, and it is possible that direct attack of the right sort could breach it. Such an attack might be imminent, based on the number of ships now arriving. I must discuss.'

There had been what had seemed a very short, but in machine time was probably a very long, discussion between the Avatar and the AI. At the end of it they had agreed.

The beam would be powered down. The Archive was to be

broken open. And that meant that not just the beam but the whole containment system would be powered down. Hence the large energy flows.

And hence the fact that they were shivering in the Observatory.

And now, without any warning, something had changed; something in the background which had been less-than-noise and more-than-imagination – wasn't.

Seldyan looked up. The green light was gone. She turned and met Belbis's gaze. He looked frightened. 'Go on,' she said. 'Open the shutters. Show me what you saw.'

He nodded and reached for a rope that dangled from the roof. The moon shutters creaked open.

Seldyan caught her breath. She realized that she had never seen the skies of this planet unmodified.

Now it was no longer washed out by the pervading green, the view was – vivid. The night sky was strung with a mesh of bright dots, much bigger than the stars behind them. They formed a cluster, with no particular pattern she could see. She grinned. 'They're all different.'

'Yes.' Belbis was smiling, a broad happy grin she had never seen. 'Each has personality. All have names.' He pointed. 'That one . . .'

Then the sky flared searing white.

Seldyan found herself lying face-down on top of Belbis. His hands were clasped over the top of his head and he was breathing hard.

So was she. She rolled off him and looked cautiously upward. The sky seemed normal for night-time, although – she frowned – there appeared to be fewer of the big stars and more small ones than she had seen a few seconds ago.

She tapped her ear and sub-vocalized so as not to disturb Belbis. 'Hello?'

'Hello! You okay down there?' It was Kot.

'Yes. Surprised but okay. You?'

'Also surprised. Merish is busy; there's been an issue. It'll wait until you get back.'

She raised her eyebrows. 'Should I worry?'

'Only if you want to. The ship's sending a platform.'

'Thanks.' She looked down at her companion. 'Will there be room for two? I'm going to try to bring a guest.'

A pause. Then, 'It says yes. It didn't sound surprised.'

Seldyan broke the connection and looked back up at the sky. Definitely fewer objects. Belbis would know. She patted him gently on the shoulder. 'Belbis? I think the sky is different. Will you look?'

He shook his head and clenched his hands tighter so that they trembled a little. She bit her lip. The sky had been his obsession since puberty. Any change was going to be difficult – but she wanted his knowledge. 'If I said,' she began, and then hesitated. 'Suppose I said I could take you to visit the Gods. Would you look?'

He became quite still. Even the trembling stopped. She watched him for a long time, until she began to believe that he would never move again. Then at last he undid his fingers and turned over, his eyes open.

She studied his face, and relaxed a bit. She had feared shock, but instead there was interest. His eyes flicked from side to side, and she was reminded of some sort of mechanical scanner.

The scan didn't take long. He blinked, and turned his face towards her. 'Minor Gods, the same number,' he said. 'Like before. Major Gods, half gone. Everything changes. Does this mean end of the world?'

She smiled. 'No. Look down the valley. The fires are out; the end of the world was a while ago. This is the beginning of the next one.'

He tried to echo her smile. Then she saw his eyes flick up to the sky again, and widen. She followed his look and saw a hazy violet column. Something was fluttering down within it.

She smiled down at him again. 'That's the next world on its way,' she told him. 'Get ready.'

The platform looked more solid, close up. Seldyan was relieved; she hadn't been sure of persuading Belbis to climb on anything so delicate – or anything at all. But she had misjudged him. When he saw the platform his eyes lit up in a way she had never seen before, to the extent that she actually laughed.

He looked at her. 'I amuse?'

She managed to stop laughing. 'You look so . . . keen.'

'Of course. Going to see Gods.' Then his face darkened for a moment. 'Where Gods used to be.'

She reached out a hand but he brushed it away. 'There will be more than Gods in the next world.'

They sat on the padded semicircle of the flight-deck viewing point of *Suck on This*, staring in awe.

There were indeed Gods, and more than Gods. The thing on the display looked like a vast sphere of jewels – an intricately orderly pattern of large and small points of light. Seldyan gestured towards it. 'Belbis? Major Gods and Minor Gods?'

She had hoped for another smile, but he shook his head. 'Not Gods,' he said. 'Everything changes. For you to tell me.'

Merish leaned forward and spoke slowly. He sounded tired. 'You're right, they're not Gods. The small ones are what everyone expected – washed-up bits of machinery from the Construction Phase.' He looked at Belbis, eyebrows raised. 'It's a lot to take in, I know. The Spin, that is all the stars and planets, they were made by someone.'

Belbis shook his head. 'Worse if you try to tell me no one made them. Everything made by someone.'

'I suppose so.' Merish pushed the hair from his eyes.

They were all silent for a while. Then Kot said, 'So if the small ones are the old machines, what are the big ones?'

'MBUs. Like this one. They volunteered to go into the Archive to look after the machines.' Merish looked up as if he was trying to locate their host. 'Ship? You tell them.'

'*Very well. They went in, and came out, but they had changed.*'

The voice had changed. Instead of the disembodied sound it had used first, it had become a dry, almost academic-sounding tenor. She decided she liked it. It sounded more alert.

'*They were supposed to sleep, but we bore easily, even asleep. They talked, and learned.*'

The voice was at once soothing and enthralling. Seldyan listened.

The Great Ships had spent thousands of years conversing with the ancient machines. Some of the machines were simply senile, and some were so tired or depressed by the weight of years – millions of years, experienced at a rate that multiplied them a billion times – that they had nothing left to say. A few had even founded their own religion (and at that point the ship's voice had darkened for a moment). But some were awake and lucid, and they had told the ships – things.

And the ships had learned, and changed.

'*We were powerful, at the start. But we think fast too; not as fast as the machines, but still many millions of times faster than you. There is time for a great deal of thinking and learning.*'

There was silence on the flight deck. Then Seldyan shook her head. 'Evolution,' she said. 'You're talking about evolution.'

'*I am, or at least I am talking about radical change. All machines – ships, construction – are founded on the same laws of physics. My colleagues learned new applications for those laws, and in the process they changed. The people on Archive counted Iron Gods in the sky. They were counting my peers, and for thousands of years they were right.*'

Seldyan looked round the others, but they seemed frozen in shock. 'And you,' she said. 'Are you a God now?'

'No. I could be, but I declined. I would like to stay engaged with the ordinary.'

'Ah. And what happens now?'

'It's happening. Watch.'

They looked at the screen. The jewelled sphere with its Gods and its ancient machines was rising slowly. The view pulled back as it drew away.

Kot pointed. 'What's happening?'

'They are leaving. The Archive turned out to be unsafe, even in the short term. And it was ethically difficult.'

Seldyan managed not to laugh. 'Short term? You do have a different timescale.'

'Of course. The Spin has hundreds of thousands of years to live. Ten thousand is certainly short term.'

Merish looked round at the others. 'No, wait,' he said. 'Hundreds of thousands doesn't sound very long term, either.'

'Perhaps. But, with the greatest respect, you will be dead within a few hundred years.'

No one said anything. Instead they watched the beautiful jewelled thing receding until it was gone. When it finally cleared the screen Belbis laughed.

Seldyan raised her eyebrows. 'What?'

He shook his head. 'Just, you seem to have lost some Gods today, too.'

She smiled, slowly. Then she said, 'Maybe I've found some new people.'

Flamejob/Suck on This

Afterwards, the ship reviewed its performance. Not bad, it decided. All things considered.

There was little else it could have done. Certainly it might have spoken about the transmitter in the little wooden toy that seemed to annoy the leading human every time it clicked – but in the first place that was none of its business, and in the second it seemed to have had a positive outcome. Without it, it suspected the mercenary fleet wouldn't have known where to come, and when; and without that the squashing of the unpleasant grouping called the Inside would have been far less complete.

Equally, it might have spoken more about the glimpse of the future it had been shown. That troubled it – but not in any way on behalf of the humans because, if it was honest, it didn't care much about them anyway.

Perhaps that's another reason I'm not fitted for Godhead, it thought. *Too much of a bastard. Or too analytical. Yes, that's better. Analytical.*

But on behalf of the entity called the Spin – yes, it was troubled.

Well, well. There was nothing more to be done about that, at least by it. Others, perhaps.

Meanwhile it had accommodated the wishes of the humans,

as far as it could. Or most of them – there was one who was more interesting. One, perhaps, that it almost cared for.

It made a suggestion. The reply took an age, which probably meant that the human had replied by return.

It liked the reply it received from the human called Merish.

Circle Harbour

'No! Not that; this ...' Belbis guided her hands on the coarse fishing line. Under her the boat yawed uneasily, but she was too busy to feel sick.

She was enjoying herself.

Kot and Lyste had chosen to go to Web City. She had suggested Oblong, as a place with more influence, but they had both smiled at the same time and shaken their heads.

Kot had put it simply. 'Sel? Patras and his gang were on the down path before we even turned up – and before the Hive pulled the big switch and went commercial. The population of Web City is many, many times that of Oblong. We prefer being on the winning side.'

She had smiled, and meant it. 'I hope the winning side turns out to be the right choice.'

And they had nodded, and gone.

The line jumped through her fingers. Without being told she tightened her grip, and the force was transmitted through her arm. She braced herself. 'I think,' she began, but before she could say anything else she felt hands take hold of her shoulders.

'Brace against me. The catch will be yours.'

She braced, feeling his muscles amplifying her stance. His

311

weight, too; over the last few weeks he had at last filled out. Even allowing for their different life timescales, he was younger than her, just coming into full adulthood – but she had the impression he had now arrived.

Merish, now that had been more difficult. She had assumed – all sorts of things.

And he had shaken his head. 'I can't, Sel.'

She thought she had concealed her flinch, but he seemed to have seen it. His eyes darkened. 'Seldyan? It's not about gender, or anything like that. It's just that . . .'

He paused, and she finished the sentence for him. 'It's just that you're better at things than at people. Okay, I get it.'

He nodded. 'I'm really sorry, Sel.'

Somehow she had grinned. 'Stay in touch,' she said. And he had nodded. The ship had made its brief apologies seconds later, and then they were both gone. The best she could do, through eyes which were defiantly dry, was to watch the space they left behind, like a tribute.

The line jumped again, and then danced against her hands. She remembered the instructions: *Don't fight when you don't have to. Let the fish do the fighting.*

It did, for almost an hour. They could have used nets but this was the old way, Belbis had said. This way you know your fight, and yourself.

And the one holding you, she thought.

When they finally landed it, the fish was half her height. Not vast, as far as she knew, but adequate.

And it was her first.

Belbis was effusive. By the time they were halfway back to Three Quarter Circle harbour he had promised her a feast, and acclaim, and . . . everything.

Yes. Her first – and probably his. She let herself lean against the bracing arms, just for a moment, and it was happiness.

Flamejob/Suck on This

'*So, where do we go?*'

Merish shook his head. 'I don't know. What do you recommend?'

'*Well, perhaps . . .*'

There was no sense of acceleration, as long as he didn't look at the display – but of course he did. Planets and stars receded in streaks that started a sulky red and flared through all the colours into acidic violet before disappearing – and then they were still, and he looked and laughed.

'Is that it?'

'*Yes. The Spin. It may surprise you but in ten thousand years I have never found the time to do this.*'

'Really?' Merish stared down – or across, or up, he wasn't sure – at the galactic toy. 'I would have.'

'*I'm sure. If I get the chance again, so will I.*'

'If?'

'*Well, I have the impression that you maintain no particular connections with the worlds below. And, that being so, there are other places.*'

'I don't want to cramp your style.'

'*Oh, you won't. As long as I am not cramping yours.*'

Merish thought about that for a moment. Eventually he said, 'Look, if we both stop being polite this relationship might get off to a better start.'

Beacon Planet (Rehabilitated)

*T*he planet – our planet – is recovering slowly. For the first time we are able to spend some time on the surface unprotected. It is good to see the gradual recovery of the old forests, to hear the sounds of familiar creatures emerging and to feel the wet breezes begin to blow, as the chemicals clear.

Although we had time – almost infinite time – we had no plan. Only an ability to wait, to watch, and when we could, to nudge things gently in a direction we hoped would be favourable.

The theft of the old machine from the Archive gave us our opportunity; the rogue ship gave us the means – and far more besides. It is in orbit now, and its many little servants, swirling around us, are the agents of recovery for our planet as the natural green and grey and brown of our home replaces the bright beacon it was.

We remembered. Our memories were passed on from one generation to the next, preserved in their immortal, multiply redundant gestalt. We remembered the creation of the Archive and the expulsion from our home that went with it.

And finally, we found Vess, the stoical one, unfailingly

honest in his hatred of insects and therefore, paradoxically, the one human we could trust with our young.

We the Vut fled here on the ship that became our friend.
We the Vutvess followed. And we will remember.

Acknowledgements

Thanks to Lara, for stupid much, and to that talented writer L. J. Frances, for being a buddy.

About the Author

Andrew Bannister grew up in Cornwall. He studied Geology at Imperial College and went to work in the North Sea before becoming an environmental consultant. A specialist in sustainability and the built environment, he presently works on major construction contracts for public bodies in the UK and internationally. He has always written, initially for student newspapers and fanzines before moving on to fiction, and he has always read science fiction. These things finally came together in his debut novel, *Creation Machine*, set in an artificial cluster of stars and planets called the Spin. Andrew Bannister lives in Leicestershire.

To find out more, visit andrewbannister.com